Strategy and History

A selection of Colin Gray's more important contributions to strategic debate, *Strategy and History* provides a unique perspective on the strategic history of the past thirty years. Written by a participant-observer of and in strategic controversies, the essays range widely over some hotly debated topics and address a number of issues which have contemporary relevance to strategists: the importance of history for strategic understanding today, the nature of strategy and why it is difficult to do well, the challenge of nuclear weapons, revolutions in military affairs, and arms control. Colin Gray argues strongly for the continuing significance of geography and culture and concludes by addressing the ethical assumptions which provide some useful guidance to the strategist. Ultimately the book shows how essential it is to maintain a strategic, means–ends perspective and defines strategy as a pragmatic activity.

This book will be essential reading for all students of strategy, contemporary history and international relations.

Colin Gray is Professor of International Politics and Strategic Studies at the University of Reading, UK. He is the author of 20 books, more than 300 articles, and several dozen reports for government. His most recent publications include *Strategy for Chaos: Revolutions in Military Affairs and the Evidence of History* (2002), *The Sheriff: America's Defense of the New World Order* (2004), and *Another Bloody Century: Future Warfare* (2005).

Cass Series: Strategy and History
Series Editors: Colin Gray and Williamson Murray
ISSN: 1473–6403

This new series focuses on the theory and practice of strategy. Following Clausewitz, strategy has been understood to mean the use made of force, and the threat of the use of force, for the ends of policy. This series is as interested in ideas as in historical cases of grand strategy and military strategy in action. All historical periods, near and past, and even future, are of interest. In addition to original monographs, the series from time to time publishes edited reprints of neglected classics as well as collections of essays.

1 **Military Logistics and Strategic Performance**
Thomas M. Kane

2 **Strategy for Chaos**
Revolutions in Military Affairs and the evidence of history
Colin S. Gray

3 **The Myth of Inevitable US Defeat in Vietnam**
C. Dale Walton

4 **Astropolitik**
Classical geopolitics in the space age
Everett C. Dolman

5 **Anglo-American Strategic Relations and the Far East, 1933–1939**
Imperial crossroads
Greg Kennedy

6 **Pure Strategy**
Power and principle in the space and information age
Everett C. Dolman

7 **The Red Army, 1918–1941**
From Vanguard of World Revolution to US Ally
Earl F. Ziemke

8 **Britain and Ballistic Missile Defence, 1942–2002**
Jeremy Stocker

9 **The Nature of War in the Information Age**
Clausewitzian future
David J. Lonsdale

10 **Strategy as Social Science**
Thomas Schelling and the
nuclear age
Robert Ayson

11 **Warfighting and Disruptive Technologies**
Disguising innovation
Terry Pierce

12 **The Fog of Peace and War Planning**
Military and strategic planning
under uncertainty
Edited by Talbot C. Imlay and Monica Duffy Toft

13 **US Army Intervention Policy and Army Innovation**
From Vietnam to Iraq
Richard Lock-Pullan

14 **German Disarmament After World War I**
The diplomacy of
international arms inspection
1920–1931
Richard J. Shuster

15 **Strategy and History**
Essays on theory and
practice
Colin S. Gray

16 **The German 1918 Offensives**
A case study in the operational
level of war
David T. Zabecki

17 **Special Operations and Strategy**
From World War II to the war
on terrorism
James D. Kiras

Strategy and History
Essays on theory and practice

Colin S. Gray

Routledge
Taylor & Francis Group

LONDON AND NEW YORK

First published 2006
by Routledge
2 Park Square, Milton Park, Abingdon, Oxon OX14 4RN

Simultaneously published in the USA and Canada
by Routledge
270 Madison Ave, New York, NY 10016

Routledge is an imprint of the Taylor & Francis Group, an informa business

© 2006 Colin S. Gray

Typeset in Times New Roman by
Newgen Imaging Systems (P) Ltd, Chennai, India
Printed and bound in Great Britain by
The Cromwell Press, Trowbridge, Wiltshire

British Library Cataloguing in Publication Data
A catalogue record for this book is available from the British Library

Library of Congress Cataloging in Publication Data
A catalog record for this book has been requested

ISBN10: 0–415–38635–7 (pbk)
ISBN10: 0–415–38634–9 (hbk)

ISBN13: 978–0–415–38635–7 (pbk)
ISBN13: 978–0–415–38634–0 (hbk)

For the small band of scholars and practitioners who strive to keep the flame of strategy alight

Strategic thought draws its inspiration each century, or rather at each moment of history, from the problems which events themselves pose.

(Raymond Aron 1970)

Theory exists so that one need not start afresh each time sorting out the material and plowing through it, but will find it ready to hand and in good order.

(Carl von Clausewitz 1832: 1976)

Contents

Preface   xi
Provenance of the essays   xiii

Introduction: holding the strategy bridge   1

PART I
Strategy, strategic studies, and history   15

1 Across the nuclear divide – strategic studies,
   past and present [1977]   17

2 New directions for strategic studies? How can
   theory help practice? [1992]   34

3 History for strategists: British sea power as a
   relevant past [1994]   54

4 Why strategy is difficult [1999]   74

5 From Principles of Warfare to Principles of
   War: a Clausewitzian solution [2005]   81

PART II
Strategic issues   89

6 Nuclear strategy: the case for a theory of victory [1979]   91

7 The Revolution in Military Affairs [1998]   113

8 Arms control does not control arms [1993]   120

PART III
Geography, culture, and ethics   135

  9 Geography and grand strategy [1991]   137

 10 Strategic culture as context: the first generation of
     theory strikes back [1999]   151

 11 Force, order, and justice: the ethics of realism in
     statecraft [1993]   170

PART IV
War and the future   183

 12 What is war? A view from strategic studies [2005]   185

     Notes   190
     Suggested reading   226
     Index   229

Preface

Strategy and History is a selection of my writings over three decades. Despite the variety of topics represented, they share two characteristics, a strategic perspective and a controversial thesis. Other features that they have in common are explained in the Introduction. The dedication of this work is heartfelt. For thirty-five years I have been applying strategic theory, directly or indirectly, from issue to issue. I recommend strongly the truth in the words I quote in one of the book's epigraphs from that most perceptive sociologist, historian, and philosopher, Raymond Aron. "Strategic thought draws its inspiration each century, or rather at each moment of history, from the problems which events themselves pose." But, as I argue in the Introduction, the inspiration provided by events needs to be educated by a grasp of the eternal lore of strategy. It is the commitment to the authority of that lore, and its application to actual and possible strategic happenings, that binds this book of collected essays and, indeed, that binds my professional record as a strategic theorist and defense analyst. This is not to claim that I have always succeeded in imposing strategic order on recalcitrant subjects, but it is to assert that I have sought to do so.

When I accepted, all too casually, Andrew Humphrys' invitation to assemble the "best of breeds" from my writings on all topics, I underestimated just how challenging that would prove to be. What criteria to apply? Readers can be reassured that there is some method in the selection. I defer discussion of content to the Introduction. The entries had to be (1) individually of high standard, (2) on topics that either in their subject matter or my treatment, or both, have some contemporary resonance, (3) on important issues or concerns, and, above all else, (4) had to present a strategic analysis. Beyond those criteria, also it was necessary to select essays that spanned the entire period, actually periods, of my professional life to date. Those years have encompassed no fewer than three reasonably distinct eras: the Cold War (–1989, or 1991, for the demise of the USSR); the inter-war period of the post-Cold War decade (1991–2001); and now the period of the so-called War on Terror (2001–). Both the scholarly pedant and the pragmatic strategist in me are well aware that one cannot wage war on an abstract noun. Nonetheless, the "War on Terror" is the fashionable term officially adopted, and widely understood, as pointing to the dominant characteristic of our current security context. Although I bow to the inevitable, I do believe, however, that this "War" will prove to be but a transient era of only modest duration.

The essays are all controversial, some much more so than others. I offer some context for, and comment on, each essay in the Introduction. The essays themselves are reprinted without amendment. They are as they were first published. It should go without saying that I do not endorse today every sentence I have written over three decades. However, I do recommend these essays as interesting discussions of significant issues in strategic theory, strategic history, and strategic policy, which have some merit beyond serving merely as illustrative period pieces.

I am pleased to acknowledge the permission I have been granted by MIT Press to reproduce my articles: "Across the Nuclear Divide – Strategic Studies, Past and Present," *International Security*, 2 (1977), pp. 24–46, and "Nuclear Strategy: The Case For a Theory of Victory," *International Security*, 4 (1979), pp. 54–87. Also, I am indebted to Elsevier for granting me permission to reprint my article, "Arms Control Does Not Control Arms," *Orbis*, 37 (1993), pp. 333–48. In addition, I am grateful to Cambridge University Press for permission to reprint, "Strategic Culture as Context: The First Generation of Theory Strikes Back," *Review of International Studies*, 25 (1999), pp. 49–69.

As well as Andrew Humphrys of Taylor and Francis who both set this venture in motion and has seen it through to publication, I must express my thanks to my friend and much respected fellow strategist, Jim Wirtz, of the Naval Post-Graduate School, Monterey, California. Not for the first time, he offered excellent advice, some of which I accepted.

I wondered whether or not to include the adjectival modifier "controversial" to the "Essays" in the title but decided that the addition would be redundant. I will allow my daughter the concluding observation in this Preface. With that perceptive wit all too characteristic of one's nearest and dearest, she commented that I must feel as if I am returning to the scene of some earlier crimes.

Colin S. Gray
Wokingham, UK
December 2005

Provenance of the essays

1 "Across the Nuclear Divide – Strategic Studies, Past and Present," *International Security*, 2 (1977), pp. 24–46.

2 "New Directions for Security Studies? How Can Theory Help Practice?" *Security Studies*, 1 (1992), pp. 610–35.

3 "History for Strategists: British Seapower as a Relevant Past," *The Journal of Strategic Studies*, 17 (1994), pp. 7–32.

4 "Why Strategy Is Difficult," *Joint Force Quarterly*, 22 (1999), pp. 6–12.

5 "From Principles of Warfare to Principles of War: A Clausewitzian Solution," unpublished essay (2005).

6 "Nuclear Strategy: The Case for a Theory of Victory," *International Security*, 4 (1979), pp. 54–87.

7 "The Revolution in Military Affairs," in B. Bond and Mungo Melvin (eds), *The Nature of Future Conflict: Implications for Force Development*, The Occasional No. 36 (Camberley, UK: The Strategic and Combat Studies Institute, September 1998), pp. 58–65.

8 "Arms Control Does Not Control Arms," *Orbis*, 37 (1993), pp. 333–48.

9 "Geography and Grand Strategy," *Comparative Strategy*, 10 (1991), pp. 311–29.

10 "Strategic Culture as Context: The First Generation of Theory Strikes Back," *Review of International Studies*, 25 (1999), pp. 49–69.

11 "Force, Order, and Justice: The Ethics of Realism in Statecraft," *Global Affairs*, 8 (1993), pp. 1–17.

12 "What is War: A View from Strategic Studies," an unpublished paper based upon presentations at a meeting in Oxford of the Leverhulme Project on the Changing Character of War (February 24, 2005), and at the Centre for American Studies in Rome (May 10, 2005).

Introduction
Holding the strategy bridge

Strategy is the bridge between military power and political purpose. Its state of repair is highly variable. Moreover, although it is a bridge that must allow two-way traffic between tasking from policy and evidence on military feasibility, it is the former that must dominate. When policy fails to command it finds itself the servant of warfare, the reverse of the only legitimate terms of the relationship.

Despite the diversity of these essays, their spread in dates of publication, and the wide range of subjects addressed, they are all about strategy and they all reflect the author's beliefs about, and approach to, war, peace, conflict, and – for the old fashioned term – statecraft. Readers may well notice some repetition of ideas and arguments, indeed it would be strange if they do not, but the similarity that is of most note, I hope, among these essays, is that they draw from and express a distinctively strategic mindset. Following Carl von Clausewitz, concerning whom more will be said throughout, I have sought to insist that the consequences of behavior must be considered. The key question for the strategist is, "so what?" In a career as a defense professional extending over thirty years and more, I have found the "so what" question to be essential and, occasionally, deadly. I have asked it to probe the sense in nuclear war plans, in maritime strategy, and in schemes for special operations, to cite but three areas of high relevance.

The title of this book carries important messages; it is not simply a convenient label. The main title reflects the fact that historical experience is literally our sole source of evidence on strategic phenomena. The future has not happened and no technological or methodological wizardry can reveal what tomorrow will bring.[1] The value of strategic history, the benefits and the perils, has been a constant concern in my writings. For example, book-end entries here, the essays, "Across the nuclear divide" of 1977 vintage and the 2005 essay on "From Principles of Warfare to Principles of War," both address the basic question of what has changed and what has not. It is encouraging to note that the US defense community, at the instigation of the current Deputy Chief of Naval Operations for Plans, Policy, and Operations, Vice Admiral John Morgan, has been investigating the issue of whether or not the traditional Principles of War have long passed their sell-by date. What is especially gratifying to one, such as myself who has beaten the drum for history and strategy for so long, is that Admiral Morgan's conceptual project has met with a hugely enthusiastic response. I am sceptical of the American ability to sustain an interest in strategy, but still one has to applaud virtue when it surfaces.

Of course, these essays can and should be read for their analysis of particular problems. However, they can be read also as a dialogue between theory and practice. Both of the epigraphs are vital and vitally complementary. On the one hand we have available a general theory of war and strategy, one composed most persuasively by Carl von Clausewitz.[2] On the other hand, as Raymond Aron insists, the history of strategic thought reflects the strategic problems of the day, albeit usually with some time lag. It has been my experience that Clausewitz's claim for the educational value of a single general strategic theory holds good across any and all strategic issues, be they ever so novel in appearance.[3] For example, the theory of strategy, following Clausewitz, is as applicable to space power and cyber power as it is to the other three geographical dimensions of war. I do not deny that my belief in the authority of, and necessity for, strategy has stirred controversy from time to time. For example, among these essays I include my 1979 piece, provocatively titled "Nuclear strategy: the case for a theory of victory." Whether or not that was an example of asking too much of strategy, readers must decide for themselves. However, I believed at the time, as I still do today, that every threat and use of military power should be directed purposively by strategy. Furthermore I believe that military power should only be exercised in a quest for advantage; why else would one fight? Since the superpowers had detailed plans to conduct the most destructive war in history, I felt that it was my public as well as my professional duty to try to hold them, the United States at least, to a strategic standard of contingent performance.

Aron's accurate claim for the authority of events in the history of strategic thought is really a necessary truth. The reason is that strategy is a practical business. In the immortal words of one of America's finest strategic theorists, Bernard Brodie:

> Strategic thinking, or "theory," if one prefers, is nothing if not pragmatic. Strategy is a "how to do it" study, a guide to accomplishing something and doing it efficiently. As in many other branches of politics, the question that matters in strategy is: Will the idea work? More important, will it be likely to work under the special circumstances under which it will next be tested?[4]

The general theory of war and strategy can have nothing to say directly about the particular problems that the course of history throws at policymakers and soldiers. But, that theory teaches, those who are willing and able to learn, how they should approach their unique challenges. In other words, strategic theory is about education, not training or doctrine. Those equipped with a Clausewitzian understanding of the nature of war and the function of strategy can turn their minds to the details of the problem of the hour, confident that they have in their intellectual armory the necessary weapons to help them prevail over ignorance, confusion, friction, and stupidity. Such, at least, is one's noble hope.

Because strategy is a highly pragmatic affair, as Brodie reminds us, it is unsurprising that the demand for general theory has never been strong. Beatrice Heuser hits the mark when she observes:

> In many respects, Clausewitz is thus providing something that few military practitioners are on the lookout for. While they tend to be in search of teachable and learnable rules of thumb that can be applied to a wide range of different situations, and can help them find short-cuts to decision making in stressful combat situations, Clausewitz mainly supplies philosophical reflections on the nature of war that are difficult to translate into simple, memorable prescriptions for action.[5]

Because strategy is a practical art, and in some respects an applied science,[6] the market for theory, and even appreciation of the value of theory, tends not to be healthy. For thirty years this strategic theorist has endeavored to serve up as much theory, in as palatable a form, as civilian officials and military professionals were willing and able to digest. Not infrequently, I misjudged my audience. Policymakers and soldiers are practical and busy people who are obliged to solve, or evade, specific and busy real-world problems. They are apt to be impatient with strategic philosophy. Whereas the theorist provides better understanding of the structure of a problem, the official seeks an answer to the pressing question, "what do I do?" Whereas policymakers should be expert at making, or postponing, decisions, and soldiers preponderantly are action people, scholars preeminently are analysts. In our efforts, we scholars of strategy often seem determined to illustrate the profundity in science fiction writer Poul Anderson's aphorism that "I have yet to see any problem, however complicated, which, when you looked at it the right way, did not become still more complicated."[7] In my experience, policymakers and soldiers cannot be relied upon to be grateful when a scholar tells them that they face a difficult problem to which there is no clearly superior solution. Especially it is true when the official client has paid a large sum of money for the study in question. Scholarship and policymaking truly comprise two different cultures, a fact and its implications that I must emphasize in the themes I now move on to identify.

All of my work as a defense professional has been performed with the aid of an enduring set of attitudes, beliefs, and concerns that have been manifest in some persisting characteristics. Whether I was analyzing Intercontinental Ballistic Missile (ICBM) basing modes, the military uses of space, maritime strategy, or the strategic utility of special operations forces, I found that my general theory of war, strategy, and statecraft would set me on what I judged to be a right enough road. My work has been characterized by

1   a strategic perspective,
2   a concern with the relationship between the theory and practice of strategy,
3   a deep respect for Carl von Clausewitz's theory of war and strategy,
4   a willingness, indeed a determination, to seek education from history,

5   recognition of the authority of politics,
6   attention to the importance of geography and culture,
7   a somewhat restrained enthusiasm for the significance of technology for strategic performance,
8   a determination to understand and explain the structure of a problem.

First and foremost these essays, indeed the entire canon of my work, are about strategy. In one way or another they are about the consequences of the threat or the use of force. By and large they are not about particular policy choices and neither are they about military behavior. As I strive to explain in the essay, "Why strategy is difficult," it is extremely hard to train strategists. In point of fact, many people who are skilled at policymaking, as well as many who are exemplary soldiers, do not really understand the strategic function at all. People have no difficulty comprehending either policy or fighting, regarded separately, but to connect the two in a purposeful way, and to keep them connected, often is a mental step too far. Indeed, with thanks to Cornelius Ryan, I would go so far as to claim that on the evidence of performance, strategy tends to be a bridge too far for many policymakers and military professionals.[8] It is not hard to see why this should be so. Politics is a profession, as is soldiering. But neither the politician nor the soldier necessarily is expert in the conduct of strategy. There are perennial efforts to make strategy a quantifiable science, but they are doomed to failure. Strategy inherently is an art, albeit a scientific one, in that some of its key enablers can and must be measured (e.g. logistics). I have waged a losing conceptual war for decades over the misuse of the adjective strategic. Strictly speaking, no weapon can be strategic. If we label some weapons as strategic, we discourage, if not outright deny, the consideration of their political consequences. It is an elementary matter of keeping instrument and effect distinct in our minds.[9]

My second theme is the difficult nexus between the theory and practice of strategy. Because of my personal professional history, I am especially sensitive to the trials and tribulations of all parties to this relationship. I have been an academic strategic theorist in three countries (the United States, Britain, and Canada), an advisor to government in two (primarily the United States, Britain), and a part-time government official (the United States). I am sufficiently old fashioned to believe both that the scholar should seek truth and that enlightenment on the nature and working of a subject is attainable. Practitioners are not generally hostile to truth, but truth is not their problem. Because strategy is a practical business, policymakers need truth that they can use. Erudite "briefings" on the dangers of particular nuclear strategies, or on the unmistakeable evidence of, and most probable reasons for, persistent violation of arms control agreements are likely to be received by officials with a yawn followed by the strategist's question, "so what?" What does it mean? Most especially, what does it mean for *my* responsibilities now? What does the briefer recommend? The scholar-briefer is probably shocked to be dragged thus brutally from the realm of truth into the rougher world of consequences. He or she probably does not appreciate that to grasp the probable nature, the structure, of nuclear war and strategy or of arms control non-compliance is really the easy task. The difficult job is reserved for the policymaker: what to do about it.[10] I strive to persuade my students that strategy, even strategic theory, is not a fine art; it is, as Brodie maintained, a " 'how to do it' study." Most practitioners need to be educated to recognize the relevance of theory to their search for workable solutions to today's problems, whereas theorists must never forget that their labors ultimately only have meaning and value for the world of strategic behavior.

Theme number three, perhaps better expressed as a characteristic, is the pervasive influence of Carl von Clausewitz's theory of war and strategy on all of my work. Bernard Brodie explained why this was likely to be the case when he wrote, unexceptionably: "His is not simply the greatest but the only truly great book on war."[11] Thirty plus years ago, I was less impressed by the great Prussian than I should have been, witness my youthful preference for Sun-tzu in the essay, "Across the nuclear divide." However, with the arrival of the Howard and Paret translation in 1976, and some maturity of understanding on my part, I soon realized that *On War* provided the basic conceptual toolkit for the education of the strategist. Clausewitz has been criticized roundly, even viciously, of late. In particular his theory of war is held by many critics to apply only to a world wherein states are the sole, or all but sole, agents. Allegedly, there was a "Clausewitzian era" which we can date, over-neatly, from the end of the first Thirty-Years' War in 1648, either to the close of the second in 1945, or possibly to the conclusion of the Cold War in 1989 or 1991. This is nonsense. A careful reading of *On War* reveals very clearly indeed that the theory it expounds is not restricted in its relevance to one or another character of belligerent. The most vital of the critics' errors has been their almost wilful misunderstanding of Clausewitz's explanation of the nature of war. He did not claim that war is the product of the dynamic, indeed unstable, relationship among the people, the commander and his army, and the government. Though he did note that those three agencies were each most closely associated with particular elements of what he termed "a remarkable trinity" (according to the 1976 Howard and Paret translation). Clausewitz's trinity comprises of "primordial violence, hatred, and enmity, which are to be regarded as a blind natural force; of the play of chance and probability within which the creative spirit is free to roam; and of its element of subordination, as an instrument of policy, which makes it subject to reason alone."[12] To date, the critics, past and present, have failed to hang a glove on him, though it certainly is not for want of trying.[13] Readers will find Clausewitz's theory of war either deeply embedded in, or at least lurking close nearby, the essays in this collection.

The fourth theme in these essays, in some cases explicit, is a willingness to seek education and inspiration from historical experience. There are two bases for my enthusiasm for history. The first, frankly, is simply personal interest. The second, more serious reason amounts to the default position: there is no alternative. To quote the excellent Brodie again, "[y]et the only empirical data we have about how people conduct war and behave under its stresses is our experience with it in the past, however much we have to make adjustments for subsequent changes in conditions."[14] Clausewitz's was an inductive theory of war. Heuser explains usefully that

> [h]e achieved a substantially greater level of abstraction than most of his peers by deriving his conclusions about war from the evidence of 130 historical battles which he had studied closely, and yet without allowing himself to become bogged down in detail.[15]

Time after time, strategic theorists and analysts have claimed that radical change in the context of war and strategy has consigned past experience to the antiquarian file. For much of the Cold War, for the leading example, most defense professionals were so obsessed with the novel problems posed by nuclear weapons that they could see little if any value in the study of prenuclear experience. The first essay in this collection was written to address that plausible fallacy. These essays reflect my agreement with the Clausewitzian arguments that "all wars are things of the same nature," and that war has two natures, objective and subjective.[16] War's objective nature comprises those qualities that do not alter, whereas the subjective is ever changing. People, including some supposedly expert, are wont to confuse change in the character of war with a change in its nature. This confusion can lead the bold theorist, as well as the hopeful official, seriously astray. Because war and strategy are unchanged and unchanging in their natures, it has to follow that we should allow ourselves to seek education from historical experience. This belief underlies all my writing.

My fifth theme is a respect for the rule of politics over war and strategy. This respect is implicit in my reverence for Clausewitz, with his dictum that "war is simply a continuation of political intercourse, with the addition of other means."[17] However, recognition of the authority of the political is so important that it warrants independent identification. All of my professional life I have conducted running battles with well-meaning theorists who have either chosen to forget that war is about politics, or who have succumbed to the temptation to believe that political problems could be sidelined by technical experts. To be blunt: politics is about relative power, and relative power is what war and strategy is all about. During the Cold War decades, the dominant RAND school of defense analysis attempted to reduce strategy to a quantifiable science. The stability of mutual nuclear deterrence was held to rest upon the calculable invulnerability to a first strike of each superpower's strategic nuclear force posture. By implication, peace and war could hang on fine calculations of weapon survivability. In the phrase of the era, our security, even our survival, could depend upon "the delicate balance of terror."[18] In truth, decisions for war or peace rest upon strength of political motivation. Indeed, much of the more rigorous of the defense analysis in the RAND genre, though notably not that authored by Bernard Brodie, who was a RAND employee of long standing, in effect all but deleted the political context.[19] The context was treated as a wholly technical one, with danger of rising or falling with changes in the rival military postures. By extension, arms control theory, analysis, and policy were pursued, indeed are still pursued, as an endeavor to achieve greater stability, that rather mysterious magical condition, by diplomacy and administration. As a bold generalization, the entire arms control effort of the past half century faltered and foundered, because it rested upon a fundamental fallacy. Specifically, arms *per se* are not the problem. Ergo, removing arms, or even just controlling them in some manner, cannot be the solution. States do not fight because they are armed; they arm because they fear that they might have to fight. The political motives come first; the arms follow. History does show, for once unambiguously, that disarmament and arms control are eminently negotiable between states who do not expect to fight each other.

The sixth theme characteristic of my writings has been appreciation of the importance of geography and culture. My position in these regards has been, and remains, controversial. I have argued that the classic theories of geopolitics, most especially those advanced in the first half of the twentieth century by the British geographer, Sir Halford J. Mackinder, and the Dutch-American political scientist, Nicholas J. Spykman, contain an important enduring wisdom.[20] Aside from geopolitical theory, in my writings I have always sought to be sensitive to the geographical context and, *ab extensio*, to the cultural also. Some of my professional colleagues have not shared my respect for geography and culture. They have argued, not implausibly, that modern technology has hugely reduced the significance of strategy's spatial dimension. The technologically effected shrinkage of space translates into a dramatic reduction in real distance and therefore time. If warfare is becoming an exercise in the information-led high-speed delivery of firepower from altitude, who cares about the geographical context? Similarly, if technology rules in the battlespace and military success is pursued by reducing the enemy to a dehumanized target set, who cares about the local culture? It is believed by many theorists that culture is both too elusive and difficult a concept to operationalize helpfully in strategy and, anyway, is unlikely to yield insights notably superior to those which can be derived from analyses of material power relations.[21] For many years my advocacy of cultural analysis for strategic theory and policy fell on fairly stony ground. But now, suddenly, defense professionals are bent on proving yet again the eternal truth in Aron's maxim. In the novel context of protracted engagement on the ground with distinctly alien cultures in the Middle East and Central Asia, the American defense community has discovered its need for cultural understanding of friends and foes.[22] However, I doubt that the current flurry of cultural awareness will long survive, let alone overcome, the long-standing American love affair with high technology.

Theme number seven, appropriately enough, given what has just been said, is a noticeably limited enthusiasm for technology as the arbiter of victory and defeat in war. Contrary to the impression I may be giving inadvertently, I am far from being a technophobe. In my career I worked for many years with sectors of the US defense community who were on, or over, the frontier of the high end of high technology. Specifically, I worked with the United States Air Force's (USAF's) ICBM program, and the MX missile and its basing mode traumas in particular; with the ballistic missile defense program in its several manifestations from SDI to the present; and with the military space program.[23] I am not, and have never been, in any sense hostile to useful new technologies. But, I have waged a long struggle to encourage those who approach military problems technologically, to think strategically as well. It has been my role to focus, time and again, on the consequences of technology. This has led me into some dangerous zones of argument. Most obviously, the insistence on strategic thought worthy of the name led me to pursue the difficult subject of the strategy in nuclear strategy. My argument in the essay on "Nuclear strategy: the case for a theory of victory" was not a gung ho push for a plan to win an all-out nuclear war. Rather did the essay express the conviction that no weapons, including those of a long-range nuclear kind, should be threatened or actually used in the absence of a plausible theory of consequential advantage. Possibly I was guilty of strategic conceptual overstretch. Certainly it is the majority opinion, even among defense professionals, that the very idea of nuclear strategy is really an oxymoron.[24] The responsible strategist in me has always rejected that position. I continue to believe that the use of any and every weapon should be directed by strategy for identified purposes. A nuclear war plan ought not to be something that one simply executes regardless of consequences when other options are exhausted. More generally, I remain committed to conducting strategic analysis in the light of the stress that Clausewitz placed on the "moral factors." In the master's words,

> [h]ence most of the matters dealt with in this book are composed in equal parts of physical and of moral causes and effects. One might say that the physical seem little more than the wooden hilt, while the moral factors are the precious metal, the real weapon, the finely-honed blade.[25]

That is a trifle too dismissive of technology to fit comfortably in the twenty-first century, but still it is a vital corrective to some of the fantasies of the technophiles among us.

Finally, theme eight is my effort down the years to approach disparate defense issues via an understanding of the structure of the issue-area in question. Far from being a brilliant method, I suspect that it reveals my true nature as a sometimes pedantic academic strategist. On occasion, I have been guilty of boring or annoying officials who had looked to me to assist them solve a current problem, when the help that I provided took the form of assistance in thinking about how to approach the topic. In effect, my official audience wanted Jomini with his formula for victory, and instead they received Clausewitz, though sadly minus the genius of the original.[26] Most of my writings have the character of trending from the particular to the general. For example, in the 1970s and 1980s I was deeply involved in the Soviet–American arms control process, sometimes at the level of quite excruciating and highly classified technical detail. That protracted exposure led me to wonder why it was that from the 1920s to the 1980s arms control had achieved so little. For another example, in the mid-1980s I wrote about maritime strategy, with special reference to the concept of "The Maritime Strategy" announced by the Reagan administration in 1986. That experience drove me to explore the ways in which sea power exerted strategic leverage.[27] For yet another case, I was appalled to discover that for all their rich, if checkered career in the twentieth century, there was effectively no, as in zero, strategic theory for special operations forces. The tactical story was well-understood, but not the strategic. No one had really stepped back to ask the strategist's question, "so what?"[28] I cite my determination to probe the structure of a problem area neither as a boast nor as advice for others. Rather it is simply an important feature of my theorizing and analysis. I can do no other.

***

With more than three hundred published articles, several dozen book chapters, and many reports to government to choose from, it has been no easy task to select these essays. Those that made the final cut succeeded, because they tried to say something important about subjects that still matter, because they demonstrate clearly several or more of the characteristics that I hope are signatures to my work, and also for no better reason than that I still like them. Although I always aspire to bring the timeless perspective of strategy to a topic, every essay has a historical, and therefore a particular policy, and intellectual context. The subject of the work and its treatment had to reflect the time of its creation. None of the entries are so inherently arcane, or address an issue so distant from contemporary concerns, as to require extensive contextual explanation here. The essays can and must speak for themselves. Nonetheless, I will provide a brief comment on each, if only to explain what the author was about.

The five essays in Part I constitute the core of the collection. They address, literally, the most fundamental matters flagged in the title of this section: strategy itself, the conduct and value of strategic studies, and the use and abuse of history by strategists. The 1977 essay, "Across the nuclear divide – strategic studies, past and present," was a plea for students of strategy to reach back beyond 1945 to mine the two and half millennia of variably accessible experience of war for our education. Modern strategic studies largely were forged and prosecuted by scholars innocent of any depth of historical understanding. After all, if the strategic world had been transformed by the nuclear discovery, what relevance could there be to prenuclear experience? Strange to note, perhaps, but whereas in the 1960s and 1970s the world before Hiroshima appeared to many people to be almost infinitely remote, today it is the Cold War with its domination by awesome nuclear possibilities that looks historically exceptional. This intellectual reacquisition of our prenuclear historical heritage has yet to be realized in a strategic studies community well-populated with the historically literate.

The next essay, "New directions for strategic studies? how can theory help practice?" was written at a time of proclaimed intellectual and political crisis for strategic studies. The end of the Cold War promoted a mini-flight from the subject. The subject in its modern guise had been the creation of Cold War, and especially nuclear, dilemmas. We students of strategy appeared to have lost our way. Of course this was all foolish, if it was not actually mischievous on the part of those who always suspected that strategic theorists were more a part of the problem than the solution. "New Directions" was a fairly bold statement of the continuing necessity for strategic studies, a claim that it supported by itemizing the ways in which the theorists of strategy could provide useful education to assist practitioners. This was an essay written, and first delivered, in hard times for the subject. I recall vividly giving the paper on which the essay is based before a distinctly unfriendly audience at the Australian National University in Canberra in 1991. I note now with much regret that I did succumb slightly to the spirit of the era and briefly expressed a preference for security over strategic studies. That was a mistake on my part, never to be repeated. Security studies is a boundary-free, indeed defying, zone that lacks intellectual or practical integrity.[29]

"History for strategists: British sea power as a relevant past," offers a straight-forward discussion of the utility of historical experience, I hesitate to use the word evidence, and provides a treatment of British sea power to illustrate my argument.[30] This item is included because of the directness of its discussion of the relationship between history and strategy or, more precisely, between the historian and the strategist. Also, the essay descends usefully from the rarefied realm of general argument to the detail of an actual historical case study.

Very occasionally one writes an essay for which the small attentive public would seem to be waiting. So it proved with the next entry, the essay that seeks to explain "Why strategy is difficult." This item is the final product of several efforts to tackle the subject in front of senior military audiences, most especially the students at the US National Defense University, in Washington DC. Strangely, perhaps, although I certainly did not discover anything new. or reveal any patent cure for the ills of the strategist, I managed to present the difficulties in a way that touched base with my official audience. Brief though it is, I believe that this essay may be the most useful one in the collection, bearing in mind, to repeat, that strategy is a pragmatic business.[31]

The last of the five essays in Part I, "From Principles of Warfare to Principles of War: a Clausewitzian solution," is both previously unpublished and the most recent in the collection. It argues that the Principles of War, to which militaries around the world pay nominal obeisance, are in fact nothing of the kind. Those Principles are strictly operational and tactical; in short they prescribe for warfare, not for war. What I offer in this essay is a new set of principles which focus not on how to fight but rather on how to wage war for political purposes, which is to say strategically. My principles reflect a strategist's concerns and address areas of persisting weakness in would-be strategic behavior. As the title proclaims, the analysis and argument are strongly Clausewitzian.

The three essays in Part II move into far murkier and more perilous waters than were traversed in Part I. In 1979, I wrote "Nuclear strategy: the case for a theory of victory," as a wake up call to an American defense community that was choosing not to think strategically about its "strategic" nuclear forces. Possibly, even probably, it was futile, or even dangerous, to think hard about how a Third World War would actually be waged, but I felt obliged to make the attempt. At least, I believed, then and now, that it is grossly irresponsible to devise nuclear war plans that cannot meet basic tests of contingent strategic desirability. It seemed to me that nuclear targeting was largely a technical exercise, a matching of military means against enemy assets in order to achieve required but arbitrary levels of damage, an efficient lay down rather than a plan worthy of the name. Just when there would be the strategic challenge of the century, perhaps of every century, strategic reasoning was distinguished by its absence. I admit to the prejudiced view that a polity has no business acquiring and maintaining forces that it cannot command strategically. The point of the essay is not so much to explore ways in which a nuclear war could be won, but instead to insist that we think strategically about the contingent use of nuclear weapons. Needless to say, the essay did not please many readers.

The second essay in the category of "Strategic issues" was written in the late 1990s to explain what was going on in the "great RMA debate" in the United States. With no significant enemy threats to provide a focus for attention, the US defense community spent much of the post-Cold War decade doing what it does best, pursuing technological dreams. The proposition was, and remains, that the information age of warfare was arriving and if exploited would enable a Revolution in Military Affairs (RMA). This was all rather enemy-independent. By mid- to late decade, RMA was the hottest idea in town (i.e., in Washington), and the quest for truth was amply fueled by the tens or even hundreds of billions of dollars that were, and are, at stake. My essay deconstructs the debate, locates different schools of thought, and generally provides a brief survival guide through the blizzard of paper that was threatening to obscure the fundamentals. The most basic of my concerns was, of course, to approach RMA strategically.[32] Notwithstanding the prodigious RMA study industry of the 1990s, there is something to recommend the rain that historian Jeremy Black has dropped on that parade. He advises that "[m]ilitary realities, however are both too complex and too dependent on previous experiences to make the search for military revolutions helpful."[33]

The third entry in the "Strategic issues" basket bears the unsubtle self-explanatory title, "Arms control does not control arms." For many years I had labored to analyze arms control proposals and to suggest new approaches and generally had striven to enhance Western negotiating performance in hope of our achieving tolerable outcomes. Eventually, belatedly, it dawned on me that I was wasting my time. By analogy, arms control and the theory of security that it expressed had about as much validity as the theory that the earth is flat. Arms control and, its big brother, disarmament, approach security problems exactly backwards. Arms are not the problem. Rather the problems are the political motives that spur polities to acquire arms. This less than dazzling insight has been either ignored or rejected by legions of people who comprise the "international arms control community." Also, it is probably worth my while noting that since we do not have the semblance of a plausible general theory of the causes of war, a mission that I believe is unachievable, we lack also for a promising theory of the causes of peace. Indeed, writing 2,400 years ago Thucydides told us all that we need to know, and all that is usefully knowable at a general level, about the causes of war. He asserted the primacy of three factors: "fear, honor, and interest."[34] The long and barren road of arms control and disarmament experience since the 1920s has been traveled by policies that were ahistorical at best.[35]

The essays in Part III reveal the importance of some of the broader themes in, and underlying, my writing: geography, culture, and ethical assumptions. "Geography and grand strategy" supports a thesis that ought not to be controversial, the proposition that geography matters greatly in statecraft and strategy. In particular, this essay emphasizes the limitations upon choice that physical geography can impose.[36] In this information age, with the elimination of distance and therefore time by electronics, it has come to be popular to assert that geography is no longer the potentially show-stopping constraint that once it was. There is some merit in that view, but only some.[37] I argue not only that physical geography continues to be an important factor in strategy, but also that in its several dimensions it is a fundamental contributor to public, strategic, and military cultures.

The second essay in Part III was designed as a major blow in the scholarly battle over strategic culture and how to study it. From being a rather eccentric interest of a few strategic thinkers in the 1970s and early 1980s,[38] culture today stands in some danger of being adopted and over praised by the US defense community. The result is bound to be an undue elevation of expectations of practical returns to effort. Policymakers and strategists are not scholars, that is not their function. They seek education that they can use, which is to say digestible nuggets that carry clear implications for probable enemy behavior. The verdict is still open on just how and when culture plays in, and as, decision making and strategic behavior. Nonetheless, despite those caveats, recognition of the cultural dimension of war and strategy is undoubtedly important, indeed on occasion it is probably vitally so. For an extreme example, it is possible to argue that Nazi culture, the quasi-religious ideology of the Third Reich, explains Hitler's determination to wage war.[39] His regime did not really have war aims in any sense that would satisfy Clausewitzian criteria. Nazi Germany waged war as an expression of its ideology, any other explanation is mere political rationalization.[40] This interpretation may or may not persuade, but it serves to illustrate my argument that culture matters deeply. This 1999 essay offers a fairly comprehensive exploration of the meaning of the concept for strategy, as well as providing some answers to critics of my approach.

In "Force, order, and Justice: the ethics of realism in statecraft," the final entry in Part III, I make an admittedly rare excursion away from explicitly strategic topics into adjacent, actually precursor, territory. The purpose of the essay is to expose the ethical code of the realist, or, in this case, the necessarily pragmatic strategist. In my career I have been accused of cynicism, amorality, immorality, and even of war crimes for my work on nuclear strategy. My accusers may have been correct, but in this essay, for once, I thought it useful to make explicit the consequentialist ethics that have helped guide my professional endeavors. We strategists inalienably are in the trade of consequences. Strategy, to repeat, is all about the consequences of the threat and use of force. Bearing the hallmark of its date of composition, 1993, the essay makes explicit reference to Bosnia, "a scenario from hell" as I called it. Over the course of thirty years I have had relatively few intellectual exchanges with moral philosophers, indeed probably too few. Those that I have had have not encouraged me to seek more. It is regrettable, but perhaps inevitable, that when philosophers and theologians join in strategic debate, they cite as authorities the strategists with whom they agree, whereas we strategists similarly tend to be guilty of looking for endorsement from the moralists who support our assumptions. I hope and believe that this short essay sheds some helpful light on the ethical dimension to strategy. I am aware that its frankness may have the effect of confirming the worst suspicions of my critics.

The single entry in Part IV, "War and the Future," has been chosen and reshaped to gather together economically most of the strands of argument and important assumptions that characterize these essays as a whole. The essay is written in a style designed to be direct, even blunt. It poses, and answers, the most important of questions about war and peace. Also it stakes a claim for strategic studies as comprising an essential venture in "peace studies." Because strategists are prodded into thought by contemporary anxieties about the future, it seemed only fair to offer readers a brief glimpse of future strategic history, as it is anticipated, albeit through a glass darkly, by this strategist.

These essays illustrate my long standing professional commitment to the duty identified in the title of this Introduction, "Holding the strategy bridge." It has been a constant struggle, nonetheless I have done my best. Perhaps the most effective way in which I can explain the value of strategic theory for strategic practice is by juxtaposing the messages in the two epigraphs of this book. Recall that Aron advises that strategic thought is triggered by the ebb and flow of historical events, whereas Clausewitz recommends a general strategic theory that is ready to hand as a vital aid to thought about the ever changing problems of the day. If we neglect strategic theory, marginalize it as irrelevant or unworldly, then we are utterly at the mercy of the perspective of the moment. A prime virtue of a history founded theory of war and strategy is that it should help protect us from the over interpretation of the meaning of today. Analysis barren of historical perspective can never be sound.

Part I

Strategy, strategic studies, and history

1 Across the nuclear divide – strategic studies, past and present [1977]

A combination of accident and design has produced a transnational strategic studies community which has only the most casual acquaintance with strategic thought and action prior to 1945. In this article it is argued both that the continuities in international politics and strategy, pre- and post-1945, are far more important than are the discontinuities, and that therefore the disciplined study of pre-nuclear ideas and events could and should much improve our understanding of the structure of current and anticipated security problems. The identity of the political players changes, as do the characteristics of particular weapons, but such policy problem categories as the utility of force for the support of foreign policy, alliance management, the conduct of an arms race, the prosecution of limited war, arms control negotiations, and the accommodation of new weapon technologies, all have long pre-nuclear histories. Nuclear-age strategic theory has suffered severely from shallowness of its empirical base.

Relatively few strategists today deny, in principle, the salience of pre-1945 thought and practice. But, historical consciousness of more than a very cosmetic variety continues to be the rare exception in contemporary strategic and arms control analysis. It is, of course, somewhat contrary to the American "style," which continues overwhelmingly to be pragmatic and optimistic in character, to suggest that the practice of bad old "power politics" may be traced back as far as human literary and archaeological records extend – the past and the present essentially are one in terms of statecraft. An historical memory that stops at a postulated great divide in 1945 encourages aspirations for "new eras" and the like. Since the past provides the only evidence upon which theories may be constructed, the time is long overdue for strategists and arms controllers (if these be separate categories) to seek out the relevant past in a systematic fashion for the purposes of policy-science today. (This is not to deny the value of historical enquiry pursued for its own sake; the trouble tends to be that historical research for its own sake requires a massive effort of translation before its findings are organized in ways at all useful for those facing contemporary policy problems.)

The development of atomic energy for military purposes produced a discontinuity in *individual* weapon lethality unprecedented in history. For once, a cliché opinion is correct. The introduction of the tactical formation of the phalanx, the stirrup, the cross-bow, gunpowder, the magazine rifle, the machine gun, the airplane, the tank, the hydrogen bomb, the ballistic missile, multiple independently targetable reentry vehicles (MIRVs) and precision-guided munitions (PGMs) – important though they have been – are all outclassed as "discontinuous" events by the development of the atomic bomb. For the first time there was a divorce between the ability to punish and the ability to defend. As early as 1945–46, it was clear to the few individuals who devoted serious attention to the meaning of atomic energy for international politics that, whether or not the atomic bomb was employed, crises and wars between great industrial powers, and even those between small powers allied to or of great interest to the atomic powers, would be conducted under the shadow of "the bomb." Clearly the world had been changed by the atomic test of July 16, 1945 and then by the employment of the "Little Boy" against Hiroshima on August 6 and of the "Fat Man" against Nagasaki on August 8. But, just how had the world changed? Was the Second World War, just concluded and apparently overshadowed, instantly to be relegated to the happy hunting grounds of military antiquarians?

For the moment it is convenient to ignore as irrelevant the probable fact that until 1950–51 the United States did not have the atomic means on hand to wage a war with the Soviet Union to a successful conclusion (by any definition of "successful"). With close to 300 atomic bombs as late as December 1950,[1] the United States could neither defend Western Europe nor, necessarily, impose (promptly, at least) what a later generation was to term "unacceptable damage." Nonetheless, looking to the longer-term, the apocalyptic visions held by many in 1945–46 were not inappropriate. The near-instant commentators upon the new age of strategy (or the dead end of strategy, perhaps) that were spawned briefly in 1945–46 and then the creators of the new strategic theory in the second half of the 1950s are both to be excused for their tendency to deny, implicitly or explicitly, the relevance of pre-atomic experience and thought. The former were grappling tentatively with total novelty, the latter with an apparently exponential growth of new and improved technologies. First and second wave theorists (i.e., those writing, respectively, in 1945–46 and in 1955–65) served well the causes of scholarship, of citizen education, and of public policy improvement. Many of the failures of thought and of execution lie elsewhere – in a later period; most particularly in a strategic studies community that was slow in producing a third wave of theory that would fill the lacunae and discipline the excesses of the second wave, and in policymakers who have declined, or were unable, to recognize the highly speculative and even ethnocentric basis of much of their theoretical working capital.[2]

Although each superpower could (of recent years, at least) inflict well in excess of 100 million fatalities on the other within a few hours at most, and presuming that the Soviet Union cannot make effective use of the civil defense facilities attributed to it by some Western analysts,[3] one of the most noteworthy features of post-1945 international politics were the degree to which they resembled pre-1945 international politics. A healthy and necessary focus upon new weapon technologies has tended to encourage an off-hand dismissal of pre-nuclear experience, although one suspects that a rather casual acquaintance with historical study and an unhealthy fixation upon the putative mechanics of the Third World War may also have contributed noticeably to the ahistorical character of much of contemporary strategic studies. Policymakers and strategic analysts do and will insist upon borrowing from the past. In an ahistoric strategy community, analogies will be undisciplined. While the purveying of distorted versions of the 1950s and 1960s are attributable, in part at least, to political and doctrinal bias, distorted portraits of say, the inter-war years often are attributable to nothing more sinister than ignorance. For an example of dubious argument supported illustratively by incorrect history, one need look no further than to the *Annual Defense Department Report, FY1976 and FY1977*. The Secretary of Defense said that "Despite frequent use of the term 'arms race', the United States has not engaged in the life-or-death competition that occurred among the European powers in the 1930s."[4]

The stakes in the arms competition of the 1930s were indeed of a "life-or-death" character, but the competition was not waged in a "life-or-death" manner by the Western powers. If one wishes to derive a single lesson from the arms race experience of the 1930s, it would be that the half-hearted conduct of a race against a wholehearted adversary is a prescription for disaster.[5] The arms race in the 1930s, in and of itself, was no danger to peace. Indeed, had the race been conducted energetically and, above all, intelligently, by Britain and France, quite the reverse would have been the case. History can never instruct policymakers as to what should be done, but a disciplined, policy science-filtered history should diminish the ease with which officials may seek intellectual comfort from simple and misleading isolated analogies.

If it is correct, or at least highly plausible, to suggest that international politics really is a continuum of historical experience, then it follows that pre-nuclear statecraft and strategy is no less the subject of the contemporary strategist, *a priori*, than are MIRVs and cruise missiles. Without in any way endeavoring to play down the importance of the quantum jump in the lethality-to-weight of projectile ratio achieved with nuclear weapons, many of the features of the post-1945 world which tend to be associated with the revolution in weaponry have, in fact, only a tenuous or partial connection with that revolution. For example, the extreme disfavor with which the general public in all NATO countries views the prospect of large-scale organized violence is a continuation of a secular trend that would seem to have been born in the mud of Flanders. Nuclear weapons have strengthened a healthy public distaste for inter-state combat, but such distaste was no less prominent a feature of the inter-war years (of the 1920s in particular).[6] It may well be correct to claim that "revolutionary" states[7] are prevented, by the prospect of nuclear use, from prosecuting their ambitions to the point of major war. However, while granting the probable sobering effect of intimations of suicide, ambitions may still be forwarded by means of the threat of force on a very large scale, as well as by the actual employment of force on a small scale (implying a readiness to escalate and a willingness to accept high risks). It is a fact that the strategic studies community has produced, and continued to produce, a literature that tends to ignore pre-1945 thought and experience.

There is some danger that two threads of contention will be confused. First, one may argue that the geometry of world power has so altered in the second half of the twentieth century – over the first half and over all previous periods – that all major political, economic, and strategic problems are distinctive to this current period. History may be fun, but it can have no policy relevance (however defined). Second, one may assert that a nuclear age must differ from all previous ages because of the revolution in military affairs wrought by nuclear physics. If the Manhattan Project (and its Soviet equivalent) had failed, what would have been the character of postwar international politics?

The superpowers and war

In summary form, one may suggest that, first, the Soviet Union and the United States would have been superpowers, contending over the control of the Eurasian "rimland."[8] Second, the preeminence of the superpowers would have meant that the United States would have been an essential "balancer" in the power scales relating to Europe. Third, the new geography of power, with the intercontinental distances dividing the principal adversaries, would have ensured the development and procurement of long-range successors to the B-29 (e.g. the B-36 and so on)[9] – the exponentially rising unit costs of which would have spurred the development of "unconventional" weapons (e.g. nerve gas). Fourth, although the inhibitions to general war would have been somewhat lower than was the case with nuclear arsenals, it is easy to exaggerate the probable propensity of both the United States and the Soviet Union to run very high risks of war in a nuclear weapon-less world.

The United States is not a superpower because it is a nuclear power of the first rank, but rather it is a nuclear power of the first rank because it is a superpower. The first detailed exposition of the superpower thesis was offered by William T.R. Fox *in 1944*, while the Manhattan Project was still top secret.[10] Atomic weapons, and a temporary monopoly of those weapons, happened to coincide with the widespread public recognition of America's superpower status. Lest the discussed arguments seem unbalanced, it is appropriate for a brief outline to be offered of the principal differences wrought in international politics by nuclear weapons.

First, no nuclear or nonnuclear power would dare to press a military campaign against a nuclear power to the attempted end of total victory. Second, no nuclear or nonnuclear power would dare to press a military campaign against a close ally of a nuclear power to the end of total victory – unless the strategic forces of that power were neutralized by the counterdeterrent of the "aggressor." Third, because of the prospective costs of nuclear war, political and military action that could be held to impinge upon the interests (not even the "vital interests") of a nuclear power would be conducted far more cautiously than would be the case in a nuclear weapon-less world. The threshold of the *casus belli* has risen markedly. Indeed, with respect to the relations between nuclear-weapon states, the very notion of the *casus belli* has lost nearly all meaning. Nuclear-weapon states do not *go to war* with each other: they might slide fearfully into combat via limited strikes for diplomatic purposes, but they could not afford the traditional unlimited implication of *going to war*.

The possibility of nuclear war, regardless of identifiable shifts in the strategic balance, the retuning of strategic doctrines, and the evolution of the arsenals, clearly strengthened greatly whatever may have been the predispositions to caution in foreign policy that were traceable to other causes. However, it would be a mistake to believe that statesmen prior to 1945, innocent of nuclear doomsday expectations, rushed like Gadarene swine down "crisis slides" into war.[11] Even before 1945, it was commonplace to observe that while victory was preferable to defeat, war tended not to pay. Short-war illusions were present in 1914, but it is well to remember that by 1914 the European political system had already endured a decade of acute international crises, none of which were permitted to slide into general war. The Anglo-French honoring of their guarantee to Poland in 1939 may seem almost trivial by comparison with the kind of immediacy of threat that would be needed to invoke similar action in the 1970s, but the Allied entry into war in 1939 was belated (in terms of a candidate *casus belli*) and fearful. It should be true that no leader could today expect to profit from major military aggression involving interests declared plausibly by a nuclear-weapon state to be vital to its security, but Hitler, and certainly the German people, did not rush joyously and unthinkingly into the Second World War. Hitler's calculations were in error, but calculations there undoubtedly were. The attack upon Poland was not intended to herald general war.

Some uses of history

The relevance of pre-nuclear thought and of commentaries upon pre-nuclear experience depend upon the character of the strategic studies in question. The closer the strategic analyst finds himself to military operations, the less relevant is he likely to find thought and experience that is distant in time. The realm of military tactics is likely to prove of policy-scientific interest only insofar as there should be lessons to be learned from the combat outcomes of asymmetries in tactical ideas and in the realm of the timely assimilation (or lack thereof) of new weapons. There is general educational value in studying the military sociology of new technology. A systematic historical study of the claims for, and realities of, the tactical performance of new weapons should promote a prudent skepticism towards extreme opinions, but the limited utility of historical study must also be recognized.

For example, an analyst seeking to make sense of PGMs for NATO's defense posture might ask what value history had for him. History-conscious strategic analysts could tell him that every weapon, or class of weapon, tends to catalyze counter-weapons; that with few exceptions, new "wonder" weapons achieve their most effective performance when employed in combination with other weapons; and that pre-war prognoses of weapon effectiveness tend to be in error. The closest historical analogue to "the PGM (claimed) revolution" was the introduction of the machine gun. Each was/is intended to prevent the tactical movement of the reigning "queen of the battlefield": infantry for the machine gun and tanks for the PGM.[12] Doctrinal argument and a wealth of supporting analyses will be forthcoming from special interests. A weapon that is doctrinally inconvenient will be disparaged. Also, new weapons tend to be fitted into existing, inappropriate military organizational forms which reflect faithfully faulty tactical conceptions. PGMs should escape this fate, given the wide diffusion of interest in their deployment. However, it should be recalled that in the British army the machine gun was thought of first as an artillery piece and that the first tanks were widely considered to be machine-gun platforms for the support of the infantry.

Without in any way reducing the burden of detailed analysis of expected weapon effects, tactical air sortie, and loss rates, and the like, it should be of some assistance to a strategic analyst to know that the particular problem of what to make of PGMs is but one example of a class of problems pertaining to the introduction of new weapons. Furthermore, it must surely be of some value to know that there is a body of *knowledge* available to be tapped concerning the past introduction of new weapons; PGMs are not machine guns, but an awareness of how effectively or otherwise previous new systems were absorbed by the military should sensitize the analyst to the kind of pitfalls that await both the enthusiast and the pessimist (and to the tactically extra-rational considerations that tend to color particular opinions). Therefore, even at the level of the consideration of a specific technology, there is some relevance in the continuity of historical experience.[13]

Paradoxically, at the politico-strategic level of concern, distant thought and experience may be both more and less salient to current policy consideration than was the experience with particular new technologies and tactical forms. Many states, in different periods, have conducted arms competitions and engaged in arms control negotiations, but only one international security system at one point in time has had to accommodate PGM technology. However, there are some near-constant factors which lend a familiarity to the set of problems faced by the interpreter of and the prescriber for "the PGM revolution." (To name but a few: military conservatism, organizational inertia, the enthusiasm of the technologist, the absence of realistic field tests, fears concerning probable counter measures... *plus ça change....*) By way of contrast, the higher-level concerns of the strategist seem, on the surface at least, to have changed remarkably little. Alliance management is a problem for the United States – as it was for the Athenians and the Spartans.[14] Naval supremacy was as vital for the Athenian Empire as for the British Empire, just as it is today for the maritime alliance of the West.[15] In 1946 Bernard Brodie saw little value in great navies in a nuclear age (this from the leading contemporary commentator on naval strategy),[16] but a majority of strategic analysts, and certainly the American and Soviet governments, do not agree thirty years later.

In short, statecraft with nuclear weapons looks very much like statecraft without nuclear weapons. Wars are fought (though not between "great powers"), force is threatened, crises are waged, arms races are run, territory is coveted, and allies are hoarded. "The rules of the road" in international politics are more restrictive than previously was the case, but the same activities are pursued; the basic competitive character of international politics has accommodated nuclear energy. The "one world or none" strain of 1945–46 was little more than an unhelpful opposition of catacylsmic/chiliastic fantasies.[17] In the long run, one suspects that the "one world" propagandists will be proved to have been correct. Strategic or political incompetence, not to mention technical accident, may well "do for us in the end." However, for a grain of comfort to the international community of strategists, the next ice age, a man-made ecological cataclysm, or even a globe-girdling virus may well accomplish the same final end. It is a duty of the strategist to ensure that no policy-created disaster occurs which could have been forestalled by a better policy science of strategy.

The paradox cited in the previous paragraphs may be false. It was suggested that the classification of policy problems, as being of one genus over many different historical periods, might in fact mislead the strategic analyst. "Decision for war" or the "basis for agreed war termination" are, stated thus baldly, potentially inclusive of all researchable periods. But, the moral and political education of leaders is very specific to period and to the embalmed beliefs of that period (resting upon the fashionable "lessons" taught by recent history).[18] As Soviet analysts think of strategic problems apparently in ways quite distinctive from analysts in the United States, so action and response differ even within one changing (rather than evolving, which suggests a movement towards higher forms) political culture. At the macro level, history shows no discontinuity in the problems faced by statesmen: when to fight, when to accommodate, how to fight (a problem typically left to the military experts, for good reasons, though often with disappointing results), and so on. The circumstances that weight political calculation are, one suspects, more local to time and culture than are those that bear upon lower level matters. Without denying variations in local color or the salience of the particular characteristics of the political systems which they serve, armies and bureaucracies do – indeed must, given their functions – have a multiplicity of features in common from Rome to the United States.[19]

Right conduct – then and now

In terms of ethical standards of strategic behavior, men are moved by the ethic of prudence. This ethic is a variable determined by the character of military technology, by the anticipated outcome of an interaction in combat of particular technologies, and by economic and political considerations. Standards of strategic behavior there certainly are, but the coincidence of calculations of enlightened self-interest with those standards leads this author to a position wherein he is unwilling to call those standards *moral*. For sound *raison d'état*, the Roman Republic destroyed Carthage and sold the surviving women and children into slavery. A "Carthaginian peace" would undoubtedly affront the moral sensibilities of Western publics today (Christian nations "do not do that sort of thing"), but the *ultima (ir)ratio* of a kindly, home-loving, and God-fearing American president is the guarantee of the assured destruction of the Soviet Union. In short, in excess of 100 million Soviet citizens would be held to account for the misdeeds of their rulers.[20] It may be objected that the Romans imposed a "Carthaginian peace," while the United States merely threatens one – for the end of preventing war (or further escalation of war). There is a legal (and ethical – i.e. temptation resisted) distinction between the contemplation and the conduct of (mass) murder. However, the assured destruction of the Soviet Union, as opposed to the threat thereof, would be far less defensible an act of state policy than was the destruction of Carthage. The former would be the last act of American state policy, the latter permitted a *Pax Romana* based prudently on overwhelming Roman hegemony in the Mediterranean.

Readers with moral antennae more sophisticated than those possessed by this writer may detect a change in the moral climate which should set the limits of permissible, expedient military action. It is my contention that if a commentator presumes a consistency over time in the moral standards that are widely accepted with respect to those actions deemed permissible in war, he will be committing no serious error. It might be noted that there is a near-global declaratory consensus upon such absolute principles of behavior as "prisoners of war shall not be shot," "prisoners shall not be tortured," and "non-combatants shall be spared." In ancient and even medieval times it would seem to have been the general case that prisoners and conquered populations were considered the legitimate and absolute property of the victor, to be disposed of as interest, convenience, whim and even perceived religious duty dictated.[21] In more recent times these particular barbarisms are no longer standard practice in the operational codes of most societies, rather they are resorted to when circumstances seem to offer few attractive alternatives. Under extreme strain of battle, soldiers of all cultures are still known occasionally to find it inconvenient to take prisoners (which is *possibly* different from shooting prisoners once taken!); waging *la guerre révolutionnaire* in Algeria, *les paras* reluctantly but determinedly resorted to systematic torture; while, in Vietnam, the United States waged a (relatively) high-technology war which was inherently indiscriminate in terms of what contemporary strategic analysts euphemistically term "collateral damage."[22]

Whether or not the television age has had a profound effect upon the permissible outer limits of military action it is far. too early to say. Certainly there is a difference in impact between a newspaper account of a search and clear operation and a dramatic movie clip in living color of a few incidents from that operation. It is widely accepted that television coverage of largely American military behavior in Vietnam did (for good or ill) promote infirmity of purpose on the home front,[23] but it seems likely that the distaste for unwanted collateral damage that the American public felt by the end of the 1960s may be confused with a rather greater distaste for a war that was being lost. One cannot help wondering what television coverage of the Somme and Verdun would have done for morale on the home front in the First World War. War is hell, but for so long as societies will pursue such ends as national independence and more-than-minimal definitions of security, and for so long as the details of some national ends are in competition between societies, then for so long must the means be accepted also,[24] Rephrased, the stability of the present international political system rests, in part, upon the threat of organized force. Nuclear weapons have undoubtedly helped dissuade super and great powers from prosecuting their interests to the point of war between each other, but the general character of international politics has remained remarkably undisturbed by the new technology.

The pre-nuclear heritage

The immediate pre-nuclear origins of nuclear-age strategic studies may easily be identified in the operational research industry that flourished in the Second World War in Britain and the United States (but which had distinguished roots in Britain in First World War),[25] in the realist vein of international relations scholarship, and in the ranks of military theorists and commentators. Although military and even strategic studies have an ancient and distinguished lineage, it is still true to say that the several perceived discontinuities imposed by the technological changes that began with the first atomic bombs have resulted in the growth of a strategic studies community that is sociologically very distinct indeed from its functional parallels in the past. This point may best be appreciated by means of a simple illustration. In the 1970s when a national military college in the United States or Britain wished to hear an authoritative exposition of the political, economic *and military* implications of new tactical nuclear weapon technologies, it tended to invite a civilian to deliver the address – even a civilian who had no direct military experience whatever. Regardless of what the largely military audience might think concerning the practicability of the civilian's views on nuclear-capable artillery, or whatever, still – in historical perspective – It was a major development that a civilian should be believed to have the most appropriate credentials for an exposition on such a subject. Prior to 1945 many civilians were opinionated, sometimes – no doubt – sensibly opinionated, on military subjects, but they were not invited to instruct the military profession on how its new weapons could be used most effectively.

The contemporary strategic (and arms control) analyst who finds his pale reflection in the separate activities of the pre-nuclear international relations scholar of a realist stripe, the operational analyst and the military commentator, tends to make only the most superficial use of pre-nuclear thought and experience. Pre-nuclear history offered a dual challenge and opportunity to the strategist in the 1970s. First, a vast library of contemporary and near-contemporary literature on the military and diplomatic experience of the day or the recent past awaited perusal. A tiny fragment of this enormous *corpus* of writing appears in the reading lists and footnotes of nuclear-age scholars. Most strategists have at least heard of Sun Tzu, Machiavelli, Saxe, Guibert, Clausewitz, Jomini, Bloch, Mahan, Foch, Douhet, Liddell-Hart, and Fuller: to cite a typical honor-roll of distinguished precursors of contemporary endeavor.

Second, the strategist today may seek to transcend the limitations, real or imagined, of the pre-nuclear "classics" of military and diplomatic thought and history, and attempt to approach the data in a more direct fashion. Contemporary literature is always, of necessity, rich in evidence that it provides concerning existing arguments and is, equally of necessity, bounded by the authors' appreciation of the needs and capacities of the target audiences for their writings and by the limits of the historical experience available as candidate data for the works in question. Few writers, over the entire length of recorded history, have been sufficiently bold or arrogant as consciously to attempt to draft books of timeless value which penetrate to the very heart of the business of the conduct of war or of statecraft. Practically every work written in the field, or even on the margins, of strategic studies that is more than a few years old, including nuclear-age literature, requires a considerable effort of translation before the reader is able to extract contemporary relevance from its pages. If one is seeking literary monuments of timeless politico-strategic wisdom one must look to Sun Tzu, Thucydides, and, to a lesser degree, to Clausewitz – not to the works on deterrence, limited war, and arms control written during the "Golden Age" of 1955–65.

There is a difference between claiming that pre-nuclear theorizing on the subject of military strategy was a very "sparsely populated" field,[26] and asserting that pre-nuclear military and diplomatic experience is not worthy of serious study. Three interlocking and highly dubious propositions would seem to command quite undue respect throughout the strategic studies community. First, it is held that pre-nuclear experience is irrelevant by definition to contemporary problems, though light anecdotal use of pre-nuclear practices may usefully be made in order to demonstrate the historical depth of the writer. Second, pre-nuclear strategic theory was intellectually unimpressive (an opinion, by and large, of a "received" character). However, even had pre-nuclear theory been a monument to prescient scholarship, it should still be deemed close to irrelevant because it was drafted for a pre-nuclear age. Third, pre-nuclear military experience should be seen as a catalogue of intellectual (and hence military) failure.

> However, by any pragmatic standard we have to concede that the system [by which new technologies were appreciated, absorbed and used by the military – prior to 1945] worked very badly. The tactical and strategic lessons presented by the experience of successive wars had to be learned over and over again, always at great cost in lives and resources and often at the cost of defeat.[27]

Brodie is correct, but – thirty years after Hiroshima – one wonders quite how the world has changed. In the 1960s and very early 1970s the United States, on the frontier of "scientific strategy," succeeded in Vietnam in fighting the wrong war in the wrong way. The fact that pre-nuclear history tends, overall, to illustrate lack of strategic foresight should encourage contemporary strategists to analyze those past errors lest they be repeated. In our *hubris*, do we imagine that the contemporary equivalent of the folly of massed cavalry charges against steady infantry could not occur?[28] Israeli practice in the opening days of the October War of 1973 demonstrated that old strategic sins continue to be committed in the newest of ways.[29] As a general rule, the case for studying manifest human failure is quite as strong as is the case for studying success.

Practically all pre-nuclear strategic writing is environment-specific and exclusive. Theorists of, and commentators on, land power, sea power, and airpower abounded, but theorists of strategy writ large were distinguished by their scarcity. This generality of environmental specialization was both a faithful testament to the unique characteristics of war on land, sea, and, later, in the air; but also it reflected the fact that commentary upon military affairs tended to be the exclusive preserve of those very closely connected with the military profession. Contemporary scholars interested in the advisory connection between civilian policy scientists and government, with regard to the prerequisites for success or the uses to which outside expertise may be put, for examples, could do a great deal worser than to add Spenser Wilkinson to their list of case studies. However, this writer cannot recall having seen a single mention of Wilkinson in the policy-relevant strategic studies literature of the nuclear-age.[30]

The essential unity of strategic problems, denying any inherent self-contained validity to land, naval, or air strategy, was of course recognized in practice in the combined operations of the Second World War. In the West, the Second World War has inspired a military-historical literature that is vast, yet which betrays implicitly the belief that its subject matter is that of a world which has vanished nearly in its entirety. One discerns almost a romantic attachment to an honest old-fashioned and "real" war: a war in which military power could be applied decisively. The "war game"-type of enthusiasm with which the Battle of the Bulge or the armored horror of the Kursk Salient is replayed in print, on film, or on boards emerged with respect to the October War of 1973. Here was a "real" war, with tanks and aircraft and front lines. While the appreciation of discontinuity has tended to persuade civilian strategic analysts to write off the Second World War as a potential source of instructive data, military practice, East and West, has shown and continues to show some remarkable continuities with pre- and actual the Second World War behavior. The Russians have returned to the "deep penetration" ideas pioneered by Marshal Tukhachevsky between 1928 and 1937 and have acquired a posture to match, while the United States, following a brief flirtation with the "pentomic division" in the middle of the late 1950s, has reverted to its old Second World War form of divisional organization. Whatever the longevity of the Second World War forms may be in American military practice (and it can be argued that they are not the forms which ought to be perpetuated), the Second World War enjoys no status at all as a supporting referent in Western strategic studies.

Hiroshima and Nagasaki preempted what might have been a flood (or even a flow) of works seeking to incorporate the lessons of the war into the general theory of the conduct of war, or into specific prognoses for future doctrine and tactical forms. The events of August 6 and 8, 1945 have been interpreted by most strategic commentators as opening an unbridgeable gulf between the present and the past. It is interesting to note that military analysts in the Soviet Union have both accepted that there has been a "military-technical revolution" of a thorough-going kind and have not ceased to maintain that, properly appraised, the history of the Great Patriotic War has an enduring military meaning.[31] The obsessive (if not retrogressive) focus on the Second World War and its lessons which permeates Soviet military literature may be explained away in terms of the searing effect of that war upon Soviet perspectives. However, those Western analysts most closely acquainted with Soviet military thought and practice seem to be agreed that contemporary and "modern" Soviet analysts and soldiers do genuinely perceive a very substantial continuity in military problems, and hence, in appropriate solutions.

Western analysts have a very mundane and eminently practical reason for studying the Great Patriotic War. Precisely, that war speaks volumes to "the Soviet way" in the conduct of war. Societies wage war not merely as their level of technological prowess dictates, but also – if not more importantly – as their very natures dictate. New technology is grafted onto old styles of behavior and old modes of thought. NATO strategists attempting to devise an effective counter to the avalanche of armor that could be moved westwards would do well to study how Soviet tank armies were handled in the Second World War and to take note of the criticisms that Soviet analysts have made of the ways in which the *Wehrmacht* handled its *panzer* armies. Western analysts might not approve, on professional grounds, of the particular meld of new technology and tactics with a traditional Soviet (and Russian) war-waging style, but they would be foolish in the extreme if they neglected to take that apparent meld seriously.

The pre-nuclear heritage for the nuclear-age student of strategy is rich and varied, both as raw and unfiltered events and, though to a much lesser degree, as reflected in the literature. The substantial neglect of this heritage may not prove well to have been a tragedy for the conduct of public policy, since even the best of all possible scholarly communities cannot guarantee political wisdom. But, this neglect does constitute a gratuitous impoverishment of the contribution of strategic studies as a policy science. A failure to attempt to bridge the nuclear divide was understandable for a period after 1945 (for perhaps a decade). One could hardly seek to relate the present to the past if there were massive uncertainties concerning the character of the contemporary strategic and political world. But, once a resilient and apparently workable theoretical framework had been devised for the accommodation of the new technologies and the new geopolitics of superpower preponderance, scholars of strategy should, without taking a full sabbatical from contemporary problems, have stood back to consider the novelty or other characteristics of the problems that they were addressing. If those problems had been found not to be substantially unique, then it might have been deduced that past eras could tell some cautionary and instructive tales.

Evidence for theory

It is easy to be misunderstood. All that is being claimed here is that a disciplined, even scientific – by James Rosenau's minimal definition[32] – study of pre-nuclear strategic phenomena should result in a cluster of strategic theories in which we could place higher confidence than is the case today. This is no mere declaration of faith: many of the errors committed in arms race management and in the conduct of arms control negotiations over the past decade should have been identified as probable errors *at the time*, had the officials concerned been operating on the basis of premises more substantial than those derived from intuition and deductive theory. Although this argument is couched in terms of the lessons to be learned from pre-nuclear experience, a study by Alexander George and Richard Smoke demonstrates that a disciplined examination of the empirical evidence of the nuclear age can yield the rudiments of an inductive strategic theory that is more promising for the education of decisionmakers than are the deductive, often intuitive and even aphoristic, propositions that tend at present to move a government down particular paths of policy action.[33]

In terms of policy relevance, the disciplined long view, which a scientific bridging of the nuclear divide should help to provide, will open to the policymaker a far wider range of experience than post-1945-focused study alone can offer. Also, this long view should help protect the policymaker from the purveyors of plausible but flawed deductive theories. For example, in and of itself, the new self-consciousness as to the systemic consequences of American arms race actions detectable in the thought of Robert McNamara was a positive development. Unfortunately, the strategic studies community had little to say to McNamara concerning the dynamics of the nuclear arms race that was worthy of his attention. Lack of inductive theory did not dissuade strategists from filling the theoretical vacuum. The American arms control community, with Robert McNamara as its most distinguished disciple, responded to the policy need by espousing and propagating (and lecturing to any Soviet citizen who would listen) a doctrine on arms race dynamics that has since been found to be incorrect in most important respects.[34] This, it must be said, occurred not at the dawn of the nuclear age; but more than twenty years after the first brief flurry of systematic speculation on the meaning of the new weapons had been disseminated. Proceeding in what has been termed an engineering mode, strategists had somehow neglected to consider the fundamental nature of the security enterprises to which their countries were committed. In the second half of the 1960s arms race theory ceased to be an esoteric sub-subbranch of strategic studies, of interest practically to nobody. Instead, it began to be milked for guidance on concrete problems of defense and arms control policy. The knowledge road could not bear the traffic that began to pass, so evidence was hurriedly, though disingenuously, tailored to fit certain propositions concerning arms race dynamics which accorded with the predelictions of the analysts and policymakers.[35] The result was not disaster, but it was policy based on false assumptions. Good arms control intentions could not substitute for lack of evidence.

Explaining the past

The pre-nuclear heritage of military thought s introduced to aspiring strategists, to a surprising degree, via the pages of one book: namely, *Makers of Modern*

Strategy, edited by Edward Mead Earle in 1941. In most respects excellent, in a few shallow and even bizarre,[36] Earle's book has tended to serve as "the book" which enables the busy contemporary strategist to feel that he has the military thought of four and a half centuries at his finger tips. As a first book to read on military thought from the 1490s to 1941 Earle is no doubt, taken overall, superb. Unfortunately, Earle is almost too good. Given the policy orientation and the ahistorical training of very many strategists, Earle's is a book which tends to be regarded as being functionally definitive (i.e. to say, it seems to be good enough for the minimal historical needs of its readers). When Earle's contributors canter from Machiavelli to Hitler, why take time to read Machiavelli, Saxe, Clausewitz, Foch, and the rest? By an accident and even an irony of history, *Makers of Modern Strategy* has served to reinforce the widespread opinion among nuclear-age strategists that atomic fission wrote *finis* to the relevance of (nearly) all previous military thought and experience. Appearing on the threshold of the nuclear age, *Makers of Modern Strategy* often is approached as a critical celebration of a defunct era. For reasons that might be worth exploring, no revised or successor volume has sought to present "military (strategic) thought from Machiavelli to Schlesinger." Edward Mead Earle intended that his book should demonstrate some not inconsiderable themes of continuity over four hundred and fifty years, even though he recognized explicitly in his Introduction that it was increasingly difficult to talk of *military* strategy.[37] Nonetheless, this work, terminating with an appraisal by the editor of the politico-military skills and ambitions of Hitler, serves to reinforce the popular opinion that works on military or strategic thought are either pre- or post-Hiroshima in focus.

It is true that some useful "linkage" work has been performed, particularly by George Quester, by Robert Osgood and Robert Tucker, and by Barry Steiner,[38] but in general the "rich lode of empirical material for the expansion and refinement of contemporary concepts," as George and Smoke describe the diplomatic and military history of the past two centuries,[39] has yet to be mined in earnest. For a contemporary strategist to delve into the Anglo-German naval race (let alone into twelfth-century arms control arrangements) is still widely regarded as a harmless, though potentially diverting, eccentricity.

Apart from the classics of military thought which should be read for their timeless qualities, the contemporary strategist in search of his pre-nuclear heritage will have to perform most of the spadework himself.[40] In much the same way that officials and politicians profess to find most academic writings interesting but only of marginal relevance to their needs, so the strategist in quest of policy scientific knowledge is almost certain to find the works of military and diplomatic historians interesting, even enlightening, but nowhere near fully responsive to his theoretical needs. The military historian, whether formed in the vintage mold of the campaign analyst, or whether conceived in the more modern image of the scholar of the relations between military institutions and society, is unlikely to be equipped adequately in order to function as a perceptive policy scientist. "Progress" in strategic studies, if such a possibility is to be admitted, seems likely to be impeded by the gulf of methods, approaches, and concerns that divides historians from social scientists. The man best qualified to examine the tactical innovations and strategic consequences of new civilian and military technologies in the American Civil War is unlikely to be a man willing to step beyond "his period" to cooperate in the amassing of a cumulative knowledge concerning the introduction of new devices and methods in different periods. Unfortunately, but of necessity, the contemporary strategist with but a cursory knowledge of pre-nuclear military history braves all the perils that beset the rank amateur when he ventures into the 1930s (or the 1830s).

Strategy in the Missile Age

It is possible that despite the presence of clear statements expressing a contrary intention, the most widely praised book on contemporary strategy, Bernard Brodie's *Strategy in the Missile Age*, may have served to discourage scholarly journeys "in quest of the wisdom of the past on the subject of war."[41] Strategists, daunted by the dimensions of Edward Mead Earle, could obtain a far quicker "fix" on their pre-nuclear heritage from the first four chapters of Brodie's work. Those chapters are witty, brilliant, and economical. They are also very contentious. For example,

> As one goes in quest of the wisdom of the past on the subject of war, one notices first of all how small is the number of general treatises on strategy even over the space of centuries. There have been many great soldiers in the past, and military historians have favored us with thousands of volumes recounting the exploits of outstanding military leaders, as well as of many of them not so outstanding. But this richness of writings in military history does not prepare us for the poverty in theoretical writings on the strategy of war. Indeed the few theorists have enjoyed an exceptional scarcity value.[42]

The context of the given quotation is an argument to the effect that the military profession, certainly prior to 1945, has been far more interested in tactics than it has in strategy. This is rather like saying that officials are far more interested in concrete proposals for action than in conceptual frameworks. Both are hardy perennial truths that stem from the very nature of the responsibilities of the men in question. The principal frailty in Brodie's argument is that it requires a baseline for assessment. If there was a "poverty in theoretical writing" (and it is by no means self-evident that this was the case – although this author agrees with Brodie), is that a poverty in quantity, in quality, or in both? If the judgment rests upon the appreciation that, say, wars from the time of Napoleon to Hitler were ill-conducted with reference to political purpose, what is the relevant standard of comparison? Ill-conduct by comparison with Korea (or Vietnam – which occurred after the date of publication)? Whether or not the wealth (in quantity at least) of contemporary strategic theorizing will produce a well-conducted Third World War, it is, fortunately, too early to say. The quality of contemporary theory *may* be reflected in the protracted absence of a direct clash of arms between the superpowers, but there is no way of being certain that this is the case.[43]

It is true that the scale of effort of strategic theorizing from the mid-1950s onwards was unprecedented. However, it is also true that this rapid-growth industry was the product of very special circumstances (including the rapid development of succeeding generations of weapons which were clearly beyond the special professional competence of the military to accommodate conceptually; and the rapid development of ancillary academic disciplines). To confront Brodie's argument directly, it is useful to pose two questions. First, are there more first-class minds studying the interface between war and politics today than was the case, say, in 1900? Second, if the answer is in the affirmative, is the numerical discrepancy reflective not of pre-nuclear "poverty" but rather of the scale and complexity of contemporary problems? As we observed earlier, the strategic studies community today is very large by comparison with times past, but the number of theoretical innovators is very small indeed (between 5 and 10 perhaps – though their identity would be disputed according to personal preference). Given the compression of comprehension time imposed upon theory-builders by the pace of technological innovation, it is quite plausible to argue that the scale of strategic theoretical activity prior to 1945, allowing for the peaks and troughs of inventiveness that characterize all streams of intellectual endeavor, was neither inappropriate to the pace of military developments, nor – historical contexts recalled – was it on a scale greatly disproportionate to that conducted today.

The rough treatment meted out by Brodie to pre-nuclear military thinkers and practitioners probably has encouraged an already ahistorical community in its intuitive preference for ignoring pre-nuclear experience. As a naval historian and theorist of the first rank, Bernard Brodie was, of course, fully aware of both the continuities and the discontinuities in strategic problems and thought effected in part by the development of nuclear weapons. However, the overall impression left by the first four chapters of *Strategy in the Missile Age* is one of an era marked by strategic intellectual "poverty" and by military malpractice. The statements in a positive vein are swamped by the generally negative thrust of the argument. Brodie's book is important both because it is one of the few works addressed to contemporary problems that does look backwards in more than a passing fashion, and because his book is not just another work on strategy. It was a landmark text: a work summarizing and transcending the debates of a decade. Moreover, it remains, in the 1970s, the first book on the subject of strategy that newcomers are requested to read. Finally, even if Brodie were correct in his implicit claim that pre-nuclear strategic theory was but a pale and undernourished forerunner of contemporary theorizing, it does not follow (and, indeed, Brodie suggests to the contrary) that pre-nuclear military and diplomatic practice offers no substantial reward to the determined scholarly explorer.

Conclusion

A deeper and more systematic training of a new generation of strategists and arms controllers in relevant pre-nuclear history may be justified on a number of grounds. Such training should enable students better to distinguish the transient from the enduring, should facilitate their understanding of the structure of policy problems (with many more cases for study), and should help them to discern inappropriate historical analogies and illustrations when they are offered. However pragmatic their apparent approach to current problems, all strategists relate the particular to the general. Whether it be the proposed sale of F-18Ls to Iran or the fate of sea-launched cruise missiles in SALT, very particular issues are processed analytically by minds that contain general frameworks relating to foreign military sales, arms race, the character and objectives of the Soviet Union (in its relation to the conduct of arms control), and so forth. This article has not argued that public policy will be improved as a direct consequence of strategists and arms controllers delving into pre-nuclear thought and practice. All that is suggested is that the paying of systematic attention to the nuclear phenomena, would allow a vast expansion in the relevant data base from which general hypotheses and premises could be constructed. Among the virtues of historical inquiry is the fact that its findings compel officials and analysts to confront evidence that transcends the bounds of their life experience – although it is not to be denied that each generation will interpret history in ways consistent with *its* actual experience.

It is possible that the argument presented here is profoundly in error; that really today's strategists and officials have no need of the policy-scientific study of history. However, on *prima facie* grounds, that possibility looks more than a little insubstantial. The case for the relevance of much of pre-nuclear strategic thought and practice to the design of policy frameworks for the proper assessment of contemporary policy problems is sufficiently robust, that the burden of proof would seem to rest upon those who claim, explicitly or tacitly, that 1945 truly marked a great divide in international political affairs.

2 New directions for strategic studies? How can theory help practice? [1992]

> Theory then becomes a guide to anyone who wants to learn about war from books; it will light his way, ease his progress, train his judgment, and help him to avoid pitfalls...[Theory] is meant to educate the mind of the future commander, or, more accurately, to guide him in his self-education, not to accompany him to the battlefield...
>
> (Carl von Clausewitz)[1]

> ...are the analyses of national security developed by scholars and decision makers part of the solution or part of the problem? Have these exercises actually made the world less safe? Have we called into existence problems that, had we defined them differently, would not have been troublesome?
>
> (Robert Jervis)[2]

Strategic studies is not a self-sustaining "multidiscipline" or field committed to the pursuit of an absolute vision of truth. Rather, strategic studies is a practical subject focused upon the means–ends relationships which political bodies, most typically governments, endeavor to manage with reference to security. Ultimately that security relates to physical security, though also it pertains to the independence of the political bodies which act strategically. An important defining characteristic of strategic studies is the salience of *force*, latent or actual, to the questions of interest in the field.

The proposition that there are security, or international security, studies, distinct from strategic studies, is a fashionable idea that is interesting but not powerfully plausible. Barry Buzan's discovery of the key role of the concept of *security*, as developed at great length in his excellent tract, *People, States and Fear*,[3] invites recollection of the British writer Philip Guedalla's observation on the writings of the leading apostle of sea power: "But if Mahan discovered nothing in particular, he discovered it very well."[4] Buzan, among others, is surely correct in stressing the need for a broad approach to enquiry; he is not correct, however, in advising that strategic studies should not be given a facelift and, in some manner, be integrated with international security studies. Properly conceived and pursued, strategic studies have always been security studies.[5] John Chipman is substantially on target when he writes that "to those who argue that definitions of strategic studies need to be widened, it is right to answer that, having been artificially shrunk in the past 40 years, they are now returning to their natural and necessary proportions."[6]

Strategy and its study, although anchored to matters pertaining to military force,[7] has meaning, finally, with reference to politics. The notion that strategic studies usefully can be separated from a much more broadly conceived "security studies" is a fallacy which should be resisted. The fact that much of what has been labeled strategic studies has been narrowly technical, and perhaps politically naive, is really beside the point. The need for better strategic studies has never been at issue. This author believes security studies to be a superior alternative label to so-called strategic studies, contested concepts though security and strategy both may be. This analysis will return to the strategic "versus" security studies question, because some significant confusions may be perpetrated inadvertently by would-be reformers of the field of enquiry.

Viewed quite strictly as an academic field of enquiry and as a subject to be taught in universities, strategic studies requires no justification other than its arguable merit for the training of minds and as a contributor to the general republic of knowledge. This article has no quarrel with the proposition that strategic studies, along with algebra, botany, or theology, can train minds – in this case train minds by the exercise of strategic reasoning. Also, this article applauds the pursuit of knowledge for its own sake. It remains the case, however, that most students of strategy understand themselves to be engaged in the pursuit of socially useful knowledge.[8] Exceptional indeed is the student of strategy who professes no interest in the utility of his scholarship for the public safety. Even more exceptional is the scholar who will argue, or perhaps admit, that his strategical enquiries have no practical merit. Indeed, it is difficult even to conceive of strategic enquiry that at some level of abstraction or by some indirect route could not lay claim to policy relevance.

The central purpose of this article is to review the theory–practice nexus and explore the level and content of theory which might indeed be useful to the public weal. Cultural setting, strategic context, working premises are all critical for this enquiry. Lest there be any misunderstanding, the author confesses: to being Anglo-American in political and strategic culture(s); that he is an active participant in the United States in the subject of this essay, as well as being an observer of the field; to believing that strategic studies can and should provide knowledge useful for official practitioners of strategy.[9] The uniqueness of the extended US defense community is a potential source of difficulty for this enquiry. No other country facilitates the co-option of civilian students of strategy for official purposes to the degree, or on the scale, of the United States. The same questions about the relationship between theory and practice can be asked of any country, but – to the best of my knowledge – only the United States formally licences more-or-less "outside" (of government) theorists as experts entitled by their recognized expertise to be live participants ("players") in actual strategy-making processes. The license in question is access to classified information. Officials in most countries guard their prerogatives as experts more jealously and effectively than is possible in the United States.

The intention here is to consider the future of the profession of strategic studies in the contexts both of its past performance and of predictable future demand for its services. Except for illustrative purposes, this article is not drafted to advance this or vilify that particular strategic idea or practice. But, since strategy is a practical art and its study necessarily bears upon the public safety, the propagation of erroneous ideas cannot be a matter of indifference. For example, what fairly can be called the dominant RAND theory of apolitical defense analysis for stable deterrence is demonstrably wrong in that it assumes away the heart of its proper subject (which is the strength of political motivation to fight, calibrated according to intensity of interests at stake).[10] Similarly, the leading, still popular, idea that arms control can serve its classic objective of reducing the risk of war is fundamentally flawed.[11] Both theories rest upon false premises and thoroughly mischaracterize their subjects in ways which exclude the political meaning of conflict. It is important to know that publicly useful knowledge cannot flow from these approaches to stable deterrence and arms control. In a defense community like that of the United States, where theory enjoys relatively easy access to the halls of practice, intellectually shoddy ideas can do real harm. Also, given that the United States is the last line of its own, as well as of many other peoples' deterrence and defense, errors in the logic which helps shape American policy and strategy is fraught with unusual peril for international security.

The two quotations which head this essay raise issues of pervasive significance. Clausewitz flags what has come to be called the level-of-analysis question. He suggests, at least as this theorist translates his meaning, that strategic theorists can help train generals, and may even identify and evaluate options, but they should not themselves attempt to write plans. Matters of expertise, authority, and intellectual integrity intrude forcefully upon this issue. In the second quotation, Jervis signals the possibility that rather after the fashion of "merchants of death" motivated to stimulate demand for their evil products, so strategic theorists perhaps are wont to discover or invent problems in need of alleviation by the skills of their trade. The overelaboration of defense planning and strategic theorizing is a familiar curse.[12] Nonetheless, before one rushes to criticize and punish the professional purveyor of bad news (is strategic studies the new "dismal science"?), it is well to remember that historical experience is far richer than is the fiction of strategic theory or even the rococo variations of some over-industrious military planners. Strategic theory and military planning are composed with some attention to plausibility and coherence; the actual course of historical events is not so constrained.

Context: of defining moments and such-like conceits

Wisely it is said that nothing fails like success. The immediate context for this discussion is, of course, the Western, really the United States, victory in the Cold War. Victory may be a politically indelicate or incorrect term in this sensitive age, but it is not an inappropriate one. The Soviet Union was overmatched and outlasted by the Western coalition. Prior to its formal demise in December 1991, the Soviet Union repudiated its defining and legitimizing ideology, abandoned its extra-territorial imperium in Europe, and bequeathed to its successor polities a "time of troubles" of uncertain duration. At present and for some time to come, at least, Russia, let alone the so-called Commonwealth of Independent States, is not a superpower, save only in the most brutal of residual military senses.

It is in no small degree ironic that the Cold War should have been won by the superpower whose political. and strategic culture is characterized by impatience and short-term thinking.[13] If by use of a time machine one could go back and ask Western statesmen and other opinion leaders in, say, 1980, 1970, 1960, and 1950 how they would choose to describe the implosion of the Soviet Empire which went critical in 1989–91, it is predictable that the answers would vary between major success and victory for Western policies. After all, what has happened recently is not that far removed from the political predictions made in 1946–47 by George Kennan with reference to the contingent promise of a policy of firm containment. It must be noted, however, that the highly competitive containment policy pursued by the United States and her allies was *always* a great deal more military in focus than Kennan favored. The US strategy that contributed critically to the historic failure of the Soviet empire was vitally non-Kennanesque.

To return to the theme of the failure of success, the almost indecent haste, with which US and NATO policy and strategy have been restructured to meet the new conditions of the 1990s, is reminiscent of some past errors in statecraft. In fact, the historical record is awash with proclaimed "defining moments," even "decisive moments," to cite a rather extensive claim made on May 7, 1991, by the US deputy national security adviser.[14] Historically defining of decisive moments, rather like "classics" in the arts, are extraordinarily difficult to identify reliably at the time. For example, only the course of subsequent events determined that disturbances in some of the American colonies in 1775, or in Paris in 1789, truly were defining moments.

Common sense should alert us to the possibility that many, indeed probably most, would-be defining moments are run over by the locomotive of history as usual. The current facts, arguable facts and probable/possible facts of change in international security conditions, are plain enough. What is not plain enough is the pattern of change. Successions of like-leaning facts constitute what usefully are called trends. But, paradoxical historical processes have a way of confronting trends with countervailing trends. The very signs of the times which proclaim that peace is breaking out are themselves alerting signals of difficulties to come; for those willing and able to read the signals, that is.

The *annus mirabile* of 1989–90 which witnessed the demise of the Soviet imperium over East-Central Europe, followed in 1991 by the all but unimaginable bonus of the then Soviet Union filing for reorganization in the face of political, social, and economic bankruptcy, were neither gifts of God nor strictly the product of processes entirely internal to the Soviet world. The West in arms should take some credit for helping to fuel the admittedly complex processes of change in the Soviet Union in the 1980s. Stalin was right when he observed that "those who fall behind get beaten." The United States sustained, indeed in the 1980s revived, a multi-dimensional competitive stance which Soviet society could not meet, even with the allocation of nearly a quarter of its economic resources to defense functions. Recognition by Moscow that the USSR was in danger of los-ing touch in high technology with the other superpower, played a significant role in the promotion of reform ideas. *Perestroika* and *glasnost* subsequently escaped central control, leading to the unanticipated political melt-down of the extra-territorial empire in Europe during 1989–90 and finally to the yet more unantic-ipated demise of the imperial state itself: but that is another story of no direct concern to this article. In retrospect it is persuasive to argue that President Ronald Reagan's Strategic Defense Initiative (SDI), announced rhetorically in 1983 and organized as a coherent research program in 1984, was the tip of the military high-technology spear which pricked Soviet pretensions to the status of first-class super power. Whether or not the SDI was believed in Moscow to have near-term promise as an integrated architecture of weapon and weapon-support systems, the technologies of all kinds to be advanced rapidly by SDI dollars had Soviet competitive loss written all over them.

It is close to being unarguable that Western, necessarily essentially American, defense policies either were successful in the eventually triumphant conduct of the Cold War, or at the least were compatible with success in that surrogate for hot war. It is perhaps just possible to argue that the successful conduct of the Western end of East–West political–strategic relations from the late 1940s to the late 1980s was performed more despite, than because of, the defense policies pursued.

The military build-up of the first half of the 1980s – embracing both the final Carter as well as the Reagan years – certainly was not a phenomenon likely to gladden the heart of defense rationalists. A series of powerfully argued, if necessarily massively speculative, articles by strategic theorists in the journal *International Security* found all but comprehensive fault with the defense policy of the Reagan administration. The general flavor of the leading edge of the criti-cism, to mix metaphors, is conveyed by the following summary critique offered in 1983 by Barry R. Posen and Stephen Van Evera:

> ... the basic direction of Reagan's defense policy seems mistaken.
>
> The strategy implicit in Administration programs and statements is unre-alistically demanding. Insofar as the Administration seems to have a grand strategy, it appears to incorporate requirements for fighting wars of every kind, all at once – global conventional war against an unspecified range of adversaries, offensive conventional operations against the Soviet homeland, and a victorious nuclear war against the Soviets. This is quite a tall order. Both counterforce operations and offensive conventional operations generate open-ended requirements that simply cannot be met.[15]

Such criticism was fair enough, if arguably a little disingenuous. The military "requirements" for the deterrence or, if need be, the conduct of global war are likely to be open-ended and unaffordable, no matter whose strategy is preferred.[16] The Reagan administration favored a more offensive strategy, if operationally feasible, at and from the sea and on land in Europe, and a more defensive strategy for the so-called strategic forces, than did its immediate predecessors.[17] Strategists of good will and equal competence and knowledge legitimately could disagree about these matters.

It would appear to be a fact, though the events at issue really are much too recent for detached and balanced judgment, that the political competitive value of the Reagan defense build-up was much greater than was the sum of its emphatically arguable parts (e.g., the MX ICBM, the B-IB bomber, SDI, the maritime strategy, and so forth).[18] It is not a demonstrated, or indeed a demonstrable, fact either that the broad directions taken by US defense policy and strategy in the 1980s were incorrect, or that the United States competed with excessive budgetary vigor. Even so careful a scholar as Stephen M. Walt can slip into the sin of unwarranted hindsight. Walt has commented that

> Interest in security affairs was also revived by the deterioration of U.S.–Soviet relations in the late 1970s and early 1980s. *Although public concern for America's international position was exaggerated*, the Iranian and Nicaraguan revolutions, the SALT II treaty, and Soviet intervention in Africa and Afghanistan helped place national security issues back on the public and academic agenda.[19]

Walt's research and writings on alliance formation stand behind that confident judgment; particularly the historical finding that "because balancing [would-be hegemonic power] is the dominant tendency in international politics, the world's most important countries are strongly disposed to ally with the United States. As a result, the United States can afford to take a relaxed view of most international developments."[20] Theories of statecraft, however, no matter how generally plausible, are always liable to fail to apply in particular cases, and Walt's logic could have led to Britain's defeat in 1940![21] "America's international position" was not corrected (perhaps overcorrected), if it needed correction, by some Hidden Hand of a balance of power mechanism. Rather, that position was corrected by the total response of friends and foes to the statecraft of the Reagan administration in the face of the Soviet menace of the day. At the very least, it would be churlish to deny that the Reagan administration did well enough – though the security outcome by the end of the decade was favorable beyond all credible prognostication – while the basis for the claim that peril had been exaggerated suffers from a fatal logic flaw. As with alleged triumphs for deterrence, how can one know how bad things might have been? Success in an international conflict can hardly help but raise doubts over whether it was purchased at too high a price, or even whether it was needed at all.

Three questions of central interest for the mandate of this article arise at this juncture. First, did US strategic choices and other defense decisions actually keep, or substantially help keep, the superpower nuclear peace for more than four decades? Second, did strategic studies have a noteworthy impact upon official choices for policy and strategy – and was that impact on balance benign or malign? Third, how much, and what, of the intellectual legacy of Cold War-era strategic studies merits preservation or just light refurbishment for future use?

The scholars among us will, indeed should, be troubled by the problems of evidence which overshadow this discussion. Cause and effect in the complicated iterative processes that link strategic ideas, defense policy, and strategic plans are notoriously resistant to conclusive investigation by tidy minds. Success has many claimants for parenthood or midwifery. Failure appears to occur as by the writ of some anonymous hidden hand. The characterization provided here thus far barely begins to do justice to the true complexity of the subject. For example, even when the community of defense intellectuals arms an official champion with potent ideas, those ideas may suffer misshaping by government, or they may fail in practice because of inept execution. It happens all the time. Those of us who are idea merchants know that it is as impossible to design policy and strategy ideas that are proof against fools as it is to find ideas that are fool-proof. It is the rare and unlucky strategic theorist who is unable to cite some not implausible excuse to avoid having to admit to mea culpa.

The question of authority of evidence is non-trivial, if there is to be intelligent speculation on the subject of how theory can help practice in the future. Many people look at the contemporary condition of burgeoning peace in what used to be known as East–West relations, for example, and see in this irenic condition proof positive of the error in past US policy and strategy practice. They neglect to notice that this possibly brief happy condition of good feeling very plausibly has been generated in good part by the hardnosed competitive position of the US-led global coalition over the course of four decades. Unsound comprehension of the causes of war and the conditions for peace cannot help but facilitate imprudent advice for future policy and strategy.[22]

The main (non) "event" of the Cold War for professional students of strategy was the non-occurrence of its termination in a nuclear Third World War. Professional satisfaction with a well done job of deterrence is marred slightly by residual and largely irreducible ignorance over just what it was that US policy and strategy "did right." By way of personal illustration of this point, recently this theorist had to draft a short bibliographical essay introducing the best books written on nuclear strategy. During the course of a long peace, major issues of strategy tend either to remain unresolved, or to be settled by budgetary fiat, the climate of opinion, political and intellectual fashion, or simply by the passage of time. The authority of combat is lacking. Looking back over the past forty-five plus years, there is no way of knowing whether this or that emphasis in the nuclear war plans, tied to different preferences in force planning, either mattered for the deterrence of war or would have mattered had a nuclear war been waged. To date, nuclear war and what does or not much help deter it, blessedly remains strictly a realm for speculative theory. Without the discipline of experience, imagination is at a premium.

It can be important for a sense of proportion, certainly for an appropriate humility and civility in debate, to remember that there is no objective discriminator of real merit dividing "the better" from "the worse" studies of nuclear strategy and deterrence. Readability, plausibility, and intellectual rigor are all positive attributes in a book. But, common sense and good judgment are not always bestowed by nature upon people who are capable of dazzling intellectual achievement. A noticeable fraction of modern strategic theory is as clever as it offends against common sense. Some of the parents of modern arms control theory positively exuded self-satisfaction at the cleverness with which they were inventing counterintuitive arguments.[23] The literature on crisis stability for stable deterrence and on limited war has been equally prone to propagate clever fallacies.[24] Although experience of bilateral nuclear war fortunately is zero, and the responsibility for successful performance in nuclear deterrence is uncertain, the twentieth century has provided a great deal of evidence of regimes for "strategic" arms limitation (including sixteen years in the 1920s and 1930s),[25] on the outbreak of major wars and on the conduct of limited war.

There is no satisfaction in registering the points that the theory of stable deterrence which helps educate the leading approach to arms control is thoroughly unhistorical and implausible, the central paradox which fuels arms control theory is exactly wrong, while the perceived lack of merit in the limited war theory generated in the 1950s and 1960s by civilian strategists may be gauged by its comprehensive rejection in the theory of "decisive force" in war expressed by Operation Desert Storm.[26]

This article is forward-, not backward-, looking, but the quality of past performance does have relevance for the likelihood of superior performance in the future. How should the current situation be characterized? Did the West survive and eventually succeed in the Cold War with more help than hindrance from the new profession of strategic studies: or, was the reverse the case? The perils to international security in the 1990s and beyond may include a dismantlement by the West of much of the political-military infrastructure which brought safety over the past decades. But, so many of the "old directions" for strategic studies in a past era did not function well even in that era, that the profession should think hard and honestly about how and what it can contribute in the future.

Adapting Clausewitz's advice, the most important step for the student of strategy is to understand the nature of the new period and not to seek to make of it something that it is not.[27] Attractive but unhistorical assumptions about the future will generate irrelevant questions and possibly dangerous answers. For example, the assumptions that past patterns of great-power rivalry miraculously are no more, or that the awful burden of Russian and Soviet history will not constrain the course of history for the Soviet Union's successor states, must serve to encourage a relaxation of Western vigil which would be unwise. Answers may be dangerous in that credulous, desperate or lazy policymakers may find them attractive, even though they address the wrong questions. Examples of flawed questions would include rigorous and imaginative study of ways to render the Conference on Security and Cooperation in Europe (CSCE) process a useful principal vehicle for security in Europe, or the energetic search for a sound negotiating position on a START follow-on regime. CSCE and START may decorate and help dignify a peaceful context, but they cannot contribute usefully to the creation or the guarding of such a benign condition.[28] CSCE posits a security community that does not exist, while Strategic Arms Reduction Treaty (START) – and the 1990 treaty on Conventional Forces in Europe (CFE) – quite literally address military balances that lack all systemic political reality.

It is sad that so many people, not excluding professional students of strategy, are willing to learn so little from the 1920s and 1930s and the 1970s and 1980s. Principal lessons from the interwar period, for instance, are that neither collective security nor arms control can work when they are needed.[29]

Theory and practice

Discussion of "new directions" for any field of study tends to reduce rapidly to rather sterile advocacy, and debate over, second-order matters. Strategists in government and outside scholars of strategy will each of them have their favorite topics, or hobby horses. Every proposed topic, new or familiar, will be more or less defensible; even the most seemingly well-ploughed fields allegedly require reworking in the light or, more likely, gathering darkness of new conditions. Understandably, properly and at least to a degree healthily, students of strategy are as disunited on the topics in need of treatment as they are on the answers they favor to such issues as can provide a focus for engaged debate. If strategic studies is a field embracing Australian professors, American think-tank analysts, German journalists, Russian soldiers and so on, one wonders whether any coherent, albeit arguable, answers are possible to the questions which provide the title to this article. Issues self-evidently important and perhaps even urgent to those parts of the US defense establishment with which this author interacts may appear trivial, atavistic, even fundamentally wrong-headed, in other perspectives.

The field of strategic studies is very much an educational endeavor, particularly for those members who either do not have access to classified information or who are citizens of countries with closed bureaucracies. Strategic study may amount to the pursuit of useful knowledge, but that utility does not have to be secured by means of a direct personal relationship between scholar and strategy practitioner. Ultimately, strategic studies – like economics (the previous dismal science, or ecology and climatology, probably the next such) – has pretensions to serve the public interest. Stated tersely, better strategic studies should yield some payoff in better policy and strategy. Public affairs, and particularly war, being what they are, there is of course no reliable correlation between excellence in strategic studies and success in statecraft and armed conflict. Well-educated generals may lack character, strategically cunning plans will prove futile if soldiers decline to fight, and so on. Strategy can fail at the tactical and operational levels of war,[30] just as superior tactical and operational skills can prove of net negative value if they are applied in pursuit of faulty strategy.[31] For example, in both world wars although the Germans were very good indeed at fighting, they were very poor at waging war.

Before considering the possible content of such new directions as strategic studies might take, it is important – indeed it is more important – to identify or revisit how students of strategy can and cannot be helpful to the world of practice. Herman Kahn popularized the proposition that "[i]t is the hallmark of the expert professional that he doesn't care where he is going as long as he proceeds competently."[32] There are grounds for arguing that much of the implicit and explicit advice for practice yielded by strategic studies over the past forty years has been less than competent, but that international conditions fortunately have proved massively permissive towards some of the less robust ideas behind policy and strategy. The 1991 START has nothing of strategic note to recommend it, but with permitted "strategic" weapon arsenals, treaty-accountable and otherwise, in the 8,000–9,000 range, does it really matter?

For a more blatant case of incompetence in, or indifference towards, strategic logic, one could cite the Intermediate-Range Nuclear Forces (INF) treaty of 1987. The fact that that treaty regime would be actively subversive of the central pillars of what passed for NATO strategy was not much noticed in the United States.[33] The guilty people who negotiated that treaty could not have known that Mikhail Gorbachev's extended empire would move into political free-fall within two years of the treaty's signing.

Strategy fulfills the bridging function between policy and military power, while grand strategy must accommodate consideration of all of the instruments of potential use for policy. Students of strategy, however, cannot afford to take policy choice as a "given" that is above their pay grade to question. Although policy is distinctive from strategy, there has to be an iterative process between the two. There is always a danger either that out of ignorance or incompetence policy will ask more of its military instrument than that instrument should be expected to deliver, or that policy will ask less of its "sword" than could, and perhaps should, be secured.

For there to be a mutually supportive relationship between theory and practice, each has to empathize with the world, including the *mentalité*, of the other. Scholars have been known to write long books and many articles which conclude, insofar as they have conclusions (more study is always needed), with such insightful gems as reminders that nuclear strategy poses dilemmas for policy choice, that nuclear war were best avoided if at all possible, that nuclear war might be difficult to control and terminate, and that there is no way of knowing whether the details of strategy and force posture really matter. Policymakers and defense planners have to make choices on deadlines often not of their own making, on the basis of knowledge that is perpetually incomplete, and in coordination with factors that are thoroughly non-strategic.

It is probably important for busy officials to be reminded that the requirements of deterrence are deeply indeterminate; that deterrent effect cannot be purchased reliably by the procurement of more firepower. But when students of strategy alert the world of practice to difficulties, complexities, and possible catastrophic developments, they do only part of their job. Ready or not, officials have to make decisions. Given that every choice of strategy and force posture is challengeable, the strategic scholar easily can outwear his welcome if he abuses the privilege of his position by constantly finding fault. The point is not that fault will not lurk in official behavior, but rather that no moral courage is required to be a perpetual critic. The critical function of scholarship is important, indeed essential. It can be instructive, nonetheless, to ask of the person who makes a living pointing to the hazards in, say, US nuclear planning and practices, just what he or she would recommend. Surprisingly often one finds that the scholar has not sought very seriously to look at the subject at issue from the perspective of the practitioner.

By way of analogy, one does not have to be an author in order to be a wise and witty book reviewer. But, the relevance, as opposed to the entertainment value of the reviews, to be improved were the reviewer to have some firsthand experience of the choices that attend the writing of a book. A scholar often is excused the passing of final judgment. He can list many options, find much to praise and criticize about each, and pen a wise-sounding "conclusion" which demonstrates his appreciation of complexity.

Because by definition the future is unknowable, the world of practice seeks flexibility to adjust tolerably quickly to change. Nonetheless, the politics of the defense budget in the United States are not friendly to honest admissions of ignorance. When political and military leaders appear before congressional committees and attempt to justify their requests, they cannot simply hide beneath the flag of a general prudence. The truth of the matter is that there is no uniquely correct defense budget and even if there were there is no analytical tool available for its reliable identification. Both strategy-making and force planning are creative exercises.[34] Competent defense analysts can justify virtually any level and mix of forces; just watch the assumptions and check the arithmetic.

Personal experience as well as common sense suggests that whatever new directions the transnational community of scholars of strategy elects to pursue, the knowledge it gains will have more public utility if theory and practice enjoy a greater measure of mutual empathy. There is enduring value in these words written by Winston Churchill on November 9, 1916 with reference to "mechanical power in the offensive" (i.e., "tanks").

> A hiatus exists between inventors who know what they could invent, if they only knew what was wanted, and the soldiers who know, or ought to know, what they want, and would ask for it if they only knew how much science could do for them.[35]

What can strategic studies do that the world of practice, albeit with some effort and no little translation, should find useful? Above all else, the theorist – for want of a better term – can help the practitioner to function holistically in a strategic manner. Most of the world of practice is absorbed in the development and application of means. The proposition that means should serve strategic ends which should advance policy goals is a notional Great Truth which somehow rarely intrudes upon the serious administrative and tactical business of the day. Not only are means frequently disconnected from ends, but different kinds of means are not considered in a properly combined-arms framework.[36]

Strategic studies, properly so-called, should help educate officials to think strategically. All kinds and quantities of military application need to be approached with some reference to the lingua franca of strategic effectiveness. For officials to be able to explain the strategic utility of, say, a special operations' capability, a nuclear strike option, or whatever, they need a persuasive grasp of the structure of the conflict at issue. No matter what the subject specifically under discussion, the strategic theorist almost uniquely should be able to relate tactical means to strategic consequences. Strategically educated practitioners can recognize when they are being fed tactical answers to strategy questions. Such people know, really know, that all military threats or actions have meaning finally only in regard to policy purposes.

The student of strategy generically is in the trade of insisting upon the explicit interconnection of means and ends; has to be a "policy scientist," a person able to understand the structure of an often complex situation (e.g., what is likely to be the future strategic significance of space systems and the control of space for the conduct of regional or general war?); should clarify level-of-analysis difficulties by way of insisting that actions and possible consequences be distinguished; and conducts end-to-end analysis focused upon the complex two-way relations between causes and effects.

Truly *strategic* analysis, for example, would be unimpressed by an explanation of a SIOP (Single Integrated Operational Plan – the US nuclear war plan) option in terms of damage expectancies to particular targets. The strategist wants to know how the design of nuclear war plans relates, or fails to relate, purposefully to the likely achievement of policy goals. War plans are not assumed to be such just because that is what they are called. Plans for the application of force are critical for strategy, but they need not be synonymous with it. Similarly, the strategic thinker will enquire as to the ends served by a START. Whether or not a treaty is equitable, verifiable, or the best that could be negotiated at the time, it will be answers with no strategic standing.

Statecraft and strategy are practical arts which require more for their successful conduct than just the power of strategic reason. The ranks of extra-governmental students of strategy are as heavily populated with would-be generals and would-be policymakers as with defense philosophers. The philosophers tend to confuse strategic studies with a branch of aesthetics and have great difficulty appreciating that in the world of action the best often is the enemy of the good enough. In strategy and strategic effectiveness there is the objective test of performance in the outcome of trial by threat and trial by combat. The test of strategy is "how well does it work" in competition with the strategy of a foe. Some notably flawed armies directed by pedestrian strategies have sufficed to win wars. The quest for strategic truth is unending, so the philosopher is never ready to make a decision or proffer plain advice.

An endearing fault among some officials is the attractive belief that deeper study can resolve important questions. Strategic theorists are not motivated to discourage the dissemination of this profitable fallacy. Policymakers would like to know both what will happen in the future and how they can cope well enough with that future. The sad truth is that the future is unknowable, no matter how many millions of research dollars are thrown at its study. Also, the rich uncertainty of what lies ahead means that study, deep or otherwise, cannot unearth demonstrably correct policy, strategy, or force postures to cope with that unknown future. But what strategic studies can do is usefully narrow the range of more or less confident assumptions behind future policy and strategy, explain the structure of generic persisting security challenges, and by means of historical illustration "isolate things that need thinking about."[37]

The aphorism that even if hospitals cannot cure people, they should not spread disease has some applicability to strategic studies. Competent strategic theory cannot provide a cookbook for assured success to politicians and generals, but it can help protect them from shoddy theory. With reference to General Robert Nivelle's promise to win the war on the Western Front in twenty-four hours in 1917, Correlli Barnett observed with characteristic pungency that "[i]n despair men turn to quacks who promise them their dreams."[38] Modern strategic studies is abundantly populated with people peddling patent remedies for national and international security ills. Whether it be to deflate claims for peace through international commerce, peace through arms control, peace through conference diplomacy, or whatever – rigorously conducted strategic studies help protect the public from "quacks" and dreamers.

It is worth noting that in addition to being unable to provide recipes for guaranteed success to their client publics, so students of strategy cannot easily transcend the limitations upon the character and content of their work which flow from culture and strategic context. Today, however, it has at long last become fashionable among strategic theorists to alert policymakers and defense planners to the perils of ethnocentricity.[39] That is a great advance. More to the point of this article, it is an advance which is sorely needed in the United States as it shifts the focus of national security policy, the balance in its strategy, and alters the structure of its military posture, away from yesterday's East–West frame of reference.

New directions for strategic studies?

The fact of change is as undeniable as its course and destination is unknown and unknowable. American political culture in particular, though far from exclusively, retains a residual faith in human progress and a conviction that change, or new directions, must be inherently good. When the cry goes up across the land for "new directions," the journalistic and scholarly wings of the broad field of strategic studies are eager to respond. Sundry visions are on offer, most of them distinctly weighted towards optimism, a few countervailing the other way.

The point has been made already in this article that new directions, major turning points, "historic" events, and the like can be difficult to identify reliably at the time. The first round of studies of alleged "lessons" of the 1991 Gulf War were completed before the appalling political trailing edge of that conflict had been appreciated in full. This is not to say that scholars today should be as dilatory as was the British Royal Navy in the interwar period. On the outbreak of the

Second World War, detailed naval staff studies of the convoy period of the Great War had not been performed.[40] As a result, many of the hard-learned lessons of 1917–18 had to be learnt anew in 1939–42.

The strategist-as-journalist, however, has to beware of the temptation to theorize from an unduly thin evidential base. Even following a very decent interval, when passions have cooled and the urge towards patriotic history and analysis is less pressing, still there can be major surprises. For example, to say that strategic judgments about the course of the Second World War were amended by the revelation in the early 1970s of Enigma-derived ULTRA intelligence would be an understatement. Also, views of American and Japanese statecraft in 1941 cannot be unaffected by the revelations that President Franklin Delano Roosevelt did not sanction the total oil embargo against Japan in August of that year, while the Japanese government as a whole was not aware of the sublime strategic folly of the Imperial Navy's plan to attack the US Pacific Fleet at Pearl Harbor.[41]

If one should be humble in recognition that important facts can pass unknown or underappreciated for many years or even decades, how much more careful should one be in the exercise of *forward*-looking strategic judgment. With so many voices speaking and word processors pounding, a few people are bound to stumble into prescient analysis. Unfortunately, neither they nor the policymakers and defense planners who might make timely use of sound theory and good advice have any way of quality-testing strategic analysis and prediction for its veracity. Those who are strapped to the "new directions" train – and this author includes himself in that happy band, notwithstanding the skepticism expressed here – should be both warned and comforted by possible historical precedents. A classic example may be found in the imprudent judgment offered to the House of Commons by Prime Minister William Pitt (the Younger) on February 17, 1792. The unlucky Mr Pitt anticipated many years of peace and prosperity in which his Sinking Fund to reduce the National Debt could accumulate healthily.

> We must not count with certainty on a continuance of our present prosperity during such an interval [from 1792 to 1808]; but unquestionably there never was a time in the history of this country when, from the situation of Europe, we might more reasonably expect fifteen years of peace, than we may at the present time.[42]

Instead of fifteen years of peace, Britain endured twenty-two years of war. Trend projection and analysis from a relatively benign present out far into the future is a perilous exercise indeed.

If strategic studies takes much of its shape and course from the political context and from political premises, what guidance is available for the field? Plainly the Cold War, with the geostrategic terms of reference of bloc-to-bloc confrontation in Central Europe, is definitively passé. No less plainly, Russia at present has few of the characteristics one should require of a superpower. The argument about America's relative decline has been not so much resolved as shunted aside and relegated by more pressing topics of fashionable debate. Strategic studies has always been a dependent, even parasitical, field, stimulated into activity by the reality or the anticipation of real-world events. The broad problems addressed by a variety of methodologies and to a range of different conclusions have derived directly from a given political framework.[43] Indeed it is a little sobering to appreciate that the modern, very substantially American, profession of strategic scholarship has known no relevant political framework *other* than superpower competition in the Cold War.

At present it is open season for the organization of hunting parties for new directions in strategic studies, because – with almost indecent suddenness – there is no settled political framework for the disciplining of strategic study. Very officially indeed, the US defense establishment has all but dismissed the Russian threat and is struggling to adjust conceptually to a world no longer ordered conveniently by two dominant menaces – Soviet blitzkrieg assault to the Channel and the latent menace of a Pearl Harbor-like surprise attack upon US strategic nuclear forces and their command system.

Western strategists are somewhat confused by the fact that yesterday's public enemy number one is down and out, even though much of his force structure remains. It is becoming fashionable in the United States to argue that although (superpower) peace has broken out, the world actually is becoming more dangerous.[44] Leading the charge for a variant of this theme, the Bush administration has reordered defense priorities in favor of readiness to cope with threats to (extra-European) regional order. It is also becoming fashionable to suggest that much of the conceptual arsenal developed by the strategic studies community was time, place, adversary, and technology specific to yesterday's superpower quarrel.

It seems to this student of strategy that relatively little has changed or is likely to change which should either threaten his professional existence or even much of the content of his work.[45] In most respects the distinguishing marks of sound scholarship in strategy, the focus on end-to-end means–ends analysis, the long view, the holistic tilt, and a sense of history are needed today more than ever. Modern strategic studies in what used, rather loosely, to be called "the West" may be the offspring of the Cold War, but the profession of strategic enquiry should survive the demise of that parent.

It is fascinating to note that none of the leading recent commentaries on "new directions" – Walt, Buzan, Chipman, and Crawford[46] – have much if anything of interest to say on the subject of "strategic" thinkers either functioning strategically or seeking to ensure that others do. While it is new-agenda time in the ranks of scholarship, and theorists debate incestuously and ingeniously the boundary problems that they find so self-absorbing (are we conducting strategic studies, security studies, international security studies, defense studies, international studies, and so forth – or, dare one suggest, does it much matter?), serious deficiencies in the house of strategy pass underappreciated. As a practicing strategic theorist, I have found it next to impossible to elicit much interest in, or even understanding of, the continuing need for excellence in the means–ends art that is strategic reasoning. Strategic, or security, studies has less need of a new agenda than it has of recognition of the importance of basic training in strategy.

People who have not functioned competently as strategic thinkers on the old agenda are simply going to perpetuate familiar means–ends errors as they transit to exciting new topics on a new agenda.

Strategic study (unlike the *strategist*) is value-neutral and topic-indifferent, though, as noted previously, by convention it should pertain to the actual or possible use of force. The necessity for sound strategic thinking is as unarguable as the subject references of that thinking must be ever dynamic. Most of the criticism of strategic studies, from within as well as from outside the profession, has neglected to notice that we have not performed very well *as strategists*.[47]

There is not, and there is not going to be, a New World Order, not even as that historically burdened pretentious concept has been clarified. According to Robert Gates,

> The New World Order is neither a Pax Americana nor a euphemism for the U.S. as world policeman. It is simply an attempt to deter aggression – and to resist it if necessary – through the collective and voluntary action of the international community.[48]

In the pantheon of noble fallacies, collective security ranks high. The unpleasantness in the Gulf during 1990–91 illustrated the general plausibility of John Terraine's judgments about the workings of coalitions in the two world wars: "inside or outside a coalition there is no substitute for strength" and "the ultimate strength of a coalition is not to be measured by the number of its members, but by the strength of its strongest member."[49]

The politically minded strategic theorist today discovers that this allegedly defining or decisive moment is both undefined and undecided. There is no definite security "order" in Europe at the moment, old or new. The CFE treaty supports or undermines, it is too soon to say which, what amounts to a vacuum. Yet again, structural arms control attempts the impossible. Arms control, like deterrence, indeed like sea power and airpower, is always specific in its referents and meaning. Further progress, if that is the suitable term, in CFE is unlikely, because the erstwhile bloc-to-bloc framework is no more. From the current chaos or absence of security assumptions for order in Europe, the strategic theorist can derive virtually any political guidance that he chooses. Any sense of history and strategic geography alerts one to the certainty of renewal of superpower or Great Power conflict. It may not much matter which mix of interests, or who, eventually secures a firm grip upon Russia and the Ukraine, balance-of-power considerations for security eventually will restore a context of international security politics as usual to Europe.

It is not particularly useful to play the "alternative futures" game, let alone to make a best guess as to the structure of international superpower and Great Power rivalries by the turn of the century. The strategic theorist does not know, cannot know, who will be in office, who will be aligned with whom, or exactly how many more intercontinental ballistic missiles the new Russia will produce. But the theorist does know how statesmen behave and why they behave as they do.

Also, the scholar of strategy understands that decisions today have a legacy, often an unintended and unpredictable legacy, value for tomorrow. The means–ends orientation of the strategic theorist, educated by a long historical view, alerts him to the identity of probable charlatans and dreamers. Never say never is sound advice. However, the strategic theorist should be able to alert the world of practice to the implausibility of some new, as well as some new-sounding but actually rather old, propositions and arguments.

It has not escaped the notice of the community of American strategic theorists that in this new era nothing actually has been deleted definitively from their agenda of professional concerns – particularly if the timeframe is allowed to include the medium- and long-terms. The political context for security in Europe has changed, is changing, radically. Problems of military security certainly have been reshaped by the upheavals in East-Central Europe, but they have not disappeared. Currently they may be in repose in equipment parks beyond the Urals, but the potential military problems of European security remain very troubling. Strategic thinkers, unlike many journalists, are expected to consider the structure of the situation, not just the political climate of the moment.

By way of analogy one might consider the case of British policy and strategy in the 1920s. The extant condition was healthy and benign indeed, but great strategic insight was not required in order to comprehend that the defense prospects of the British Empire rested unreasonably upon a permanence of fine security weather.[50] The political context for security can shift massively from one decade to the next; as happened from the 1920s to the 1930s, and from the early 1980s to the early 1990s. The strategic theorist cannot predict a regular cycle in these matters, but he does know – really know, that is – that bad times return.

A part of the strategic theorist's responsibility to his society is to challenge the arguments of the purveyors of claims for "the end of history,"[51] the arrival of a "post-nuclear era,"[52] the obsolescence of major war,[53] the abolition of conventional war,[54] the banishment of force as a practicable instrument of statecraft, and so on. Society has to be protected against its understandable wish to believe that, *this time*, things will be different – peace truly will last, transnational economics will vanquish old fashioned military concerns, and the like.

Many and probably most of the criticisms leveled at strategic studies of recent years are either true but second-order in kind (e.g., they reflect upon poor performance by students of strategy), or are simply misconceived. For example, in her often insightful article in this journal, Neta C. Crawford advances the canard that

> The dominant paradigm of security studies [realism or neo-realism] could not foresee the changes in the Soviet Union or the changing relationship between the superpowers because its assumptions were incapable of even suggesting that this was an alternative, let alone believe that the changes were real once they began to occur. Realism must be modified (or possibly partially abandoned) to account for change of this sort.[55]

This is just wrong. Unreconstructed realists such as myself have been weaned on the rise *and fall* of empires. The fact that most realists and neo-realists did not predict the fall of the House of Lenin in the 1980s was a failure in prescience, not of paradigm. The ending of the Cold War has occurred for reasons fully explicable without strain by realist argument.

Crawford advises also that "one way to get more theory and better theory is to step back from policy analysis and ask basic questions about security and test our basic assumptions rather than continue to repeat them without question."[56] This is an example of false alternatives; of a misconceived choice rather than of flatly false judgment. Well conducted strategic, or security, studies *never* adopt and repeat assumptions uncritically. The advice in effect to take a time out to consider our intellectual navels is not well taken. Scholars true to their calling do not conduct policy analysis of a kind or in a way indifferent to basic questions. Indeed, it is the very sensitivity of the scholar of strategy to the importance of those basic questions and assumptions that renders his work valuable to official clients or to the public at large. Good policy analysis is attentive to its assumptions, just as good strategic study will embody genuinely strategic argument.

Conclusions

How can theory help practice in the universe of strategy?

First, strategic theorists can do for practice what practice needs but cannot readily do for itself. Few practitioners have the time, the training, or even the inclination to think strategically. Strategy guardianship cannot be entrusted to the tacticians in government. Strategic concepts and the sustained exercise of means–ends analysis can help officials muddle through with a practical opportunism that at least is informed by some disciplined sense of purpose. The strategic theorist should open in accessible form to the harried practitioner whatever of cumulative wisdom has been winnowed from the harvest of strategic history. Clausewitz advised that "[t]heory exists so that one need not start afresh each time sorting out the material and plowing through it, but will find it ready to hand and in good order."[57] The strategic theorist's reach will exceed his grasp in that regard, but what is a strategist's heaven for?

Second, the strategic theorist can help the practitioner by providing the kind of conceptual education which fits the evolving context for policy. The problems of deterrence and the content and relevance of deterrence theory, for example, require a comprehensive safety check when they are applied to issues of regional stability in the 1990s.[58] Virtually all of the assumptions, the conceptual working capital as it were, derived by theorists from the protracted Soviet–American, and heavily nuclear, nexus, need to be revisited for their roadworthiness *vis-à-vis* distinctly non-Soviet strategic-cultural climes. Deterrence theorists and defense planners need to consider the implications, for example, of a non-nuclear Iraq purposefully assaulting a nuclear Israel in the hope of catalyzing a wider and politically different war. Similarly, the US failures either to deter Iraq prior to August 2, 1990, or subsequently by compellence to persuade her to withdraw from Kuwait, should serve to flag potential softness in the American (and Western) way of deterrence theory and practice. The honest and competent strategic theorist, though in some measure the prisoner of his culture and the willing servant of his polity, has an obligation to provide useful truths about strategic matters. The wise strategic thinker is open to the revelation that ideas can work well enough in practice, even though they do not perform convincingly in theory. By way of a leading example of this phenomenon, Lawrence Freedman has noted that "[extended nuclear deterrence] is one of those areas where a policy has worked far better in practice than an assessment of the theory might lead one to expect."[59]

Third, as guardians – not the only guardians, but as guardians nonetheless – of the quality of strategic education for those in need of such education for the fulfillment of their official responsibilities, strategic theorists can help sort the ephemeral from the enduring, the fashionable and merely trendy from the items of more lasting importance. Politicians and journalists may inhabit a succession of short terms, but the strategic theorist has purchased a ticket for a longer journey. The theorist should be able to advise as to the salience of the strategic tools and methods of the 1970s and 1980s for the changed context of the 1990s. Although the details of adversaries, specific issues, and technologies, *inter alia*, will change, the strategic theorist will be alert to the inappropriateness of claims for the utter historical novelty of events asserted by those who lack historical perspective. Politicians and the decision-makers for foundation grants are inclined to respond to the headlines of the day.

To the noteworthy degree to which strategic studies is fueled financially and by the lure of political access by patronage from policy institutions and the foundations, there is likely to be some pull towards the new, or allegedly new, almost as an end in itself. Old ideas and "old thinking" tend to be deemed blameworthy because they are old. It is a matter of historical record that the old ideas generated by the strategic studies community in the Cold War worked well enough for that period in the most important of respects. "New thinking" may or may not be superior to "old thinking," but whatever its merit the newness of the thoughts is irrelevant. It is the fit of ideas with conditions that matters, not the age of ideas.

Fourth and finally, strategic theorists can, in the inimitable words of that great strategic thinker, Clint Eastwood, remind those in need of reminding that "a man has to recognize his limitations." The beginning of wisdom in the approach to strategic practice reposes in frank appreciation of ignorance. Strategic theorists actively concerned for national and international security – as contrasted with those absorbed with the intellectual beauty, or apparent novelty, of their own creations – can advise the world of practice both as to those things which cannot be foreseen and the ways in which the strategic effects of unwelcome surprises can be minimized. The strategic theorist should not himself seek to function as a defense planner, but he can develop guidance in aid of *fault-tolerant* defense planning.[60]

The strategic theorist should not waste his time and effort endeavoring to predict the precise condition of Russia, let alone of the world, in 2000 or 2010. Instead, he should help the realm of strategic practice by developing principles for the guidance of defense planners who must cope with uncertainty. A defense community cannot foresee the future, but it can adopt the strategic policy, and purchase the forces necessary, to protect against many plausible unwelcome futures. The strategic theorist, in short, can play an invaluable role in helping the world of practice to manage risks.

3 History for strategists
British sea power as a relevant past [1994]

Historians and strategic theorists have much to learn from each other, but there is little doubt that the two express different cultures and seek distinctive truths. Historians are apt to find uniqueness, where strategic theorists will seek out, and almost certainly find, patterns in behavior. A study of the British experience with sea power over the past four centuries yields a rich haul of strategic history for careful exploitation by theorists. Provided general propositions about the land and sea, and later the air, are recognized always to have applicability governed by local detail, the realms of strategic theory and history can cooperate to mutual advantage. Viewed in the context of statecraft and conflict as a whole, British sea power over several centuries is a treasure trove of historical evidence which positively beckons for broad-gauged interpretation.

For a familiar refrain, the continuities in the structure and terms of statecraft and strategy from period to period are deeply impressive. The detail of technology and political forms certainly have altered massively, but in the fields of strategic ideas, key features of geography – and broadly of geopolitical relationships – and the general warp and woof of the politics of strategy and security among states, continuities dominate discontinuities. For example, the significance of the Bosphorus and the Dardanelles straits as a critical geostrategic chokepoint can be traced at least from the fifth century BC through to the late 1980s and the end of the Soviet–American rivalry.

Although most naval engagements throughout history have occurred close to shore, also it is true to claim that oared galley warfare in the narrow waters of the Mediterranean comprised a distinctive, even unified, historical experience. It would not be true to claim, however, that the geography and technology of ancient and medieval sea warfare were so distinctive in their tactical and logistic details as to have no operational or strategic value as a long case study (or series of case studies) for the strategic theorist. Closely dependent though galleys were upon sustenance from the shore, land power did not eclipse sea power in strategic value. Rather, geophysical conditions in the Mediterranean prior to the modern era meant that continental powers were able to extract more strategic value for their sea power than could their successors in modern times. A related fallacy is the notion that the maturing of airpower has, or will, render (surface) navies obsolescent. All things are possible for the distant future, but to date the advent of airpower has had the paradoxical net effect of making great navies greater still.

It is unmistakable that, in quite sharp general contrast with the ancient and medieval eras, in modern times continental states and coalition persistently have failed to solve the strategic problems posed by great maritime foes. The geographical and political cultural differences between Britain and the United States are many and profound, but nonetheless the practical continuities in statecraft and strategy are vastly impressive. Of course it matters that the United States is a continental-size power an ocean away from Europe (and Asia), and not a small offshore island, but the theme of a balance-of-power policy *vis-à-vis* would-be hegemons in Eurasia dominates the Anglo-American experience in its entirety. The US practice of superior sea power as a vital enabler for a forward continental policy has been thoroughly reminiscent of its British predecessor, even when the complications of airpower and nuclear weapons are added to the stew.

There is much that strategic theorists and contemporary US defense planners could learn from the British practice of sea power as a principal agency supporting its statecraft for four centuries. Above all else, perhaps, Americans can allow British strategic history to remind them of the hard cases when continental allies, as well as British expeditionary forces, failed in the field. The succession of short terms that tends to be the actual (non)perspective of defense planners, and the shifting policy guidance that should provide meaning to the activity of planners, have a way of discounting the future. History reminds those willing to be reminded that bad times always return and that every warfree period actually is an inter-war era. Finally, on a more positive note, both the British experience with sea power and now the like American practice speak to what dominant maritime power can contribute to help build, protect, and advance an international order characterized by respect for humane values.

History and strategy

After the fall of the great Russian naval fortress of Sebastopol on September 8–9, 1855, the realization gradually dawned in the Allied capitals that their combined arms had failed to wreak sufficient harm to the Russian state to cause the Tsar to accede to a peace of surrender.[1] The technological conditions of the mid 1850s were, of course, unique. Partially steam-driven naval power and superior armaments on the Allied side confronted a great continental state prior to its acquisition of strategic railroads. The tactical and operational feasibility of the Anglo-French (and Turkish) strategic designs of 1854–56 have nothing to say in detail to any other period. Yet, the structure of the grand-strategic problems faced by sea-based and continental power in those years are of permanent interest.

Contemporary strategic studies is respectful but wary of history. There is a disciplinary–cultural divide of no small significance. On the one hand, strategic theorists tend to be unduly interested in the general at the potential expense of the particular, for the professional comfort of historians. On the other hand, historians are overly prone to retreat into the rich singularity of detail at the possible expense of a general wisdom, for the professional comfort of strategists. In this analysis I seek to bridge the disciplinary–cultural divide by examining the validity of cross-historical theory and understanding, with particular reference to the British experience with sea power.

The British case virtually selects itself as the repository in modern times of strategic experience with the limits and possibilities of typically superior sea-based power. By no means is my thesis a theory explaining the strategic value of sea power that can be based upon three and a half centuries of British history. Nonetheless, the British record in managing sea power–land power relations is so instructive that it warrants unusual attention. It may be objected that Britain as a sea power was not so much an exemplar as an extraordinary phenomenon. Further, the objection might be registered that there is as much to be learnt about the theory and practice of strategy and statecraft from the experience of Britain's foes seeking to conduct conflict with the aid of generally second-rate naval instruments. The first objection is probably well-founded but is beside the point. Extraordinary or not, the British (and hence the foes of the British) experience with sea power is an unusually rich vein of phenomena to be mined and refined. The second objection is no more sound. British performance as a maritime state can be studied properly only in a context that has to include the strategic options, cultures, and styles that opposed her over the centuries. Britain is not by any means the only modern polity worth studying by theorists of strategy.

Geoffrey Till advises, "the chief utility of history for the analysis of present and future lies in its ability not to point out lessons, but to isolate things that need thinking about."[2] The British experience with the strategic value of sea power is of interest for the purpose of this essay precisely because, as Till says, the study of history has the ability "to isolate things that need thinking about." In his seminal examination of galley warfare in the Mediterranean in the sixteenth century, John Guilmartin warns strongly against seeking to derive a general theory of sea power only from the British experience with "fighting sail" from the period bounded by the First Anglo-Dutch War (1652–54) and the fall of Napoleon.[3] Of course he is right. It is natural enough that an Anglo-American author, looking ultimately to explain the strategic utility of sea power for the United States in the mid-1990s and beyond, should have the perspective provided by a tradition of dominant and open-ocean sea power. However, one can focus upon the British experience yet still be sensitive to the strategic-cultural and other differences between first- and second-rate sea powers and between conflict in confined waters and on the open ocean, and to differences among eras wherein marine propulsion was by oar and wind, by wind alone, by coal and oil generated steam, and – in small measure, overall – by nuclear reaction. The protracted British case in the strategic value of sea power is useful for the scope and variety of experience which it encompasses, including the experience of Britain's foes over the centuries, not necessarily for any model it might provide for the future and certainly not as a mold for navies for all time.

Few students of strategy would agree with Henry Ford's dismissive axiom, "history is bunk." Yet, few of those students are comfortable with analyses and theories that straddle the nuclear divide of 1945. It is easy to recognize an unchanging human nature, an unchanging physical geography, and unchanging impulses to compete for security. It is less easy to determine either the meaning of changing economic and technological conditions for the choices open to statesmen, or the salience of the choices exercised in one technological era for those in another.

History is a storehouse that lends itself to abuse by raiding parties on behalf of almost any persuasion among strategic theorists. Alfred Thayer Mahan was determined to put "maritime interests in the foreground" of his writing and to correct or balance the "tendency [among 'historians generally'] to slight the bearing of maritime power upon events."[4] So far did he succeed that he overcorrected for the tendency that he may well have perceived accurately. So abundant is the historical record, yet so uncertain are causal relationships and so many are the levels of analysis – policy, grand-strategic, strategic, operational, and tactical – that the determined raider is unlucky indeed if he cannot locate examples to illustrate the plausibility of virtually any argument.

Analysis based on history is vulnerable to the biasing effect of the necessarily selective treatment of often uncertain data, conducted honestly or otherwise, by scholars who cannot help but have points of view. Moreover, it is all very well to assert the permanence of strategic principles, but many a general, admiral, and government have seen strategic enterprises founder on the rocks of logistic and tactical infeasibility. For example, galleys, for reasons of the necessity to sustain a large crew while remaining lightly burdened, absence of navigational aids and general unseaworthiness, were obliged to operate both close to land and close to a thoroughly reliable (i.e. in friendly hands) water supply on shore.[5] Plainly, naval squadrons whose cruising radius was limited by their ability to carry drinking water only for two or three weeks, and which could not venture out of the shelter of land on to the open sea save at major hazard, were operational and strategic instruments of distinctly limited value. For a further example of the critical importance of logistic details, it was not until Admiral Sir Edward Hawke organized the contemporary equivalent of the fleet train in 1759 that the British Royal Navy operationally and tactically was capable of imposing an effective close blockade of the French Biscay and Breton ports – weather permitting, another non-trivial factor in the age of fighting sail, as indeed always.[6] Prior to 1759, generally it had been British naval policy to blockade Brest via distant observation from the western Channel ports. This traditional practice of distant observation had failed to provide an effective grip on the French battlefleet in 1756–58, while its repetition in the War of American Independence was to have disastrous consequences for the balance of naval power off the American coast.

For a landward example, the strategic problem posed between 1914 and 1918 by the need to invest the continental "fortress" of Imperial Germany and Imperial Austria–Hungary was obvious even to a dim intelligence. The German army, the mainstay – in Clausewitzian terms the "center of gravity" – of the Central Powers, had to be beaten or at least worn down in the field, while the only logistically feasible field for the principal British effort on land was Belgium and northern

France.[7] After Allied setbacks in the spring and summer of 1915, and certainly after the launching of the German offensive against the French army at Verdun in February 1916, Britain had no practicable choice but to bear an ever heavier burden of the fighting on the Western Front. It is worth noting that the United States proved to be exceedingly suspicious of the ulterior objects that its European co-belligerents might have in mind in their fluctuating interest in pursuing the defeat of the Central Powers in secondary (other than France) theaters of war. It was made very plain indeed in 1917 that a continuation of the principal concentration of Allied effort upon the Western Front would be a condition for the dispatch and employment of a large American Expeditionary Force.[8]

Notions of the strategically desirable are relatively unchanging, but the question of feasibility must be ruled by the details of supply, influenced by technology, and generally dominated by the quality and quantity of the military instrument to hand. The relationships among policy, grand strategy, strategy, operations, and tactics are all of an interactive kind. It does not suffice to say that forces and their tactics must be able to implement a strategy that relates military power effectively to the ends of policy. The policymaker and the strategist, no matter how wise their chosen policy and strategy, always must have an eye to the practicality of their designs. The first duty of the statesman *vis-à-vis* his armed forces in, or towards, war is so to set the political stage for the conflict that those forces stand a reasonable prospect of success. The forces should not be dependent for victory upon some *deus ex machina:* "wonder weapons" introduced at the eleventh hour, the break-up of a hostile coalition, repeated gross military errors on the part of the enemy, or even upon the working of cunning deception plans to achieve tactical surprise.

An historically wide-ranging work of analysis and theory can founder on tactical and logistic details that have changed dramatically from period to period, but the opposite peril also applies. Works of theory may ascend to so high a plateau of generality that, while secure against tactical invalidation, the "lessons" derived from historial study are of a stupefying obviousness and practical inutility. It has been a hallmark of successful statesmen and military leaders that they knew when to break the rules (divide the fleet, engage in a *mêlée* battle via "general chase" rather than rigidly forming in line-of-battle as required by the Permanent Fighting Instructions, and so on). Knowledge of how to apply general precepts is much more important than are the principles themselves.

It is not enlightening or helpful to be advised by careful historical study to have a genius in command. Genius by definition is rare and is difficult to identify prior to its unmistakable demonstration in action. Or, there is much to be said for the advice that "[t]he best strategy is always to *be very strong* ... at the decisive point" (obedient to the principles of concentration and economy of force).[9] Admiral Isoroku Yamamoto's violation of this precept (*inter alia*, including the principle of simplicity in operations) helped critically to lead the Imperial Japanese Navy to defeat at Midway in June 1942. Yet. since the location of the decisive point is determined by interaction between rival military machines, the ability to identify at will, and enforce the location and timing of, the decisive point is unlikely to be wholly reliable.

The strategic significance of particular features of physical geography has varied greatly as the identity, and hence location, of the major players in the politics of international security has altered, as technologies of many kinds have increased or decreased the cruising range of ships, and as economic, political, and military intercourse has expanded from the eastern Mediterranean to encompass the entire world. To cite a case of continuity in importance, the maritime defiles connecting the Aegean and the Black Seas, the Bosphorus and the Dardanelles, retained a strategic significance which defied time, technology, and changing polities. Those defiles were critical to Greek security against Persia; vital for Athens' food supply from the Crimea;[10] provided refuge for the fleet of the Byzantine Empire and served as the protected central hub (interior lines, *à la* Jomini) from which the Byzantines, and later the Ottoman Turks, flexibly could choose to concentrate in the Aegean or the Black Sea (a two-sea fleet on the cheap, courtesy of control of the Bosphorus and Dardanelles chokepoints); were essential for the security of Venetian and Genoese trade with Asia; and in more recent times were the key to keeping Russian sea power out of the Mediterranean, keeping Anglo-French sea power out of the Black Sea for the succor of a hard pressed Russian ally (1915), and in the Cold War were critical for the confinement of the Soviet Black Sea Fleet. The advent of airpower certainly has modified the geostrategic significance of the guarding of the maritime defiles of the Bosphorus and the Dardanelles. In recent decades neither NATO nor the Soviet Union could be optimistic over the wartime survivability of surface fleets in the confined waters of the Aegean and the eastern Mediterranean. Since the early 1940s, the air balance has been critical for the determination of permissible risk-taking in forward deployment in restricted waters. Eric Grove makes an essential point when he asserts, "[s]ea power and airpower are indivisible."[11]

The relevance of sea power to the rivalries and wars of particular states and coalitions has depended far more upon geostrategic context than upon contemporary level of technological development. The parable of the whale and the elephant or, if one prefers, the tiger and the shark, who have enormous difficulty coming to grips to reach the sources of each other's strength in order to force a decision, is as relevant for Greece in the fifth century BC as it was for Soviet–American rivalry. Notwithstanding the contrasts in basic transportation and other technologies as between the fifth century BC and the twentieth century AD for many decades continental Sparta could not effectively oppose the system of war devised by maritime Athens, while the land power Germany of the Third Reich was strategically baffled by the Straits of Dover and an insular, sea power enemy on the flanks of its continental empire.

Unlike Germany, Sparta was able to solve its strategic problems after Athens had overreached itself with its Sicilian expedition (415–413 BC). The Athenian disaster in Sicily emboldened Persia to assist the Spartans and Corinthians so that they could assemble sufficient sea power to challenge Athens in its own realm of strategic excellence. Nazi Germany, far from solving its problems of bringing superior land power to grips with a maritime enemy, fatally compounded its difficulties by undertaking a great adventure in the East for which, again, its system of war (particularly its logistic reach) was thoroughly unsuited. To press the analogy further, both maritime Athens and continental Germany had to ruin themselves by overextension in their own medium of general excellence, before they were weak enough to be liable to definitive defeat; which is say defeat in the war as opposed to the loss of a battle or even a campaign. Persia did not dare subsidize Sparta's maritime war against Athens prior to the Athenian catastrophe at Syracuse in 415–413 BC. The sea-based power of the Western members of the Grand Alliance against Nazi Germany became competitive in land warfare only following Germany's gross continental overextension in the war in the East and with the achievement of air superiority early in 1944.

Far from being eclipsed in strategic importance as a result of the maturing of air, missile and other space technologies, some of the ideas of maritime strategy, in addition to retaining their value for operations on earth are applicable to military operations in space. The marine ocean and the space ocean – admittedly with the important exception of weather, which does not exist (save for the consequence of variations in solar activity, and the problems that terrestrial weather can pose for space launch activity) in the latter – as well as the desert on earth have some geostrategic features in common. There is more to learn about military space operations from Sir Julian Corbett's 1911 book, *Some Principles of Maritime Strategy*,[12] than from any number of much more recent tracts on airpower, let alone on the geophysically mysterious, hybrid concept of aerospace power.

Technological change necessarily modifies the tactical and operational application of sea power. Yet, the case for affirming continuity in the relevance of the sea–land nexus in crisis and war from the time of Themistocles to the present day is far stronger than any claim for bounding the terms of reference in accordance with one or another technological or political great divide. There are many candidate fences for the bounding of the historical experience relevant to the future.

First, there was the shift from a preponderance of oar power to virtually all sail power in the late fifteenth and sixteenth centuries, married both to revolutionary advances in the science of navigation and to the adaptation of gunpowder artillery for shipboard use. Naval tactics altered dramatically as ships became artillery platforms rather than merely platforms for infantry combat at sea. Second, in Western perspective, there was a great divide between ancient/medieval and modern times, with the reorientation of the most important lines of conflict in European security politics from those states that bordered the closed sea of the Mediterranean to those on the fringe of the open Atlantic.

Third, one might employ as a breakpoint for historical evidence the wholesale change from sail to steam power in the third quarter of the nineteenth century, as marine and naval science applied the fruits of the industrial revolution. Fourth, there is a case for fencing-out allegedly irrelevant historical experience via focus upon the change in transportation economics as between land and marine effected by railroads and the internal combustion engine. Speaking in 1904, the British geographer, and occasional geopolitical theorist, Sir Halford J. Mackinder (1861–1947), concluded that the internal unification of the continents by the railroad was effecting the end of a 400 year long Columbian Era characterized by the preponderance of sea power over land power.[13]

Fifth, it is possible to argue for the exclusion of historical evidence prior to the maturing of airpower. In its strategic significance, airpower came of age during the Second World War. Airpower, as well as sea power, helps shape the course and outcome of war. When airpower in its many forms is interrogated for its meaning, no problems of substance arise. As a general rule airpower has functioned as an adjunct to land and sea power; it has been an expression of, and has expanded the nature and effectiveness of, each. Even in some cases wherein airpower appeared to be strategic in operation, in the particular sense of independently decisive, it transpires on closer investigation that the air campaign in question was conducted from advanced bases seized and held by some mixture of sea and land power. The argument developed here is sensitive to the possibility that the maturing of airpower either has, or is about to, invalidate analysis framed in a traditional sea–land framework.

Sixth, the clearest and probably most popular and defensible criterion for inclusion or exclusion of historical experience is that provided by the nuclear revolution heralded in 1945.[14] Seventh, and typically rather vaguely related to the sixth suggestion, the emergence after the Second World War of a bipolar Soviet–American standoff could be taken to herald the beginning of prudently usable historical experience. Eighth and finally, there is a view that the conclusion of the Cold War in 1989–90, and the demise of the Soviet Union itself in December 1991, ushered in a new era which will, or might function in the security realm with terms of reference very different even from those of the 1970s and 1980s, let alone from distant centuries.

These suggestions comprise only a sample of the breakpoints that could be selected for the fencing-out of arguably irrelevant historical experience. The importance of the historical changes just cited is not seriously in doubt. But, none of those changes, *including the nuclear revolution*, have so far changed the missions statesmen endorse for their sea power that previous wars and insecurity conditions hole only an antiquarian fascination. Mackinder's thesis that the twentieth century would see a closed world that must favor land power over sea power did not point to a change with boundary-for-evidence implications for examination of the sea–land strategic nexus. Mackinder predicted that every shoreline would be held by organized security communities increasingly better able to move people and material efficiently and rapidly by land.[15]

The closed-world argument of Mackinder was correct and strategically important. However, it did not imply the eclipse of sea power that he predicted and feared. The twentieth century to date has seen the critical influence of sea power in *grande guerre* demonstrated twice, while the world war which might have been, between East and West, bore much promise of being structured in part by familiar sea power–land power factors. Furthermore, the influence of land power on sea power is at least as significant and interesting as is the influence of sea power on land power. The Persians, the Spartans, the Macedonians, above all others – to date – the Romans, and in non-trivial measure the Germans, sought to command the sea *from the land* It was, however, in the thousand-year struggle between Christian and Muslim sea power in the narrow waters of the Mediterranean that the significance of land power for sea power was demonstrated most persuasively. In the Mediterranean of late antique, medieval, and early modern times, the high road to superior sea power was the control of coasts and therefore of naval bases. This contrast with modern navalist beliefs was dictated by the weather and physical geography of the Mediterranean, as well as by the marine and navigational technologies of the long period in question.

Sea power is a direct product of the resources of the land – people for crews, wood or iron and steel (and other metals) for construction, food and water for shipboard supplies, and so forth.[16] If rival states are deprived of coastline from which sea power can be projected, they can pose no maritime threat. Notwithstanding definitive naval victory in the first war with Carthage (over the control of Sicily), Roman strategic culture remained thoroughly land-minded. Apart from periodic difficulties with piracy, prior to the final time of troubles of the Western Empire, the Roman Republic and Empire had scant need of a large navy of dedicated warships because the Mediterranean was *mare nostrum* for Rome; a sea totally bordered by Roman territory. Nonetheless, the leading modern historian of the Imperial Roman Navy has pointed out that "we are dealing with the Romans, so generally and with some justice considered a landbound folk, but these same Romans developed the control and organs of sea power to their highest refinement in antiquity."[17]

Roman statesmen had the precedent of Alexander the Great (ruler of another land-minded empire, Macedon) solving the problem of the Persian maritime threat to his lines of communication by eliminating that threat, at source, from the land. Of more recent vintage, Adolf Hitler briefly was intrigued in the fall of 1940 with a landward project against Gibraltar (Operation Felix), but Generalissimo Francisco Franco declined to cooperate.[18] A powerful strategic incentive behind the British offensive in Flanders in 1917 (Third Ypres, or Passchendaele) was the Royal Navy's insistence that the German U-boat bases in Flanders had to be seized from the land. As early as January 1, 1915, Winston Churchill, then First Lord of the Admiralty, informed the Commander-in-Chief of the British Expeditionary Force (BEF) as follows:

> The battleship *Formidable* was sunk this morning by a submarine in the Channel. Information from all quarters show that the Germans are steadily developing an important submarine base at Zeebrugge. *Unless an operation can be undertaken to clear the coast*, and particularly to capture this place, it must be recognized that the whole transportation of troops across the Channel will be seriously and increasingly compromised.[19]

During the Cold War US defense planners considered the influence of a NATO preponderant at sea on an effectively landlocked, continental Soviet enemy. Nonetheless, American grand and military strategy also had to consider what a Soviet victory on land in Western Europe would have meant for Soviet sea–air power (Soviet submarine bases at Brest, Lorient, La Rochelle, La Rota?); what such a victory would have meant for difficulty of American access to European and north African waters, territory, and airspace; and how Soviet sea power could have had direct and indirect influence over the military effectiveness of NATO land power.

Although there is some historical support for the proposition that "it is easier for land power to take to the sea than for sea power to take to the land,"[20] this notion warrants the judgment that it is a persuasive fallacy. Certainly one should not be blinded by the British experience into believing that thalassocracies enjoy inherent and abiding competitive advantages over continental imperia. There is considerable potential for misunderstanding in this much-quoted judgment by Field Marshal Viscount Montgomery of Alamein, "From the days when humans first began to use the seas, the great lesson of history is that the enemy who is confined to a land strategy is in the end defeated."[21] The Field Marshal was not claiming that land powers have always been beaten by sea powers Rather did he mean that land powers confined to a continental strategy always have been beaten *eventually* Furthermore, there are some abiding reasons why the plainly discernible advantage in modern times (post 1500) of sea power over land power is likely to continue. Significantly, Martin Wight noted that

> Mackinder's most cogent examples of the ultimate superiority of land power are drawn from classical history. Perhaps he did not sufficiently consider that the states-system of classical antiquity grew up round a sea enclosed by land, while the modern states-system has grown up on a continent surrounded by the ocean.[22]

Mahan and Mackinder, though they adopted contrasting geostrategic perspectives, nonetheless agreed on the dependence of sea power upon the resources of the land. In his discussion of "The Elements of Sea Power" Mahan gave pride of place to geographical position. His first sentence under that heading proceeded as follows:

> It may be pointed out, in the first place, that if a nation be so situated that it is neither forced to defend itself by land nor induced to seek extention of its territory by way of the land, it has, by the very unity of its aim directed upon the sea, an advantage as compared with a people one of whose boundaries is continental.[23]

The reasoning in this point was the principal motive force impelling Queen Elizabeth I to expend scarce English assets in direct support of the revolt of the Spanish Netherlands against Madrid. In 1585, Elizabeth reluctantly dispatched a modestly sized body of soldiers for continental campaigning, and initiated the policy of financial subsidization of continental allies, practices that were to be hallmarks of British statecraft for nearly four centuries. It would be an error to believe that there are land powers as contrasted with sea powers in some thoroughly exclusive sense. In practice, strategic geography and economic necessity or opportunity indeed have inclined states in one or the other direction. However, great naval strength can be accumulated by a traditional land power, just as a formidable army can be raised by a sea power. It was Mackinder's great fear in the early decades of this century that a land power, or a continental coalition inadequately distracted on its landward frontiers, would have the economic resources for the development of overwhelming sea power.[24] Mackinder, in company with many commentators before and since, was prone to overestimate the ease with which great naval power could be developed from nominally adequate resources. The infrastructure for a first-class navy takes decades to construct.

Mahan drew the wrong lesson from the brief, though prominent, treatment he accorded Roman strategy in the Second Punic (Hannibal's) War of 218–201 BC. The Roman conduct of that war does indeed demonstrate the utility of command of the sea. No less important was the example provided of how a well-found, land-minded state can turn to the sea of strategic necessity as a vital complement to its traditional orientation towards continental campaigning. To a lesser degree, Sparta had done the same (one should recall the seemingly definitive eclipse of Athenian naval power at Aegospotami in 405 BC by Lysander), as had Alexander the Great when he created Macedonian naval strength out of the landward defeat of the base structure of the Persian Fleet on the Levantine littoral (333–332 BC). The sources of Roman, Spartan, and Macedonian sea power were scarcely at all those specified canonically by Mahan, with his emphasis upon the links in the chain among domestic production, colonies, maritime trade, and, inevitably, a fighting fleet. These were *naval powers*, as contrasted with true or "natural" sea powers.

A maritime focus for strategic analysis can incline scholars to wax unduly lyrical about the natural inclination to the sea, and hence the organic and enduring character of the sea power of such thalassocratic states as Athens, Carthage, arguably Byzantium and Genoa, Venice, and Britain. Important though the distinction may be between a "merely military" naval power and a natural sea power,[25] the potential of the former to pose serious maritime threats to the latter should not be despised. It so happens that the greatest naval power of the 1990s, the United States, is far from being a natural sea power. The American merchant marine is distinctly unimpressive in size, and the country's style in strategic thinking and practice has tended to be continentalist rather than classically maritime.

Virtually all of the elements necessary for an understanding of sea power–land power nexus can be gleaned from the British experience over 400 years in modern history. Nonetheless, there are strategic cautionary points of value to learn from ancient and medieval times, wherein maritime Athens, Carthage, Persia,[26] and – much later – Byzantium lost to continentalist Sparta, Rome, Macedon, and Ottoman Turkey. These cases do not illustrate anything as simple as the superiority of land power over sea power. On the contrary, perhaps, they show how land powers can, and have, taken to the sea – or have bribed or intimidated maritime allies – in order to neutralize and then defeat the strategy of a true sea power. Strategic history is not a repetitive tale of sea power versus land power, but rather the saga of how each can be exploited to generate strength for decision against the other in a medium where there is a common unit of campaign account.

The remainder of this essay treats the question of the relevance of historical experience for the present and the future with the argument focused, with an important caveat, upon the British experience from the Elizabethan period to the 1940s. The caveat is that it is easy to forget that bodies of water can be either barriers or highways, depending upon who, if anyone, "commands" them. Britain did not win its first world war (the Seven Years War, 1756–63), or its 22-year-long struggle with Revolutionary and later Imperial France, because it was a true sea power or because a sea power somehow is beyond the strategic grasp of a land power. Britain won those wars because it made fewer significant errors in grand strategy than did its French enemies. There were linked formulae, perhaps broad principles, for grand and national military strategy which go far to explain British success. When pursued competently, those principles tended to produce performance in the conduct of war superior to that by a France which lacked a suitable policy-strategy system. In the first three years of the Seven Years War, again in its maritime war with France (and Spain, from 1779) from 1778 to 1783, and arguably yet again in the 1790s, Britain showed that it was at least as capable as France of pursuing faulty strategy.

The British experience

One should resist any temptation to read the modern British experience in statecraft and strategy as all-purpose validation of allegedly eternal precepts concerning sea power–land power relationships. As with Americans during the early campaigns in the Pacific in the Second World War, the British worked for, and generally deserved, the luck that was theirs. The incompetence of the enemy, nonetheless, frequently was critical for national survival. This is not to deny that in modern times there have been persisting reasons why continental powers have tended to find insuperable difficulty understanding either how to transmute land power into sea power, or otherwise how to offset hostile sea power. Overall, the problem of composing and executing military strategy suitable for assault upon the strategy of an essentially maritime enemy has proved beyond solution by continental statesmen. The Spaniards, the French, and the Germans failed in both grand and military strategy to solve their problem with the British Isles. Nonetheless, as noted already, the Spartans, the Macedonians, the Romans, periodically the Arabs, and certainly the Turks did succeed in resolving their maritime difficulties, albeit through the excellent education provided by painful experience.

The relevance of the protracted British historical example to the American situation is in good part a function of the geography of the Western alliance structure that the United States has led. Too much can be made of the idea that the United States inherited Britannia's trident. Geopolitics is about possibilities, not about geographically determined policies and policy outcomes. Soviet maritime powers could have been forcibly confined to Eurasian coastal waters not by US naval strength *per se*, but rather by American naval strength applied to chokepoints or zones that would be chokepoints precisely because the relevant landforms were in friendly hands. Operating unilaterally at transoceanic range, the US Navy and Air force probably could have rendered hazardous Soviet naval passage into the Atlantic from the Barents Sea, the Baltic, and the Mediterranean, as well as passage into the Pacific and the Yellow Sea. However, the potential for the landlocking of Soviet naval power was at least as much a result of political as of physical geography. Should some among Norway, Denmark, Iceland, Britain, Turkey, Spain, Portugal, and Japan have ceased to be active and reliable allies of the United States, then the four-centuries-long British analogy for US maritime strategy in the Cold War would have lost some of its relevance.

Geostrategically appreciated, Britain itself is a breakwater, physically located so as to canalize the seaborne trade of southern Europe with northern Europe and well-placed to interdict at will, subject to capability, the maritime traffic of the great *entrepôts* of northern and western Europe with their transoceanic sources of supply and their markets.[27] The measure of safety that reposes in mere distance, subject to the caveat already provided concerning the balance of maritime strength, poses the enemies of the United States a difficult logistic problem. Yet, US policymakers cannot forget that their country, while strategically advantaged by oceanic separation from Eurasia, also is handicapped in comparison with its functional British predecessor by the geopolitical fact that American territory is not itself a barrier against bids for maritime *Weltpolitik* stemming from continental Eurasia. While recognizing the geopolitical and geostrategic dissimilarities between the Britain of the alleged Columbian Era and the United States of the 1990s, the relevance of the British experience to the structure of the US security context remains impressive.

Periodically, Britain was threatened by the possible emergence of a dominant power or coalition on the continent at least nominally able to use a large fraction of its economic assets for a great maritime challenge. Speaking in 1911, the British Foreign Secretary, Sir Edward Grey, warned that a Britain aloof from European balance-of-power politics could find itself challenged by the need to meet what would amount to a Five-Power standard in naval strength.[28] In part, though only in part, to arrest the maturing of this recurring danger, generally it was British policy to seek alliance with the second strongest power or coalition in Europe. The purpose was to tip the balance of power against the aspiring hegemon and keep it occupied in an expensive ground war. Britain would contribute as little by way of direct land power as its allies could tolerate, consistent with satisfactory conduct of the continental contest. British statecraft typically was indifferent to the political complexion of allied states. Alliance ties were made and unmade expediently for management of the balance of power. Britain's interest in the balance of power in Europe did not focus narrowly upon the idea that landward distraction would fatally inhibit a continental foe from building a truly first-class navy. Particularly with reference to France in the eighteenth century, Britain understood very well that the hindrances to French sea power were much more numerous, and substantial, than just the periodic fact of continental military distraction.[29]

In the eighteenth century, following a useful period of alliance with France after the Peace of Utrecht in 1713 (in which period Britain used France to accelerate forcibly the decline of Spanish sea power, much as it had sought to use France against the Dutch in the 1670s), Britain successively allied, again, with Austria in the 1740s in the War of Austrian Succession (1740–48) and with Prussia in the Seven Years War (1756–63). In the period 1815–1914, following the war with France (1793–1815, with brief pauses in 1802–03 and 1814–15), Britain generally eschewed formal alliance entanglements. In the nineteenth century the principal foe was France – in the 1890s it was the Franco–Russian Alliance – a status transferred to Germany in the First Morocco Crisis of 1905. (Even while Anglo-French armies and navies were allied in the disciplining of Russia in the Crimean War, Britain's Royal Navy constructed major warships in competition with the French Navy.) In the words of Winston Churchill

> For four hundred years the foreign policy of England has been to oppose the strongest, most aggressive, most dominating Power on the Continent, and particularly to prevent the Low Countries falling into the hands of such a Power... Observe that the policy of England takes no account of which nation it is that seeks the overlordship of Europe. The question is not whether it is Spain, or the French Monarchy, or the French Empire, or the German Empire, or the Hitler regime. It has nothing to do with rulers or nations; it is concerned solely with whoever is the strongest or the potentially dominant tyrant.[30]

It should be recalled that the United States intervened in the First World War as a co-belligerent in 1917 and was enthusiastic in its alliance with the totalitarian Soviet Union, as well as with democratic, but imperial, Britain, from 1941 until 1945. Similarly, the thirteen American colonies had no terrible *crise de conscience* over accepting direct military assistance from monarchical France and Spain in 1778 and 1779. Notwithstanding the ideological cast to American political culture, US policymakers have obeyed in practice the ancient precept that "the enemy of my enemy is my friend." In support of a rather dim vision of a "new world order," the United States of the early 1990s embraced the "terrorist" state of Syria as an ally of temporary convenience and deemed it expedient not to dwell upon China's record of domestic oppression. *Plus ça change...* In the twentieth century the United States has acted three times to restore or sustain a balance of power in Eurasia when the British weight in the scales, for the same purpose, manifestly was inadequate (1917, 1941, 1947).

British statesmen had to resolve the grand and military strategic conundrum of how much effort to allocate directly to continental power balancing (British soldiers, hiring of (German or Portuguese) mercenaries, subsidization of allies) and how much to allocate to maritime endeavors. British historian Piers Mackesy notes that in the Great War with France from 1793 to 1815, Britain "ranked as a great power not because of its army but because of its wealth, which it used to keep the armies of the other great powers in the war."[31]

Over the past 100 years too much has been made of the proposition that there is a traditional British way in warfare. As expounded by Julian Corbett and Sir Basil Liddell Hart (1895–1970), and revived lately by Daniel A. Baugh,[32] this "British way" allegedly entailed the blockade of continental ports, distant "blue water" maritime operations (to acquire the colonies and overseas trade of continental powers cut off by the Royal Navy from access to the world beyond Europe), subsidies to allies, symbolic ground-forces' commitment to the continent, and peripheral raiding around the continental littoral to exploit the flexibility of sea power for surprise maneuver.[33] Corbett and Liddell Hart, for example, confused necessity with strategic grand design. Those theorists neglected to appreciate the extent to which geostrategic circumstances altered, if not priorities, at least the operational application of priorities in defense planning.

The British way in warfare which approached a navalist's ideal was rarely attained or sustained in practice, and the repeated exceptions to its exercise are at least as instructive as its occasional reality. Britain was a small, if increasingly wealthy, country during the course of the most virulent century-plus of Anglo-French antagonism in modern times, from the 1680s until 1815. Since for reasons of domestic politics Britain could not introduce conscription for the army, it simply could not maintain a first-class Navy, plus adequate garrisons for the growing empire overseas, plus a large army of occupation in Ireland (and, until the 1750s, in the heavily Jacobite-loyal parts of Scotland also), as well as an army first class in quantity for continental campaigns. Variations on this theme of manpower shortage applied even with conscription (1916 and 1939) to the two world wars of this century, as well as to the war; of the French Revolution and Empire.

The British military commitment in the Iberian peninsula against the Napoleonic Empire (1808–14) under Lieutenant General Sir John Moore, and resumed under the general who became First Duke of Wellington, was close to comprising the maximum feasible British land power effort, about eight divisions (including German and Portuguese troops). British Empire forces under Field Marshal Sir Douglas Haig's command in 1918 totaled 59 divisions. While there is ample ground for questioning the massive dispersal of Imperial Army assets to "Eastern" and colonial theaters throughout the First World War (East Africa, Gallipoli, Mesopotamia, Palestine, Salonika), there is a little doubt that having borne the brunt of the fighting on the Western Front from mid-1916 until the end of hostilities, the well of British manpower was running dry in 1918.[34] The case of the Second World War is even the Second plainer.

The principal British military effort in that war, as it had been in the rearmament program of the 1930s, was devoted to the Royal Air Force (RAF), not to the army or the navy. For a variety of reasons, including prestige and longer-term imperial security as well as immediate strategic advantage, by late 1944 Britain and its empire was waging three massive continental campaigns simultaneously, in France and the Low Countries, Italy, and Burma. Field Marshal Sir Bernard Montgomery was obliged to direct his 21st Army Group from Normandy to the Elbe in the knowledge that it comprised, quite literally, Britain's last army; there were no British reserve divisions. John Terraine makes the telling point that in the

First World War the British Empire suffered 38,834 fatalities among officers, a loss of the nation's elite that contributed strongly to the inter-war determination in Britain that "never again" must it wage large-scale continental warfare; while in the Second World War the RAF suffered 55,573 aircrew (largely officer) fatalities.[35] Dependence upon airpower had been touted misleadingly as an alternative to the slaughter of continental land warfare *à la* 1914–18.

Time after time, maritime Britain was obliged to make a maximum feasible continental effort. Because Britain never prepared ahead of time for continental campaigning on a large scale, its army, typically pared to the bone in peacetime, was never as effective as it should have been in continental warfare. Indeed, Britain's peacetime neglect of its army drove its grand and military strategy towards heavy dependence upon continental allies. Britain's greatest ever commitment to continuous and very large-scale continental warfare, from 1914 to 1918, stands as a classic illustration of how not to raise and employ a mass army. This is not to demean the monumental achievement of the British army in utterly transforming its character in the course of two years and then beating through attrition (i.e. hard fighting) the finest, or at least what had been the finest, army in the world.

Repeatedly, British statesmen have been attracted to a fairly pure form of maritime warfare. Provided the enemy of the day had an important overseas economic network, as was true of Spain, the Netherlands, and France (though in differing degree), it is not difficult to see why Britain preferred to have land war waged on the continent, the dying performed by allies (or by German mercenaries), the commercial profits of war accrue to London (some of which could be invested in the bribery of continental allies), and permanent colonial advantage follow from the success of British naval arms.

The strategic problem for Britain, recurrently, was that continental allies failed to play their part adequately in occupying the attention of the aspiring hegemonic power on the Continent. Allies either went down in defeat or were in serious danger of so doing. The British army, which eventually was to triumph over a somewhat dispirited enemy in the 100 days campaign of Fall 1918, had its origins in a mere six-division commitment in August 1914, one division of which was withheld in Britain against a nonexistent German invasion menace. Until the era of long-range bombardment by aircraft and ballistic missiles, offshore Britain had to design its grand strategy so that some suitable weight of land power could threaten the would-be hegemonic foe of the day. In principle there should have been a fairly direct inverse relationship between the scale of danger to Britain's vital interests and the quantity and quality of continental distraction provided successively to the Spaniards, the Dutch, the French, and the Germans. Frequently, however, there was the danger that the enemy would succeed on land, despite substantial British and British-allied effort, or that the enemy might decide to resolve its continental problems by dealing a fatal maritime stroke at the British paymaster of the anti-hegemonic coalition.

In common with ancient Athens and, with suitable provision for a robust nuclear deterrence, the United States of the Cold War, British statesmen of the

Columbian Age knew that if they maintained the ability to command the sea, the scale of peril to Britain was limited. The first principle of British strategy always was to maintain command of the Channel. This principle first found systematic operational expression in the War of Austrian Succession (1740–48) and thereafter (following precedents from the time of the defeat of the Great Armada in 1588) in the form of a concentration of superior force by a Western Squadron off the island of Ushant, or in Plymouth and Torbay. If the wild blew strongly from the West, the Royal Navy could not safely maintain station on a lee shore for the close blockade of the French Navy in Brest, but neither could the French beat out to sea.

Looking to the eastern approach to the Channel and the Thames, British statesmen were extremely sensitive to the issue of who controlled the Scheldt estuary. Prior to the development of Cherbourg, Antwerp was the only continental port on the Channel and southern North Sea capable of hosting a mass of hostile shipping of deep draught. Antwerp was close to Britain, and – unlike Brest and the other Biscay ports of France – when an East wind blew an invasion fleet could sail to Britain, while the British Fleet could not put to sea from the Thames or beat up the Channel. In the late 1850s, however, the France of the Second Empire invested in both a deepwater Channel harbor in Cherbourg and a steam-driven fleet capable of ignoring the vagaries of the wind.

A great continental foe undistracted militarily on land would not necessarily be able to construct a first-class fleet, but the possibility repeatedly was an attention-getter in London. Critically important though it was that a continental balance of power be maintained, Britain had an absolute need for maritime superiority in its home waters. Security against invasion was the first strategic priority, just as an effective working command of the Atlantic approaches to continental Europe was the *sine qua non* for all overseas military efforts.

Loss of, or a condition of temporally alternating, local maritime command can be dangerous, as the US Marine Corps learned in August and September 1942 on Guadalcanal, and – if not retrieved – even locally fatal, as the Athenians learned in their great expedition to Sicily in 415–413 BC, and the French discovered in Egypt in 1798–1801. Yet, disasters or near disasters can be survived, always provided command of the center of gravity of national strength is not lost. Athens was obliged to fight *à outrance* for the security of its grain supply route to the Black Sea and eventually lost through incompetence. Britain occasionally and briefly (e.g. in 1779) lost command of the Channel, but the French never succeeded in exploiting that fact. Imperial Japan lacked the strategic reach and weight ever to place the United States in a position from which it would have been obliged to withdraw from the contest. Had Japan identified the US fleet carriers as the operational center of gravity of American resistance in the Pacific, and had it seized Hawaii and Ceylon (and perhaps Madagascar) early in 1942, the course of the Second World War and not simply of the Pacific War, might have been very different. However, contemporary naval doctrine, the continentalist outlook and ambitions of the army-dominated Japanese government, and the firm determination of Tokyo to wage a limited war render this hypothetical case distinctly fanciful.[36]

The British experience in the balancing of maritime effort with direct continental endeavor speaks to recent US strategic problems also. There is an obvious geostrategic parallel with the NATO commitment; there is the question of the priority to be accorded protection against the worst eventuality (then invasion, more lately nuclear assault upon the homeland); and there is the residual issue of what to do should a major part of grand strategy collapse in ruins. Modern British history provides several partial parallels for the hypothetical defeat of NATO on what used to be its Central Front in Europe. The question of continental commitment by sea-based power is a hardy perennial topic. Throughout most of the twenty-two years of the last of its military struggles with France, Britain, in common with the United States of recent decades, was as supportive of a coalition strategy as military and diplomatic circumstances permitted. Britain did not eschew from choice a sustained commitment to continental warfare after 1795. The strategic problem was that France made a habit of rapidly defeating the European powers whose armies British forces might join in the field, if they could reach them, that is. After the French conquest of the Netherlands in 1795, the British army had a problem of access to European battlefields, not to mention logistic difficulty operating far from the coast. With the collapse of British hopes of Russia and the Fourth Coalition in 1807, Britain could only wage war at sea, or more or less immediately from the sea and readily sustainable by sea power, as in Portugal, for example.[37] As in June 1940, the defeat of continental allies left a Britain deficient in ground forces with no practical option but for a time to foreswear major continental campaigns against the principal strength of the enemy.

Valuable hindsight

Students of contemporary strategy who look backwards often are content simply to repeat obvious, if important, generalities about the sea power–land power connection. The beginning of wisdom is to appreciate the merit in Paul Kennedy's judgment that "the conflict with France also confirmed the limitations of sea power, the necessity of watching carefully the European equilibrium, the desirability of having strong military allies in wartime, the need to blend a 'maritime' strategy with the 'continental' one."[38] So far certainly so good. However, beyond these bland desiderata for prudent statecraft lies a set of quasi-permanent problems. How much national effort should be devoted to the direct, local bolstering of continental allies? What forms should that direct effort assume? What if the continental allies decline to make what British or American statesmen and attentive publics regard as a sufficient defense effort? Could a forward continental military commitment be so substantial that its potential loss in combat actually would imperil either the nation's survival or at least some values of critical importance later in the conflict? In the event of a victory in Europe for hostile land power, how would or could a United States preponderant over most of the world's oceans, and possessing a thoroughly convincing nuclear counterdeterrent, conduct war thereafter? How would the United States reach the enemy's center of gravity (with long-range air and missile power, perhaps, or from space)? Where would a continental enemy's power be reached, grasped, and overcome?

The relevance of the British experience for US policy and strategy in the 1990s extends beyond the hard-eyed world of geostrategy and *realpolitik*, to considerations of ideology and ethics. Albeit necessarily imperfectly, Britain pioneered and practiced, while her sea power protected, humane values in political intercourse. However amoral and ruthless British statesmen and admirals may have been, it was an existential fact that British grand-strategic success in peace and war tended to support the preservation and advancement of individualistic, democratic values. This is neither to deny that the "balancer" in a fluid balance-of-power system sometimes had to be agile in its affiliations, nor is it to fail to register that the Japanese actions against Port Arthur (February 8, 1904) and Pearl Harbor (December 7, 1941) had distinguished precedents in the British surprise attacks on Copenhagen (April 2, 1801 and September 2–7, 1807), not to mention the preventive action taken forcibly to neutralize the French fleet at Oran (July 3–4, 1940).

Naturally, Britain served herself in pursuing a generally consistent anti-hegemonic, balance-of-power policy towards continental Europe. Moreover, of course the British economy prospered as a result of the protection offered overseas trade by a superior Royal Navy. Nonetheless, the *Pax Britannica*, like its far antecedent *Pax Athenica* (but unlike the very genuine *Pax Romana*), and its successor *Pax Americana*, the disciplinary writ of all of which tend to be exaggerated,[39] served interests far more extensive than those of the home superstate only. Athenian and British wealth, influence, and arrogance were resented widely in their time, as have been those facets of American performance since the Second World War. Tracts on the arrogance of power have been drafted against each of these three great sea powers. The charge has been valid, yet dwarfed in significance by the fact that each helped forge in their own self-interest an international order which advanced a general peace and prosperity. Furthermore, these states have stood for an idea of individual human worth that has proved both exceedingly precious and in need of much muscular support.

Cause and effect are often difficult to trace, but it is worth noting the judgment of a biographer of Mackinder. Writing of the continuing validity of Mackinder's geopolitical concepts after nearly half a century, W.H. Parker claimed, persuasively: "But the great geographical realities remained: land power versus sea power, heartland versus rimland, centre versus periphery, an individualistic Western philosophy versus a collective Eastern doctrine rooted in a communal past. Mackinder died [March 1947] but his ideas lived on."[40] It is easy to be cynical about British, Athenian, or American policy motives. It is less easy to be cynical about the consequences for political and other humane values of British, as contrasted say with German, success in statecraft. The United States can learn both positive and negative lessons from the British way in statecraft and strategy *vis-à-vis* the dangers of unchecked continental-based power. Also, Washington can recognize that while it is balancing power for the sake of US national security, it happens also to be the contemporary torchbearer and first cohort of the praetorian guard for a concept of human dignity that has always been under assault. More often than not that assault has come from states and empires whose political philosophies have been the products of distinctively continental experience. Writing of the British way with coalition warfare, John Terraine judged that "the ultimate strength of a coalition is not to be measured by the number of its members, but by the strength of its strongest member."[41] The Persian Gulf in 1990–91 attested to the wisdom in Terraine's point.

The long and full British experience in managing strategic relations between sea power and land power invites extensive attention by strategic theorists. Objectively speaking, few of the strategic concepts or classes of activity of interest fail to apply to British strategic history. Subjectively viewed, that British experience is recent, readily accessible, to a degree familiar to most strategic theorists and commentators, and is characterized in its essentials by continuity to the present.

4 Why strategy is difficult [1999]

My aim is to relate the nature of strategy to the character of its artistic application and to the unknowable context of the twenty-first century. The immodesty, even arrogance, of this endeavor is best conveyed through an anecdote about a meeting between Hannibal Barca and an armchair strategist. Hannibal suffered from what in this last century has been the German failing – winning battles but losing wars. Hannibal won all of his battles in the Second Punic War except, sadly for a Carthage that did not deserve him, the last one, against Scipio Africanus at Zama in 202 BC. He is reported to have had little patience with amateur critics.

> According to Cicero (de Oratione), the great general when in exile in Ephesus was once invited to attend a lecture by one Phormio, and after being treated to a lengthy discourse on the commander's art, was asked by his friends what he thought of it. "I have seen many old drivellers," he replied, "on more than one occasion, but I have seen no one who drivelled more than Phormio."[1]

The theme of this article lurks in the ancient strategic aphorism that "nothing is impossible for the man who does not have to do it." When I was contributing to the *Defense Guidance* in the early 1980s its basic direction for the Armed Forces could be reduced to "be able to go anywhere, fight anyone, and win." To repeat my point, to those who do not have to *do* strategy at the sharp, tactical end of the stick, the bounds of feasibility appear endless.

True wisdom in strategy must be practical because strategy is a practical subject. Much of what appears to be wise and indeed is prudent as high theory is unhelpful to the poor warrior who actually has to do strategy, tactically and operationally. Two classic examples make the point.

Carl von Clausewitz advised us that there is a "culminating point of victory," beyond which lies a decline in relative strength.[2] Great advice – save, of course, that political and military maps, let alone physical terrain, do not come with Clausewitz's "culminating point" marked. Imagine that you are a German and that it is anytime between late June 1941 and late August 1942. You have read Clausewitz. Where is the culminating point – at Minsk or Smolensk, on the Dnieper, Don, or Volga? How can you find a culminating point of victory until adverse consequences unmistakably tell you where it was?

The other example of great strategic wisdom that is difficult to translate into practical advice is the insistence of Clausewitz (and Jomini) that "the best strategy is always to be very strong; first in general, and then at the decisive point."[3] Naturally the challenge is not to comprehend the all but sophomoric point that one needs to be very strong at the decisive point. Rather it is to know the location of that point. What did Clausewitz's advice mean for Germans in the late summer and fall of 1941? Did they need to concentrate their dissipating strength on the Red Army in the field, on the road to Moscow, or both?

For a tougher call, consider the American military problem in Southeast Asia in the second half of 1965. General William Westmoreland somehow had to identify military objectives to match and secure the somewhat opaque political objectives. Mastery of the arguments in the classics of strategic theory was unlikely to be of much practical help.

The argument

Before expounding the central elements of my argument, which appear pessimistic, let me sound an optimistic note. Terrible though the twentieth century has been, it could have been far worse. The bad news is that the century witnessed three world wars – two hot, one cold. The good news is that the right side won each of them. Moreover, threats to peace posed twice by Germany and then by the Soviet Union were each seen off at a cost that, though high, was not disproportionate to the stakes nor inconsistent with the values of our civilization. Western statecraft and strategy in two world wars was not without blemish. One needs to remember the wisdom of Lord Kitchener who said during the First World War: "We wage war not as we would like but as we must." Strategically, notwithstanding errors, the Western World did relatively well. Now for a darker view.

My key argument is organized around three reasons why it is difficult to do strategy well:

- its very nature, which endures through time and in all contexts,[4]
- the multiplicity and sheer variety of sources of friction,[5]
- it is planned for contexts that literally have not occurred and might not occur; the future has not happened.

This argument is essentially optimistic, even though that claim may appear unpersuasive given that the high-quality strategic performance is always challenged by the nature of strategy – not only by its complexity but by the apparent fact that whatever can go wrong frequently does. Also, strategy can fail because it may apply the wrong solutions to incorrectly framed questions because guesses about the future were not correct. If, despite this, the bad guys were beaten three times during the course of the twentieth century, there are grounds for hope.

Before explaining the many sources of difficulty for strategy, it is necessary to highlight the recurrence of a serious fallacy. Lest this point appear unfairly focused on the United States, I will sugar coat the pill by citing an American who got it right, and two others – one American and one German – who got it wrong. Samuel Griffith, who got it right, was a scholar of Chinese military theory from Sun Tzu to Mao. He once observed that "there are no mechanical panaceas" when commenting on a *Newsweek* report in July 1961 about a fuel–air explosive to destroy bunkers.[6] The American and German, who got it wrong, allowed themselves to be seduced by the promise of "mechanical panaceas." One must hasten to add that these two warrior-theorists were exceptionally able men. The point is that, writing ninety years apart, they made almost the same mistake.

The issue underlying both views is whether much of the fog and thus friction that undoes applied strategy can be thwarted by modern technology. Writing in 1905, Lieutenant General Rudolf von Caemmerer, a member of the great general staff working under Field Marshal Alfred Graf von Schlieffen, offered this claim:

> The former and actually existing dangers of failure in the preconcentrated action of widely separated portions of the army is now almost completely removed by the electric telegraph. However much the enemy may have succeeded in placing himself between our armies, or portions of our armies, in such a manner that no trooper can get from one to the other, we can still amply communicate with each other over an arc of a hundred or two hundred or four hundred miles. The field telegraph can everywhere be laid as rapidly as the troops marching, and headquarters will know every evening how matters stand with the various armies, and issue its orders to them accordingly.[7]

Caemmerer proceeded to admit that the telegraph might dangerously diminish the initiatives allowed to army commanders. The irony is that poor communications, lack of coordinated action, and a general loss of cohesion by the all important armies on the right wing of the German assault in early September 1914 allowed an Allied victory with the miracle on the Marne.[8] The telegraph was a wonderful invention, but it could not reliably dissipate the fog of war.

An American example of a functionally identical error is drawn from the magical "system of systems" invoked by Admiral William Owens, former Vice Chairman of the Joint Chiefs of Staff. In 1995 he wrote, "The emerging system...promises the capacity to use military force without the same risks as before – it suggests we will dissipate the fog of war."[9]

New technology, even when properly integrated into weapons and systems with well trained and highly motivated people, cannot erase the difficulties that impede strategic excellence. A new device, even innovative ways to conduct war, is always offered as a poisoned chalice. Moreover, scarcely less important, strategy cannot be reduced to fighting power alone.[10] Progress in modern strategic performance has not been achieved exclusively through science and technology.

Consider this argument: strategists today have at their disposal technological means to help dissipate the fog of war and otherwise defeat friction that previous generations could only imagine. Modern strategists can see over the hill, communicate instanteously with deployed forces around the world, and in principle rapidly destroy enemy assets wherever they are located – at least in fine weather and provided no innocent civilians are colocated with the targets. The problem is that war cannot be reduced simply to the bombardment of a passive enemy.

Despite electro-mechanical marvels it is no easier – in fact it is probably harder – to perform well as a strategist today than a century ago. Consider the utility of railroads, telegraph, radio, and aircraft to the strategist. The poison in the chalice of each is that other polities have acquired them; each has distinctive vulnerabilities and worse (recall the radio intercepts of First and Second World War); and none of them can address the core of the strategist's basket of difficulties.

Strategy is not really about fighting well, important though that is. To follow Clausewitz, it is about "the use of engagements for the object of the war."[11] The fog of war and frictions that harass and damage strategic performance do not comprise a static set of finite challenges which can be attrited by study, let alone by machines. Every new device and mode of war carries the virus of its own technical, tactical, operational, strategic, or political negation.[12]

To tackle the fog and friction of strategy and war is not akin to exploring unknown terrain, with each expedition better equipped than the last to fill in blanks on the map. The map of fog and friction is a living, dynamic one that reorganizes itself to frustrate the intrepid explorer.

Why so difficult?

Field Marshal Helmuth Graf von Moltke – victor in the wars of German unification – had it right when, in *Instructions for Superior Commanders*, he wrote that "strategy is the application of common sense to the conduct of war. The difficulty lies in its execution."[13] The elder Moltke was rephrasing the words of the master. Clausewitz advises that "everything in strategy is very simple, but that does not mean that everything is very easy."[14] Why should that be so? Five reasons can be suggested.

First, strategy is neither policy nor armed combat; rather it is the bridge between them. The strategist can be thwarted if the military wages the wrong war well or the right war badly. Neither experts in politics and policymaking nor experts in fighting need necessarily be experts in strategy. The strategist must relate military power (strategic effect) to the goals of policy. Absent a strategic brain – as was the case of the United States and NATO *vis-à-vis* Bosnia and Kosovo – one is left with an awkward alliance of hot air (policy statements) and bombardment possibilities (the world is my dartboard view of aerial strategists).[15] Strategy is difficult because, among other things, it is neither fish nor fowl. It is essentially different from military skill or political competence.

Second, strategy is perilously complex by its very nature. Every element or dimension can impact all others. The nature of strategy is constant throughout history but its character continually evolves with changes in technology, society, and political ideas. Success in strategy is not really about securing a privileged position in any one or more of its dimensions – such as technology, geography, or leadership – because it is always possible an enemy will find ways to compensate for that strategic effect from its special strengths. This is a major reason why information dominance in a technical–tactical sense cannot reliably deliver victory. Triumph in war does not correlate with superior technology nor mastery in any allegedly dominant dimension of conflict.

Third, it is extraordinarily difficult, perhaps impossible, to train strategists. Consider these words of Napoleon Bonaparte:

> Tactics, evolutions, artillery, and engineer sciences can be learned from manuals like geometry; but the knowledge of the higher conduct of war can only be acquired by studying the history of wars and the battles of great generals and by one's own experience. There are no terse and precise rules at all; everything depends on the character with which nature has endowed the general, on his eminent qualities, on his deficiencies, on the nature of the troops, the technics or arms, the season, and a thousand other circumstances which make things never look alike.[16]

Napoleon was in a position to know. Like Hannibal he was good at winning battles, but he failed catastrophically as a strategist. Like Imperial Germany, Nazi Germany, and the Soviet Union, Imperial France pursued political goals that were beyond its means. That is a failure in strategy.

Basic problems in training strategists can be reduced to the fact that no educational system puts in what nature leaves out, while the extraordinary competence shown by rising politicians or soldiers in their particular trades is not proof of an aptitude for strategy. The strategist has to be expert in using the threat or use of force for policy ends, not in thinking up desirable policy ends or in fighting skillfully.

Fourth, because strategy embraces all aspects of the military instrument (among others), as well as many elements of the polity and society it serves, the maximum possible number of things can go wrong. To illustrate, sources of friction that can impair strategic performance include those familiar to the military realm (incompatibilities among the levels of military activity and specialized functions such as operations, logistics, and weapons production) and, conceivably the most lethal of all, a mismatch between policy and military capabilities. In the world of strategists, as opposed to that of tacticians, there is simply much more scope for error.

Finally, it is critical to flag an underrecognized source of friction, the will, skill, and means of an intelligent and malevolent enemy. Andre Beaufre defines strategy as "the art of the dialectic of force or, more precisely, the art of the dialectic of two opposing wills using force to resolve their dispute."[17] Recall Clausewitz's dictum: "War is thus an act of force to compel our enemy to do our will."[18] Yet it is easier to theorize about new ways of prevailing than to speculate honestly and imaginatively about possible enemy initiatives and responses.

Further thoughts

There is a sense in which this article reinvents the wheel. It is no great achievement to appreciate that strategy is difficult to do well. Indeed, my point is not dissimilar from that made by Lawrence Freedman, who takes 433 pages in *The Evolution of Nuclear Strategy* to state that there is no truly strategic solution to the dilemmas of nuclear strategy.[19] When armchair strategists tell military practitioners that their task is difficult on the level of strategy, they should not expect much praise. After all, strategy does have to be done. Academics can vote undecided and write another book. Practicing strategists must make decisions regardless of the uncertainty.

Next, one must stress the strategic ignorance of even practical people. Clausewitz wrote, "It might be thought that policy could make demands on war which war could not fulfill; but that hypothesis would challenge the natural and unavoidable assumption that policy knows the instrument it means to use."[20]

The challenge is that before undergoing trial by battle, no one really knows how effective military power will be. Every passage of arms remains unique. A capability that appears lethally effective in peacetime exercises will not translate automatically into a violent elixir to solve political issues. That the armed forces appear lethally potent against a conventional enemy in open warfare could prove irrelevant or worse in urban areas. In peacetime, militaries train against themselves, and that has to comprise a major source of uncertainty concerning future effectiveness.

It is vital to recognize potential tension in three sets of relationships: between politicians and commanders, between commanders and planners, and between commanders and theorists (recall Phormio's efforts to educate Hannibal). Military professionals must simplify, focus, decide, and execute. Politicians, by virtue of their craft, perceive or fear wide ramifications of action, prefer to fudge rather than focus, and like to keep their options open as long as possible by making the least decision as late as feasible. Although commanders are gripped by operational requirements, planners – especially if unschooled by real operational experience – are apt to live in an orderly world where a model of efficiency and compromise is acceptable, indeed is a driver.

The tension becomes acute when a soldier who is only a planner finds himself in a position of high command. The classic example is Dwight Eisenhower, a superb staff officer and military politician who lacked the experience and the aptitude for command, let alone supreme command.[21] As to the terrain between theorists and doers of strategy, the former are skilled in the production of complexity and are unlikely to enjoy the empathy for operational realities that makes strategic ideas readily useful. For example, the nuclear strategist might conceive of dozens of targeting options yet be unaware that his theory passed its "culminating point of victory" – actually its "culminating point of feasibility" – at a distinctly early stage. A president thoroughly uninterested in matters of nuclear strategy until suddenly confronted at dawn some Christmas with the necessity for choice cannot likely cope intellectually, morally, politically, and strategically with many options. Probably he would find it useful to have alternatives: shall we go now, shall we go later, shall we go big, or shall we go small. But those broad binaries may be close to the limits of presidential strategic thinking. Many strategists have presented seemingly clever briefings to policymakers and senior officers whose eyes crossed and brains locked at the sight of the third PowerPoint slide.

The many reasons why strategy is so difficult to do well can be subsumed with reference to three requirements. For strategic success, forces must

- be internally coherent, which is to say competently joint,
- be of a quantity and provide a strategic effect scaled to the tasks set by high policy,
- be employed coercively in pursuit of military objectives that fit political goals.

Competence cannot offset folly along the means–ends axis of strategy. Military history is littered with armies that won campaigns in the wrong wars.

Since the future is unforeseeable – do not put faith in the phrase "foreseeable future" – we must use only assets that can be trusted. Specifically, we plan to behave strategically in an uncertain future on the basis of three sources of practical advice: historical experience, the golden rule of prudence (we do not allow hopes to govern plans), and common sense. We can educate our common sense by reading history. But because the future has not happened, our expectations of it can only be guesswork. Historically guided guesswork should perform better than one that knows no yesterdays. Nonetheless, planning for the future, like deciding to fight, is always a gamble.

To conclude on a positive note, remember that to succeed in strategy you do not have to be distinguished or even particularly competent. All that is required is performing well enough to beat an enemy. You do not have to win elegantly; you just have to win.

5 From Principles of Warfare to Principles of War

A Clausewitzian solution [2005]

> Theory cannot equip the mind with formulas for solving problems, nor can it mark the narrow path on which the sole solution is supposed to lie by planting a hedge of principles on either side. But it can give the mind insight into the great mass of phenomena and of their relationships, then leave it free to rise into the higher realms of action.
>
> (Carl von Clausewitz)[1]

The problem

The problem with the long traditional Principles of War is that they are not what they purport to be. They are Principles of Warfare, not Principles of War. The Principles do not so much require changing for a better fit with a new strategic context, though that might be useful, but rather subordination to a true set of Principles of War. It is the purpose of this essay to provide just such a set.

To focus on the Principles as they have been, and are still, presented (typically, mass; objective; offensive; surprise; economy of force; maneuver; unity of command; security; and simplicity) would be to concentrate on an admittedly important, but essentially second-order, topic: how to fight well. These Principles advise for an activity, fighting, in which America tends to be proficient. Americans are good at warfare. Unfortunately, they are less gifted in their performance at levels above the tactical and operational. The national record in war and strategy leaves much to be desired.[2] Political and strategic culture are prominent among the reasons for this dichotomy between skill in warfare and its lack in strategy and war as a whole. However, if US performance in war is to improve markedly, a necessary step is a conceptual transformation, founded upon a set of Principles that really would provide the essential basis for a theory of war. With a great deal of assistance from Carl von Clausewitz, this essay seeks to take a bold step towards effecting such a transformation. Of necessity, the main body of this analysis is devoted to clearing the ground of the debris of false assumptions and bad habits of thought which impede understanding and impoverish national performance.

A catalog of confusion

It is no small matter to reinvent the Principles of War. Especially is this the case when their overriding limitation, an indifference to strategy and politics, is powerfully characteristic of American strategic culture and national style in military behavior.[3] To compose the new set of Principles so that they secure a tight grip on the subject of war, a number of popular conceptual errors must first be corrected. These function as a catalog of confusion. Unless these fallacies are recognized and corrected, there is little prospect of any marked improvement in American strategic performance.

In order to draft a set of Principles of War worthy of their title, six major sources of confusion must be removed.

1   *The distinction between war and warfare needs to be appreciated and applied.* War is a relationship between belligerents; it is the whole context for warfare. Warfare is defined as "the act of making war."[4] The traditional Principles of War are heroically misnamed. They are not Principles of War at all. Instead they are Principles of Warfare. This most vital point is complementary to Antulio J. Echevarria's recent complaint that Americans have confused a theory of battle with a theory of war.[5] The classic Principles pertain strictly to the tactical and operational levels of military behavior; they pertain to warfare.

2   *The nature and the character of war are clearly distinctive concepts.* The former is eternal, while the latter is ever changing, albeit at a variable pace at different times and in different places. Failure to grasp the empirical point that war has a permanent nature is proving to be one of the most damaging sources of misunderstanding among American defense professionals today. Contemporary debate is awash with studies and speeches on the allegedly changing nature of war. To be blunt, if war changed its nature it would become something else. In other words, it is an impossibility. War cannot change its nature. Clausewitz argued thus in a manner that should have settled the issue for all time. He explained that war has two natures, objective and subjective. The former is enduring in all times and places, regardless of belligerents, weapons, and purposes. The latter refers to "the means by which war has to be fought," and they are ever variable.[6] The nub of the matter was expressed with characteristic clarity by Clausewitz when he stated that "all wars are things of the same nature."[7] Also, he observed most tellingly that "war, though conditioned by the particular characteristics of states and their armed forces, must contain some more general – indeed, a universal element with which every theorist ought above all to be concerned."[8] A profound conclusion follows if Clausewitz is judged correct in his claim for the essential unity of the phenomenon of war through the ages. Logically, the Principles of War, though not of warfare, ought not to be changeable if they are properly framed.

3   *There is a vital unity between war and peace.* War is about the succeeding peace; it can have no other meaning. War is not an end itself, whereas warfare is only acceptable to our society if it is waged to secure strategic leverage for a clear

political purpose.[9] American strategic experience over the past century, not excluding the present, reveals a persisting failure to grasp the umbilical connection between war and peace. So well known is Clausewitz's argument that "war is an instrument of policy,"[10] that it all but beggars belief that time after time the United States has failed to wage warfare effectively as an instrument of policy. This seemingly endemic, possibly cultural, inability to comprehend the continuity of politics through warfare finds significant expression in the over enthusiasm of the defense community for the material means of war, treating them in effect, and indeed the act of making war, autonomously. The next item makes this point even more explicitly.

4 *The military instrument and its employment too often is regarded as an end in itself.* Another way of phrasing this claim is to assert that the United States has a damaging habit of failing to function militarily in a strategically purposeful manner. It would be only a slight exaggeration to claim that America "does not do strategy."[11] The misleadingly titled Principles of War, past and present, contribute not at all to the correction of this appalling confusion.

The current drive for a transformation keyed to comprehensive netcentricity, whatever its merits, is in danger of comprising yet another essentially tactical, possibly operational, rolling achievement. It does not have to be so, but the contemporary signs are not entirely reassuring.[12] The defense community seems wedded to the fallacy, mentioned already, that the nature of war can change and means and ends continue to be confused. American defense debate persists in misusing the adjective strategic. This is not a trivial error. No weapon or action is inherently strategic, and the strategic level of war is not a linear continuation upwards from operations and tactics. Strategy is the bridge between military power and policy, whereas strategic effect refers to the consequences of the threat or use of military power. Strategy and tactics are different in kind. If tactics, which is to say the exercise of military power, is confused with strategy, Americans condemn themselves to fighting adrift from navigation by strategy and policy. Again, the Prussian theorist sought to educate us when he wrote, "tactics teaches *the use of armed forces in the engagement*, strategy, *the use of engagements for the object of the war*."[13] And yet the US defense community repeatedly has focused on tools rather than purposes. When we talk today of netcentric warfare, attention is drawn to the instrument, not its purpose. Principles of War need to be drafted in a way that encourages a shift of focus from action itself to the intended political consequences of action, via the intervening and enabling bridge of the concept of strategic effectiveness.[14]

5 *Technological change frequently is confused with change in the nature of war.* History, our sole source of empirical data on war and warfare, appears to show that technological innovation is only one among the dynamic factors that promote military transformation. Moreover, such innovation tends to be less important than political, social-cultural, and doctrinal factors. In addition, new technologies can deliver their military potential only when they are embedded in appropriate organizations and are employed by a suitable doctrine keyed to the idea and reality of a combined arms team.[15] New military technologies, as well as

some civilian ones (e.g. railroads, food canning, the electric telegraph, the internal combustion engine, and so forth), can matter profoundly for evolution in the means and methods of warfare. However, it is the way in which new technologies are employed that is the engine of change, not the machines themselves. Historical study also tells us that new technologies are apt to be employed in different ways by different societies.[16] Distinctive ways of war will be partly attributable to unique cultural contexts and partly to the individual geopolitical and geostrategic circumstances of the societies in question.[17]

Because technological change, especially in weaponry and means of transportation, is visible and therefore obvious, and pertains to the actual point of the spear of strategic history, its significance is easily exaggerated. Indeed, the exaggeration extends to the claim that material innovation changes the nature of war. Often, that erroneous claim reflects nothing more than the casual misuse of language. As noted earlier, many people refer carelessly to the changing nature of war, when what they mean is war's changing character. Nonetheless, a defense community, which is heavily technocratic, populated overwhelmingly by technophiles, and has long been committed to a machine-centered and dependent way of war, is prone to harbor extravagant expectations of the implications of new technology. The sound argument that technological change can be a vital dynamic of military transformation, all too readily becomes an unsound argument when change in the material context of war-making is expected to rewrite the whole book on war.

6   *The differences between regular and irregular warfare are so obvious (at least, they should be) that there is a powerful tendency for officials and theorists to fail to grasp what these modes have in common.* Appreciation of a set of Principles of War, properly drafted, could hardly fail to help correct this error. Today's technophiles are inclined to reject past experience on the grounds of its material irrelevance. So, also, today's theorists of countersurgency, indeed of irregular warfare in general, are apt to exaggerate the uniqueness of their concerns. In 1991, Martin van Creveld proclaimed *The Transformation of War*, and as a consequence retired Clausewitz, allegedly as the theorist of an era now past, that of inter-state warfare.[18] More recently, albeit developing ideas first aired in the 1980s, theorists would have us believe that war has entered its fourth, highly irregular, generation. A prominent prophet of Fourth-Generation Warfare (4GW), Colonel Thomas X. Hammes, USMC, registers the peculiar claim that a defining characteristic of 4GW is its focus on warfare as a struggle between the political wills of the belligerents.[19] It is true that today's information technologies enable both regulars and irregulars to conduct netwar to erode their opponent's determination, but this technical evolution is not a matter of great moment for the nature of war. The 4GW school has confused technical novelty and the current prevalence of irregular conflict, with change that would be truly profound. 4GW is rediscovery of the wholly familiar. Clausewitz defines war as "*an act of force to compel our enemy to do our will.*"[20] Ideally, in his view, that enemy will be rendered "powerless" to offer further resistance. In practice, however, most wars, both regular and irregular, are concluded when one belligerent decides that it has had enough. Even the "total" war of 1914–18, a contest of industrial-age attrition,

was ultimately a battle of wills rather than resources. Common understanding of true Principles of War, as contrasted with the Principles of Warfare which today continue to masquerade as such, should go a long way towards helping to prevent the confusion of changes in the popularity of irregular modes of warfare, with the dawning of a new era. Of course, regular and irregular warfare differ profoundly. But also they have much in common. Specifically, they share a necessary obedience to the basic and enduring lore of war and strategy.

A solution

This essay began with the claims that the United States lacks a theory of war and that the current Principles of War are misnamed. Those Principles are all about waging warfare, an activity at which the US military generally excels. Admittedly, its record in counterinsurgency does leave much to be desired, and in that respect certainly there is scope for some light amendment to the traditional Principles. However, suggestions for improvement to the existing lore of warfare is not my purpose. The challenge rather is to augment the Principles about combat with a new set that treats war as a whole and which relates force to its political purpose. In order to highlight the conceptual contrast, I will preface my new list of Principles of War with the Principles that are now authoritative in the US Army.

---

9   Principles of War[21]

The nine Principles of War as defined in the Army Field Manual FM-3 Military Operations

Principle	Definition
Mass	Concentrate combat power at the decisive place and time.
Objective	Direct every military operation towards a clearly defined, decisive, and attainable objective.
Offensive	Seize, retain, and exploit the initiative.
Surprise	Strike the enemy at a time, at a place, or in a manner for which he is unprepared.
Economy of force	Allocate minimum essential combat power to secondary efforts.
Maneuver	Place the enemy in a position of disadvantage through the flexible application of combat power.
Unity of command	For every objective, ensure unity of effort under one responsible commander.
Security	Never permit the enemy to acquire an unexpected advantage.
Simplicity	Prepare clear, uncomplicated plans and clear, concise orders to ensure thorough understanding.

Whatever their merits and limitations, the nine Principles are robustly military and offer advice for tactics and operations. Some of the more sophisticated unofficial lists of the Principles have been "slanted to serve senior politico-military policymakers and strategists, rather than practitioners of operational art and tacticians," but the product remains overwhelming a guide to good practice in the conduct of warfare.[22]

This essay concludes with a list of ten Principles of War. These are not intended to supersede the traditional list but rather to provide the appropriate theoretical context for them. It will become readily apparent that my ten items are far from original. As the title of this essay proclaims, they are largely, though not entirely, derived from Clausewitz's theory of war. Given the novelty of this enterprise, I have not worried overmuch about some overlaps and redundancies among items; future refinement will smooth the rough edges. Similarly, I have chosen clarity over elegant parsimony, and hence have elected not to try and reduce each Principle to a single-word title, after the taut fashion of the traditional Principles.

Principles of War – new style

1 *War is a political act conducted for political reasons.* Even though war has its own grammar, as Clausewitz insists, which can trip up overambitious policymakers, there can be no strictly military realm.

2 *There is more to war than warfare.* Although war must be characterized by organized violence, belligerents employ many of the policy instruments available to them. War can be prosecuted in several ways, among which the battlefield may not be the most important.

3 *There is more to strategy than military strategy.* Belligerents devise and implement grand strategy, seeking to exploit their nonmilitary as well as military assets.

4 *War is about peace, and sometimes vice versa.* Wars are not autonomous happenings. They are launched and conducted solely for the purpose of solving political problems and securing thereby a more satisfactory political context. The whole conduct of war must be directed to achieve a desirable peace. Of course, this is often frustrated by the like ambitions of the enemy.

5 *Style in war-fighting has political consequences.* Although war has a grammar of its own which must be respected,[23] insofar as is practicable, it should be waged militarily in such a manner as not to sabotage its political goals. The United States has a disturbing history of winning wars in such a way that the succeeding peace is heavily mortgaged or even lost.[24]

6 *War is caused, shaped, and driven by its contexts.* Context-free analysis of future war, or warfare, is nonsense. When it is conducted it is a meaningless technical exercise. War has to be studied, and defense plans

drafted, in the dim light of prudent guesswork about the political, social-cultural, strategic, and technological contexts. Defense professionals are apt to forget that war is not self-referential.

7 *War is a contest of political wills.* Mercifully, few wars are prosecuted to the very bitter end. Instead, typically they endure until one belligerent decides it has had enough. This general fact means that the social context of war is truly vital. Military victory is only a means to a political goal. In warfare against irregulars it is unusual for military victory to be feasible. Such conflicts have the dominant character of a violent struggle of political attrition.

8 *"War is nothing but a duel on a larger scale": take the enemy into account.*[25] Enemy-independent planning is an occupational pathology among defense professionals. The theory of war and strategy applies universally. Every belligerent performs on all of war's many dimensions simultaneously. Each combatant seeks to exploit its strengths to try to offset its weaknesses, and each strives to conduct its war effort grand strategically to the disadvantage of the enemy.

9 *War is a cultural undertaking.* It is not only a cultural undertaking, as some anti-Clausewitzian theorists assert erroneously, but also a cultural influence necessarily as universal as it is widely variable in content.[26] These Principles of War are designed to be culture-neutral, but the ways in which they are realized in the practice of statecraft, strategy, and war-waging are inalienably influenced, or more, by local culture. Thirty years ago, Bernard Brodie warned that "good strategy presumes good anthropology and sociology. Some of the greatest military blunders of all time have resulted from juvenile evaluations in this department."[27]

10 *War requires the ability to adapt to failure and to cope well enough with the consequences of chaos, friction, and the unintended consequences of actions.* The prudent strategist does not seek the perfect plan, but rather the plan that is tolerant of faults, which, if it fails, should fail gracefully and which, in failure, would not render a new plan infeasible.[28] In an 1812 memorandum on the *Principles of War*, Clausewitz noted "that we cannot be readily ruined by a single error, if we have made reasonable preparation."[29] Even aside from actual errors, war usually is so traumatic an experience that generally it follows a course and has consequences quite unintended and unexpected by the belligerents. To go to war is to roll the iron dice.

Much work remains to be done to refine new-style Principles of War. However, these Principles do address and provide an answer to the most serious problem by far that faces the US defense community. They are crafted to compel due focus of attention upon the whole enduring nature of war.

Part II

Strategic issues

6   Nuclear strategy
The case for a theory of victory
[1979]

For good or ill, or even perhaps for some of both, 1979 is almost certain to see the most intensive debate over strategic postural and doctrinal issues since the days of the mis-projected missile gap back in 1959–60. SALT II is bringing it all together: the state of the balance, predictions of trends, the relevance (or otherwise) of strategic forces to superpower diplomacy, developments in high technology, Soviet intentions and Soviet performance, and the character of a desirable strategic doctrine.

The great SALT II debate, when finally joined, will probably cast as much shadow as light because much of the argumentation will avoid reference to truly fundamental issues. Indeed, a similar problem besets the quality of debate over individual weapon and related program questions (i.e. does the United States need a follow-on (to *Minuteman* III) ICBM, and if so of what kind? – or, does the United States need a civil defense program? – and so forth). Much of the earnest and even occasionally rather vitriolic debate over SALT, the MX-ICBM, cruise missiles, and the like, is almost purely symptomatic of disagreement over basic strategy – indeed, so much so that if attention were to be focused on the latter, then the generic, though not detailed, solutions to the former problems should follow fairly logically. As a somewhat inelegant axiom, this author will argue that a defense community which has not really decided what its strategic force posture is for, has no business either engaging in strategic arms control negotiations, or in passing judgment on the merits of individual weapon systems.

A need for strategy

Notwithstanding the popular, and indeed official, nomenclature which classifies our centrally based nuclear launch systems as *strategic*, the fact remains that there is an acute deficiency of strategic thinking pertaining to those forces. To many people, apparently, it is not at all self-evident that there are any issues of operational strategy relevant to the so-called strategic nuclear forces. Strategic nuclear war, presumably, is deterred by the prospect of the employment of those forces; while, should such a war actually occur, again presumably, each side executes its largely pre-planned sequence of more and more punishing strike options in its Single Integrated Operational Plan (SIOP) and then dies with the best grace it can muster. This author has difficulty seeing merit (let alone moral justification) in executing the posthumous punishment of an adversary's society, possibly to a genocidal level of catastrophic damage, and hence has some difficulty discerning the value of such an option brandished as an intended pre-war deterrent.[1] Of course, the US Government has not been planning to *execute* even a rough facsimile of genocide for many years. But official, and even Presidential, language (and perhaps thinking),[2] and war planning, have long been recognized to be somewhat different activities. This author is not confusing post-NSDM 242 nuclear weapon employment policy (NUWEP) guidance with assured destruction thinking,[3] although he believes that both would prove fatal to the US prospect of success in the event of war. In addition, this author does not accept the argument that US war plans are in good order: the real deficiency lies in the strategic forces that have been acquired to attempt to implement them (though there is considerable merit in that argument).

Absurd and murderous though mutual assured destruction (MAD) reasoning is to a strategic rationalist, one has to admit that the world, perhaps fortunately, is not ruled by strategic rationalists. Readers should be warned that this author does believe that there is a role for strategy – that is, for the sensible, politically directed application of military power in thermonuclear war. However, it is entirely possible that politicians of all creeds and cultures are, and will be, deterred solely by the undifferentiated prospect of nuclear war – which may be translated as meaning the fear of suffering societal punishment at an unacceptable level. Even if one suspects that the politician, a rank amateur in strategic analysis, will be deterred where a professional strategic analyst would advise that he should not be, there remain good reasons for listening to the cautionary words of the professional.

First, however unlikely the possibility from the perspective of American political culture, there could come to power in the Soviet Union a leader, or a group of collegial leaders, who would take an instrumental view of nuclear war. Whether or not such a group already is in place is very much a moot point. It could be profoundly imprudent simply to assume that strategic analysis has no bearing on the likelihood of occurrence of nuclear war. In a political context where a decision to act or not to act was finely balanced, military confidence and promises, or the lack thereof, could have a large influence on the political decision. *One of the essential tasks of the American defense community is to help ensure that in moments of acute crisis the Soviet general staff cannot brief the Politburo with a plausible theory of military victory.*

Second, it should not be forgotten that an important role for strategic analysis is the underpinning of a strategic doctrine which makes for the orderly management of, and choice between, defense programs.[4] If sufficient deterrent effect is believed to repose simply in the undifferentiated threat of nuclear war (of doing a lot of damage in a short space of time), on what basis does one choose what to buy? The essentially arbitrary guidelines for the "required" levels of assured destruction make some sense on this reasoning. (i.e. nobody claims that some "magic fraction" of threatened damage is needed for deterrence – even if annual

Posture Statements do lend themselves to being misread in that fashion – but, some doctrinal guidance, beyond simply doing a lot of damage, is required for the provision of rules of thumb and for the suggestion of appropriate measures of merit).[5] Unfortunately, arbitrary doctrinal guidance for force sizing (and even quality) devised for the convenience of orderly administration tends to acquire an aura of strategic authority that was not originally intended and which it cannot bear.[6]

Third, and most important of all, it is sometimes easy to forget that a central nuclear war really could occur. Whatever the pre-war feelings, thinking, and even instincts, of a politician may have been, in the event of war it is safe to predict that he would demand a realistic war plan. The promise of imposing catastrophic levels of damage on Soviet society may, or may not, have merit as a pre-war declaratory stance, but the politician would find that his learning curve on nuclear strategy rose very rapidly indeed following a deterrence failure.[7] Killing people and blowing down buildings, on any scale, cannot constitute a strategy – unless, that is, one has some well developed theory which specifies the relationship between societal damage, actual and threatened, and the achievement of (political) war aims. Unless one is willing to endorse the proposition that nuclear deterrence is all bluff, there can be no evading the requirement that the defense community has to design nuclear employment options that a reasonable political leader would not be self-deterred from ever executing, however reluctantly.

Several years ago, Kenneth Hunt argued that among NATO's more important duties was the need to guarantee to the Soviet Union that it could not avoid having to initiate a "major attack" should it move westwards in Europe.[8] NATO's function, on this theory, is not to defend Western Europe (at least, not directly); rather, it is to impose a high threshold for military-political adventure – to compel Soviet leaders, of any degree of intelligence or rabid hostility, that there are no relatively cheap or risk-constrained military options available. A similar logic underlies the policy positions of a major school of thought on strategic nuclear issues: all that we should, or need to, ask of the US strategic nuclear posture is that it be capable of inflicting a lot of punishment on Soviet society. Precisely how much punishment, and of what kinds, we need to promise, must be a matter for conjecture, but fortunately for the robustness of a nuclear deterrent regime, precision is not required. Essential to this thesis, are the beliefs that nuclear war cannot be won, that there is no way in which damage in such a war can be held down to tolerable levels in the face of an adversary determined to impose major damage, and that notwithstanding the many differences between the superpowers in strategic culture, each side should have no difficulty identifying, threatening, and, if necessary, effecting a level of damage that the other would find unacceptable.

Strategic debate of recent years on SALT and strategic forces' issues has become so polarized and has involved such a high level of polemical "noise," that the transmission of signals between contending camps has been difficult. It is a considerable oversimplification to assert that there are two schools of thought on nuclear deterrence – there are not: there are many. However, while admitting the many nuances that separate the exact philosophies and policy prognoses of individuals, it is useful to recognize that the impending major debate over SALT II is being nurtured by what amounts to a fundamental dispute over the requirements, and even the place, of a deterrent policy. It is argued that, the premises of the two loose coalitions of policy contenders drive the debate that surfaces all too often with reference to specific defense and arms control issues[9] – at a level of detail where the policy action (or inaction) advocated, can have integrity only if it is related to basic assumptions and explicit *desiderata* (it is analogous to discussing strategy without reference to war aims).

Assured destruction and its descendants: a sickly breed

The first school of thought,[10] which currently holds policy-authoritative sway in Washington (though it is not unchallenged within the government), may be thought of as the heir to the assured destruction ideas of the mid- to late 1960s. In 1964–65, the US defense community substantially abandoned the concept of damage limitation. It was believed that, strategic stability (*the* magic concept – far more often advanced and cited than defined),[11] largely by virtue of a logic in technology (a truly American theme), could and should repose in what would amount to a strategic competitive stalemate. Each side could wreak unacceptable damage on the other's society, and neither could limit such prospective damage through counterforce operations or through active or passive defenses. Ballistic missile defense (BMD), in principle, if not in contemporary technical realization, did of course pose a potentially fatal threat to this concept. A good part of the anti-ABM fervor of the late 1960s, which extended from Secretary of Defense Robert McNamara to local church and women's groups, can be traced to the strange belief that the goals of peace, security, arms control, stability, and reduced resources devoted to defense preparation, could all flow from a context wherein societies were nearly totally vulnerable and strategic weapons were nearly totally invulnerable. It is important to note both that US operational planning never reflected any close approximation to the assured destruction concept,[12] and that the legatees of MAD reasoning in the late 1970s have made some adjustments to the doctrine for its better fit with contemporary reality.

The adjective "strange" was applied to MAD reasoning in the paragraph above from the perspectives of the historian of strategic ideas and of the sociologist of strategic culture. A detached observer might well ask and observe as follows:

- Is MAD a matter of a logic in technology (wherein offense-dominance is a physical law), or is it more in the nature of a self-fulfilling prophecy?
- If one side to the competition pursues the assured destruction path, how great a risk is it taking, should the other side, for whatever blend of reasons, chooses differently?
- MAD and its variants assume a noticeable measure of functional convergence of strategic ideas. But, strategic sociology tells us that each security community tends to design unique solutions to uniquely defined problems.[13]

- History may not tell us much with assurance, but certainly it suggests that technology cannot be frozen through arms control regimes: some qualitative boundaries upon its inventory expansion may be accomplished, but the slender historical arms control record suggests that politicians are as likely to freeze the wrong, as the right (i.e. stabilizing!), developments, and that prohibitions in one area serve to encourage the energetic pursuit of capabilities in other areas.[14]
- Although the existence of nuclear weapons encourages nuclear-armed states to be extremely careful in their mutual dealings, the fact of nuclear weapons has yet to be transcribed into some absolute injunction against war. The late Bernard Brodie has offered the thought that

> if it is not yet an established fact it is at minimum a strong possibility that, at least between the great powers who possess nuclear weapons, the whole character of war as a means of settling differences has been transformed beyond all recognition.[15]

Notwithstanding some recent claims by Raymond Garthoff,[16] it is not at all certain that Brodie was correct with respect to the Soviet Union, while – even if he were correct – it remains the case that a nuclear war could occur. Mutual assured destruction, whatever its (highly dubious) merits as a pre-war deterrent declaratory stance, clearly has no appeal as an operational guidance. Indeed, MAD is the antithesis of strategy – it relates military power to what? – to the punishment of a society for the sins or misjudgments of its rulers.

- The pre-war deterrent focus of MAD reasoning is appealing, but the historian in him/her is distressed by the realization that the advent of nuclear weapons has affected, but has not transformed the character of, international politics. Insane, drugged, or drunk American chief executives might seek to punish Soviet society, but a more responsible leadership has to be presumed to be likely to wish to adhere to an ethic of consequences (rather than revenge).

Pre-war deterrence: a misleading focus?

The second school of thought embraces a coalition of people who are convinced: that Soviet strategic-nuclear behavior is difficult to equate even with a very rough facsimile of MAD reasoning; that the technical-postural basis for the American MAD thesis of the late 1960s has been eroded severely;[17] and that the theory of mutual assured destruction, even as amended officially in the 1970s in favor of greater flexibility, appears to have little of merit to offer as an operational doctrine. To state the central concern of this chapter, US official thinking and planning does not embrace the idea that it is necessary to try to effect the *defeat* of the Soviet Union. First and foremost, the Soviet leadership fears *defeat*, not the suffering of damage – and *defeat*, as is developed below, has to entail the forcible demise of the Soviet state. The second school of thought is edging somewhat tentatively towards the radical thesis that the theory of nuclear deterrence espoused, for example, by Bernard Brodie from 1946 until 1978, a theory which stressed the "utility in nonuse [of nuclear weapons],"[18] and has had extremely deleterious effects upon the quality of Western strategic thinking and hence upon Western security. Above all else, our attention has been directed towards the effecting of pre-war deterrence, at the cost of the neglect of operational strategy.[19] Incredible though it may seem, it has taken the United States' defense community nearly twenty-five years to ask the two most basic questions of all, pertaining to nuclear deterrence issues. These are, first, what kinds of threats should have the most deterring effect upon the leadership of the Soviet state? and, second, should pre-war deterrence fail, what nuclear employment strategy would it be in the United States' interest actually to implement?

The debate has yet fully to be joined, but this revisionist school of strategic theorists sees little merit in contemporary official US deterrent policy (though the trend, as is discussed later, is mildly encouraging). The argument launched in public in late 1973 by the then Secretary of Defense James Schlesinger concerning selective nuclear targeting[20] served, in retrospect at least, more to encourage persuasive fallacies than it did to focus attention upon the real problem. Our real problem, according to this view, is that the United States (and NATO-Europe) lacks a theory of victory in war (or satisfactory war termination). If, basically, one has no war aims (one has no image of enforced and favorable war termination, or of how the balance of power may be structured in a post-war world), on what grounds does one select a strategic nuclear employment policy, and how does one know how to choose an appropriate strategic posture? The answer, in this perspective, is that, one does not know.[21] The answer, provided by the first school of thought is that, one chooses an employment policy (at least at the declaratory level), with roughly matching equipment, that has little, if anything, to do with the intelligent conduct of war. By definition, it is assumed that nuclear war cannot be waged intelligently for rational political ends: the overriding function of nuclear weapons is the deterrence, not the waging, of war.

The second school of thought objects to the above reasoning on several grounds. First, the heavy focus upon nuclear threat, as opposed to nuclear execution, has encouraged a basic lack of seriousness about the actual conduct of a nuclear war – which feeds back into an impoverished deterrent posture and doctrine. Second, although peace may be its profession, one day – arising out of political circumstances that no one could foresee with any confidence – SAC might discover that war is its business, and it would be better for our future if, in that event, SAC were guided by some theory of how it should wage the war to a tolerable outcome. As noted earlier, the somewhat irresponsible ideas that pass for orthodox nuclear deterrent wisdom, with their bottom-line focus upon damaging Soviet economic assets, would (as a prediction) evaporate in their official appeal in the event of a deterrence failure. Fundamentally, they are not serious. SAC does, of course, have plans to wage a central war in a fairly serious way. But, it is very large and – (1) US strategic weapon acquisition policy (under four Presidents) has failed to provide SAC with the means to prosecute the counter-military war very effectively, and (2) US counter-military planning (however well or poorly it could be executed) continues to be deprived of the overarching political guidance that it needs – a definition and a concept of victory.

Superficially, at least, Schlesinger's strategic flexibility, as reflected in NSDM 242 and eventually in actual nuclear employment plans,[22] marked a noteworthy improvement in the quality of US deterrent policy. A richer menu of attack options, small and large, would provide a president with less-than-cataclysmic nuclear initiatives, should disaster threaten, or occur, in Europe or elsewhere.[23] Selectivity of scale and kind of attack, it was and is still argued, enhances deterrence because it promotes the vital quality of credibility. As far as it goes, that line of thought has much to recommend it. Few would deny that a president should feel less inhibited over the prospective dispatch of (say) 30 (or even 130) reentry vehicles, than he would over the dispatch of 1–3000 – particularly when the targets for those 30–130 reentry vehicles had been chosen very carefully with a view to inflicting the minimum possible population loss on the Soviet Union. This theme of restraint, selectivity, and usability – all in the interest of enhancing credibility for the improvement of deterrence – attracted predictable negative commentaries from quarters prone to argue that a more usable nuclear deterrent was a nuclear deterrent more likely to be used[24] (similar arguments surfaced in connection with the protracted debate over enhanced radiation weapons). As Herbert Scoville explained: "[a] flexible strategic capability only makes it easier to pull the nuclear trigger."[25]

The second school of thought has no quarrel whatsoever with the ideas of flexibility, restraint, selectivity, minimal collateral damage, and the rest. But, it does have some sizable quarrel with strategic selectivity ideas that are bereft of a superordinate framework for the conduct and favorable termination of the war. Against the background of a fairly steadily deteriorating strategic nuclear balance,[26] the selectivity thesis simply adds what could amount to bigger and slightly more effective (i.e. the Soviets pay a higher military price) ways of losing the war. With a healthy strategic (im)balance in favor of the United States on the scale of, say, 1957 or 1962, one can see some logic to strategic flexibility reasoning. However, in the late 1970s and the 1980s, there are many reasons why a Soviet leadership might be less than fully impressed by constrained US strategic execution, and might well respond with a constrained nuclear reply that would (and indeed should) most likely impose a noteworthy measure of escalation discipline upon the United States.[27] Selective nuclear options, even if of a very heavily countermilitary character, make sense, and would have full deterrent value, only if the Soviet Union discerned behind them an American ability and will to prosecute a war to the point of Soviet political defeat.

Targeting the recovery economy

Of very recent times, much of the nuclear strategy debate has narrowed down to a dispute over the validity of the thesis that *the real* (and *ultimate*) *deterrent* to

Soviet risk-taking/adventure is the threat that our strategic nuclear forces pose to the Soviet recovery economy. Orthodox assured destruction thinking has evolved since the late 1960s. Notwithstanding the worthy deterrent motives of their authors, it is a fact that the last several annual Posture Statements of Robert McNamara endorsed a mass murder theory of nuclear "war" (to stretch a term). In the event of a central nuclear war, our declaratory policy was to kill tens of millions of Soviet citizens and destroy Soviet industry on a heroic scale.[28] Fortunately, under Presidents Nixon and Ford, killing people and blowing down buildings *per se* ceased to be strategic objectives (though, to repeat, this is not to impugn the motives of the MAD theorists of the 1960s – they wished to deter war: a highly ethical objective – it is only their judgment that is challenged here). Instead, it was noticed (belatedly – though welcome for all that) that recovery from war was an integral part of the Soviet concept of victory[29] – ergo, the United States should threaten the post-war recovery of the Soviet Union.[30]

The counter-recovery theory was not a bad one, but in practice several difficulties soon emerged. First, and most prosaically, American understanding of the likely dynamics of the Soviet post-war economy was (and remains) far short of impressive. In the same way that arms controllers have been hindered in their endeavors to control the superpower strategic arms competition by their lack of understanding of how the competition "worked," so our strategic employment planning community has found itself in the position of being required to be able to do that which nobody apparently is competent to advise it how to do. To damage the Soviet recovery economy would be a fairly elementary task, but to damage it in a calculable (even a roughly calculable) way is a different matter. Furthermore, the discovery, year by year through the mid- to late 1970s, of more and more Soviet civil defense preparation, threw into increasing doubt the "damage" expectancy against a very wide range of Soviet economic targets.

Second, it appears that the counter-economic recovery theme is yet another attempt to evade the most important strategic question. Should war occur, would the United States actually be interested in setting the Soviet economy back to 1959, or even 1929? Such an imposed retardation might make sense if it were married to a scheme for ensuring that damage to the American economy were severely limited. However, no such marriage has yet been mooted in policy-responsible circles.[31] Third, it is possible that the posing (even credibly posing) of major economic recovery problems to the Soviet Union might be insufficiently deterring a prospect if Soviet arms could acquire Western Europe in a largely undamaged condition to serve as a recovery base; if the stakes in a war were deemed by Moscow to be high enough; and if the Soviet Union were able, in the course of the war, to drive the United States back to an agrarian economy.[32] It is difficult to disagree with Henry Kissinger's comment on massive counter-population strikes.

Every calculation with which I am familiar indicates that a general nuclear war in which civilian populations are the primary target will produce casualties exceeding 100 million. Such a degree of devastation is not a strategic doctrine: it is an abdication of moral and political responsibility. No political structure could survive it.[33]

Targeting the Soviet state

Nonetheless, the counter-recovery theme of the 1970s has prompted an interesting line of speculation. Namely, perhaps the recovery that should be threatened is not economic in character, but rather political.[34] Some revisionists of the second school of deterrence theorists argue that any kind of counter-economic strategy is fundamentally flawed because it leads into Soviet strength. The Soviet Union, like Czarist Russia, knows that it can absorb an enormous amount of punishment (loss of life, industry, productive agricultural land, and even territory), recover, and endure until final victory – provided the *essential assets of the state* remain intact. The principal assets are the political control structure of the highly centralized CPSU and government bureaucracy; the transmission belts of communication from the center to the regions; the instruments of central official coercion (the KGB and the armed forces); and the reputation of the Soviet state in the eyes of its citizens. Counter-economic targeting should have a place in intelligent US war planning, but only to the extent to which such targeting would impair the functioning of the Soviet state.

The practical difficulties that would attend an endeavor to wage war against the Soviet state, as opposed to Soviet society, have to be judged to be formidable. However, one would at least have established an unambiguous and politically meaningful war aim (the dissolution of the Soviet political system) that could be related to a postwar world that would have some desirable features in Western (and Chinese) perspective. More to the point perhaps, identification of the demise of the Soviet state as the maximum ambition for our military activity, encourages us to attempt to seek out points of high leverage within that system. For examples, we begin to take serious policy note of the facts that:

- The Soviet peoples as a whole have no self-evident affection for, as opposed to toleration of, their political system or their individual political leaders.
- The Soviet Union, quite literally, is a colonial empire – loved by none of its non Great Russian minority peoples.[35]
- The Soviet state has to be enormously careful of its domestic respect and reputation, so fragile is the system deemed to be (evidence of Soviet official estimates of this fragility is located in the very character of the police state apparat that is maintained, and in the extreme sensitivity historically displayed in response to threats to Soviet authority in Eastern Europe).
- The entire Soviet political and economic system is critically dependent upon central direction from Moscow. If the brain of the Soviet system were destroyed, degraded, or – at a minimum – isolated from those at lower levels of political command who traditionally have been discouraged from showing initiative, what happens to the cohesion, or pace of recovery, of the whole?
- The peoples of Eastern Europe and the minority republics in the Soviet Union itself, respect the success and power of the Soviet state. What happens in terms of the acquiescence of these peoples in Soviet (and Great Russian) hegemony if Soviet arms either are defeated, or are compelled to wage a long and indecisive struggle?[36]

Improbable though it may seem to many, this discussion is beginning to point towards a not-implausible theory of victory for the West. The alternative theory of deterrence/war waging proposed by some people within the second school, by way of contrast to the mass murder, punishment theme of the first school, comprises essentially, the idea that the Soviet system be encouraged to dissolve itself. We resist the external military pressure of the Soviet Union, and effect carefully selected kinds of damage against the capacity of the Soviet state to function with authority at home. Soviet leaders can reason as well as Western defense analysts that large-scale counter-economic strikes would not serve Western interests (if only because of the retaliation that they would invite), whereas a war plan directed at the destruction of *Soviet* power would have inherent plausibility in Soviet estimation.

The decline (but not fall) of assured destruction

The essential backcloth to this counter-political control strategy has to be the ability to deny the Soviet Union any outcome approximating military victory in a short war. No matter how intelligent our ultimate goals may be for the Third World War, if the Soviet Union can (or believes that it can) win a rapid campaign against NATO–Europe[37] and, if need be, could escalate to do unmatchable damage to US strategic forces, while holding virtually all American economic assets at nuclear risk, then the second school would have failed to think through the totality of the deterrence problem. Needless to say, scarcely less significant a weakness in orthodox deterrence thinking than the fact that it focuses upon the threat of effecting the kinds of damage to the Soviet Union that should not be of interest to American policymakers actually to execute, is the fact that it discounts totally the intra-war self-deterrent implications of the vulnerability of American assets. Foreign policy, in good part, is about freedom of action. Mutual assured destruction thinking, which still lurks in our declaratory policy and, presumably, in our war plans, virtually ensures self-deterrence and denies us the freedom of strategic-nuclear action that is a premise of NATO's strategy of flexible response.[38]

It is no exaggeration to claim that still-orthodox punishment-oriented deterrence thinking stemmed to a notable degree from a group of theorists who tended to think of the superpowers as though they were two missile farms: the attainment of an assured destruction capability by both sides would encourage the establishment and endurance of a technologically imposed peace.[39] The idea was fundamentally apolitical, astrategic, and was contrary to what the Soviet Union discerned, very sensibly, as its self-interest. Overall, as John Erickson has observed, American thinking on mutual deterrence, with its technological premises, reflects a "management" approach by way of contrast to "the Soviet 'military' inclination."[40] This author has difficulty understanding how a country like the United States, which has accepted obligations to project power at great distances in support of forward-located allies, could have seen any noteworthy attractions in the mutual hostage theory of deterrence. Of all countries, the United States needs a credible strategic force posture married to a theory of feasible employment. The catastrophic retaliation thesis, whether or not preceded by very selective nuclear employment options, is an idea it would be hard to improve upon were one seeking to minimize the relevance of (American) strategic weapons to world politics. It is probably appropriate largely to dismiss the deterrence-through-punishment ideas of the 1960s (or, at least, as formalized and codified in the 1960s) as the products of a defense community that was neither trained nor inclined to think strategically.[41] After all, the codification of the mutual punishment theory of deterrence as explicit policy – between 1964 and 1968 – coincided exactly, and scarcely totally by chance, with gross *strategic* mismanagement in, and concerning, Vietnam. The same Department of Defense policymaking hierarchy that could not (or would not) design a theory of victory for Vietnam,[42] similarly abandoned such an apparently extravagant notion in the realm of strategic nuclear policy.

Until the mid-1960s, it is probably true to say that the quality of American strategic thinking concerning central war execution was a matter of relatively little importance: defeat for the Soviet Union was virtually implicit in the sheer scale of the strategic imbalance (i.e. even if the United States, in the event of war, had executed a foolish strategy, it would have done so on so massive a relative basis that the Soviet Union could not possibly have emerged from such a conflict with any net profit). But, as the capabilities of the two sides approached rough equivalence in the early to mid-1970s, the quality of strategic thinking, as reflected in actual plans, could easily make the difference between victory and defeat, or recovery and no recovery.[43]

The strategic debate referred to repeatedly in this chapter thus far is in a curious condition – with neither side quite sure of which positions are really worth defending. Notwithstanding the high polemical noise level, there has been a very notable narrowing of real differences of opinion over the past 3–4 years. For prominent examples:

- There is now widespread endorsement of the thesis that Soviet strategic thinking differs markedly from American. Indeed, recognition of what in the West we term a "war-fighting" focus (on the part of the Soviet Union) has helped greatly to promote insecurity in the minds of many over either the inherent wisdom, or the practical advisability (or both), of a punishment-oriented theory of nuclear deterrence. It is many years since commentators in the United States have written about "raising the Russian learning curve."[44]

- Today, there is virtually universal agreement that, notwithstanding the many and accelerating weaknesses in the Soviet system, most of the major military balances have been moving to the disadvantage of the West. There is no consensus over whether or not those trends will continue into and through the 1980s, nor as to whether or not those adverse trends constitute cause for alarm as opposed merely to concern.[45]

- To the knowledge of this author, in the United States' defense and arms control community today there are no strong adherents to anything approximating the pure theory of mutual assured destruction. But, those who have disengaged from the arguments of Robert McNamara's *Posture Statements* for 1968 and 1969 seem to be uncertain as to what other doctrinal haven there might be available, while many of those who have rejected MAD reasoning outright are less than confident that they have identified any superior alternative.

A catalogue of confusion

The admittedly unsatisfactory designations, "first school" of thought and "second school" of thought, have been employed here because there is a considerable danger of unintended misrepresentation and undue simplification should any less neutral titles have been chosen. At this stage in the chapter, it may be safe to introduce the claim that the "first school" corresponds roughly to a focus upon "deterrence through punishment," while the "second school" tends to focus upon deterrence through the expectation of a militarily effective prosecution of war. Alas for neatness of description, neither group closely approaches its ideal type.[46]

The first school has recognized the immorality, inflexibility and plain incredibility of having a strategic force posture preprogramed to deliver only massive strikes against Soviet economic assets *per se*. However, because it rejects any thoroughgoing "war-fighting" alternative as being certain to stimulate the arms competition, perhaps to render war more likely (through the believed consequent increase in strategic instability), and to make the prospects for negotiated measures of arms control far less encouraging, it has endeavored to design what might be termed "assured destruction with a human face." In place of the grisly (though superficially anodyne) prose of 1967–68 vintage McNamara, we are told about the deterrent virtues of strategic flexibility and the ultimately dissuasive merits of impairing Soviet economic recovery to a catastrophic degree. However, as observed above, the first school has yet to cope adequately with the rather obvious critical point that strategic flexibility and counter-recovery targeting are options that two can exercise. An intelligent strategy, if feasible, would be to design nuclear threats and employment options that the adversary either cannot or dare not match (or overmatch). Also, the first school has been increasingly overtaken by developments both in American weapon laboratories and, above all else, in the force posture that the Soviet Union is deploying. There is no logical reason why one should shift from a selective punishment thesis as a consequence of observing the Soviet strategic developments of recent years (if one endorses the punishment thesis); but it does appear that many commentators have been uneasy and defensive in a context where the Soviet Union is apparently challenging every major tenet of the American theory of strategic stability.[47]

First-school adherents are obliged by the contemporary climate of opinion in the United States to endorse the proposition that there should be an "essential equivalence" in strategic prowess between the superpowers, but what can this mean when there are very large asymmetries in strategic doctrine? Does it mean that the United States should invest in strategic capabilities that it deems to be destabilizing (say, hard-target counterforce and civil defense), solely in order to provide a perceptual match with Soviet capabilities?[48] In practice, first school theorists are finding it very difficult to resist venturing into program regions which really have no place in their philosophy. The result, as may be seen in the curious mix of half-heartedly promoted programs and ill-assorted ideas that constitute current strategic policy, is something for nearly everybody. Because the official theory of nuclear deterrence is so uncertain, one sees the following:

- A new commitment to civil defense, qualified near-instantly by assurances that the new commitment will be neither very expensive nor so serious as to pose a threat to strategic stability.
- A commitment to preserve a survivable ICBM leg to the strategic forces triad, but one that will pose as little (and as late) a threat to fixed site Soviet assets as the domestic SALT-related traffic will permit.
- A commitment to the devising of a new strategic nuclear employment doctrine, but not one which challenges any of the basic premises of the deterrence through punishment thesis.
- A commitment to *second-strike* hard-target counterforce prowess, on a scale which should fuel little first-strike anxiety in Moscow.[49]
- A commitment to a SALT process, and to a SALT II outcome, that has no reference to a stable strategic doctrine that has political integrity.[50]

As the period of intense debate over SALT II begins, it is fair to note that the United States Government sees merit in strategic flexibility, in *some* counterforce, in *some* degree of direct protection for the American public (though not much), and in the ability, in the last resort, to blow down large sections of the urban Soviet Union. This may be sufficient for deterrence, but a defense community should be capable of providing strategic direction that has more political meaning.

Revisionist claims: myths and reality

The second school of deterrence theory waxes eloquent on the absence of strategy in official policy, and indeed on the rarity of strategic thinking within the defense community,[51] but remains slightly abashed at the boldness, and even apparent archaism, of the logic of its own position. Today's revisionists are challenging the mature judgment of the finest flowering of American strategic thought. In policy terms at least, "The Golden Age" of American strategic thought extended roughly from 1956 until (at the outside) 1965.[52] The author of probably the single most highly regarded book to appear in this period[53] has written as follows:

> The main war goal upon the beginning of a strategic nuclear exchange should surely be to terminate it as quickly as possible and with the least amount of damage possible – on both sides.[54]

Of course, the best prospect of all for minimizing (prompt) damage lies in surrendering preemptively. If Bernard Brodie's advice were accepted, the West would be totally at the mercy of a Soviet Union, which viewed war in a rather traditional perspective. The second school of nuclear deterrence is concerned lest its debating adversaries, neglecting the degree to which their ideas rest upon an unacknowledged measure of US firepower (if not strategy) superiority, which no longer exists, may mislead American policymakers into ignoring the possibility that nuclear age crises and wars can be *lost*, in a quite unambiguous fashion.

The various arguments of the second school (really a loose coalition) of strategic theory do, it must be admitted, lend themselves fairly easily to grotesque misrepresentation. For example, responsible theorists of the persuasion do *not* claim:

- That the Soviet Union believes that it *will* win a thermonuclear war (instead, it is claimed that there is an impressive apparent consensus among Soviet authorities to the effect that victory (and defeat) is possible).[55]
- That the Soviet Union either wants or expects to have to wage a central war with the United States. Military power can be most useful, and cost-effective, when the mere promise of its exercise achieves desired deterrent and compellent outcomes. It is very likely indeed that the Soviet Union sees its strategic forces largely in a counterdeterrent role – functioning to seal off local conflicts from influence by US strategic forces. However, any Soviet skepticism over the likelihood of central war does not (to the best of our knowledge) spill-over into defense programs and doctrine in the form of weapons and ideas that make little or no military sense. Because war is possible, one prepares sensibly for it.
- That the Soviet Union anticipates achieving ultimate victory in war at little cost (much, though by no means all, of the argument of recent years in the United States concerning Soviet civil defense is really beside the point). Cautious committeemen in the Politburo could not afford to assume that T.K. Jones' optimistic studies (in Soviet perspective) were even close to the mark.[56] Second-school theorists, by and large, anticipate Soviet expectation of the necessity of accepting human and industrial loss on a catastrophic scale. However, catastrophic loss need not be an intolerable loss – and may indeed be loss of a kind that the Soviet Union is willing to absorb, if the political stakes in the conflict are high enough (and if the alternatives to extreme measures of military action are very unattractive in their likely returns). It is fundamental to the Soviet theory of victory that the essential (and as much else in the) homeland be preserved. It is a sobering thought that the loss of 30 or 40 million people might well be compatible with a context defined by a Soviet leadership as victory: it would depend very much on who was among that 30 or 40 million.[57]
- Any certain knowledge concerning the requirements of deterrence or the proper conduct of thermonuclear war for a politically acceptable outcome. What is claimed is that the ideas of the 1960s (the assured destruction of people and industry) and the 1970s (small- and large-scale attack options of

a carefully constrained nature, counter-economic recovery targeting, and the currently increasing interest in even more counter-military options (than in the past – which was fairly extensive) cannot withstand critical examination, given the adverse evolution of the major East–West military balances, and the more mature Western understanding of the Soviet approach to the waging of war.

Counter-military targeting

Newspaper reports in late 1978 and early 1979 suggested that the Department of Defense was attracted to the idea of a substantially counter-military targeting doctrine, in contrast to the counter-economic recovery theme.[58] However, intra-governmental opposition to this idea is substantial, in part for reason of its budgetary implications, and in part because it offends some still fairly authoritative notions pertaining to the sacrosanct concept of stability. In 1978, a State Department publication claimed that "it is our policy not to deploy forces which so threaten the Soviet retaliatory capability that they would have an incentive to strike first to avoid losing their deterrent force."[59]

Counter-military targeting is not, of course, even close to being a novel idea in US war planning. Indeed, one may speculate to the effect that counter-military targeting already comprises the lion's share of strategic resource allocations in SIOP planning – a thought supported amply by the bevy of official commentaries offered in 1974–75 in support of the "Schlesinger shift" in targeting, largely following the guidance provided by NSDM 242 (of 1974). If there is a shift impending in favor of (still more) large counter-military strike options in the SIOP, one can speculate that such a shift might imply the paying of heavier attention to Soviet projection forces or, at a more basic level, a commitment to purchasing the ability to neutralize a far higher fraction of really hard Soviet military (and political) targets than is the case at present.

For the US Government to endorse a full-fledged war-fighting doctrine in the strategic realm would constitute a doctrinal revolution. Such a doctrine would deny the validity of the stability theory that has informed US defense and arms control policy since the mid-1960s.[60] Strategic stability, in the standard formula, requires that societal assets (people and industry) be near totally vulnerable, while strategic weapons be invulnerable. The Soviet Union has always believed in the value of the assured destruction option *vis-à-vis* the United States, but not in *mutual* assured destruction. It is too early to be certain, but even if the United States under President Carter *might* be willing to shift its declaratory focus (and eventually its actual targeting plans) – and to invest in actual military capability – more toward military targets than is the case at present, it is unlikely that it will be able to overcome its fundamental skepticism over the wisdom of approaching a central nuclear war as one should approach (or did approach, in pre-nuclear days) non-nuclear war. Pending the occurrence (and resolution in favor of change) of a sophisticated debate over the worth of still-fashionable ideas concerning crisis and arms race instability, American strategic policy will be shifted at the margin rather than rewritten. Also, a particular strategic posture, even one as large as that to be maintained in the 1980s by the United States (with the blessing of SALT II), is not omni-competent.

At the present time the United States does not have a strategic posture capable of seeking a military outcome to a war in which Western political authorities could place any confidence. Moreover, on the record extant, the interest of the Carter Administration in purchasing such a posture rapidly has to be judged to be distinctly lukewarm. Carter's record on the character and timing of the MX ICBM program, on the B-1 bomber (aborted), and on civil defense, would have to fuel incredulity over the likely postural matching for any proclaimed new strategic doctrine with a war-waging, as opposed to a pre-war deterrent, orientation. If, as (almost certainly over-) reported, the US Government should inch towards a very heavily counter-military strategic nuclear employment doctrine, it will need to understand the requirements and limitations of such an approach. A non-defense professional might be somewhat puzzled by this discussion. As a general rule, he might observe, US war planning surely has *always* been oriented most heavily towards Soviet military targets (strategic forces, projection forces, command and control targets, and war-supporting industry and transport networks) – so what is new? The answer lies in the scope of the military targeting, in its ability to cope with a much harder target set than before, and in its design for separation from civil society. Anybody who sought to argue that the United States suddenly had discovered counter-military targeting as an interesting option, would of course be guilty of misleading his audience. For example, Richard Burt of *The New York Times* wrote recently that

> The Carter Administration has revised the United States strategy for deter-
> ring nuclear war by adopting a concept that would require strategic forces to
> be capable of large-scale precision attacks against Soviet military targets as
> well as all-out retaliatory blows against cities.
>
> The new strategy, which has emerged after months of debate in the
> Pentagon, represents a significant departure from the long-held concept that
> the United States needs only to threaten all-out retaliation against Soviet
> cities to deter Moscow from launching a nuclear attack.[61]

Clausewitz wrote of war that "[i]ts grammar, indeed, may be its own [i.e., war should be waged in a way that makes military sense, given its unique dynamics], but not its logic."[62] A US SIOP oriented towards different kinds of military targets should be guided by a political logic – what are our war aims? A rewriting and recomputing of the SIOP in an even more heavily counter-military direction than is the case at present could place the United States in a somewhat worse position than that occupied by the (major) allied politicians of the First World War – there could be a determination to do *military* damage to the enemy (which is very sensible), but a lack of commitment to the idea of prosecuting the war to the point where the enemy is defeated militarily (unlike the First World War). The question of just how the military damage to be wrought is to be translated into political advantage could easily be evaded.

It may be ungenerous to proffer such a negative (or, at least, skeptical) verdict, but it does seem that the official (at least in the Department of Defense) redirection of US strategic nuclear targeting preferences continues to neglect factors that bear upon the issue of desired war outcomes. As noted earlier, a counter-political control strategy cannot succeed unless a Soviet military offensive, at the theater and/or intercontinental levels, is thwarted. However, it would be foolish to wage the military war without taking proper prior account of the Soviet perspective upon Soviet vulnerabilities. There is considerable danger that the United States, looking to the damage promise of an inventory of cruise missiles and (much later) MX ICBMs, will neglect the very important political criteria for strategic targeting. A theory of victory over the Soviet Union can be only partially military in character – the more important part is political. The United States and its allies probably should not aim at achieving the military defeat of the Soviet Union, considered as a unified whole; instead, it should seek to impose such military stalemate and defeat as is needed to persuade disaffected Warsaw Pact allies and ethnic minorities inside the Soviet Union that they can assert their own values in very active political ways. It is possible that a heavily counter-military focused SIOP might have the same insensitivity to Soviet domestic fragilities as may be found in the counter-economic recovery orientation of the 1970s.

In important respects, a heavily counter-military SIOP would be the kind of war plan that the Soviet Union is well equipped to counter. Notwithstanding its apparent war-waging focus, the American authors and executors of such a doctrine would be unlikely to have considered the conduct of war as a whole: really they would still be seeking, very substantially, to be responsive to pre-war deterrence needs. With a clear political war aim – to encourage the dissolution of the Soviet state – much of the military war might not need to be fought at all. The apparently resolute determination of the American defense community not to think through its deterrence needs, which would involve addressing the question of war aims, promises to produce yet another marginal improvement in doctrine (after all, US strategic forces have always been targeted against Soviet military power – whatever annual Posture Statements may have said).[63] It may be worth reminding American policymakers in 1979 that the United States had a counter-force doctrine in Vietnam. A focus upon counter-military action, bereft of an overarching political intent, save of the vaguest kind, is unlikely to serve American interests well, except by unmerited luck.

The war-fighting theme which now has limited, though important, official support in Washington, comprises no more than half of the change in thinking that is needed. It is essential for pre-war deterrent effect that Soviet leaders not believe they could wage a successful short war. But, for reasons that none could predict in advance, war might occur regardless of the prewar theories and the postures of the two sides. In that event, it will be essential that the United States has a theory of war responsive to its political interests.[64] Because a counter-military focus in the SIOP is not informed by a clear goal of political victory against the Soviet state, the United States is unlikely to be able to wage an intercontinental nuclear war in a very intelligent fashion. In the Second World War, American wartime leaders declined to attempt to look beyond the battlefield, so long as the war was still in progress, with results of impressive negative educational value for succeeding generations. How much more intelligent it would be to have explicit war aims that should, in and of themselves, have considerable pre- and intra-war deterrent value.

One hesitates to criticize the reported current trend in official thinking, so healthy a change is it in its war-waging focus from the murderous and impolitic counter-economic themes of the 1960s and (most of the) 1970s. Nonetheless, the point has to be made that there continues to be an absence of political judgment overseeing US strategic nuclear employment policy and, *ergo*, there is a neglect of strategy. A possible change in the 1980s in strategic employment orientation towards the counter-military, is fully compatible with a US defense community which would not be able to bring itself to think of thermonuclear war in terms of victory or defeat. The US defense community, substantially coerced in its thinking by the adverse trends in the major East–West military balances, has progressed from a counter-economic, to a counter-military focus in its nuclear employment reasoning (although the mechanical details of war planning may well have focused more upon Soviet military assets than the US defense community generally understood to be the case), but it has yet to accept a *strategic* focus and advance to a counter-political control thesis. Unlike Soviet defense analysts, Western commentators continue to be bemused by the reality-numbing concept of "war termination." Wars are indeed terminated, but they are also won or lost. Moreover, if the US defense community envisages (as it must, realistically) the sacrifice (presumably unwilling) of tens of millions of Americans in a thermonuclear war, that sacrifice should be undertaken only in a *very* worthwhile cause. If there is no theory of political victory in the US SIOP, then there can be little justification for nuclear planning at all.

Stability and the need for defense

The principal intellectual culprit in our pantheon of false strategic gods is the concept of stability. For more than fifteen years, influential members of the US defense and arms control community have believed that it is useful, or even essential, that the Soviet Union have guaranteed unrestricted strategic access to American societal assets. Such unrestricted access *was* believed to have a number of stabilizing consequences. In and of itself it should limit arms competitive activity (such activity as remained would stem from "normal" modernization and from efforts to offset counterforce-relevant developments on the other side),[65] while – more basically – it should promote some relaxation of tension, in that the Soviet Union would, belatedly, be assured of its ability to deter (through punishment) the United States.[66] (This theory has some features in common with the view that the four-fold rise in oil prices in 1973–74 was "good for us" – compelling us to confront the implications of our own profligacy in the energy consumption field.)

Analysts of all (or perhaps most) doctrinal persuasions have come at last to accept the view that the Soviet Union does not relax as a consequence of its achieving a very high quality assured destruction capability: the excellent reason for such continued effort is that the assured destruction of American societal assets plays no known role in Soviet deterrent or wartime planning – save as a threat to deter American counter-economic strikes. In addition, Soviet planners probably see considerable political coercive value for a postwar world in a very large counter-societal threat. Backward though it has seemed to some, the Soviet Union has provided unmistakable evidence of believing that wars, even large nuclear wars, can be won or lost. The mass-murder of Americans makes a great deal of sense in terms of the authority structure of a postwar world (since the Soviet Union cannot consummate a victory properly through the physical occupation of North America), but such a grisly exercise has little or nothing to do with the prosecution of a war (save as a counterdeterrent threat).

American strategic (and arms control) policy, since the mid-1960s, has been misinformed by stability criteria which rested (and rest) upon a near-total misreading of Soviet phenomena. Soviet leaders are opportunists with a war-waging doctrine as their strategic *leitmotiv*. Supposedly sophisticated self-restraint in American arms competitive activity, designed so as not to stimulate "destabilizing" Soviet responses, has simply presented the Soviet Union with an upcoming period of strategic superiority of uncertain duration. The American stability theorem held only for so long as both sides endorsed it. There is legitimate dispute today over the quality of Soviet strategic programs, but no one, to the knowledge of this author, disputes the contention that the Soviet Union is seeking both to protect its societal assets (assured survival, not mutual assured destruction) and to pose the maximum threat to American strategic forces, compatible with the adequate manipulation of Western hopes and fears for the future for the purpose of discouraging a strong American competitive response. Unlike the Soviet Union, the United States has declined to recognize (courtesy of its still-authoritative stability theory) that an adequate strategic deterrent posture requires the striking of a balance between offensive and defensive elements. There is a painful irony of several dimensions in this American intellectual failing.

First, among the more pertinent asymmetries that separate the United States from the Soviet political systems, is the acute sensitivity of the former to the *personal* well-being of its human charges. It is little short of bizarre to discover that it is the Soviet Union, and not the United States, that has a serious civil defense program.[67] Second, potentially the strongest element in the overall Western stance *vis-à-vis* the Soviet Union is its industrial mobilization capacity. Reasonably good American BMD carries healthily terminal implications for Soviet opportunism or adventure. A BMD system that works well enables the United States to wage a long war and to mass produce the military means for eventual victory. So great is American mobilization potential, *vis-à-vis* the extant strategic posture, that US defense policy, logically, should endorse a defensive emphasis. Such an emphasis is the guarantor of strategic forces in overwhelming numbers *tomorrow*.

Third, if US strategic nuclear forces are to be politically relevant in future crises, the American homeland has to be physically defended. It is unreasonable to ask an American president to wage an acute crisis, or the early stages of a central war, while he is fearful of being responsible for the loss of more than 100 million Americans. If escalation discipline is to be imposed upon the Soviet Union, even in the direst of situations, potential damage to North America has to be limited. Damage-limitation has to involve both counterforce action and active and passive defenses. The claim that actually to protect (even very imperfectly) Americans and their industry would be destabilizing, is a doctrinal cliché whose shallowness merits uncompromising exposure. Since virtually all Western commentators recognize that the Soviet Union is not moved in its strategic policy by assured destruction criteria, and since no one can deny that an American president could not threaten, or implement, even highly intelligent strikes against the Soviet body politic if American society is totally open to Soviet retaliation, the stability concept is in need of fundamental redefinition. As long as American society is essentially unprotected by BMD, air defense, and civil defense, the United States will have to lose any process of competitive escalation against the Soviet force posture anticipated for the 1980s.

Fourth, even if the arms controllers' argument were correct, that a defensive emphasis would stimulate the Soviet Union into working harder so as to be able to overcome it through offensive force improvement,[68] so what? Generically, the claim that this or that American initiative will catalyse Soviet reactions tends to be accorded far too respectful a hearing. Certainly it is sensible to consider adversary reactions and to take a full systemic look at possibilities, but a country as wealthy (and as responsible for international security) as the United States should not be deterred by the mere prospect of competition from undertaking necessary programs (e.g. an MX ICBM, deployed in a multiple protective structure (MPS) mode, will certainly have some noteworthy impact upon Soviet arms competitive activity, but such recognition does not constitute proof of the folly of deploying MX/MPS).[69] Crude though it may sound, the United States would probably achieve more in the field of arms control if it decided to achieve and sustain a politically useful measure of strategic superiority,[70] than if it continues its endorsement of the elusive quality known as essential equivalence.

Superiority for stability

If it is true, or at least probable, that a central war could be won or lost, then it has to follow that the concept of strategic superiority should be revived in popularity in the West. Superiority has a variety of possible meanings, ranging from the ability to dissuade a putative adversary from offering resistance (i.e. deterring a crisis), through the imposition of severe escalation discipline on opponents, to a context wherein one could prosecute actual armed conflict to a successful conclusion. There is certainly no consensus within the United States defense community today over the issue of whether or not any central war outcome is possible which would warrant description as victory. However, a consensus is emerging to the effect that the Soviet Union appears to believe in the possibility of victory, and that the time is long-overdue for a basic overhaul of our intellectual capital in the nuclear deterrence field.[71] At the very least, most defense analysts would endorse the proposition that it is important for the United States to be able to deny the Soviet Union victory on its own terms.

There is a need for Western strategic thinkers to address and overcome the emerging tension between the (probable) requirements of high-quality deterrence, and the still-authoritative and inhibiting ideas of crisis and arms race instability which have directed the US defense community away from programs that speak to Soviet reality. A false choice has misinformed the structure of our thinking. The historical record of the arms competition since the mid-1960s shows that the choice has not been between, on the one hand, a measure of US restraint which would facilitate Soviet acquisition of an assured destruction capability – an achievement that would promote the prospects of arms control negotiations intended to codify a more stable strategic environment – and, on the other hand, an absence of American restraint which would serve to stimulate Soviet counter-vailing programs and which would be doomed to failure anyway. Instead, the choice has been between a measure of American restraint which facilitated the Soviet drive to achieve a not implausible war-winning capability, and a relative absence of restraint which would greatly complicate the life of Soviet defense planners. Overall, the evidence suggests that the Soviet Union has not been seeking a deterrent, as that concept and capability has been (mis?)under-stood in the West for nearly twenty years. The choice the United States confronts today is whether or not it will tolerate Soviet acquisition, unmatched, of an emerging war-fighting capability which might, with some good judgment and some luck, produce success in crisis diplomacy and in war.

The instability arguments that are leveled against those who urge an American response (functionally) in kind are somewhat fragile. For example, there is good reason to believe that the Soviet Union would be profoundly discouraged by the prospect of having to wage an arms competition against an American oppo-nent no longer severely inhibited by its long-familiar stability theory. In addition, an American war-fighting-oriented strategic posture, if well-designed, should not contribute to crisis instability. The fact that the United States might pose a theoretical first-strike threat to much of the Soviet strategic posture, should not give aid and comfort to the "use them or lose them" argument. A central purpose informing US strategic posture would be its denial of any plausible Soviet theory of victory. Why the Soviet Union would be interested in starting a war that it would stand little, if any, prospect of winning is, to say the least, obscure.

The contemporary debate over strategic doctrine, whatever its eventual effect may be upon US war planning and declaratory policy, has registered a qualitative advance over most of the strategic thinking of the past fifteen years. The debate has focused upon what might be needed to deter *Soviet* leaders, *qua* Soviet leaders, and some (still unduly limited) attempt has been made to consider oper-ational, as opposed to pre-war declaratory, strategy. Theories of pre-war deter-rence, however sophisticated, cannot *guarantee* that the United States will never slip into an acute crisis wherein a president has to initiate strategic nuclear employment or, *de facto*, surrender. In such a situation, a president would need realistic war plans that carried a vision of the war as a whole and embodied a theory of how military action should produce desired political ends. In short, he would be in need of strategy. Fortunately, still orthodox wisdom notwithstanding, there is no necessary tension between a realistic wartime strategy (and the posture to match) and the pre-war deterrence of undesired Soviet behavior.

7 The Revolution in Military Affairs [1998]

Introduction: what is going on?

Way back in 1952, two of the world's leading social anthropologists – A.L. Kroeber and Clyde Kluckholn – discovered more than 300 distinctive definitions of the concept of culture. (I know that because, for my sins, I once intended to be a social anthropologist!) Recent debate on the Revolution in Military Affairs (RMA), especially in the United States, does not show quite as much rich variety in definition as the anthropologists have managed over culture, but the conceptual and practical confusion is almost as great, nonetheless. My task, as I understand it, is to help clarify the confusion.

What is going on is that the American defense community has "discovered" information power, or the power of information. In some ways, this is a triumph for common sense. You may recall that, writing in the fifth century BC, Sun Tzu advised that:

> Thus it is said that one who knows the enemy and knows himself will not be endangered in a hundred engagements. One who does not know the enemy but knows himself will sometimes be victorious, sometimes meet with defeat. One who knows neither the enemy nor himself will invariably be defeated in every engagement.

Obviously, information matters. It was always so. Nonetheless, Karl Marx told us, persuasively for once, that quantity changes quality. The claim is that today, and even more plausibly, tomorrow, armed forces – which is to say the US armed forces – have an information edge that should be decisive over any and every rival. Space-based and airborne gatherers of intelligence will yield a "dominant battlespace knowledge" for exploitation by information-led weapons and warriors.

The debate about the RMA

What we are discussing as a possible RMA can be neither true nor false. There is no acid test for an RMA. The question is whether, on balance, it is useful to approach the changes that we discern and predict as offering us, and perhaps our enemies, some revolutionary challenges. Definitions are necessary to clarify what we talk about, but they cannot be true or false. Any commonsense definition of RMA requires that there should be what amounts to a radical change in, if not a complete transformation of, the terms on which warfare is conducted. But, who is to say which changes qualify for the radical label, or even – to muddy the water further – when warfare becomes something else. We lack agreed definitions of RMA and indeed of war itself. If war is organized violence for political ends, would cyberwar in the "infosphere" of cyberspace truly qualify? Wherein lies the violence, or force, in information warfare (I-war)?

Careful study is always to be preferred over careless study, but the RMA debate has generated more opinions than knowledge. Unsurprisingly, historical scholarship has a way of producing the answers that historians seek. With respect to RMAs in history some scholars find RMAs wherever they look, and the more they look, the more they find. Other scholars, operating with essentially the same database, find that really there are no RMAs; the concept is not useful. They discover that change in military affairs is fairly constant over time, that every apparent great change has a lengthy, and often diverse, provenance, and that, overall, history is not punctuated by great discontinuities. With the same database of twentieth-century strategic history, therefore, you can choose to find one, several, or even many RMAs, or you can elect to be impressed by the seamless web and the flow of history. The choice is yours; it is not dictated by the data.

The American defense debate is driven by a mix of fueling elements of which one needs to be aware. A person totally unfamiliar with defense debate in the United States might make the mistake of equating repetition of concept and volume of debating noise with strategic truth. Just because RMA is the subject of several hundred journal articles and hundreds of conference speeches, it does not follow, necessarily, that the concept is either very useful or of a lasting significance.

Defense debate is fueled by the need of defense thinkers to find new sounding topics to talk about – it is the Watergate investigation principle of "follow the money" – as well as by the triggering effect of real-world "events." The principal event triggering the RMA debate was, of course, the Gulf War of 1991. In the absence of new events in the real world, however, defense debate on a subject goes stale. After all, without the inspiration of evolving, or revolutionary, events, it is difficult to find new and interesting things to say. I have myself participated in several defense debates, for example on ballistic missile defense/Strategic Defense Initiative (SDI), nuclear strategy, nuclear ethics, maritime strategy, and so forth. The tide comes in, and the tide goes out, with the "concept, or strategy, du jour." Sometimes the tide brings in matters that provide lasting nourishment, and sometimes it does not.

Schools of thought

If you "surf" the waves that comprise the current debate about RMA and information warfare, I suggest that you look for no fewer than seven poles in this distinctly multipolar controversy. These seven poles constitute seven schools of thought, each of which is a magnet for particular theorists and institutional interests. My seven poles, schools, or magnets (for a truly mixed metaphor) are not necessarily mutually exclusive.

School one: cyberwar, or strategic information warfare. Without necessarily condemning bombs and bullets to the garbage can of history, there is a growing dedicated band of "cyberwarriors" who predict that we will have to fight for the control of cyberspace: with cyberspace defined as "the global information infrastructure," or, if you prefer, as "the sum of the globe's communication links and computational nodes." Although the conduct of nonviolent political warfare is as old as strategy itself, the idea of waging nonviolent cyberwar against the information infrastructure of an enemy's state and society certainly is novel. It should be needless for me to add that the principal citizens of "Byte City" are going to be G-8 folk like us, and that the bad news aspect to the good news of our cyberpower is that we are the ones who are most cybervulnerable.

School two: information-led warfare: The radical vision. Complementary to the true cyberwarriors, who would wage bloodless electronic combat, are those who favor the eventual comprehensive restructuring of the armed forces to reflect the (allegedly) new centrality of truly high-quality "information." The "bombs and bullets" version of I-war does not ask, "what can better information do for the armed forces that we know and love?" Instead, the question takes the form: "what character of armed forces best fits the mould of a country that can enjoy the benefits of dominant battlespace knowledge?" This can be a difficult leap of the imagination to effect, even a dangerous one, but if the center of your military universe is not the army, navy, or air force of today, but rather is a reliable supply of information about friendly and enemy forces, the question then focuses upon how best to exploit a condition of information dominance.

I must hasten to add that I am merely reporting here, I am not endorsing. Probably I do not need to underline the point that the radical vision of information-led warfare can have traumatic impact upon patterns in defense expenditure. Investment strategy to implement a radical vision of this RMA would emphasize advanced conventional munitions, multispectral active and passive sensors – especially on space systems and on unmanned aerial vehicles – long-range, and preferably low observable, delivery platforms, "Internetted" digital communications, data management and visual display systems, and just-in-time, on-call, logistics. Needless to add, perhaps, the bolder the investment strategy, the greater the risks that are run. Obviously, there could be a large regret factor should the strategic experience of the next few decades demonstrate painfully that the radical vision of the RMA was massively flawed. Every military revolution comes with costs as well as benefits, with new vulnerabilities as well as new sources of leverage. At this juncture I might remind you that yesterday's RMA, generally known as the nuclear revolution, has not gone away. Indeed, it will be strategically logical for the enemies of information-rich, cybercompetent, countries to seek ways in warfare that are asymmetrical to "conventional" information-led combat.

Old-fashioned weapons of mass destruction have a kind of brutal simplicity, and reliability, that is likely to appeal to the cyberchallenged.

School three: information-led warfare: the digital overlay. It is probably the majority position today to endorse the "vision," if that is the correct term, of a future that is much like today only more so. The sunk costs in existing systems and approaches, in the context of recognition of the technical and political uncertainties about future conflict, not to mention plain old conservative habits of mind and some emotional attachments, all can argue for making haste slowly. Military history shows that several RMAs may coexist albeit uneasily, that armed forces are likely to have to wage different kinds of conflicts in the same period, and that large mistakes in the design and equipment of forces can prove exceedingly expensive. Unfortunately perhaps, this approach – which amounts to the position that the truth lies somewhere in the middle – may not be as safe as it appears. It is not that difficult to sound responsible and wise when you adhere to what might be called a measured scepticism, but sometimes the truth lies at one or the other end of the spectrum. For example, in the late 1940s it was not wholly unreasonable to predict that the next great war would resemble the Second World War, only with an atomic overlay that would not, itself, yield decisive results. That vision, though accurate for the late 1940s and despite its apparent reasonableness, had the flaw that it was wrong. If you decline to buy the military power that you might have bought, had you not feared that it was the wrong choice to make, you risk being on the embarrassing end of a true military-technical shortfall if someone else buys that military power and that power "works."

School four: much ado about nothing much. There is a noisy and growing band of apparent, though most typically only apparent, "Luddites," at least extreme sounding sceptics, about this alleged RMA. Such scepticism can have both analytical and emotional origins. Even when the reaction to the proposition of an I-war RMA is fairly obviously rooted in personality, at least in personal experience, the acceptable language of dissent is, of course, analytical in character. Your true position may be to the effect that "this is not war as I knew it, and know it, and I do not like the idea of an airpower that is increasingly unmanned or of a seapower that leans heavily in favour of arsenal ships that are just floating missile platforms." As always there are more and less legitimate forms of, and content to, dissent. The most acceptable face of scepticism about the I-war RMA hypothesis, or hypotheses, simply takes the form of an assertion of the complexity of war and defense planning. The broadly sceptical school of thought says that better information is always nice to have, but it cannot translate into a magical military sword. Why not? Because war, or defense, has many dimensions – human, political, economic, ethical, geographical, military operational, and so forth – and an RMA offers improvement, even dramatic improvement, only on one or two of those dimensions. As Barry Watts has explained in a brilliant reconsideration of Clausewitz' complex concept of friction (in a monograph for the U.S. National Defense University), the enduring human dimension of war, to cite but one such critical dimension, ensures that this RMA will not abolish the fog of war or the fog of crisis.

School five: air is the real revolution. There is a view that holds that the real revolution, that RMA enthusiasts are in peril of missing, lies in the full maturity of airpower. "Douhet was right," in other words. The airpower that this school celebrates tends to be the airpower that has pilots, rather than hypersonic long-range cruise missiles that dispense smart submunitions. You can interpret the performance of airpower in the Gulf War as plain proof that American (at least) airpower has become the leading edge of military power to which other kinds of power increasingly will be subordinate or adjunct. Or, you can interpret the performance of airpower in the Gulf War as evidence of just how expensive and difficult it is to wage an air war for decisive effect.

School six: space is the real revolution. A small but growing body of commentators has begun to assert that the real revolution either lies with, or is enabled critically by, space systems. Most of the information that fuels this alleged RMA is collected by space vehicles or is transmitted via space vehicles. Of course there are alternative ways to deploy sensors, but the highest of high "ground" generally offers unique and dramatically superior performance. If space control is lost, this RMA simply will not work. In the view of this school of thought, space systems either are the real revolution, or at least they comprise the most key among key contributing elements to the RMA. If you lose the war for space, or in space, you lose the war (on land, at sea, and in the air).

School seven: a revolution in security affairs. Finally, a small but influential body of opinion is advancing the view that a revolution in security affairs is well underway and dwarfs in significance whatever may be the merit in an alleged information-led RMA. This revolution in security affairs is about the sources and fundamental character of conflict, not merely about the military instrument that is the subject of RMA speculation. The real revolution, we are told, is in political loyalty and pertains, above all else, to an alleged crisis of the nation state, and especially to a crisis in the ability or inability of the state to deliver security. Supposedly, states are failing, or failing to provide the nonmilitary forms of security that, so the argument proceeds, matter more and more to people, world-wide. The wonderful military capabilities that the I-war RMA might provide will matter little for the problems of, say, economic, environmental, or cultural insecurity.

What is the RMA debate about today? In the United States the relevant big ideas – of RMA, I-war, information-led warfare – now have been aired sufficiently for interested people and organizations to sort out some considered responses. I will highlight three areas of lively current debate:

How important is technology in war? No one is arguing that technology does not matter. But, always provided you are not fighting with the equivalent of spears against machine guns, does modern history suggest that a technological edge is particularly vital in the outcome of wars? Some people are distinguishing between a military technical revolution (MTR) and a true RMA. You may have state-of-the-art weaponry and support equipment, but do you plan to wage war in a state-of-the-art way? Popular TV series are wont to confuse "weapons with which the war was won," with "weapons that won the war."

Investment strategy. How aggressively should we seek to buy this RMA? How much near-term readiness should be sacrificed on the altar of tomorrow's technology?

Vulnerability. Or, is there a hostile ULTRA "Enigma" variation in our future? How might a peer or "niche" competitor buy into this RMA – and is the entry price quite modest? For example, what might a cybercompetent enemy do to harass and delay the workings of "just-in-time" logistics? Or, to risk being unduly crude, what would exposure to electromagnetic pulse (EMP) do to an "RMAed" fighting force in the war of 2020 or so?

On any reasonable criterion of significance, this is an important debate. The stakes are very high indeed. At the highest level of concern, the subject of the RMA is the prevention, conduct, and outcome of wars. In addition, our subject is the cost of defense preparation and the many dimensions of the cost of war itself. An information-led RMA could have profound implications for the scale of casualties in war, if, that is, both sides agree to terms of engagement that produce only military surgery by tactically sharp instruments. Also, this debate is about money, jobs, and the health of many different organizations.

Concluding thoughts

I will conclude with four thoughts.

- Some of the literature on information-led war appears to equate bombardment with war. "Dominant battlespace knowledge" is apt to be deployed for the precise acquisition of targets and the subsequent application of firepower precisely against these targets. Firepower, especially precise firepower, is important. But we must never forget the wise words of Rear Admiral J C Wylie USN: "The ultimate determinant in war is the man on the scene with a gun."

- Strategy and war have many dimensions, of which the technological is only one. Technological improvement, even radical technological improvement into the RMA or MTR zone, does not, however, necessarily guarantee a radical improvement in strategic effectiveness. The military value of a RMA may be limited, even negated, by human limitations of leaders, the unpopularity of a cause, and so forth. Strategy and war are whole phenomena that cannot be transformed by movement on one dimension only. The Wehrmacht was an outstanding fighting machine, but its merits as a fighting machine merely enabled it to do the strategically – and politically and ethically – wrong things very well.

- I-war may be evaded by enemies who resort to crude and old fashioned options, such as nuclear (and other mass destruction) threats and action, and who are able to fight in terrain that is unfriendly for Western soldiers – which is to say in huge sprawling cities. Even if Ralph Peters exaggerates when he says, "the future of warfare lies in the streets, sewers, high-rise buildings, industrial parks and the sprawl of homes, shacks and shelters that form the broken cities of our world," he still makes a noteworthy point.

- Finally, I would note that information itself is simply that, or even less. It may just be data causing the soldier's information indigestion or overload. You will recall that intelligence sank no U-boats; men in ships and aircraft had to do that. A soldier who is a true "information warrior" may be so fascinated by what he is seeing on the display on his laptop, that he fails to notice that his virtual battlespace is about to be violated by a real warrior with a machete who has crept up behind him.

8 Arms control does not control arms [1993]

In 455, the Eastern Roman Emperor Marcian prohibited the export of all weapons, and materials for making weapons, to the barbarians.[1] *Plus ça change* ... The 1968 treaty on the Non-Proliferation of Nuclear Weapons (NPT) and the 1987 Missile Technology Control Regime (MTCR) bear more than a casual resemblance to Marcian's policy enunciated 1,500 years earlier.

But then, as now, a mixture of politics and greed rendered control over the supply of weaponry an expedient of only temporary and partial value, at best. In the same way that the problem with Americans is that they form a distinctly uncivil society rather than a domestically heavily armed one, so the dominant problem for international security is not armaments but rather the motives of communities to acquire and use them. Lethal instruments are not unimportant, but they acquire their significance from politics. The Huns and other barbarians no doubt found the Roman supply blockade of weapons to be an inconvenience. Today, the NPT and the MTCR similarly are inconveniences, but only inconveniences, to would-be acquirers of nuclear weapons and missiles.

But if politics subverts arms control, so does it facilitate arms control. Speaking in the House of Commons on July 13, 1934, Winston Churchill claimed that "it is the greatest possible mistake to mix up disarmament with peace. When you have peace you will have disarmament."[2] If Ronald Lehman, Director of the US Arms Control and Disarmament Agency, was correct when he lent encouragement to the speculation that 1985–95 may prove to be a "golden decade" for arms control,[3] it will be because of Churchill's dictum, that is, because 1985–95 proves to be a golden decade for peace.

Unfortunately, this ironical proposition – that when peace breaks out arms control is sure to follow – has yet to achieve the popular respect it deserves. Consequently, the arms control community is not responding to the outbreak of East–West peace in relevant ways. Generals and admirals often are accused of responding to the onset of peace with an unseemly scamper to find new missions for their favored forces. The arms control community in these post-Cold War 1990s is guilty of a like scamper. The problem has changed; all that remains constant are the purported solutions.

But how good are arms control solutions?

Paradoxes

The control of arms is often confused with the much narrower idea of arms control. Arms control, as the term is commonly used, refers to a distinct body of ideas and approaches to the military dimension to international security. According to this body of ideas, arms control can be bilateral or multilateral; it can be formal or tacit; it can be structural or operational. Recent fashion in arms control theory holds that it can even be competitive or cooperative. And naturally there exist competing notions as to what is most effective in advancing arms control: building arms to parley or self-restraint in arms to parley.

But it is important to put aside these variants and come to grips with the core idea of arms control – and to suggest what is wrong with it. Too often, the debate over arms control has been mired in technical detail (or loaded with extraneous political baggage), and the enterprise itself has escaped close scrutiny as a result.

The heart of the arguments for and against the integrity of arms control theory and the attempted practice of arms control can be summarized via the stark opposition of two paradoxes.

On the one hand, the argument for arms control says that it is a process of limited cooperation between potential enemies. The parties involved are motivated to cooperate, despite their enmity, lest their similar interests (e.g., in survival) be overcome by the dynamics of an unbridled antagonism. Rephrased, the first paradox holds that enemies have some interests in common and need to cooperate because of the awesomely terrible damage to those interests that they fear might flow from their enmity.

On the other hand, to state the rival paradox, the argument against arms control holds that the political hostility which renders it relevant to a strategic relationship also, and to approximately the same degree, renders arms control unachievable. Rephrased, the second paradox claims that pairs or groups of states that appear to need the benefits of arms control are denied those benefits, precisely for the reasons that they need them.

Supporting the first paradox, characteristically, are two fundamental propositions, in no matter how modified a form: that weapons bring about war and that, therefore, the control of weapons makes for peace. The less significance weapons and competition in weapons are believed to have as causes effecting, irritants promoting, or triggers precipitating war, the less important arms control must be to antagonists seeking peace. These two fundamental propositions are the center of gravity for arms control theory and also its central fallacy. Arms control theory postulates a cause-and-effect nexus between armaments and conflicts that does not stand up well under either historical inquiry or theoretical challenge.

- *The political ownership of weapons and the political incentives to use them are vastly more important than is their technical character.*

Indeed, it is remarkable that so much public and private thought and behavior on arms control should rest upon so shaky a conceptual foundation. It ought to be a less than blinding insight to notice that the political ownership of weapons and the political incentives to use them are vastly more important than is their technical character. Yet this truth is hardly ever noticed. Thus, the remainder of this essay is devoted to suggesting that arms control ideas and policy – as contrasted with ideas and policies for the control of arms – express a fallacious theory of peace.

Specifically, the remainder of this essay will attempt to demonstrate the validity of five closely connected propositions. These are

States do not threaten war, or go to war, because they are armed. Rather, states arm, and counterarm competitively, because they anticipate the possibility of war.

If weapons or military behavior are not the problem, the control of weapons or military behavior cannot be the solution.

Because weapons are only instruments of political forces and desires, arms control can never withstand the traffic of heavy political antagonism and must always fail to meet reasonable expectations for utility.

It is a mistake to believe that truly useful measures of arms control are negotiable. The net benefit of arms control for international peace with security is always liable to be trivial or even negative.

Arms control is an instance of the wider fallacy that there are technical and administrative solutions to political problems.

The desirability of controlling arms and the elegant neatness of some of the theory surrounding arms control has no bearing whatsoever upon its feasibility. The theoretical flaws in the theory of arms control must prove fatal for arms control activity of all kinds.

History

Disarmament and arms control are ideas with a long, if undistinguished, genealogy. For example, fourteen years before the Emperor Marcian felt strong enough to proclaim the weapons blockade against the barbarians, his predecessor, Theodosius II, agreed with the Persians (in AD 441/442) that neither empire would further fortify border installations in the Euphrates highlands of eastern Anatolia. For a better known case of medieval arms control: the Second Lateran Council in 1139 anathematized the use of the bow, and particularly the crossbow, in wars between Christians.[4] Nearly fifty years earlier, Pope Urban II had spoken vehemently against the use of those weapons in terms familiar to those who today argue that taboos against particular weapons can help deter their acquisition or employment. (Anathematization, or taboo promotion, finds a modern advocate in Lewis A Dunn.[5]) However, none of these historical cases had a noteworthy effect in stopping wars.

Perhaps the clearest empirical demonstration of the error in arms control is provided by the four-plus decades of historical experience in the 1920s and 1930s and the 1970s and 1980s. Both of those protracted episodes in arms control illustrate the same basic points: states which share a common expectation that major war among them is all but unthinkable find it possible to sign-on for quite drastic regimes of arms limitation. But, conversely, arms control regimes worthy of the name cannot function when they are needed, and they fail for the same reasons that they are needed.

The practice of arms control in this century grew directly out of what many people believed the experience of the Great War of 1914–18 had to teach. Those who should have known better confused the obvious association of war and armaments with the not-at-all-obvious causation of war by armaments. In the immediate aftermath of the First World War, sophisticated and liberal opinion sought and found the roots of the recent tragedy in conveniently general social processes (e.g., the arms race, or militarism) rather than in specific human error. Consequently, though the protracted bids for arms control and disarmament in the postwar era were motivated in important part by considerations of political economy, they were also driven by the popular conviction that disarmament would "cause" peace.

Success. An arms control process, even a disarmament process, "worked" in a promising way in the 1920s (by and large), and, with gathering momentum, after 1986–87. In the 1920s, when deep political peace was not merely a fact and an expectation, but was even legislated to be so (by the Kellogg–Briand Pact of 1928), the ever-more comprehensive taming of competitive armaments appeared to be eminently achievable. Likewise, today, when a true political peace characterizes Russian–American relations, virtually any and every measure of arms control and disarmament seems possible between them, subject only to prudential considerations bearing upon the capabilities of third parties. Indeed, since there is no longer a political relationship of antagonism between Russia and the United States, and since it is not obvious that they even have a strategic relationship describable as such, it is a little puzzling to understand how an arms control process between them makes sense. There is no shortage of candidate solutions to that puzzle,[6] but none of them stands up well under close scrutiny.

Failure. Many and important differences exist, of course, between the security contexts of the inter-war and the Cold War eras. Nonetheless, in their basic structures, the arms control experiences of the two periods – especially the great power and superpower arms-limitation experiences – yield an all-but-common pattern. Neither produced an arms control process that could accomplish useful objectives.

In the 1930s, an era radically less arms control friendly than the 1920s, both the World Disarmament Conference (1932–34) of the League of Nations and the Washington–London system of regulating naval arms collapsed in the face of sharply deteriorating political conditions in Europe and Asia.[7] The naval arms limitation regime of the inter-war years – embracing the Washington treaty of 1922, the London treaties of 1930 and 1936, and even the Anglo-German naval agreement of 1935 – was irrelevant to Europe's slide into war in Europe and paradoxically made a minor contribution to Japanese paranoia and antagonism in East Asia.

As a general rule, arms control agreements in the Cold War era licensed competitive behavior much as usual. In the 1970s and through most of the 1980s, Soviet–American arms control negotiations achieved next to nothing of significance for the proclaimed goals of crisis- and arms-race stability. In particular, the idea that an effective prohibition upon the development and deployment of strategic missile defenses would break a purportedly upward-spiralling arms-race action and reaction of offense and defense was shown not to be true: The Anti-Ballistic Missile (ABM) Treaty of 1972 had no discernible effect upon the competition in strategic offensive arms. Even as late as 1987, the Intermediate-Ranged Nuclear Forces (INF) Treaty was defended in part by the argument that it would not really damage the nuclear pillar to NATO's strategy and security.

In sum, one generation of would-be arms controllers (in the 1920s and early 1930s) sought to identify and constrain "aggressive" or "offensive" weaponry, whereas a later generation (in the late 1960s, 1970s, and 1980s) targeted "destabilizing" weaponry. Both generations were supported by the vague but right-sounding proposition that some kinds of arms, particularly arms purchased for the energetic prosecution of military competition (arms races), somehow cause wars to occur.

In fact, however, there are and can be no aggressive, offensive, or destabilizing weapons. Weapons do not make war; national leaders do. And there certainly have been aggressive, offensively minded weapons-owners, bent upon changing international political conditions in their favor.

As a result, arms control has repeatedly benefited or suffered depending upon whether political relations were improving or deteriorating. But as a result too the substantial hopes for arms control could not be fulfilled when they were most relevant – in the 1930s and the 1970s/early 1980s. Arms control itself was not able to shape, or help shape, dynamic political relations in significant and positive ways.

- *The positive glow that attaches viscerally to arms control serves effectively to deter almost all root-and-branch inquiry.*

Yet it would have been subversive of politically correct thinking in any of those decades to suggest that the problems of peace with security had infinitely more to do with Japanese capital ships, German submarines and panzer divisions, and Soviet MIRVed ICBMs, than with capital ships, submarines, panzer divisions, or MIRVed ICBMs *per se*.

The current scene

Much the same is true today. To observe the new international-security debate regarding the post-Cold War world is to find many of the same people and institutions who have praised arms control for decades and to see them shifting direction but not changing their mode of transport. A visitor from another planet might be excused for concluding that these arms control cognoscenti, fresh from triumph in the Cold War, were now turning their ideas and methods to a new agenda. The latter, alas, is true; but not the former. The plain fact is that arms control, however defined, does not have a historical record of glittering accomplishment. Indeed, an unvarnished history of arms control would tend to promote the conclusion that, having so faint a past connection to international security, it is unlikely to have a substantial one in the future.[8]

Arms control glitters attractively only when its ideas are viewed in isolation as ideas. Adhering generally to pleasing concepts, spokesmen for arms control have not had to suffer a rigorous audit or to contend with fundamental theoretical challenges. The positive glow that attaches viscerally to arms control serves effectively to deter almost all root-and-branch inquiry. One can criticize this or that negotiating position or approach to negotiations, but it is not politically correct, on the Right as well as the Left, to argue that the emperor of arms control has no clothes. Familiarity breeds acceptance. After all, how could so many politicians and commentators be wrong?

Nevertheless, it is the contention here that the case against arms control's contributing a net security benefit is not even a close one. On the contrary, it is the critique provided here of orthodox, if evolving, arms control theory that fits the readily ascertainable historical facts, while the orthodox theory itself does not.

Theory

As noted at the outset, arms control in recent decades has been viewed as a process of limited cooperation among putative enemies and actual antagonists: a process that carries the promise of reducing the risks of war, reducing the damage that might otherwise be suffered in war, and reducing the burden of peacetime defense preparation.

The intellectual history of arms control since the Second World War has seen four phases of fashionable opinion, though there has, of course, been substantial overlap and parallelism among them. Phase I, which can be identified approximately with 1946–56, typically was the era of grand schemes for nuclear or, more grandly still, for general and complete disarmament.[9] Phase II, which was the main event, extended from 1956–57 until 1983–84 and had as its center of intellectual gravity the limitation of allegedly destabilizing arms.[10] From 1983–84 until 1989–90, a noticeable Phase III emphasized operating practices and the security of command arrangements for arms, rather than the structure or size of arsenals.[11] Finally, the front-window of arms control in the post-Cold War era (post-1990) has been dressed with a Phase IV fashion for arms control as a pillar strengthening, indeed helping to create, would-be political communities in an essentially cooperative environment.[12]

These four phases identify only the cutting edge of fashionable opinion in the various periods. The full spectrum of views and approaches can be found in all eras, if one looks hard enough. But the frontier ideas in all phases suffer from the same fatal malady: a misunderstanding of the basic relationship between weapons and political conflict, which leads to the ingenious provision of more or less elegant answers to the wrong questions.

The arms control theory expressed as Phases II and III from the late 1950s to the late 1980s (bearing upon arms limitation as well as operational arrangements and procedures for forces) was very much the product of defense analysis. Indeed, the thesis that allegedly vulnerable strategic nuclear forces would be crisis-unstable and, through a "reciprocal fear of surprise attack,"[13] could trigger the very war they were designed to deter was the intellectual keystone of modern arms control. Much as an allegedly ever-escalating arms race is supposed to drive policy for war (rather than functioning as a surrogate for war), so tactically vulnerable strategic forces are deemed to be potent fuel for war because they are cursed with a high first-strike incentive. States would strike first for fear that they would be unable to strike second.

This theory of crisis instability and the vulnerability analyses on which it was based were singularly uncommunicative on two central matters. First, the defense-analytical reductionists never explained why a state would strike first in order to achieve, at best, a massively Pyrrhic victory, rather than waiting and hoping that the Pyrrhic example would impress the putative enemy also. Second, the vulnerability analyses reduced war to a military-technical exercise virtually bereft of political meaning.[14] If the incentives and disincentives to fight are pre-ponderantly political, albeit modified by a careful net assessment of military prospects, how much integrity can there be in a theory of crisis stability that focuses exclusively upon the characteristics of the rival armed forces? More-over, how much merit is there likely to be in an arms control theory that bor-rows and seeks to apply a wholly military-technical vision of stability in time of crisis?

The slide into war

The postulate of war-prone rival military postures overshadows all arms control enterprises, even though it is devoid of empirical support. In no important sense have the armed forces of rival polities or coalitions "detonated into war" because of their military-technical characteristics. Even July/early August 1914 is not an example of runaway armed forces dictating high policy. That was a crisis of several weeks' duration that concluded with the players allowing war to occur for political reasons which seemed good, persuasive, and popular at the time.

"Never say never" is good advice; so there is something to be said for the design and operation of armed forces with a mind to their not being accident-prone or inviting to putative surprise-attackers. However, there is nothing in modern history or persuasive strategic logic to suggest that the central concern of modern arms control is a very real one in practice.

What is of very real concern in practice is that arms control regimes can have negative consequences if a slide into war takes place. Medieval examples as well as recent ones show that arms control agreements occasionally have had an unfortunate effect upon the terms of engagement, and particularly the initial terms of engagement, of wars they were powerless to avert.

For example, the naval arms regime of the inter-war years had potentially fatal consequences for Britain and her allies once war broke out. Writing in 1941, Bernard Brodie noted pointedly and with only slight exaggeration that "Great Britain and the United States, between whom no antagonism worth mentioning existed, proceeded to disarm each other in an unsettled world, relying completely, as Admiral Beamish put it, 'upon faith, hope, and parity, with parity said to be the most important of all.' "[15]

The legacy of naval arms control for 1939–42 was a British Royal Navy with ships insufficient in number (and in some cases ill-designed) to support a maritime strategy for global war.[16] As the result of a fifteen-year "building holiday" (1922–36), the Washington–London system bequeathed Britain only fifteen capital ships. Combat loss, plus routine and nonroutine maintenance, meant that there were occasions in 1939–41 when the real number of British battleships and battle cruisers was as low as nine. Those nine ships had to escort or cover Atlantic convoys against the serious menace of German surface raiders, perform like duties *vis-à-vis* the Italian fleet in the Mediterranean, and help deter Japanese aggression in East Asia. And the potentially negative consequences for maritime Britain of the restrictions of the 1930 London treaty upon trade-defense ships (cruisers and destroyers) were, if anything, even more serious than the capital-ship restrictions negotiated in 1921.

Stability

Although the notion of an automatic slide into war has no support in history, the key or master concept for arms control has been "stability" – presumably to prevent such a slide. People of all political and doctrinal persuasions agree that an arms control process should, via its ability to help stabilize a strategic relationship, contribute to peace with security. But the meaning of stability that has inspired Western arms control theorists and would-be practitioners has been overwhelmingly technical.

Unfortunately, that technical approach has not rested upon an adequate understanding of the causes of wars. Because the problems of security are preponderantly political, they cannot be evaded by legal, ethical, administrative-managerial, or technical-military approaches. Those approaches, severally or ensemble, can express prior political wishes, but they cannot reshape political reality independently. There is no autonomous arms control process that can transform the lead of conflict into the gold of international cooperation.

Specifically, the notion that through an arms control process states can help fire-proof a strategic relationship is almost certainly wrong. Arms do need to be controlled, but they cannot be usefully controlled by the activities now typically identified as arms control. The reason, simply, is that the use of arms is not an autonomous military decision.

- *Some arms control regimes have the ecumenical effect of disarming both the rogue polity of the day and the needed guardians of the security order.*

If the arms control search for stability has not rested upon an adequate understanding of war, neither has it been noticeably refined or revisited in the face of evidence that America's adversary-partners understand it differently. Alexei Arbatov, a member of the Soviet Strategic Arms Reduction Treaty (START) delegation in 1990, has noted that "only at the final stage of talks did the Americans and Soviets arrive at a common definition of strategic stability, albeit a general and vague one."[17] In other words, superpower negotiations on strategic arms limitation – SALT and START – proceeded for more than twenty years before rough, and only rough, agreement was possible on the meaning of the enterprise's key goal.

Finally, the arms control concept of stability has not been crafted on the basis of careful historical analyses of so-called arms-race phenomena.

Arms control regimes are often based on the fantasy that they can lock-in benign military conditions. In fact, states decline to be locked into regimes of arms control, or regime-compliant behavior, when it no longer serves their needs and is unenforceable by others. After all, Weimar and Nazi Germany were allegedly "locked-in" to a 100,000 man army by the treaty of Versailles. And the NPT supposedly locked Iraq into nonnuclear status. It is a familiar story. Arms control works when polities are not strongly motivated to break out of its confining embrace.

Some arms control regimes have the ecumenical effect of disarming both the rogue polity of the day and the needed guardians of the security order. For example, in the Five Power Treaty of 1922, the ratios in the standard displacement of capital ships (5:5:3:1.75:1.75 for the United States, Britain, Japan, France, and Italy respectively) had the strategic result of destabilizing the balance of power in the Western Pacific. Stability in the numerical relationships translated into an American inability to discipline Japanese ambitions on the mainland of Asia and particularly in China. More recently, the parity principle approximated in the SALT I package of 1972 had undesirable implications for the protection that the central strategic forces of a distant United States could yield via extended deterrence. Thus, a somewhat mindlessly "stable" military relationship can be distinctly harmful to the protection of the political interests that really provide the fuel for conflict.

Today, "lock-in" is one of the prime rationales for the treaty on Conventional Forces in Europe (CFE). But anyone who believes the current official US policy line – that INF, CFE, and START lock-in political gains for peace by exploiting what may prove to be but a fleeting window of opportunity – ignores both history and common sense. One cannot today predict confidently how military balances may need to be structured for the future security of Europe.

Lessons

The political feasibility of arms control in the post-Soviet, post-Cold War world is testament to its relative impotence, not to its vitality. Where was arms control accomplishment when it was needed? Arms control can only till fields already cleared by hard political labor. It can rush to the aid of political victors who will permit it to bandwagon with them, but who strictly do not need it. The fault is not with this or that arms control policy or policymaker: the fault lies in the erroneous premise underlying the entire field of arms control thought and activity, that weapons make war.

Mention has been made of the historical continuities in arms control experience, and US policy for the control of arms may be more realistic in the future if it rests upon an understanding of how persistent have been the flaws in previous efforts. Policymakers and the general public should examine the future in the light of the past. After all, theory and policy towards strategic arms control can appeal for insight to two major and long-lasting historical precedents. Those precedents are the inter-war experience with naval arms limitation, a process concluded by pre-war crises, and the SALT–START era of 1969–89, a process concluded in its original strategic meaning by political peace. These two lengthy episodes of arms control-in-action tell much the same story. Specifically, the inter-war experience with naval arms limitation and the effort in the Cold War to practice arms limitation for strategic nuclear weapons yield the following lessons:

Arms control is negotiable only in an unusually permissive political climate and collapses, or slips into remission, when the political climate becomes more antagonistic. Lesson: arms control is feasible only when it is not needed.

Arms control cannot achieve its widely advertised and over-advertised objectives (such as, making the world safe), nor can it even assist significantly in their achievement. Indeed, an arms control regime is as likely to fuel political antagonism as to prevent or alleviate it. Lesson: arms control attempts the impossible and therefore fails, though not always in ways that are innocuous.

When arms control proves negotiable, it is negotiated to the near exclusion of strategic rationales, so as to serve broad political agendas and political appearances. Parity, and other such nonstrategic concepts, create arms-limitation regimes that are more likely to exacerbate serious military challenges to peace with security than to lessen those challenges. Lesson: regardless of the foreign policies that it should serve, arms control is prone to reflect the immediate political needs of negotiators and to have a political logic of its own.

With reference to likely strategic need, arms control constraints tend to misshape both military posture overall and the design of particular classes of weapons. Thus, "treaty cruisers," and "treaty ICBMs and SLBMs" may be explicable in terms of arms control but will not necessarily make tactical, operational, strategic, or foreign-policy sense. Lesson: arms control is likely to have more effect upon the military instrument – in both its treaty-accountable and treaty-evasive aspects – than it is upon the political demand for the deterrent or war-fighting utility of that instrument.

When arms control agreements are pending, the legislators in democracies are reluctant to fund weapons that may have to be abandoned. Lesson: democratic polities have such enduring problems arming and parleying simultaneously, that authoritarian adversary-partners enjoy a systemic advantage when an arms control process is a factor in security relations.

Authoritarian countries cheat on arms control agreements. Germany, Italy, and Japan cheated between the wars, while the USSR cheated extensively and systematically in the 1970s and 1980s. Neither between the wars nor more recently have democracies been able to design and implement timely and effective compliance or safeguards policies. Lesson: arms control regimes are likely to be unexpected in some of their consequences because, *inter alia*, their formally equal terms will be unequally observed.

Severe legal regulation of some classes of weapons motivates the parties to focus attention upon unregulated, or less regulated, weapons. Lesson: arms control regulation influences navigation of the course, but not the fact, of politically driven military competition.

These tentative lessons are not necessarily true for all cases, but they fit almost equally well the sixteen or so years of negotiated arms limitation experience in the 1920s and 1930s, and the SALT–START years. That is an impressive fit of explanation with a diverse body of evidence.

Conclusions

The intellectual shallowness of the arms control experience is thus truly astonishing. Arms and the competitive acquisition of arms are considered to be important causes of war simply by virtue of their technical and military-operational character. Specifically, the belief has been that arms are a challenge to crisis stability, while competitive arms acquisition is a problem of arm-race stability. Arms control has thus been an effort to sidestep apparently intractable political difficulties and to work instead upon the lethal instruments of state policy, which are thought to be both a trigger for hostilities and a more or less long-term aggravating factor in political relations.

At best, these ideas must be judged with the "Scotch verdict" of "not proven." More likely, however, the twin ideas of crisis- and arms-race stability that drive arms control theory and rationalize arms control practice are simply not true. This is not a fine scholastic point. To put it bluntly: the arms control theory which, in different manifestations, has achieved all but universal acceptance, and which has legitimized and ultimately helped direct countless man-hours of effort, is false and cannot be useful in the ways advertised. Perhaps this arms control tool-kit that "works" only in the most friendly of international conditions may be judged a grand-strategic instrument of ceremonial if not substantive importance.

But the record of arms control in the twentieth century has been as extensive as it has been barren of achievement for the overriding goal of peace with security. The problem has not been hostility among states, because it is the very antagonism among polities that yields to an arms control process its fundamental purposes – to reduce the risks and destructiveness of war. Louis J. Halle penetrated to the heart of the matter when he wrote: "We must suppose that there has been something fundamentally wrong at the conceptual level to account for so consistent a failure on so large a scale over so long a period."[18]

This essay identifies and discusses what is so fundamentally wrong with arms control. Whether the case at issue is two superpowers competitively negotiating arms limitation, or a would-be community of states more or less cooperatively seeking to mold their military environment, the same basic fallacy is at work. Policy, which is to say politics, drives armaments, their acquisition and use, far more than it is driven by them. Discovery of ever-more-elegant alleged uses for an arms control process cannot succeed in negating or otherwise evading the point that arms control puts carts before horses.

- *Military-technical understandings of what is stable or unstable are simply wrong, as the historical record amply demonstrates.*

Seven general arguments organize and highlight the historical and philosophical case against arms control.

First, the facts of political antagonism that stimulate interest in arms control are the very facts that condemn the enterprise to futility. The collapse of arms control arrangements in the second half of the 1930s, as Europe and Asia slid towards war, and the apparent triumph of arms control now that the Cold War is over have to be registered as powerfully suggestive illustrations of this argument.

Second, whether or not states can agree on arms control regimes, the connections between competitive armaments and political conflict is precisely the opposite of that postulated by arms control theory. States, governments, societies, and communities make war or anticipate the possibility of war, and as a consequence they arm themselves.

Third, the theory and practice of arms control both reflects and encourages the erroneous notion that skilled technicians can effect what would amount to safety engineering for national and international security. The better texts on arms control acknowledge in passing the deeply political nature of the subject, but typically they then proceed to recommend the military, technical, administrative-managerial, and legal "fixes" suitable for problems of military, technical, administrative-managerial, and legal kinds.[19] If the problems of security that cause states to arm were technical, administrative, or legal, then the problem-solvers of arms control would have important contributions to make. Unfortunately, international security politics cannot be reduced to international engineering, administration, or law.

Fourth, the transnational community of arms control scholars has discovered and sought to apply an almost wholly valueless master concept in the slippery notion of stability. Military-technical understandings of what is stable or unstable – in the forms of crisis stability or arms-race stability – are simply wrong, as the historical record amply demonstrates. There has been no notable correlation between great crisis instability (in military terms) and the outbreak of war, or between so-called arms-race instabilities and the onset of fighting. Again, it transpires that what is wrong with a technically oriented approach to the control of arms by means of arms control is that the superordinate political dimension to the subject is unduly discounted or even ignored altogether. An unstable military balance is not a menace to peace. Instead, actual or impending major military advantage on the side of a revisionist power is a threat to peace. "Unstable" military balances in favor of such non-revisionist powers as the United States or Israel are a guarantee of peace. To repeat an elementary claim advanced earlier, it is the political identity of the owners of arms that matters, not the military-technical condition of military balances.

Fifth, the health of arms control regimes will wax and wane with the political climate, but those regimes do have the ability to impair flexibility in military preparation. If that limitation on flexibility finds compensation in a positive contribution made by arms control to peaceable relations, or even if the impaired flexibility is tolerably matched by constraints among all regime participants, this charge will carry little weight. But it so happens that democracies have neglected to negotiate arms control arrangements that supported their foreign-protection duties during the declining years of arms control regimes, have failed to craft treaties that allow for suitable flexibility in the face of unexpected developments, and in practice have elected to condone extensive and sustained non-compliance by politically unsatisfied treaty-partners.

Sixth, although it has been a rare event for an arms control regime to wreak massive harm, the opportunity costs of the arms control approach to the control of arms has been anything but trivial. As a variant of Gresham's Law, unsound but popular ideas deny time and effort to more worthy ideas. Indeed, so persistent has been the pattern of failure, that the burden of proof has to be laid upon those who would go forth to do battle with the dragons of war and insecurity, armed preeminently with what logic and the balance of evidence suggests are the cardboard weapons of arms control. No matter what the era, what the issues, who the state participants, or which the precise approaches selected, there is no escaping the central fallacy that condemns arms control to failure, namely, weapons are only a politically subordinate component part of the whole problem of security. Political communities with deeply antagonistic interests are prone to fight, whether or not they are well or even adequately armed.

There are many ways in which arms can be controlled. The approach known as arms control, which focuses upon the negotiation of measures of limited cooperation among potential foes, is among the least productive. Instead, the control of arms is achievable by policies designed both to balance the power of possible rogue states and to diminish the political incentives for conflict. The essential triviality, at best, of arms control as commonly understood can be readily appreciated when the question is posed: "How in fact have (German, Japanese, Soviet, Iraqi, and so forth) arms actually been controlled?"

Finally, the arms control process has proved in practice to be a gratuitous hindrance to the efforts by democracies to make sensible defense provision for national and international security. Every decade in this century has shown how difficult it is for a democracy to function competently at the level of strategy. The proper political management of the military instrument to support tolerable balances of power is a first-order task that democracies have cultural difficulties effecting steadily and well. Arms control encourages much that needs to be discouraged in democracies and particularly in the United States. Notwithstanding the paying of a token obeisance to the primacy of policy, the theorists and would-be practitioners of arms control have sought a technical peace. The arms control community has promulgated the fallacy that with the engineering know-how of stability theory, military confrontations can be significantly fire-proofed against accidental or inadvertent explosion. Very often, though certainly far from invariably, arms can be controlled. They cannot be controlled, however, by the application of reductionist apolitical notions of stability.

Arms control as advocated and practiced by the United States for decade after decade in this century has been a notable failure. Nonetheless, in the latter half of the century, the arms that mattered most to Americans, which is to say Soviet arms, were controlled very effectively. The true relationship between arms and politics revealed by the conclusion of the Cold War (arms control followed peace, not vice versa) should stimulate a wholesale reappraisal of how arms can best be controlled.

Part III

Geography, culture, and ethics

9 Geography and grand strategy [1991]

As a limitation upon the power of states, nothing has proven to be more pervasive and enduring than geography. Indeed, when explaining the direct and indirect influence of geography upon statecraft and strategy, the terms of geographical reference can become so all embracing that there is danger of a deterministic element creeping in to ambush the unwary.[1] With particular, but not exclusive, references to limitations upon the power of states, this article explores several major aspects of the influence of geography upon choice of, and performance in, grand strategy.

Physical and political geography provide opportunities, challenges, and dangers, and help condition the frame of reference for official and public debate over national choices in policy and grand strategy. The Anglo-American colonists, who founded what was to become the great continentwide United States of America, defined the hostile physical and political geography of North America as a set of challenges to be overcome. National destiny has a way of looking manifest only either in retrospect, or in the mouth of a propagandist for expansion at someone else's expense. In the first half of the eighteenth century the Anglo-Americans shared North America with the rather military empire of New France in Canada (and through the Mississippi River System), with the northernmost ramifications of New Spain, and with some militarily still powerful and diplomatically adept Indian confederacies.[2] Geography, broadly understood, has shaped US policy, strategy, and culture, but it certainly did not in any reliable fashion dictate the outcomes of the great wars by which empire first was won in 1763, and then was lost 20 years later.[3]

Other things being equal, which is not always the case (e.g. the menacing approach of a mass immigration or invasion by Hunnic tribes), the generally well-established territorial basis of a security community carries major implications for policy choice and strategy. One can always find exceptions, but it is a tolerably accurate rule in statecraft that neighbors tend to be enemies while neighbors-but-one tend to be allies. Proximity breeds issues for dispute, provides territory contiguous to both parties, which facilitates combat, and triggers incentives to sign up allies which are able to distract the neighbor elsewhere. For example, from late medieval times to the present, Britain has been allied with Burgundy against France, with Austria or Prussia (or both) against France, with France and

Russia against Germany, and now, functionally at least, with China against Russia. From the 1590s to the 1940s, England's continental foes sought to outflank her via landings in Ireland or Scotland. The second half of the nineteenth century brought recognition in London that the eventual emergence of the United States as a great naval power would outflank Britain's global geostrategic position comprehensively.[4] That position long rested upon the fact that any rival naval power would have to evade, or fight its way through, a geostrategically very advantageously home-based Royal Navy in order to reach blue water.

History is replete with examples of polities maintaining both powerful armies and powerful navies. However, in the overwhelming majority of historical cases there was a little real doubt, at least for long, over which environment, the land or the sea, required first call upon a country's security potential. The geographical circumstances of individual states and of their enemies have not determined the details of grand strategy, but they have shaped the policy and strategic problems in need of solution.

To cite the British case again: Britain's insular situation (once the Irish and Scottish backdoors were closed) did not in some literal sense mandate that Britain maintain a superior naval fighting instrument. But, that insular situation did require that Britain: (1) either so involve herself in continental campaigning that continental enemies would lack the disposable assets to fashion superior maritime strength, (2) or bribe and otherwise support continental allies to fight on land so that, again, enemies would not be at liberty to menace British interests on or from the sea, (3) or find sea power allies willing and able to protect the British Isles from invasion and British maritime commerce from harassment, (4) or herself provide a superior fighting fleet, with that superiority greatly assisted by the continental distraction of actual or potential enemies.

The purpose of the previous paragraph is to remind readers that a country potentially fatally vulnerable at or from the sea has a range of grand-strategic alternatives. Typically, Britain has pursued simultaneously 3 of the 4 options just cited: she committed her own military strength on a modest scale to the continent;[5] she provided tangible incentives to continental allies to adhere to an anti-(continental) hegemonic coalition;[6] and she maintained a fighting fleet that no continental foe could face in battle with a reasonable prospect of tactical success.[7] With some adjustments for changing circumstances, Britain's grand strategy for the 1990's is entirely recognizable from the outline just provided.

Britain's insular geographical setting mandated that, by one grand-strategic means or another (and generally by a mix of instruments), maritime security had to have first call upon those resources of society that could be mobilized for defense functions. However, the physical and political geography, which yielded Britain major competitive advantages *vis-à-vis* the sea power of European continental states, were not without its significant limitations. Victory at sea is a precondition for victory in war between maritime and continental states or coalitions, but it is not synonymous with it.[8] The challenge to the leaders of a state plainly superior in naval strength is to find ways to translate that superiority into strategic effectiveness over the ability or the willingness of the enemy to continue the war. It is commonplace to note that the Battle of Trafalgar was won by the Royal Navy in 1805, but that Napoleon did not fall, finally, until 1815.[9]

Airplanes, and cruise and ballistic missiles have extended the tactical reach of sea-based power over the land and of land-based power over the sea, but the broad limitations that pertain to geographically specialized fighting forces are distinctly familiar as among, say, the 1800s, 1940s, and the 1990s. Notwithstanding the addition of nuclear menace and of combat in and from the air and space environments, Soviet–American strategic relations have carried the potential for a land power–sea power standoff that would be immediately recognizable to Pitt the Younger. The ancient truth that sea powers could only be defeated at sea and land powers could only be defeated on land plainly is in need of nuclear amendment. However, the very mutuality of the probability of holocaust tends to depress the strategic significance of the nuclear revolution.

To summarize, courtesy overwhelmingly of their particular geographical settings, states tend to be maritime or continental in their security orientation.[10] It follows that states tend to be uneven in the relative excellence of their land as contrasted with their naval forces. The statecraft and strategy of maritime and of continental states has been and remains very much oriented towards exploiting the strengths of superior land or sea power so as to overcome the limitations of the national or coalition instrument of excellence.

Geography and strategic culture

Strategic studies is an interdisciplinary field of enquiry. Borrowing carefully from the discipline of social anthropology, an increasing number of students of strategy – of different primary disciplinary affiliations – have become persuaded that the complex idea of culture has a great deal of explanatory value for their developing field.[11] Specifically, the proposition that a national security community has a reasonably distinctive strategic culture has found growing favor. Geography does not determine national strategic culture in some simple and mechanistic fashion, but the geographical circumstances of all kinds of a community cannot help but play a large role in the course of that community's historical experience. Strategic culture may be understood to be a set of socially transmitted attitudes, beliefs, and preferred procedures that members of a society learn, practice, and teach to new members.

It is close to self-evident both that geographical factors (location, size and character of national territory, character of neighbors, and so forth) must permeate defense thinking. Although some of those geographical factors are subject to change and to a changing significance as technology and trade flows (*inter alia*) alter, one is not talking here about policy choices or fairly casual opinions that shift with fashion or the appearance of new information. For example, it is reasonable to observe that the very long-standing Soviet proclivity, to be less than careful in abiding by supposedly solemn international agreements, reflects cultural predisposition rather more than conscious, and very often repeated, decisions to cheat.[12] To avoid even the appearance of prejudice here, one could balance that Soviet example with the historical evidence of an American practical preference (theoretical aspiration is another matter) for the waging of war against an enemy's society rather than against his armed forces. In the Second World War the USAAF endeavored to conduct precision bombing but was condemned by technical necessity to be less than discriminate. The Gulf War of 1991 was really the first conflict in American military history wherein long-range firepower truly could be applied in a very discriminating manner. The American way of warfare can be traced in the punitive raids by seventeenth-century Anglo-American settlers against Indian societies (whose warriors wisely declined to stand and fight), in General William Tecumseh Sherman's great raid through Georgia and the Carolinas in 1864, in General Curtis LeMay's purposeful fire-storming of flimsy Japanese cities in 1945, to the nuclear war plans of the 1950s (and since).[13] Countries develop identifiable approaches to defense and war, indeed sometimes even unique philosophies of war, which express their successful learned responses to geographically conditioned, but not determined, historical experience.[14] Writing of *The Soviet Military System in Peace and War*, Christopher Donnelly observes

> Yet just as individuals are conditioned by the environment in which they grow up, so are governments conditioned by the same environment, and reflect, as well as reflect upon, national characteristics. These characteristics are shaped by geography, climate, historical experiences, and religious beliefs, which in turn determine economic circumstances, national prejudices, ideals or ideologies.

He proceeds to note that

> the Soviet military system is greatly influenced by the Russian attitudes to distance and space, to discipline and authority, and to time and work, as well as by the ideology of Marxism–Leninism and, of course, by the national experience of war.[15]

Russian geography has dominated Russian military history. This has been true in the sense that a harsh climate and a (eventually, following the conquest of a great empire) vast continental extent of territory have yielded problems and opportunities for expression in national (or imperial) strategic preference. It has also been true that geography has limited the operational and strategic choices (and their feasibility) of Russia's enemies.

The state of research into strategic culture is still in its infancy, but early results are promising. It transpires that the question, "what was the Athenian (Spartan, Roman, Byzantine, Venetian, British, American and so on) way in statecraft and war," if posed with due empathetic respect both for the known or inferable motives of historical figures and institutions and for the richness of experience, actually can yield new insight. For example, when confronted in the late 440s with the extraordinary scale of threat posed by Attila's Huns, the eastern Roman empire brought rapidly to full maturity a system in statecraft and strategy – involving a mix of intelligence gathering, bribery, hostage-taking, and the corruption of barbarians to employ against barbarians – which, as valuable supplements to the more traditional tools of grand strategy, came to characterize Constantinople's handling of its barbarian (*inter alia*) problems for centuries to come, at least when the empire was relatively weak.[16]

If Byzantine strategic culture is judged unduly arcane to make the point, consider the conditioning effect of British and US national geographies upon strategic culture. The Anglo-American colonists were very much the heirs to, and indeed the carriers of, English strategic traditions.[17] But, the national feat of conquering a continental size homeland, as well as the very prolonged experience of the frontier,[18] left a mark on American strategic culture that was radically different from its British roots. As Denis Brogan once wrote, "[s]pace determined the American way in war, space and the means to conquer space."[19] The logistical excellence that has come to be a hallmark of the American approach to defense and war was the plain product of continental necessity.[20] One might add that the logistical and engineering spirit that has characterized the US Army, also has found worthy expression in a US Navy which, relatively short of secure naval bases in the Second World War in the Pacific, (re)invented the ability to resupply itself at sea and to create forward bases on tropical islands very rapidly.[21] The "fleet train" was not exactly an innovation in principle or practice,[22] but it was an innovation on the scale with which it was applied; certainly it confounded Japanese strategic expectations.

The roots of American (or British) strategic culture can be identified with social and ideological-religious factors in addition to considerations properly identifiable as variably geographical in kind. However, the American and British preferred ways in statecraft and war have been, and remain, so obviously heavily conditioned by geography that fear of appearing deterministic should not deter one from allowing geography its substantial due. As a very large continental size country effectively with insular location, the United States has a first-order maritime strategic problem but very much a continental outlook upon security problems. In its structure, US defense policy in the late 1970s and 1980s was dominated by the mixture of a continentalist focus upon NATO's European Central Front (optimistically, a 90-day war), and the prospects for a high-technology intercontinental holocaust should defeat impend in the field in Europe. The US Navy's maritime strategy in the 1980s,[23] not unnaturally, somewhat ambiguously harbored an alternative vision of protracted, global and non-nuclear conflict. But, comprehension of a significantly maritime view of the structure of conflict is culturally alien to a large fraction of the US defense community.

Some recent scholarship on the subject of the allegedly "British way in warfare" as it, again allegedly, matured from the time of the Commonwealth to the demise of Napoleon is rather friendlier to the heavily maritime postulates of Julian Corbett and Basil Liddell Hart than has been fashionable since the 1930s.[24] For apparently excellent reasons, Michael Howard and Paul Kennedy have argued powerfully for the importance, if not primacy, of continental allies in British grand strategy,[25] certainly in the second Hundred Years' War with France.[26] Unfortunately for the authority of that continental and coalition focus, it is less than obvious that historical facts adequately can support it. Howard and Kennedy may have fallen into the same generic error as did Corbett and Liddell Hart. In short, they pressed the variegated British grand-strategic theories and practices *vis-à-vis* continental foes into an elegantly simple, but possibly, certainly arguably, overly procrustean, mold. As the NATO Alliance is perceived almost visibly to age in the aftermath of German reunification and with the Soviet Union all but *hors de combat* for a while, historically framed or illustrated arguments about British grand strategy, about British approaches to the balance of power on the continent, should be expected to assume some new prominence. The argument has yet to be fully joined with reference to the events of the first half of the twentieth century, but the growth in respectability of a more maritime view of the British way in statecraft and strategy in the eighteenth century may yet lend itself to exploitation by those who would plunder history for the dignifying of contemporary argument.

Limitations on power: nuclear weapons and grand strategy

The four geophysical environments for conflict – land, sea, air, and space – are distinctive as to technologies, tactics (and hence doctrines, that is how to fight), and operational art but not with respect to strategy or policy. The military instruments of the grand strategies of particular countries are skewed broadly for reasons of the geographical considerations already cited in favor of one or more of the environments.

There are circumstances in which each of the principal forms taken by military power – land power, sea power, airpower, and (one day) space power – either has been, or might have been, truly independently decisive. For example, had the United States executed its SIOP-62 preemptively in 1961 or 1962, it is unlikely that North America would have suffered much, if any, damage by way of Soviet retaliation.[27] Similarly, for a rather more mixed case, it would seem in retrospect that both the B-29s of the USAAF and the submarines of the US Navy had Imperial Japan in a stranglehold by mid-summer 1945. However, respectively, the era of "splendid first strike" options has long gone, and the redundantly "decisive" capabilities of the USAAF and the US Navy, without the excuse for surrender provided by the atomic bomb, might not have sufficed to awe Japan into surrender prior to suffering invasion.

Even in the nuclear age it is a general rule that war, and perhaps deterrence, is a combined-arms phenomenon. The nuclear fact has wrought much of its own tactical, operational, and strategic negation. Simplemindedly viewed, nuclear weapons are the most powerful military instruments ever invented for use and abuse by states. But, in practice, political, operational (prudential), and even ethical restraints have served vastly to limit the nominal power of these weapons. Independent, or very highly reliable allied, possession of nuclear weapons is essential if the use of nuclear weapons by would-be enemies is to be deterred. However, the potential utility in the initiation of nuclear warfare has so far eroded that a well-known strategic theorist can write fairly plausibly of the functional emergence of a "postnuclear era."[28] Moreover, so unfashionable have nuclear weapons become that the long-standing Soviet diplomatic campaign for the effective, if not quite literal, denuclearization of NATO in Europe, is judged by experienced national security professionals to be a nontrivial possibility (or danger).[29] In common with many other developments in the history of weapons technology, the lion's share of the tactical, operational, and hence strategic, value of nuclear weapons was lost when their possession was shared with other countries. The small residual danger that, in militarily desperate circumstances, nuclear-armed states might have unreasonable recourse to their nuclear arsenals guarantees that the deterrent value of nuclear weapons will never be zero. But in the closing years of the century it is an open secret that whatever the merits would be in continuation by NATO of a nuclear-dependent strategy of flexible response, they would not include the provision of operationally interesting nuclear use options.

The raw physical power that is potential in nuclear arsenals is not only exceedingly limited in its utility for grand strategy (the inconvenience of mutual nuclear deterrence), it is also, by association (i.e. the escalation danger), restrictive in its effect on the utility of the non-nuclear armed forces of super and great powers. This is not to claim that armed force generally is of declining utility as an instrument of policy, nor is it to argue that conventional combat between nuclear-armed states or coalitions must deteriorate into a process of explosive nuclear escalation. It is suggested here that the relative greatness of the greatest of states in the post-1945 era, though perhaps symbolized by the engines of nuclear destruction, actually has been diminished in most strategic contexts by the pervasive, if latent, nuclear fact.

The argument that nuclear weapons have been "essentially irrelevant" to international security since 1945,[30] popular and expert perceptions to the contrary notwithstanding, may well contain a germ of truth, but as presented to date it falls short of being wholly persuasive. It may be true that nuclear arsenals have overdeterred superpower adversaries who were not strongly motivated to fight anyway. Nonetheless, the possibility that some "Balkan trigger" in Central Europe, the Middle East, East Asia, or the Caribbean could propel the great coalitions into nuclear holocaust has been an enduring psychological reality for policymakers for four and a half decades.

It remains important to understand what can and cannot be achieved by superior fighting power on land, at sea, in the air, and from space. The delivery of nuclear weapons by missile or aircraft (or by spacecraft) could not serve magically to substitute for the inability of a maritime coalition to wage war successfully on land or of a continental empire to practice sea denial conclusively. If, as argued above, the nuclear fact is all but neutralized by its mutuality (admittedly an important qualification), some distinctly traditional reasoning pertaining to the operational reach and strategic effectiveness of land power and sea power, with (tactical) airpower adjuncts, assumes significance.

Sea power and land power are operational complements for strategic effect. A continental empire can be harassed and economically weakened by inimical sea-based action, but that empire cannot be defeated by such action and is unlikely to be brought to accept tolerable terms for the cessation of hostilities as a consequence of maritime events. Similarly, dominant land power may run riot to the water's edge, but offshore states, able to enforce geographical terms of engagement which place the line of contact effectively in the coastal waters of the continental power, will have centers of gravity immune to continentalist action. In the same way that one should note that the only one of the seven wars with France that Britain lost between 1689 and 1815 was the war wherein France was not distracted from maritime/colonial ventures by continental campaigns (1778–83), one should also register the fact that coalitions led by maritime powers have won all of the great struggles of modern history. This latter claim requires the absorption of the fates of the first three coalitions against revolutionary and Napoleonic France, and of the Anglo-French Alliance against Nazi Germany, into the frameworks of the great wars of which they were critical parts.

The geographical realities that limit the political-decision potential of superior land power or of superior sea power pose an enduring challenge to grand strategy. States need to deter war; not narrowly to deter war on land, in the air, and so forth. Similarly, states and great coalitions of states sensibly cannot plan to win campaigns on land, at sea, in the air, or in space treated in isolation. Instead, policymakers functioning at the level of grand strategy have to deter or win war writ large, in all relevant environments. Success on land, in the air, and at sea, let alone through intercontinental nuclear bombardment, is barren and futile unless it generates strategic effectiveness over the ability or willingness of the enemy to fight on. There is nothing about the ramshackle continental empire, that is the Soviet Union and its "allies," which should incline one to believe that the strategic superiority of maritime over continental coalitions demonstrated in the modern era has come to a close. Sir Halford Mackinder predicted the close of what he termed the Columbian epoch (dated from approximately 1500), as great continental states unified and exploited their vast territories with railways.[31] However, Mackinder's analysis, though not his geopolitical framework, went astray with his failure to appreciate fully the meaning for the structure of international security of the addition of continental-size sea power (the United States) to the maritime order of battle.

Geography and the character of conflict

Every conflict is shaped by its geographical setting and, with few exceptions, has the participants express war aims in terms of physical or political geography. It has been common indeed for states to misunderstand their geostrategic problems and to misread their geostrategic opportunities. As a result, policymakers have failed either to fashion a military instrument suitable for resolution of the difficulties posed by geography, or have neglected to bribe or otherwise acquire allied military instruments capable of meeting the national deficiency. For example, misapplying the lessons of their three Dutch wars, the English began their second long period of antagonism with France, greatly overoptimistic concerning the strategic effects that superior sea power could wreak.[32] As a state dependent for its prosperity upon overseas trade, the Dutch could be defeated in maritime wars of quite brief duration.[33] France, though ever somewhat ambivalent over the strength of her maritime interests,[34] could not be defeated in war as a direct consequence of defeat at sea. France certainly was at risk to ultimate defeat (which is to say to more or less severe military disadvantage, not to defeat 1940-style) through the adverse working of the financial attrition inflicted by lengthy conflicts.[35] However, Britain found it expedient in war after war to augment the damage she could inflict via sea-based power, with a variety of continental commitments.

It is worth recalling Carl von Clausewitz's judgments, that

> The first, the supreme, the most far-reaching act of judgment that the statesman and commander have to make is to establish ... the kind of war on which they are embarking: neither mistaking it for, nor trying to turn it into, something that is alien to its nature.[36]

Elsewhere, Clausewitz notes that

> No one starts a war – or rather, no one in his senses ought to do so – without first being clear in his mind what he intends to achieve by that war and how he intends to conduct it. The former is its political purpose; the latter its operational objective.[37]

With those thoughts in mind, one might consider the strategic geography of the Second World War. Through a series of policy, grand-strategic, military-strategic, and even operational blunders, the high command of the Third Reich, military as well as political, thrust its country into combat on such grossly disadvantageous terms that no amount of tactical superiority on the battlefield could offset the top-level failures. Thoroughly misunderstanding the political resiliency and strategic options, in succession, of Britain, the USSR, and the United States, Adolf Hitler committed the cardinal sin for military statecraft: he placed his generals and admirals in a strategic context where they could not win.[38] By way of the tersest of summaries, Nazi Germany, functioning almost as a parody of an opportunistic continental power, attempted the geostrategically impossible. With the executive instrument of a truly short-range military establishment, Germany endeavored to discourage or defeat the two countries (Britain and the USSR) whose national geographical settings (insular/maritime and sheer space with a very poor communications infrastructure and climatic extremes) facilitated the protraction of hostilities.

There was a pattern of Germany policy ambition exceeding German military reach and of Germany military reach exceeding German military grasp. The logistical nonsense that was the modified Schlieffen Plan (as actually implemented in

1914; the purer conceptions, with a much weightier right wing, would have fared even worse)[39] was succeeded in the next great war by a logistical insouciance towards the invasion of Russia that was quite breathtaking. In both world wars, Germany bid for swift continental victory against coalitions willing and able to deny Berlin advantageous temporal and geographical terms of strategic engagement. Indeed, in the case of the First World War, Germany never achieved a campaign success in the West such as might have had genuinely strategic consequences. The collapse of Imperial Russian in 1917 occurred too late in the war for Germany to be able to exploit it with high confidence of achieving success in the West.[40]

To fight Britain did not necessarily require the ability to wage global war, but at the very least it required a military reach capable of bridging the channel. It is true to argue that in the 1930s Hitler did not intend to fight Britain. Explicitly learning from some of the errors in Imperial German statecraft, Hitler sought, pro tem, a free hand in Europe in fair exchange for respect of Britain's overseas interests.[41] But statesmen must be judged by the consequences of their policies and not by their intentions. Hitler misjudged Britain's willingness to fight to restore the balance of power in Europe, neglected to provide himself with armed forces capable of exerting a fatal level of pressure against an insular enemy, and then, admittedly with the enthusiastic backing of the military professionals on the general staff,[42] and committed the Napoleonic error of a fatal overextension on land with an invasion (*Fall* Barbarossa) whose necessary geographical scope exceeded the logistical reach of his army and air force.

Geography does not dictate choice in policy or strategy, but its pervasive influence via culture certainly predisposes states and their military establishments towards particular ways in warfare. Similarly, the objective aspects of geography (insular or continental location, defensibility of frontiers, identity and strength of neighbors), cultural preferences aside, can have a logic all their own. The problems and opportunities posed by the newly united Germany's central location in Europe dominated the structure of German strategic planning from 1871 until 1914.[43] Ironically, the extremities of geostrategic vulnerability felt by Imperial Germany have been paralleled since 1948 by the state of Israel. The two (plus)-front war problem inherent in German and Israeli geographies produced strategic cultures that opportunistically equated battles, campaigns, and war. Israel has proved to be at least as incompetent in the realms of grand and military strategy as was Imperial and Nazi Germany, but Israeli tactical and operational excellence thus far has kept the wolves outside the doors. Israel's opportunistic offensive victories have been utterly unmatched by grand-strategic vision.

Appearances to the contrary notwithstanding, perhaps, this is not to pass negative political judgment on Israel for the many wars or, really, the one war with many campaigns she has been obliged to wage. Rather, the points simply are, first, Israel, like Germany, wins campaign after campaign, yet has no very plausible theory of victory in the war as a whole; second, the short-war, operational opportunism that has been the hallmark of the Israeli and the Germany way in warfare, is largely to be explained with reference to geography.

As geography shapes national approaches to, styles in, and of course comparative state advantages and disadvantages for war, so also must it influence the character of every conflict. Truly insular polities, be they naturally so, as with Britain and Japan, or artificially contrived, as with imperial Athens or the early modern Dutch Republic, occasionally can be discouraged via continental disasters or the harassment of maritime trade into accepting a disadvantageous peace (witness the brief Peace of Amiens of 1802–03). But, as a general rule, a polity has to discover a theory of victory in war that can reach and defeat the pivot of the strategy system of the enemy. In the final volume of his magisterial history of the Peloponnesian War, Donald Kagan concludes that

> The Peloponnesian War was one of those classic confrontations between a great land power and great naval power. Each entered the war hoping and expecting to keep to its own element and to win a victory in a way that conformed to its strengths at a relatively low cost. Within a few years events showed that victory would not be possible in that way for either side. To win, each had to acquire the capacity to fight and succeed on the other's favorite domain.[44]

The problem for grand strategy, whether in the Peloponnesian War, the Napoleonic wars, or the Second World War, was not necessarily for the engaged polities to become great naval or great land powers if they were not such already. Instead, the grand-strategic problem was to acquire the use of the missing instrument of excellence. In short, most states in most periods have had to approach the problems of *grande guerre* in a coalition context.[45]

The influence of geography upon the character of conflict is pervasive at all levels of analysis: policy, grand strategy, military strategy, tactics, and technological choices and performance.[46] Geography influences high policy in that, for example, Imperial Japan believed she could seize, fortify, and hold a very far-flung maritime defense perimeter in the Central Pacific to such good military effect that the United States would elect to acquiesce in that (defensively motivated) expansion.[47] By way of stark contrast, at the sharpest, distinctly tactical, end of war, the combination of poor logistic planning, generally fierce resistance, autumn rains, winter cold, unmetalled roads (if any), and sheer distance, took a toll upon a *Wehrmacht* at its peak of fighting effectiveness in 1941 from which it never really recovered.[48] Russian physical geography and climate effected progressive demotorization upon a German army that even in its prime had been none too extravagantly equipped in that way. The Soviet army was progressively motorized from 1943 to 1945, in noteworthy part courtesy of American lend–lease shipments.[49]

Geographical factors highlight the salience of a point so obvious that frequently it is ignored. Specifically, war is a contest between two or more independent but interacting wills. An enemy will be motivated to apply the military principles which help guide combat distinctive to each environment. The good book on the philosophy of war claims that "defense is *the stronger form of waging war*."[50]

This is a general truth applicable only to land operations (a qualification not rendered explicit by the great man). Another good book argues that "defence is insured only by offence."[51] For reason principally of the distinctive character of the geophysical environment in question and never forgetting the necessary synergism between offense and defense, it is true to claim that although defense is the stronger form of war on land, offense is the stronger form of war at sea,[52] in the air, and in low earth orbit. It may prove to be the case that the energy and time required in order to climb the gravity well out from earth, in order to attack space platforms (say) at geosynchronous altitude (at 22,300 miles), will yield an enduring advantage to the defender against many, though certainly not all, predictable kinds of threats.

The geography of space is quite as distinctive as the land, maritime, and air environments with which defense theorists are much more familiar.[53] Thoughtful works on space and grand strategy, on principles of space warfare, and even on the influence of space power on history will have to be very sensitive to the unique geographical features of the environment at issue and to the implications of those features for strategy, operations, and tactics.[54] For example, a well-designed architecture of space-based sensors (multispectral) could yield what would amount to total real-time, all-weather surveillance of any portion of the surface of the earth of interest. What use might Napoleon have made of that?

Conclusions

It might seem that this essay either has been defending a proposition that no sensible person would attack, the notion that geography is important for grand strategy, or, formal disclaimer notwithstanding, really has been purveying a noxious "essentialism" (i.e. essentially geography drives policy and strategy). At least by intention, this article has sought to build upon the commonsensical point that geography is important as a source of limitation upon, and opportunity for, the power of states, in order to identify ways in which that importance is made manifest. Throughout history people have always known that geography mattered, but still they committed errors in statecraft, strategy, and operations that flowed from geographically conditioned misleadingly narrow insular or continental worldviews.

The United States exploited its geographical situation and logistical excellence for the purpose of waging truly global coalition warfare very effectively indeed between 1941 and 1945. Yet in the 1960s, the United States restricted herself to the conduct of a form of warfare in southeast Asia with geographical restraints against most of the kinds of maritime and ground-force action which might have isolated the battlefield sufficiently for success to be possible.[55] The physical and political geography of southeast Asia could not determine US policy and strategy. But that geography had the implication that if Washington was set upon protecting South Vietnam from North Vietnamese aggression: the Cambodian port of Sihanoukville had to be blockaded, as did the North Vietnamese port of Haiphong; the Laotian panhandle had to be sealed off; enemy forces had to be denied Cambodia as a sanctuary; overland North Vietnamese supply routes from China required thorough harassment; and the long North Vietnamese coastline had to be menaced seriously with the threat of assault from the sea. The point here is neither to advocate these measures (comfortably in retrospect), nor to claim that assuredly they would have sufficed to produce some facsimile of victory. Rather, the point is that the geography of the region mandated that most, if not all, of the forceful measures just cited had to be adopted if the United States and Saigon were to stand a reasonable prospect of success in the war. US amphibious warfare doctrine in the Second World War emphasized the value in isolating the battlefield.[56] The duration and cost of the Guadalcanal, or indeed the Gallipoli (to step back a generation), campaign illustrate what can happen when the enemy is able to manage a process of battlefield reinforcement. In 1942 the United States could not isolate Guadalcanal, any more than the Allies could have isolated the Gallipoli peninsula in 1915. But in the mid- to late 1960s the United States could have done a great deal to isolate South Vietnam from North Vietnamese infiltration. The US Joint Chiefs of Staff, if not President Johnson, knew what the geography of the region implied for sound strategy and operations, but they chose to acquiesce in a style of war that they knew could not deliver success.[57]

To summarize, it has been argued in this article that (1) geography, broadly understood, is a major contributor to national strategic culture, a better understanding of which should aid predictability in international security affairs, (2) Geography shapes a principally maritime or continentalist strategic worldview, which suggests what national grand strategy needs to accomplish by way of adding, through coalition diplomacy, military or naval excellence to a polity's unilateral assets. (3) Geography functions both as a source of limitation and of opportunity for statecraft and strategy. However, in different historical eras either continentalist or maritime-centered coalitions have enjoyed systemic competitive advantage. For example, it was not a matter of chance alone that the great land powers of antiquity tended to defeat their maritime rivals, while in modern times the great land powers, without exception to date, have all gone down in ruin.[58] (4) Nuclear weapons have reduced the greatness of great powers, even as they have helped redefine that status. The inconvenient possession of nuclear weapons by countries of East and West has reduced great-power freedom of military action and may have undermined radically the legitimacy and utility of *grande guerre* as an instrument of policy. (5) The geography of international security relations today is at least as important as ever it was in days of prenuclear innocence. The maritime-continental standoff between the superpowers has been uncannily Mackinderesque in structure,[59] nuclear weapons, ICBM's, and space platforms notwithstanding. (6) Each of the four geophysical environments (land, sea, air, and space) is distinctive as a theater of conflict. The forms that combat can take and the objectives that can be pursued are both unique to each environment. For example, it is in the nature of the land to be controlled and of the sea to be uncontrolled. The land can be occupied and fortified, as to a degree can earth orbit, but the sea and the air cannot be. (7) Geographical considerations permeate and help shape every conflict. For example, any power seeking the definitive overthrow of the Byzantine Empire learned both that it had to assault the strongest fortifications of the age (i.e. the triple land-walls of Constantinople erected by the Emperor Theodosius II in the first half of the fifth century),[60] because the imperial capital was the key to the empire,[61] and that Constantinople could be taken only if it was invested thoroughly, and assaulted, by land and by sea.[62] For another example, the particular geography (including weather) of Anglo-French conflict from 1689 to 1815 meant that the key to British security and success was adoption and competent execution of a fleet deployment scheme that ensured that a Western Squadron (later the Channel or Home Fleet) always would command the mouth of the English Channel.[63] Prevailing westerlies and an absence of French deep-water ports on her channel coast meant that occupation of the "Ushant position" by a Royal Navy, which was tactically superior as a fighting instrument, rendered Britain as safe against invasion designs or fleet-scale French adventures into colonial waters as historical experience and a geostrategically logical system could ensure. The British system in fleet deployment was not thoroughly weather-proof or fool-proof, but it was fault-tolerant.

Only in the late 1970s and 1980s did the study of geographical factors in statecraft and strategy begin to claw back at least some of the scholarly ground that it lost in previous decades (since the late 1940s). Anybody who writes about geography and grand strategy, let alone about geopolitics,[64] virtually issues a hunting license for careless, or perhaps just suspicious, reviewers to level charges of determinism. The argument in this article has been anything but deterministic. Far from claiming that some reified geography mandated this or that course of action, the argument rather has been to the effect that physical geography, which helps shape cultural geography, provides limitations that sometimes are overcome and opportunities that sometimes are taken. The public official who disdains geographically flavored argument is a public official riding for a fall. Disdain for geography can leave your soldiers with tanks whose tracks are too narrow for soggy terrain; with summer clothing in winter conditions; and with problems of reach and grasp that a cavalier and optimistic approach to long-range transportation and logistics all but invite.

Grand strategy is many things. Among others, it is politics, economics, technology, and ideology. But grand strategy also is, and is about, geography. Be it Flanders in 1914, Berlin and Cuba in the early 1960s, or the Falklands in 1982, the relevance of geographical factors, perceived and objective, for grand-strategic choice and capabilities, demands more sophisticated and more steady recognition.

10 Strategic culture as context

The first generation of theory strikes back [1999]

Three generations of scholars in rapid succession have addressed the concept of strategic culture.[1] In minor part this chapter is a critical commentary upon third-generation scholarship by a representative of the first generation. In major part, however, the chapter is a belated development of first-generation enquiry. The analysis proceeds from a reexamination of vital matters of theory, through explanation of the postulated universality and ubiquity of culturally stamped behavior, to an attempt to chart a better way forward in research. The discussion addresses the connection between strategic culture and strategic behavior.

There is a sharp difference of view between third-generation theorists such as Alastair Iain Johnston and first-generation theorists such as this author, over what comprises the proper domain of culture and possibly, though less certainly, over how culture may shape impulses to act. At the very least, the time is overdue for debate to be joined. The subject of strategic culture matters deeply, because it raises core questions about the roots of, and influences upon, strategic behavior. By strategic behavior, this author means behavior relevant to the threat or use of force for political purposes. I will argue that recent (third-generation) scholarship on strategic culture is seriously in error in its endeavor to distinguish culture from behavior. Nonetheless, that error has been committed for the praiseworthy reason of finding reasonable tests for the influence of culture. Furthermore, we of the first generation of scholarship on strategic culture, though, I believe, fundamentally correct in our understanding of the subject, could be insufficiently critical of the friction that intervenes between cultural preference and behavior.

So limited is the empirical and theoretical scholarship currently available on strategic culture, that we would probably be best advised to look more for complementarities of approach than to try and elect one or another view the methodological winner. Strategic culture should be approached both as a shaping context for behavior and itself as a constituent of that behavior. The theoretical, let alone empirical, difficulties raised by the latter approach obviously are severe. Readers could do a lot worse than consider this discussion of strategic culture with reference to the key distinction drawn by Martin Hollis and Steve Smith between "explaining and understanding international relations."[2] To clarify, one can think of strategic culture as being "out there" as a rich and distilled source of influence which might "cause" behavior. Alternatively, or perhaps just in addition, one can regard strategic culture as being in good measure socially constructed by both people and institutions, which proceed to behave to some degree culturally.

The methodologically awesome qualifier "to some degree" is the nub of the problem. It is not the case, however, that to see all strategic behavior as culturally influenced behavior is to explain everything and therefore to explain nothing. There is vastly more to strategy and strategic behavior than culture alone. Nonetheless, the dimensions of strategy cited below are expressed in behavior by people and institutions that both have internalized strategic culture and in part construct, interpret, and amend that culture. In other words, the strategic cultural context for strategic behavior includes the human strategic actors and their institutions which "make culture" by interpreting what they discern. Arcane though it may sound, this discussion bears directly upon such matters as whether, why, and how, people, polities, and would-be polities fight.

Definitional clarity usually is useful, but one needs to remember that the price of clarity can be clear error. In calling this article "strategic culture as context," I accept, actually I even welcome, a key dualism in social-scientific definitions of context. To be specific, context can be considered as something "out there," typically in concentric circles, meaning "that which surrounds."[3] Alternatively, or methodologically perilously, as well, one can approach context as "that which weaves together" (from the Latin, *contextere*: to weave together). In this discussion strategic culture can be conceived as a context out there that surrounds, and gives meaning to, strategic behavior, or as the total warp and woof of matters strategic that are thoroughly woven together, or as both.

Ideas and behavior

In the mid-1970s, a small number of strategic theorists came to believe that strategic ideas and some strategic behavior were much more the products of educational processes of social construction than the professional literature on defense matters then recognized. Those scholars were much taken by Bernard Brodie's claim that "good strategy presumes good anthropology and sociology. Some of the greatest military blunders of all time have resulted from juvenile evaluations in this department."[4] This ranks among the wisest of observations in the entire history of strategic thought. The fact that Brodie rediscovered the obvious does not detract much from its luminosity.

It is probably accurate to say that the initial, if you will, first-generation, literature on the startlingly familiar yet strangely under-explored notion of strategic culture was more workmanlike than truly scholarly.[5] That probability noted, still it seems that the study of strategic culture has advanced boldly into avoidable conceptual, methodological, and practical ambush. The most prominent and influential of the latest generation of theorists on strategic culture is Alastair Iain Johnston. Although almost any scholarly work on strategic culture is granted importance because of its rarity, Johnston's work is especially significant both because it has been legitimized by publication in prestigious outlets and because it contains errors of a kind that, if allowed to pass unchallenged for much longer, are apt to send followers into an intellectual wasteland.

How should we think about strategic culture, and why does it matter? Strategy can have many dimensions,[6] of which one is the cultural. Culture or cultures comprises the persisting (though not eternal) socially transmitted ideas, attitudes, traditions, habits of mind, and preferred methods of operation that are more or less specific to a particular geographically based security community that has had a necessarily unique historical experience. A particular community may well contain more than one strategic culture, just as there tend to be military cultures associated with particular missions or geographical environments.[7] Furthermore, strategic culture(s) can change over time, as new experience is absorbed, coded, and culturally translated. Culture, however, changes slowly. Scholars who prefer to look only to recent history as the determining influence upon contemporary strategic culture would be well-advised to change concepts. If strategic culture is held to be significantly reshapeable on a year by year, or even on a decade by decade, basis, then culture probably is unduly dignified, even pretentious, a term to characterize the phenomena at issue.

The dimensions of strategy interpenetrate. Everything a security community does, if not a manifestation of strategic culture, is at least an example of behavior effected by culturally shaped, or encultured,[8] people, organizations, procedures, and weapons. A critic would be correct in observing that if strategic culture is everywhere it is, in practicably researchable terms nowhere. That critic, however, would have missed the point (that, for example, Germans are Germans and, it is postulated, have had certain strategic cultural tendencies). In their strategic behavior, Germans cannot help but behave except under the constraints of Germanic strategic culture, even when they are unable to adhere strictly to the dominant ideas and preferences of their strategic culture. Hitler sought to draw strength in 1942–45 from the common German belief that theirs was the historic duty of protecting Europe from the barbarians to the East. This belief, or myth, had power over contemporary German imagination.

By far the most persuasively plausible definition of culture that I have uncovered is that offered by sociologist Raymond Williams. Williams claims that the definition of culture has three general categories: the "ideal," the "documentary," and the "social." Respectively, Williams' categories include values pertaining to some "timeless order," " 'the artefacts' of intellectual and imaginative work in which human thought and experience are variously recorded," and finally he advises that culture "is a description of a particular way of life which finds expression in institutions and ordinary behaviour."[9] In other words, culture is ideal, it is the evidence of ideas, and it is behavior. Should doubts remain over the authority for my preferred usage, both the Oxford and Webster's dictionaries define culture as embracing ideas *and* patterns of behavior.

Essential to a properly holistic understanding of strategy, and especially to a grasp of the ways in which culture can manifest itself, is the proposition that strategy has several, or many, dimensions. These dimensions apply to, indeed play on, strategy in all periods. This conceptual structure effectively is unmoved even by radical changes in the details relevant to each dimension (e.g. the ethical, or the technological, dimension will play distinctly in each strategic condition). The importance of this inclusive view of strategy and war is its insistence that strategy comprises all of the dimensions identified, and that there are practical limits to what excellence on just a few dimensions can achieve (e.g. better weapons, superior geographical position, and so forth), if one is massively disadvantaged even on just one or two of the dimensions (e.g. poor leadership, unpopularity of a conflict at home, which translates as a low score on the political command and social dimensions). I choose to group strategy's dimensions into three clusters. The first category, "People and Politics," comprises of people, society, culture, politics, and ethics. The second category, "Preparation for War," accommodates economics and logistics; organization (including defense, force, and more directly, war, planning), military preparation and administration (including recruitment, training, and many aspects of armament), information and intelligence, strategic theory and doctrine, and technology. The final category, "War Proper," groups military operations, command (political and military), geography, friction (including chance and uncertainty), the adversary, and time.[10]

Anyone who seeks a falsifiable theory of strategic culture in the school of Johnston commits the same error as a doctor who sees people as having entirely separable bodies and minds. In his writings about Chinese strategic culture. Iain Johnston's apparently methodologically progressive determination to consider culture distinctively from behavior for the purpose of studying the influence of the former on the latter transpires paradoxically to be a scholarly step or two backwards. There is an obvious sense in which positivistically he is seeking to explain how the cultural context (as "that which surrounds") does, or does not, influence the realm of action. From the perspective of methodological rigor it is hard to fault him. The problem is that we cannot understand strategic behavior by that method, be it ever so rigorous. Strategic culture is not only "out there," also it is within us; we, our institutions, and our behavior are the context.

Whatever the sins of omission and commission in the first generation of writings about strategic culture, those writings were plausible on the most important matters; moreover, even with hindsight and in the light of some fierce criticism, they still look plausible. What did those theorists attempt to say? On the basis of familiarity with strategic history, they hypothesized that (1) different security communities and sub-communities tend to exhibit in their strategic thought *and behavior* patterns that could be collectively termed cultural and that (2) strategic culture finds expression in distinctively patterned styles of strategic behavior. When Johnston criticizes my early work on strategic culture for being deterministic,[11] he misunderstands the nature of the subject in dispute. Johnston's real source of unhappiness with my writings on strategic culture lies in his dislike of my definition of the concept. I conflate strategic ideas and strategic behavior, to the effect, according to Johnston, that my theory is tautological and therefore unfalsifiable.[12]

Johnston commits several errors. First, he requires "a notion of strategic culture that is falsifiable or at least distinguishable from nonstrategic-culture variables."[13]

Reasonable though that requirement should be, Johnston does not understand a point raised by anthropologist Leslie A. White: "Culture is not basically anything. Culture is a word-concept. It is man-made and may be used arbitrarily to designate anything, we may define the conception we please."[14] Even scholars can forget that definitions are neither right nor wrong. Second, although definitions necessarily are arbitrary, a definition driven by the needs of theory building rather than by the character of the subject is unusually likely to lead scholars astray.

There is something to be said for restricting the concept of culture to the realm of ideas, to the assumptions that lie behind strategic behavior, but there is sense in Robert B. Bathurst's words when he writes, to adapt, "[s]trategic culture, here, refers to those prominent patterns of... [strategic] behaviour which are indicative of social ways of seeing and responding to 'reality'."[15] Similarly, in an invented conversation, Clyde Kluckholn and William H. Kelly's "Second Anthropologist" advises that "what the anthropologist does is to record the distinctive ways of behaving which he sees and those results of behavior which are also characteristic. These constitute the culture of the group."[16] Finally, for a variant, anthropologist Marvin Harris informs us that "[c]ulture...refers to the learned repertory of thoughts and actions exhibited by the members of social groups – repertories transmissible independently of genetic heredity from one generation to the next."[17]

The traffic between ideas and behavior in strategic affairs is continuous, hence my preference for the idea that context is more about "that which weaves together," than it is about "that which surrounds." As the intellectual history of strategy, including its manifestation in national or sub-national strategic culture, bears the stamp of particular perceptions and interpretations of strategic history, so the domain of strategic behavior is shaped by the strategic attitudes and ideas that we know as strategic culture. In the practical world of strategy, strategic ideas apply to strategic experience, while strategic experience constitutes ideas in action, albeit as modified by the constraints of imperfect practice.

Johnston's approach flags some important concerns. For example, up to a point he is correct to signal the perils of determinism in sweeping claims for the explanatory value of the concept of strategic culture. Also, his work is useful in reminding us of the probable facts that a security community may have several strategic cultures, that culture evolves over time, and that strategic culture may comprise more a litany of canonical idealized beliefs than a set of attitudes, perspectives, and preferences that are operational as real guides to action. Furthermore, Johnston is partially correct when he alerts scholars to the difficulties posed by a concept of strategic culture that comprises so extensive a portfolio of ingredients, and is so influential upon behavior, that it can explain nothing because it purports to explain everything.[18] Nonetheless, it would seem that Johnston read the score rather than listened to the music. We first-generation scholars of strategic culture, albeit with exceptions, were not advancing a culturally distinctive theory of strategy, at least we did not think that we were. At times, some of us, myself included, may well have appeared both careless in our all too implicit causalities (connecting cultural preference and particular behavior), and perilously tautological. It is useful to have those weaknesses signalled clearly, so that scholars speak more plainly. Although the written products of our speculation may have seemed somewhat deterministic, by and large all that we intended was to remind our readers and official clients that there was a notably Soviet–Russian dimension to the Cold War foe; we were not competing with some "black-boxed" superpower "A" or "B" that was beyond culture. Probably, we over-signaled the cultural argument, but that is not unusual when arguments are novel.

Johnston does not grasp the nature of strategic culture. He objects to a theory that is effectively untestable because its evidential domain is pervasive. The problem, though, does not lie so much in poor methodology and casual conceptualization on the part of people like myself – though that charge may well have merit – but rather with Johnston's overly simple view of strategy. Although each dimension of strategy can be discussed in isolation, all dimensions function synergistically to constitute the strategy whole.

On balance, it may be desirable to fence-in the concept of strategic culture with reference to ideas, attitudes, traditions, and preferences for kinds of action, and to consider the actual behavior of a strategic culture, or cultures, as the realm of "style."[19] It is important to understand that even when a particular security community is performing missions that are not long preferred, if not actually alien, it must behave in a culturally shaped manner. Germans cannot help but be Germans, whether they are waging war as they would prefer or as they must. Culture is behavior, because those responsible for the behavior necessarily are encultured as Germans, Britons, and so forth.[20]

One should resist the suggestion in some recent scholarship that somehow strategic culture, or cultures, can be sidelined and offset by other influences upon strategic choice.[21] The idea of strategic culture does not imply that there is a simple one-for-one relationship between culturally traceable preferences and actual operational choices.[22] The claim rather is that culture shapes the process of strategy-making, and influences the execution of strategy, no matter how close actual choice may be to some abstract or idealized cultural preference. This simple, but crucial, point can elude the intellectual grasp even of careful scholars. For example, in a recent major review of "culturalist" theories of security, Michael Desch draws an invalid distinction between culturalist theories and realist theories of national security.[23] Desch does not seem to understand that "realist" analysis and policy is undertaken by particularly encultured people and organizations. Perhaps the point is too obvious to attract scholarly notice.

The unity of cultural influence and policy action denies the existence of the boundaries needed for the study of cause and effect. If there is cause in the effect, how can cause be assessed for its effect? Happily the problem lies with the question, not with the answer. Strategic culture and patterns of strategic behavior, if one elects to separate them conceptually, are related integrally much as strategy, operations, and tactics are related. Just as all strategy has to be "done" by operations which consist of tactical behavior, so all strategic, operational, and tactical behavior is "done" by people and organizations that have been encultured supranationally, nationally, or sub-nationally. As the anthropologist Edward T. Hall has emphasized, culture, in this case strategic culture, provides context for events and ideas.[24] Some societies (e.g., Russian) are high-context, some are low-context: that is to say that some societies take a relatively complex and organic view of events, seeing sub-texts and sub-plots and subtle interconnections, while others (e.g., American) are prone to see simple oppositions (e.g., particular weapons are either stabilizing or destabilizing) and to approach each event on its isolated merits.[25] But, even a low-context strategic culture is still a strategic culture.

In practice, polities cannot afford to listen to much idle speculation of the scholarly kind suggested in Johnston's work. The policy interest in scholarship in strategic culture lies not so much in prediction of how culture "out there" might influence behavior, because behavior can be triggered by many factors. Instead, the vital contextual question, that is cultural, is "what does the observed behavior mean?" It is more modest to seek to interpret than it is to predict, but strategic cultural scholarship is as likely to be useful in the former role as it will be unduly challenged in the latter.

Strategic culture matters deeply for modern strategy, because the culture of the strategic players, individuals, and organizations influences strategic behavior. One may not wish to endorse completely John Mueller's claim for the power of ideas when he asserts that

> the grand strategies of the major contestants [in the Cold War] and therefore the essential shape and history of that conflict were chiefly determined by differences in ideas and ideologies that emanate from domestic politics, not by structural differences in the distribution of capabilities at the international level.[26]

Mueller concludes his innovative essay with the bold claim that "domestic changes that lead to changes in political ideas may be far more important influences on international behaviour than changes in the international distribution of military capabilities."[27] For example, a radical change in Soviet ideology in the mid- to late 1980s led to a no less radical change in Soviet foreign policy, even though the military capabilities of the United States registered no matching radical change in those years: in other words, that change in Soviet ideology was not coerced by the international correlation of forces.

Strategy is universal, but cultural

The nature and purpose of strategy is permanent and universal; it is also, in its particular historical form and content, inescapably cultural. Johnston laments that "[m]uch empirical work on strategic culture has also been hampered by a lack of methodological rigour."[28] Alas, the concept of strategic culture, in common with the idea of paradox,[29] expresses an important pervasive, yet in detail typically elusive, truth about the nature and practice of strategy. It is in the nature of strategy to be subject to a paradoxical logic, just as it is in the nature of strategy to reflect the culture of its particular maker and executor. Strategic culture, like paradox in strategy, is a useful notion provided one does not ask too much of it.

In discussing Sun Tzu, historians Barry S. Strauss and Josiah Ober draw attention to his pithy advice on "the issue of ideology, by which we mean the matrix of unexamined assumptions, opinions, and prejudices that every human being brings to the decision-making process."[30] The authors note that "Sun Tzu reminds us that sense [as in common sense] is usually idiosyncratic and seldom crosses cultural lines." It is powerfully plausible to postulate that people and the institutions through which they function are educated by their distinctive contexts to bear more or less particular cultural preconceptions. Just as friction in war cannot be eliminated by technological advance, in part because people must employ the new machines,[31] so "people, being of the human condition...are necessarily enmeshed in a network of preconceptions."[32] Why should this be so? In her brilliant pioneering study, *Politics and Culture in International History*, Adda B. Bozeman advises

> that each society is moved by the circumstances of its existence to develop its own approach to foreign relations. This means that diplomacy, as for that matter every other social institution, is bound to incorporate the traditions and values peculiar to the civilization in which it is practiced.[33]

Similarly, Bathurst argues that people cope with incoming data in files that organize their understanding of the world. Moreover, in Bathurst's words,

> [c]ultures teach us to see according to the labels on the files.... [I]t follows that a nation's wars are congruent with that nation's political and social structures. The way it chooses, defines and perceives its enemies, estimates their intentions and plans to counter them necessarily comes from its unique expression, arising out of its systems and organisations.[34]

Bozeman and Bathurst are persuasive to the point where one wonders how they could possibly be wrong. To be German, American, Russian, at a particular time is to be "encultured" in particular ways. Those ways will vary modestly among, say, Germans at different times in German history, and there may be noteworthy distinctions among Germans even in the same period. Nonetheless, it is reasonable to postulate the presence of some important cultural features among people who share a common heritage, particularly if they are of a similar age. At least until the mid-1940s, Germans believed that they were the Eastern bulwark of European civilization. Until perhaps 1968, Americans had great difficulty even conceiving of their country losing a war. In the winter of 1942–43, the Soviet defenders of Stalingrad believed that History was with them, both "scientifically" – compliments of Marx, Lenin, and Stalin – and essentially morally because they represented Mother Russia. The alternative to the argument just advanced is close to absurd. How can there be a Strategic Person "beyond culture"? A noteworthy strain in American defense analysis during the Cold War expressed transcultural confidence that it had unlocked the universal mysteries of, for example, strategic stability in the nuclear age. Needless to add, such arrogant positivism was itself profoundly cultural.[35]

In an effort to criticize theorists of the first generation on strategic culture, Johnston stumbles over reality, though without quite realizing what he has uncovered. In his words,

> To date, many of those who have explicitly used the term strategic culture have tended to define it in ways that make it unfalsifiable and untestable. Especially egregious in this regard is what could be called the first (and most influential) generation of studies in strategic culture. Definitionally, this literature subsumed both thought and action within the concept of strategic culture, leaving the mechanically deterministic implication that strategic thought led consistently to one type of behaviour. The literature also tended to include everything from technology to geography to ideology to past patterns of behaviour in an amorphous concept of strategic culture, even though those variables could stand as separate, even conflicting explanations for strategic choice. This left little conceptual space for non-strategic culture explanations of behaviour.[36]

I believe that Johnston is wrong, but he is wrong for the right reasons. The point is that strategic culture does indeed emerge from the kind of mixed stew of ingredients that Johnston finds, and finds so methodologically frustrating, in the early literature on the subject. To adapt Dennis Kavanagh's definition of political culture, "we may regard the strategic culture [political culture, in original] as a shorthand expression to denote the emotional and attitudinal environment within which the defence community [political system, in original] operates."[37] Ideas about war and strategy are influenced by physical and political geography – some strategic cultures plainly have, for example, a maritime or a continentalist tilt – by political or religious ideology, and by familiarity with, and preference for, particular military technologies. Strategic culture is the world of mind, feeling, and *habit in behavior*. Johnston is systemically wrong in two respects in conceiving of culture as clearly distinctive among "conflicting explanations for strategic choice." He errs in failing to recognize a cultural dimension to all that human beings think and feel about war and strategy. Culture is the context that "surrounds" and the context that "weaves together." Johnston fails to spot the absurdity of the opposition that he postulates when he complains that there is little conceptual space remaining for explanations of behavior beyond strategic culture. Let us state the methodologically appalling truth that there can be no such conceptual space, because all strategic behavior is effected by human beings who cannot help but be cultural agents.

Occasionally, an overwhelmingly maritime strategic culture, like the British in the First World War, is obliged to play an uncharacteristically major continental military role. However, the fact of the huge British continental commitment of 1914–18 did not alter the dominant British strategic culture, notwithstanding the infantry experience of a whole generation of Britons. Indeed, exaggerated claims for a traditional British maritime orientation in strategy were pressed in the 1920s and 1930s in ways that overstated the culturally strategically extraordinary character of the size and responsibility of the British Expeditionary Force (BEF) of 1916–18.[38] Strategic culture explains why the continental role was, certainly psychologically was, so different for Britain, as contrasted with some other great powers, it does not explain why Britain chose to wage war as a continental power in those years. In other words, strategic culture provides context, even where the final choice is all but counter-cultural.

For another example, although the United States has joined and, in one case, even led three coalitions in the twentieth century, and notwithstanding the fact that the third of those coalition commitments is now nearly of fifty years' duration (i.e., NATO), isolationism, certainly unilateralism, remains a potent icon and impulse for policy in the United States.[39] There is a decidedly hollow ring to Richard Holbrooke's bold claim that "the United States has become a European power in a sense that goes beyond traditional assertions of America's 'commitment' to Europe."[40] Even when security communities function strategically in ways flatly contrary to a dominant tradition – Britain in 1916–18, or America's repeated involvement in entangling alliances – those actions do not produce a seismic shift in strategic culture. Furthermore, when a preponderantly maritime culture commits to continental warfare on the largest of scales, or when an isolationist culture becomes a partner in coalition-style strategic ventures, the stamp of those basic moulds will be seen in the ways behavior is adapted to the practical needs of the uncharacteristic roles. For example, Hew Strachan has shown how resistant to revolutionary change was the traditional "British way of war," even under the greatest of pressures of continental military crisis in the First World War.[41]

Cultural preconceptions are inescapable, but they are not of some malign necessity pathological. To be encultured as a German or American may be unavoidable, but there is nothing about being a German or American that requires one to fail to recognize the cultural distinctiveness of others. I may be British and American, but I do not have to believe that all the world thinks and feels as do Britons and Americans. Cultural reductionism, even stereotyping, and their polar opposite, ethnocentrism, are to a degree unavoidable.[42] In strategy we have to deal with human beings – Germans, Chinese, and so forth – collectively, and we can only interpret incoming information with reference to what we know in our culture of their culture (which is an unavoidable brand of ethnocentrism). Nonetheless, while recognizing ethnocentrism as a cardinal sin against the gods of sound strategy, some cultural reductionism and stereotyping is inescapable and can even yield judgments of tolerable accuracy.

The term cultural preconception has pejorative connotations that can mislead the unwary. Whereas many American soldiers entered the Second World War with scant respect for a German army which their preconceptions told them was bound to be rigidly teutonic in action, British soldiers – trained by experience in 1914–18 and 1940–41 – were apt to hold the accurate preconception that the

German army was formidable in its tactical flexibility.[43] The British were correct, as Americans learnt in Tunisia, Italy, and later in France. For another example, during the Napoleonic wars British admirals and generals typically held strategic cultural preconceptions about their French foe at sea and on land that were good enough to provide an accurate overall frame of reference within which campaigns and battle plans could be prepared with reasonable confidence. When Vice Admiral Horatio Nelson planned the apparently reckless ploy of attacking the Franco-Spanish line of battle in three, then two, columns off Cape Trafalgar in October 1805, he rested his plan upon preconceptions about the enemy that expressed the wisdom of great experience. Nelson knew his enemy.[44]

Even if one elects to restrict the concept of strategic culture to the mind and the emotions, and to treat strategic behavior as activity that can flow from several motives or influences, including the cultural, whence can strategic cultural notions emerge? Strategic culture may be regarded as the zone of ideas, but ideas about strategic matters have to derive from intellectual and emotional interaction with experience, widely understood and however gathered and processed. Since there may be contending orientations and schools of strategic thought, strategic culture or cultures appears existentially as those working "assumptions underlying everyday life"[45] that provide "the emotional and attitudinal environment." The policymaker, the military professional, and the concerned citizen cannot approach contemporary challenges in a strategic cultural void. Human beings are encultured as people who live in communities, and because, alas, those communities are communities for security, humans have no choice other than to undergo a process of strategic enculturation.

Culture is as culture does: explaining and understanding strategic culture in modern strategy

It may appear paradoxical to some readers that an article drafted to explore the salience of specific local contexts for the making and execution of strategy is so abstract. But, in the absence of a scholarly consensus about the meaning and functioning of strategic culture, detailed historical case studies can illustrate nothing much beyond the conceptual apparatus preferred by the theorists in question. Because strategic culture, no less than culture itself, is a contested concept, no amount of rigorous empirical historical enquiry will liberate scholars from the perils of arguable definitions. Nonetheless, there is a useful way to understand the nature and behavioral implications of strategic culture.

Because of its nature and content, strategy attracts "interested" scholarship. In the same way that a British scholar, even though he should be culturally self-aware, cannot help but be British, so theorists and other commentators of every political affiliation can hardly help but be interested in the strategic choices that must affect the public, and their personal, security. Even if a scholar's preponderant interest lies in the value of a book for his professional résumé as the agent of his personal advancement, choice of strategic topic, and the character of argument developed, is likely to express some more or less overt commitment to the value of national or international security. Scholars, scarcely less than politicians and generals, cannot be de-cultured, as opposed to accultured, or somehow rendered indifferent to the practical consequences of strategic debate. Strategic theory should be honest, but it can hardly be disinterested. Even when the strategic theorist seeks evidence and inspiration from temporally far distant contexts, the essential unity of all strategic experience guarantees the feasibility of a current policy agenda. Two modern historians of antiquity address directly the issue of an enduring historical unity to strategic matters.

> Can modern policymakers really derive lessons from ancient warfare?... [T]he advent of modern technology has in no way lessened the strategist's need to adapt his military plan to social and political realities. The second half of the twentieth century has seen a series of startling defeats handed to great powers by warriors whose strategic insight made up for their inferior weapons. Algeria, Vietnam, and Afghanistan are cases in point. Evidently, technology has not replaced strategy as the determining factor in military strategy. *We believe it is precisely the technologically low level of ancient warfare that makes it so valuable an object of modern study.*[46]

Whether or not one agrees with Strauss and Ober – plainly something provided adequate compensation for inferior weapons in Algeria, Vietnam, and Afghanistan[47] – their approach, though obviously self serving to ancient historians arguing for the contemporary utility of their historical expertise, is instructive. In *Anatomy of Error*, Strauss and Ober affirm the universality of strategy in time and place, the value of a policy agenda as a focus and guide for scholarship, and the salience of strategic history, even temporally far distant strategic history, for general strategic enlightenment today.

It can be difficult to talk about the ubiquity and importance of strategic culture, without appearing reductively to claim that strategic culture is the golden key to strategic understanding. For reasons explored here already, strategic culture is not, and cannot be, such a golden key: strategic culture offers context, not reliable causality. A dominant culture need not be associated with a particular national group, some cultural pluralism is possible, even likely. Strategic cultures change over time, albeit probably slowly (otherwise the phenomenon would not merit description as cultural), and strategic choices occasionally are made that contradict the dominant culture.[48]

Six general points serve to help advance understanding of the nature and working of strategic culture.

1   *Strategic behavior cannot be beyond culture.* Strategic behavior can be eccentric from some viewpoints, incompetent, unsuccessful, even contrary to cultural norms, but it cannot be a-cultural, beyond culture. A de-cultured person, organization, or security community would have to be deprogramed even of the process of learning about, and from, his or its own past. The proposition of extra-culturality is ridiculous. It is not at all ridiculous to postulate a person,

organization, or security community which treats a strategic issue in isolation from any context but its apparent own, though even in the case of such extreme pragmatism – which is perhaps a distinctive culture – the actor would need to know enough beyond the issue to recognize a strategic matter for what it is. To claim, for example, that the United States is a pragmatic problem-solving culture, although it affirms the existence of a socially programed broad approach to challenges, does not imply that all American players in the process of strategy-making must agree on the details of the solutions preferred. Overall, culture is context. In the absence of such context events must lack meaning.

2 *Adversity cannot cancel culture.* Strategically encultured Americans, or Russians, do not cease to be so encultured just because they are obliged to function strategically under conditions of severe constraint. Plainly, the grimmer the national circumstance, the less the scope for exercising strategic cultural preferences. Nonetheless, even when the enemy has the initiative, one does not cease to be socially strategically programed. The USSR was ideologically hollow at the core, with the quaint pseudoscience of Marxism–Leninism contrasting ever more starkly with the unmistakable absurdities of Soviet life. That USSR, however, was in notable part the product of the distinctive beliefs and rhythm of Russian culture. Central authority in Russia has collapsed precipitately three times in this century (1905, 1917, 1991). In adversity or in triumph, Russians have to be Russians. Even when Russians behave in an arena unpreferred by their strategic culture, for example at sea, they are apt to behave in ways, and for purposes, that are culturally characteristic.[49] In the 1980s, US maritime strategists, unsurprisingly, sought to find and comprehend a Soviet maritime strategy that matched or sought to offset US maritime strategy, much as US theorist-practitioners of arms control sought in vain to find a matching Soviet concept of strategic stability. In neither instance did the dominant school among Americans appreciate suitably that Russian strategic culture, with ideas and in behavior, organized its strategic world differently. As land animals, Russians conceived maritime operations very much as adjuncts to continental enterprises.

This is not to succumb to the relativist trap of what has been called "ethnic-chic," with particular reference to an alleged sinological fallacy.[50] Chinese, or Germans, do not necessarily respond to strategic stimuli in some noticeably, let alone eccentrically, Chinese or German ways. But Chinese and Germans are socially educated distinctively in their strategic assumptions and, even when they are obliged to act responsively under duress, are likely to assess distinctively their options and the consequences of exercising each of them. The greater the pressure upon an individual or organization to act, and the more hastily the decision is taken, the greater is the likelihood of behavior manifesting what Bathurst usefully calls "cultural instinct."[51] When there is little time to explore the details of the pressing case, the strategist then is obliged to go with what he knows already and to act according to what he judges, and feels, to be correct: "Culture Rules."

3 *Strategic culture is a guide to action.* Strategic culture has to be a guide to strategic action, whether or not the kind of action that culture prefers is practicable.

Moreover, unlike strategic theory, which, as Clausewitz argues, "need not be a sort of *manual* for action" that would "accompany [the future commander] to the battlefield,"[52] strategic culture is on the battlefield inalienably because it pervades the combatants and their military organizations. Soldiers carry their culture with them into battle. It may well be the case that one can locate, as did Johnston with Ming dynasty China, a polity that has two or more cultures, at least one of which is more a set of ideal standards than a practical manual for behavior.[53] However, strategic culture, or cultures, has to be a guide to action as well as comprising, existentially, descriptive reality, notwithstanding the frequent fact that an adverse strategic necessity can subvert or utterly overthrow its influence. The prescriptive character of strategic culture flows inexorably from the nature of strategy. If strategy is about what works in the world to bridge the potential chasm between political ends and military agents, it has to follow that strategic culture is at least contingently prescriptive.

4 *Strategic culture expresses comparative advantage.* For a particular security community the same blend of comparative advantages (e.g., easy access to the open sea) and disadvantages (e.g., absence of "natural" frontiers on land) that yields a dominant strategic culture, also yields a distinction between the kind of strategic activities that that community will tend to perform either well or poorly. This is not to deny the possibility of strategic cultural pluralism, or the (generally slow) evolution of culture under the press of new experience. For example, for reasons that one can at least ultimately call cultural, the United States is relatively poor at the conduct of special operations, whereas Israel, Britain, and the former USSR are relatively competent.[54] If technology and technique, which is to say tactical prowess, were all that there were to the effectiveness of special operations forces, then the US Army's Delta Force, Green Berets, and Rangers, and the US Navy's SEALS, would be as good as anyone's special forces. The problem for US special forces is that the US armed forces as a whole are not friendly to less than wholly regular troops, and that US organizations for strategy-making and execution are not receptive to the strategic and operational promise in special operations.[55] The leading difficulty lies with military cultures and strategic culture. Times appear to be changing in the United States in favor of special operations' capabilities, but cultural resistance to allowing special warriors to wage war in their own kind of way remains powerful.[56]

When dominant security communities are obliged either by adverse circumstances or by eccentric policy and strategy-making to behave in culturally radically atypical ways, success will be unlikely. A security community is unlikely to perform well at unfamiliar tasks; for example the Germans and the Russians in surface naval warfare. After all, the strategic cultures that focus upon land warfare are the cultures pressed by long and painful experience to devote far more resources to continental than to maritime affairs. Also, there are physical reasons why particular communities have evolved their individual dominant strategic cultures. Both Russia and Germany have had strategically chronic problems securing access to the open sea.[57]

A security community can behave in ways massively contrary to the strategic preferences implied by its dominant strategic culture; Britain and the

United States did exactly this, respectively in the First World War and in Vietnam. Even though the Great War was won, general public and much military expert opinion in the inter-war years came to believe that never again should Britain wage mass continental warfare, a form of conflict popularly deemed to be lethally unBritish.[58] In Vietnam, the US armed forces waged the American way of war in accordance with a dominant American strategic culture that favored mechanized combat of all kinds, but they waged a form of war that probably could not succeed.[59] The American offense against its dominant culture, therefore, lay not in the chosen acts of military commission *per se*, but rather in their strategically inappropriate application. To resort to Clausewitz, because the United States could not settle upon a plausible military objective to fit a sound and stable political objective,[60] strategy failed. "Engagements" could not advance "the object of the war." American politicians and American soldiers were punished by American society because they waged an American-preferred way of war in a context where that way of war could not deliver victory, in a cause deemed by many people to be unAmerican. It is common for strategic failure to be punished politically, at home as well as abroad. When that failure is delivered by armed forces directed to conduct forms of war that offend dominant cultural preferences, however, the domestic political backlash is apt to be severe and protracted.

5   *Strategic culture can be dysfunctional.* Strategic cultures can contain strongly dysfunctional elements. It is possible for scholars to be so fearful of the accusation of ethnocentrism that they embrace a cultural relativism that blinds them to evidence of functionally irrational (as contrasted with unreasonable) ideas and behavior. Societies are apt to run high risks of strategic failure when it appears that the broad precepts of a dominant strategic culture knowingly have been flouted. Security communities, however, can have such notably dysfunctional elements in their strategic cultures that, even when polities act congruently with their culture, they are likely to fail badly. In my early writings on strategic culture I believed that strategic culture evolved as an expression of generally successful adaptation to challenge. In other words, the dominant strategic culture of Germany should comprise ideas, attitudes, and habits that worked well for Germans. That logic seemed compelling because, given the long time frame implied by the quality or dimension deemed cultural, it ought to be the case that maladaptive strategic cultures would vanish in more or less bloody a fashion.

On further reflection, the issue of the dysfunctional element in strategic culture appears more complex. To identify the characteristics of, say, a dominant Russian strategic culture is not necessarily to identify a culture that maximizes the prospects for Russian strategic success. It is probably more accurate to claim that Russian strategic culture has contributed massively to the three wholesale Russian/Soviet collapses of the twentieth century and might have yielded an utterly irretrievable collapse in 1941–42. It is possible to argue that Russia's historical survival, notwithstanding periodic catastrophic or near catastrophic shocks, demonstrates that its dominant strategic culture has been good enough to meet the traffic of historical challenges. But also, one could argue that the constituents of Russia have been sufficiently robust as to be able to survive the behavioral consequences of a somewhat self-destructive culture.

The qualities functional and dysfunctional, like concepts of offensive and defensive or stabilizing and destabilizing, can have no meaning out of specific historical context. The machine-mindedess that is so prominent in the dominant American "way of war" is inherently neither functional nor dysfunctional. When it inclines Americans to seek what amounts to a technological, rather than a political, peace, and when it is permitted to dictate tactics regardless of the political context, then on balance it is dysfunctional. Having said that, however, prudent and innovative exploitation of the technological dimension to strategy and war can be a vital asset. At the very least it is important for a security community to avoid being caught on the wrong end of a true technical deficiency, because then one is obliged to find operational, tactical, human, or other compensation on a heroic scale. For example, if enemy tanks are immune to our anti-tank artillery, and if friendly airpower cannot provide reliable protection, then we leave our infantry to their courage, skill, and terrifyingly personally deliverable devices, when confronted by hostile armour.

Strategic cultures obviously pass at least minimal tests of consistency with community survival. Strategic culture, the assumptions that underlie, but do not dictate, strategic behavior, has to make sense to its human agents and client organizations. It is tempting to argue that security communities acquire and have their histories shaped by strategic and military cultures that obviously have worked for them. The proof is existential, if perilously circular. The community endures over decades, even centuries, so, self-evidently, the dominant strategic culture has to have been of net positive functional value – in the past, at least. After all, strategic culture in part is a celebration of community beliefs about historical strategic experience, and no community knowingly is going to enshrine advice for failure. Even when communities celebrate their apparent failures, those failures are apt to be tactical (e.g. the Alamo), at most operational (e.g. Dunkirk, Stalingrad), and are rendered into heroic fable for purpose of public inspiration. Strategic attitudes and beliefs can be simultaneously functional and dysfunctional (e.g. Nazi Germany's racial doctrine), and objectively dysfunctional and irrational, yet culturally inescapable in the short term (e.g., extreme Russian centralization of political and military authority).

6 *Strategic cultures can be variously categorized.* The study of modern strategy has yet to yield careful classification of strategic cultural orientations. Some recent theoretical writing on strategic culture is unhelpful in probing the subject. Instead of focusing on the question of whether ideas and behavior are separable, with only the former being the zone of (strategic) culture, the beliefs and behavior of the human and organizational agents of culture(s) can best be understood with respect to six nonexclusive categories of strategic cultural discrimination.

- *Nationality* (the security community as a whole). Distinctive historical experience encultures peoples more or less differently. Information is received and coded culturally, and strategic choices are made and exercised by people and organizations equipped with dominant national (or sub-national) strategic cultural lenses – bearing in mind that those national cultural lenses have been ground by historically distinctive experience.

- *Geography*. The physical characteristics of each distinctive geographical environment, notwithstanding technological change, yield noticeably distinctive strategic cultural attitudes and beliefs. In the insightful words of J.C. Wylie,

> [T]he connotation of the word "strategy" is not the same to the soldier as to the sailor or airman. The reason for this is elusive but very real. It has to do with the environment in which the conception is set. Where the sailor or airman think in terms of an entire world, the soldier at work thinks in terms of theaters, in terms of campaigns, or in terms of battles. And the three concepts are not too markedly different from each other. This state of mind in which the soldier derives his conception of the strategic scene is brought about primarily by the matter of geography.[61]

- *Weapons and functions*. In addition to being, for example, an American sailor, a person may be a naval aviator, submariner, or intelligence specialist, each of which professional orientation yields what can fairly be called a cultural influence all its own. Special operations forces provide distinctive functions which often should work synergistically with and be complementary to the entire "joint" effort of military power. Nonetheless, there is an unconventional mind-set for the special warrior that has a cultural quality.[62]

- *Simplicity–complexity*. Following the suggestion of anthropologist Edward T. Hall, and political scientist and naval intelligence professional Robert B. Bathurst, one can broadly categorize strategic cultures with reference to their attitude to simplicity and complexity of context. One can classify monochronic, one-thing-at-a-time cultures, and polychronic, everything-is-interconnected cultures. Bathurst argues persuasively that the United States adheres to the former tendency, while Russia/the USSR is an exemplar of the latter.[63] Rephrased, some strategic cultures favor holistic analysis, others are wont to be more Cartesian, dissecting strategic problems for discrete, sequential treatment. There is an empirical difficulty with this candidate discriminator in that most of the strategic-cultural speculation that is sensitive to this test of complexity has focused on American and Soviet/Russian phenomena. We need case studies of other cultures.

- *Generation*. Individuals and age cohorts of individuals are apt to have their strategic worldview shaped by particular historical experience. In addition to being, say, an American sailor who is a career submariner inclined to monochronic decisionmaking, a person also will have his strategic culture influenced by strategic education at the hand of the events that touched his life and imagination with special impact. Such events can be truly personal, or they can be historical context (in the sense, for example, that all contemporary Americans shared a virtual, if not actual, presence at the Berlin and Cuban crises of the early 1960s). Different generations, or age cohorts, will have their attitudes shaped by some different strategic-historical cultural influences. When looking back from today to the Second World War, for instance, it is easy to forget that the policymakers and leading military commanders of the 1939–41 period were nearly all survivors of the Great War of 1914–18, and that they had learnt about modern war from that experience. All people have some strategic cultural equivalent(s) to the example just given, even if it is not as traumatic. This is not to say that matters of age cohort overwhelm or negate strategic culture. It is to say, however, that a dominant strategic culture will be reintegrated by each generation in the light of its own distinctive experience: "Culture evolves."

- *Grand strategy.* For reasons that warrant classification as cultural, strategic cultures and sub-cultures can be categorized according to grand strategic preference. A pattern of reliance upon one or several of the range of instruments of grand strategy (overt military power, diplomacy, espionage and covert action, positive and negative economic sanctions, and so forth) is apt to characterize particular strategic cultures. In practice it is not usually a question of a polity neatly picking the winner from among its array of instruments; rather it is a matter of selecting the appropriately weighted mixture of grand strategic instruments. Particular national level strategic cultures can be approximately categorized according to their pattern of preference when choosing among instruments.

All dimensions of strategy are cultural

The distinctive experience of particular security communities finds social expression in more or less distinctive patterns of enduring assumptions about strategic matters, and those patterns warrant description as cultural. Strategically encultured people will behave in ways influenced by their cultural pattern of assumptions. Strategic culture need not dictate a particular course of action, indeed domestic and external constraints frequently will prohibit such behavior. But the effects of strategic culture will be more or less strongly stamped upon strategic behavior of all kinds. Maritime Britain functioned as a major continental power from 1916 until 1918, but that brief continental performance did not cancel or deny the contrary character of Britain's dominant strategic culture. Actions taken apparently out of strategic cultural character are apt to confirm the rule rather than to change it.

Rarely can conceptual and empirical problems have posed such synergistic difficulties as with strategic culture. If culture is everywhere, then, inescapably, culture is nowhere. Plainly, cultural enquiry in the field of strategic studies is in urgent need of a few working rules. Above all else, strategic culture should be approached as the context that can provide understanding of what behavior means. Unfortunately, however, to repeat, context means both "that which surrounds" and that which "weaves together." It is as certain as anything can be in the social sciences, that Iain Johnston is wrong when he tries to separate ideas from behavior. Culture is as culture does: we are culture, we are part of our context. However, recent scholarship certainly is correct when it points to the real or apparent confusion of cause and effect of culture and policy and when it complains about tautologies between cultural influences and culture in behavior. Particularly strategically encultured polities will not be allowed by objective or subjective circumstance always to indulge their culturally preferred policy choices.

The scholastically effective solution to these dilemmas simply is to command that strategic culture is the realm of ideas and attitudes, which leaves the zone of strategic behavior amenable to assay for strategic-cultural influence. Aside from the minor fact that this methodologically convenient distinction contradicts common linguistic usage, not to mention the best of anthropological theory, it offends against the evidence of experience. Nonetheless, readers are recommended not to pick either this author's, or Johnston's, approach to strategic culture, but rather to move on to a creative accommodation of the two, if that is possible.

11 Force, order, and justice

The ethics of realism in statecraft [1993]

The current Bosnian tragedy, or crime and tragedy in the view of many, highlights in the starkest fashion the dilemmas that moral judgments pose for statecraft. Indeed, the events of 1992–93 in the former Yugoslavia demonstrate all too clearly just how ill-prepared are both politicians and the general public to handle moral impulses, ethical considerations, and genuinely complex conflict cases.

People are confused over the salience of moral judgments to international behavior. For an obvious example, is a polity akin to a moral person? Individuals in society and within a system of law would be at least morally in error were they to observe a crime taking place that they might be able to prevent or arrest, yet choose to do nothing. Should a like standard apply to international "society"? Is there sufficient rule of law in international society for this question even to make sense?

As a general rule, for understandably human reasons, international politics are personalized and moral judgment is leveled at the authors of state policy. Also as a general rule, however, moral judgment plays an all but trivial role in the determination of high policy. That is not to say that ethical considerations are irrelevant to policy choice and execution, but rather that ethical reasoning for international behavior is fundamentally different from the functionally similar reasoning that helps govern individual human behavior.

Public vs. private morality

Public and private behavior are different. Two examples may serve to make the point:

First, the United States, a peace-loving democracy, develops war plans for contingent actions against other countries: American citizens, as private individuals, do not develop plans, contingent or otherwise, for the conduct of battle against their neighbors. Why do they not? The answer, of course, is that they live within a political and legal framework enforced by police agencies that is deemed legitimate. Self-help is not the rule for personal survival, though occasionally it can be the applicable exception. In foreign affairs, the United States is both its own last line of defense as well as being the much favored protector for other polities.

By way of a second example, consider the paradox of Adolf Hitler, a leader whose public behavior expressed a megalomaniacal drive for gain, yet whose private life remained rigorously austere. Hitler's quite genuine disapproval of private vice (drinking, smoking, personal immorality) coexisted with public policies of the utmost criminality (a word chosen carefully for both its legal and moral meaning).

Force, order, and justice are the three concepts that must pervade all discussion of ethics in statecraft. The issues, perennially, are where the emphasis is to be placed and exactly which definitions of order and justice should apply in particular cases. Much of the public debate about foreign policy is unduly fixated upon only one of these three central concepts. To apply the familiar aphorism, a near exclusive focus – upon either the merit, force, order, or justice – is worse than a crime, it is a mistake.

Ethics: alternative approaches

There are two rival coalitions of beliefs which translate into approaches to the ethical dimension of international politics. One coalition of beliefs may be labeled the consequentialist, the other the absolute or deontological. The former coalition holds that the dominant ethical argument over a policy must pertain to its actual consequences. The latter coalition of beliefs in contrast adheres to an absolute ethic that purportedly should govern behavior. The contrast is between an approach that finds right conduct in beneficial results and an approach that discerns right conduct in good intent. The deontological approach finds moral authority in the good that is intended or in the evil that is opposed.

A further distinction of some significance is that between alternative "objects" for beneficial consequences. A statesman seeking good results (an inherently disputed concept) may have in mind good results for himself and perhaps his or her close personal circle, good results for his or her political community, or good results for all of humankind. To ignore the case of policy decisions taken for the personal benefit of politicians, the question remains of whether there is a moral obligation to seek the general benefit of people everywhere, or only the benefit of one's fellow citizens and their friends and allies. In practice the issue is rarely posed so starkly. Nonetheless, the issue is central to, and persistent in, statecraft.

It is the thesis of this essay both that states pursue their interests as best they are able to identify and measure those interests, and that there is a moral and an ethical aspect to that pursuit. By moral I refer to the believed "rightness" or otherwise of means and of ends. By ethical I mean a concern that the consequences of official behavior should be beneficial. It is a sub-thesis of this essay that statecraft cannot be guided by the standard of *Moralpolitik*, because that standard, in fact, cannot provide practical guidance for the strategic world of statecraft.

In effect, a policy dominated by absolute moral judgment would have to be indifferent to success (i.e., to consequences or outcomes). What would matter would be that the policy would be right in an absolute moral sense.

In any particular case of local or regional conflict, the operative question would be, "which side has the right, or the majority of the right, on its side?" As a heroic bid for the realist mantle, such an approach could claim that it is only realistic for the United States to support just causes and that injustice lies at the root of many conflicts. The long-standing "Theory of American Exceptionalism, of the United States" as a (perhaps *the*) "city on a hill," encourages the notion that America is true to herself only when she stands for liberty and justice (if those *desiderata* are locally locatable). Moreover, so the argument goes, the United States succeeds only when her policy follows her moral compass.

The argument just advanced can be presented in a way that invites ridicule. There is, however, much to be said in favor of statesmen consulting their – and the relevant publics' – moral compass. An ethic of consequences that is bereft of moral guidance is an ethic likely to lead statecraft into self-destructive practices (i.e. doing much more harm for the ultimate purpose of doing good than the national or global community will tolerate).

It is not entirely illusory to talk of moral force. People imbued with an ideology that provides moral meaning to their actions are apt to show a determination and resilience in some contrast to actual material relationships. Readers may recall the Napoleonic aphorism that "the moral is to the material as three is to one." Studies have shown, for example, that the indoctrination of German soldiers with Nazi ideology had positive consequences for their military effectiveness in the war in the East. Ideological conviction can make a good army better and can compensate for some deficiencies in numbers and weaponry, but it has its practical limits.

Moral imperative vs. strategy

Prominent among the problems with *Moralpolitik* is the fact that the (moral) imperative to decide and to act is all but utterly disconnected from (means–ends) strategic considerations. One must say "all but" because, as just noted, there is some strength to be found in moral conviction alone. A significant difficulty arises, of course, when ideas of justice and hence of just conduct clash. The case of Palestine springs to mind as an obvious example.

The undisciplined pursuit of virtue through statecraft, however, that is defined from culture to culture, can lead in practice to limitless harm. Was the evil empire of the USSR so evil that any and every means was acceptable to oppose or destroy it? More to the point perhaps, wherein exactly lay the evil of that USSR? Did it lie in the affront that the Soviet Union constituted to humane values (as we define them or as we may believe are, or should be, truly universal)? Or, was it the international consequences of the domestic regime that comprised the evil most relevant to US policy?

The truth of the matter is that all foreign policy is made at home and that the domestic character of a political regime does have implications for the external policies and methods of the state. It is also true that recognition of the sovereign independence of states is a long-standing fundamental principle of international law. It is a very general rule, indeed, that states should not intervene in each others' domestic affairs, almost no matter how atrociously conducted those affairs are judged to be.

A foreign policy driven by a moral imperative would have to sort out just which "society" it was seeking to improve. Would America the Good seek to punish wrongdoing and advance virtue in the society of states, or in the society of all of humankind regardless of state boundaries? In other words, would the objects of morally driven US security actions be politically organized communities or individuals?

Public debate on foreign policy is frequently cast in moral terms. Behind that pervasive fact lies both the reality of our common humanity and disparate cultures as well as the paucity of "strategic" expertise. In our personal judgment we are all authorities about behavior, but few of us are experts in the means–ends issues that pertain to those judgments.

Moral outrage at "ethnic cleansing" in Bosnia leads quite naturally and under-standably to a conviction that something should be done by somebody to stop that outrage and to punish the guilty parties. The moral outrage is unrelated to judgments over the feasibility or overall wisdom of an attempt to stop the perceived evil. But that is not to say that the moral outrage lacks consequences for the likelihood of an operation proving feasible.

Unsurprisingly, the purveyors of essentially absolute moral judgments have a way of finding supporting consequentialist authority. Whether it was moral philosophers debating nuclear deterrence in the early 1980s, or seemingly every-body debating military intervention in Bosnia in the 1990s, each absolute moral stance somehow succeeded in locating technical authorities and arguments that suggested the practical, consequential, wisdom of their predetermined, utterly strategic, positions.

It would seem to be the case that few people are comfortable simply advancing ideas that allegedly are morally correct. In addition it is necessary or strongly desirable to affirm the consequential practicality of favored beliefs. Public dis-course is littered with the claim that "policy 'brand x' is morally wrong and by the way will not work." Rare indeed is the claim that "policy 'brand y' is morally right and by the way will not work," at least when the morally right course of action is being urged. It is not legitimate to advocate policies which, no matter how morally correct, genuinely are recognized to be forlorn hopes. Given the complexity of most international issues and the wide range of opinions available among "experts," it is a poor policy idea indeed not to armor its moral imperative with some pragmatic justification.

Authority for obligation

All traditions in moral and ethical argument require authority for the rules applied and the judgments rendered. Debate over the dilemmas of US policy towards Bosnia has manifested what amounts to a classic array of resorts to authority. Moral authority for the policy preferred, whether that preference be for intervention or non-intervention, is claimed in the name of a choice, or mix of choices, of the following:

- the national interest
- order – local, regional, and/or global
- God
- international law
- precedents
- reason, common humanity, human rights

These six sources of authority for moral judgment and ethical reasoning are neither exhaustive nor mutually exclusive. Statesmen are rarely short of legitimate sounding and not implausible arguments which purport to explain why the course of action selected is correct and probably morally imperative as well. It is a reasonable assumption, amply supportable by historical evidence, that people and polities prefer to do good to doing evil. It is also a reasonable assumption that people and polities are skilled in persuading themselves that that which they are able to do is that which they really want to do, and that that which they want to do is a morally acceptable course of action. Indeed, the expedient circularity in that logic could suggest a greater cynicism than often is the case.

Politicians with actively sensitive consciences typically find that the sources of moral authority most relevant to them can function as pliable counselors rather than as masters. With only rare and arguable exception, politicians as a breed are consequentialist in ethical tradition. To a pragmatic politician, some undesirable means can be justified in terms of desirable ends (the "area bombing" of urban Germany for the intended purpose of hastening the end of the war), while some desirable ends (bring peace, order, and good government to the former Yugoslavia) are judged irrelevant because they appear to be unattainable at reasonable cost.

Every country in every historical period has a few "belief politicians," sometimes with charismatic leadership qualities, who take the moral high ground on issue after issue. Often such voices of conscience have considerable nuisance value to the government of the day. Consequentialist reasoning has a way of appearing weak and shifty when confronted with the assertion of moral certainties. Notwithstanding the Western legal tradition of state sovereignty, there is rather more recent tradition of moral recognition of the rights of man on a global scale.

Strategic argument about means and ends, let alone explicit reference to perceived relative intensity of national interest, can appear thoroughly cynical or pusillanimous in the face of a policy argument that is framed within a moral imperative.

Within a particular political culture there usually is not much useful scope for disagreement over moral interpretation of the facts of evildoing abroad. Over the contemporary case of US policy towards Bosnia, for example, all major camps of opinions agree that: atrocities on the grand scale have occurred and continue; and all local ethnic groups are guilty, but that the Serbs are more guilty than the rest (moral distinctions have a distressing tendency to reduce to issues of quantity).

Where the camps divide is over the question of whether some moral "imperative" to intervene is, or is not, offset by a like moral "imperative" not to intervene in the absence of robust belief that such intervention would do more good than harm.

Clausewitz: common sense over theory

As Carl von Clausewitz advised, theory must never be allowed to stand in the way of common sense. The historic practice of statecraft, on behalf of all polities in all accessible periods, yields a pattern of behavior just as plain as speculative theory about morality and ethics, as a guide to policy, tends to be complex. Statesmen differ in their political culture and in the problems they face, but the practical role of morality and the contribution of ethical considerations has been as steady as its detailed content has varied.

The morality of realism

From Pericles to Henry Kissinger, hard-nosed "realists" have recognized the multi-faceted salience of ethical judgments to their prospects of success as statesmen. Just causes do not triumph because they are just. But just causes have a widely perceived legitimacy that can multiply the capacity of a society for collective action and can facilitate the acquisition of allies.

There is not – and never can be – a rigid set of ethically derived principles, beliefs, and precepts which comprise a realists' – or a geopoliticans' – code. Theory can only prepare the judgment for its specific application to an actual historical case ("shall we use the atomic bomb against Japan?"; "should we intervene militarily in Bosnia?"; and so forth). In other words, historical study and a search for theoretical understanding of how to succeed in statecraft function to educate people rather than to solve unique problems.

What follows are ten historically founded generalizations, framed as advice, that command widespread respect among realist thinkers and doers. These ten precepts are presented for the purpose of highlighting how realist statesmen reconcile the sometimes competing, though often complementary, demands of force, order, and justice. Overall, these points demonstrate how ethical argument pervades realist logic.

Precept no. 1: Distinguish between personal and collective morality. States and other collectives are not moral persons; still less are they moral persons with moral purposes.

Frequently it is affirmed that people must never be treated as an expendable means to allegedly higher ends. In practice, as well as ethically justifiably in theory, individual citizens (albeit statistically and not by certain choice of particular people, and also in some senses willingly) are "sacrificed" for the security of their community. Similarly, some variable, but not arbitrary, measure of communal expropriation deprives citizens of a fraction of their property – the universal phenomenon known as taxation.

Social, political, and legal contexts alter the moral meaning of behavior. "Private" taxation is called theft (or piracy). "Private" defense can be a murder. This is not to suggest that there are no constraints with moral force upon the behavior of polities, but it is to claim that people do things on behalf of their state and society that they would never do, let alone be sanctioned to do, on their own behalf.

The old adage that "necessity knows no law" (e.g., a hungry person will steal, a desperately insecure person will kill) is expressed by this first precept. States will do what they have to do in order to protect their political independence and the physical security of their citizens. Citizens, domestically, generally benefit from abstention from adopting extreme measures of self-help for security.

Precept no. 2: Behave prudently. Because international life if fraught with a wide range of perils, and because foreign assistance against those perils is more or less uncertain, prudence has to be the *Leitmotiv* of responsible statecraft. The prudent statesmen is alert to the dangers of the "security dilemma" – a situation wherein our overly self-regarding quest for national security translates into perceptions of growing insecurity abroad, and hence, spiral-like, inadvertently to new insecurities for us.

But, the prudent statesman also is alert to the damage that can be wrought by wishful thinking. At the present time, for example, a prudent American statesman has to assume that he is in an inter-war, as well as a post-(Cold) War, period. The prudent statesman is both sensitive to the emerging trends of the 1990s and respectful of the historical record of statecraft.

Prudence in statecraft requires consequentialist thinking and can be presented as a moral obligation placed upon government by society.

Precept no. 3: Distinguish between normal and extraordinary times. Properly viewed, "realist" theory for statecraft is not a crass prescription for brutal *Realpolitik*. Quite to the contrary: realist thinkers recognize that in their foreign activities most polities, most of the time, over most issues, behave in a generally cooperative manner in the context of settled rules, regulations, and expectations (even "laws," in some cases).

The realist statesman and theorist, therefore, do not claim that international life is a heroically anarchic *mélèe* for which dark and "dirty" deeds are perennially appropriate. The realist argues, rather, that the polity always must be prepared to take measures in self-defense that indeed would register as large-scale crime were they taken by individuals or private bodies for personal or group advantage.

In extremis, states say that they are willing to punish a state-foe to the very limit of the damage that a nuclear arsenal could inflict – assured destruction of his society. The state threatens to do evil in order to do good. This issue was debated emotionally and none-too-rigorosly in the early 1980's when the churches tackled the knotty problem of the moral tolerability, or otherwise, of implicit nuclear threats *for deterrence.*

Virtually every ethical tradition – certainly those that are consequentialist but even some that are focused upon rules of right conduct – recognizes the sanction of necessity for desperate measures of self-defense.

Precept no. 4: Do "good," if the price is low. To repeat, states are not moral persons charged with promoting some vision of "good." Nonetheless, individuals have consciences, reason ethically, and recognize moral rules of conduct. Theories of more or less popular sovereignty vary in detail from polity to polity, but still it is valid to claim that the institutions of state are expected to function for the net general welfare, certainly domestically and even – provided the cost (American lives, money, reputation at stake) is low – abroad. (This logic abuts the region of national interest analysis that is discussed briefly below.)

Precept four says that realists expect and require states to function to the advantage of their societies in ways that can be presented fairly in ethical terms. This precept also implies that realists are not opposed, or even necessarily indifferent, to states seeking to promote their notions of "good" abroad, if the cost is low (in balance with the lack of intensity of national interest).

Precept no. 5: Avoid "evil" acts, if it is prudent to do so. The logic supporting this fifth precept is the same as advanced precept four. Indeed, these two items of "advice" are listed separately principally for reasons of emphasis and clarity. History, common sense, reason, and even law and some ethical traditions may affirm that necessity knows no law, but purportedly necessary acts which offend domestic, allied, and neutral opinion, and which inflame passions among the enemy, can prove exceedingly imprudent.

The "realist" statesman frequently will find it realistic not to order behavior that offends his conscience. Every circumstance will be distinctive. State behavior that is expedient for the achievement of immediate objectives may be profoundly inexpedient for the securing of longer-term goals.

The classic dilemma arises when statecraft is obliged both to achieve victory in war today, yet to build the basis for a lasting peace tomorrow. It should not be supposed that the temptation to license expedient and ugly acts is unique to "realist" policymakers. In times of crisis and of war it is often the general public rather than the government – obliged to reason strategically in means–ends terms – that is eager to wreak death and destruction upon enemies who possibly have been demonized (evil aggressors) and dehumanized (as by racialist stereotypes).

Precept no. 6: Regard the well-being of the state and order among states as values as well as a means to protect values. States and patterns or relations among states can come in a wide range of possibilities with reference to their promotion of human values. Nonetheless, it is only within a state, with its systematized sets of duties and obligations among people and institutions, that any facsimile of "civilized" life is possible at all.

Raison d'ètât can be an amoral and cynical creed, but also it can help protect the principal vehicle that provides for the security and tolerable liberty of the individual. In the 1930s, for example, the British government preferred, in effect, to condone Japanese and Italian aggression, because the British Empire could not be defended simultaneously against Germany, Japan, and Italy.

Moral choices are rarely between right (oppose Italian imperialism in Ethiopia) and wrong (condone that imperialism). Instead, moral choices reduce to the need to make priorities among a shifting set of more or less unsavory options.

War is not always the worst outcome, but it must appear high on anybody's list of evils. Settled relations of influence among states or coalitions of states, a neutral characterization of order, have positive value making for low risks of war occurring. War can be launched by predetermined design, but war out of uncertainty, even chaos, should not erupt or emerge from a settled international condition (like the Cold War "order" in Europe, as a case in point).

Precept no. 7: Balance power, oppose the growth of immoderate power. Ideally, power is unbalanced in favor of a satisfied polity; as is true today with regard to the temporary primacy of the United States.

Belated endeavors to redress imbalances of power in Eurasia explain the underlying reasons for US participation in the three world wars of this century (two hot, one cold). The "order" identified above as a value (in precept six) is most likely to endure if it rests upon a balance of power or, as suggested here, a healthy imbalance against would-be rogue polities. "Order" by balance/imbalance of power and right conduct viewed narrowly morally, rather than broadly ethically, often will be in a state of tension, not to say contradiction.

There is a raft of American commentators, of several doctrinal persuasions, which divides the world's political players into "good guys" and "bad guys." Not infrequently, political players, useful to the ethically impeccable US mission of balancing Soviet power, did not pass major tests of political correctness. The supreme example of this phenomenon, and of much derivative self-delusion (since Americans psychologically had to deny what they could not afford to admit), was the wartime Grand Alliance of necessity with Stalin's USSR.

Precept no. 8: Recognize that justice can reign only within a system of order, and that order requires the ultimate sanction of force. This precept, as with all plausible realist theory, is not so much an argument as a description of the ways things have been, remain, and almost certainly have to be.

Laws or rules may be formal or tacit, but without them people and institutions cannot know what are their duties and obligations to others and what are their own contingent "rights." The realist commentator probably will not disagree with those from other ethical traditions over notions of "the good life," or even over ideas of right conduct. The realist will, however, insist that judgments on right conduct be tied umbilically to the record of, or to calculations concerning, consequences.

It may be "right" to punish the wicked, but what if such punishment can be anticipated to cost the lives of innocent people on, say, an adverse 10:1 ratio? Realists are wont to emphasize the salience of order to the actual achievement of justice and to focus upon the necessity of the state as the framework within which most human rights must be secured, protected, and advanced.

Theorists of realism are not dismissive of global and transnational challenges to the relevance of traditional state-centric forms of political organization, but they tend to judge extra-state bodies and "rules" as so thoroughly immature and unreliable as to offer enticements more perilous than promising.

The relations among justice, order, and force are intimate and complex. Plainly, an "unjust" order, domestically or internationally, can be sustained for a while by force. An order deemed generally to be just, however, should need the backing of force largely in latent form.

Competent theorists of realism in international politics do not claim, let alone advocate, that states maximize their influence by any and every means available to the limit of practical effectiveness. Instead, realists claim simply that, in the last resort, each state has to make the full range of provision for its own survival and for the future security of its citizens. From time to time such provision must include the threat or use of armed force. Prevention, being vastly preferable to cure, states work day-in, day-out to design and manage a system of tolerable international order that reduces the risks of war.

The concept and policy recommendation of a (favorable) balance of power is a leading idea relevant to risk reduction.

Precept no. 9: Pursue national interests prudently and strategically with a view to consequences. Statesmen endeavor to identify and pursue national interests. Providing state policy is conceived and implemented with due respect for the interests of other polities, success in defense of (legitimate) national interests is ethically either innocuous or praiseworthy. Statesmen are not necessarily indifferent to the plausible characterization of their deeds, or of the consequences of their deeds, as just or unjust. But, statesmen assuredly do not conduct national-interest assessment with principal or even heavy reference to notions of right conduct. As international issues arise, they are not weighed on a moral balance scale, any more than policy responses are classified on a range from most just to most unjust. The literature of political science is weighed down with commentaries pedantically skeptical of national-interest reasoning. In the real world what happens is that statesmen ask "what is the US interest in issue 'X,' how intense is that interest, and what – if anything – might the United States do about it?"

This theorist favors a simple four-level scale: national interests can be of a kind classifiable as (1) survival, (2) vital, (3) major, and (4) other. Survival interests are those that bear directly upon the political or the physical survival of the US polity; vital interests are interests (in principle) plainly worth fighting to protect; major interests are non-trivial interests that it is difficult to persuade oneself or the public should be protected by force; while other interests are interests about which one cares, but about which one does not care enough to pay any very noticeable price in American lives or money.

In 1993, Bosnia lies four-square in the region of "other" American interests. As a general rule, all "right conduct" issues that are fairly strictly such, by definition, fall into category four, "other" interests. Americans do care about atrocities abroad, but they do not care enough to undertake expensive expeditions with deeply uncertain outcomes in order to try to halt such abominations.

Americans are not alone in this; all peoples reason similarly. In reply to the question, "how does one distinguish among survival, vital, major, and other interests?" the most basic useful answer is to the effect that Americans are most likely to be willing to fight, indeed they *should* fight, if the answers to one or more key questions are positive. Specifically, the best test of the true intensity of national interest lies in the answers to these questions: (1) is the balance of power threatened?; (2) are Americans in peril?; and (3) is the US reputation on the line?

It is a matter of historical record, as well as of prudent realist statecraft (conducted competently or otherwise), that the United States will fight to protect its good name as a protecting power (Vietnam in 1964–65), or to restore a favorable regional balance of power (*inter alia*, Persian Gulf 1991). But it will not fight to stop mass murder in Uganda, Cambodia, Iraq, or Bosnia.

Precept no. 10: When possible, exploit politically the justness of a cause. Often, when a government is criticized for failing to attend competently to the political requirements of a policy, what really is meant is that policymakers have failed to make an ethically powerful case. With reference both to the claimed inherent justice of deeds themselves and to the consequences of those deeds, there is always an ethical argument to be made in favor of, as well as against, high policy.

Indeed, there are times when tough-minded consequentialist arguments would be none too persuasive, the strategic prospects looking distinctly bleak. Winston Churchill's heroic public speeches in the 1940–41 period essentially were moral declamations of the necessity of opposing Nazi evil. They were not lectures on grand strategy (just how could Britain, without allies, defeat Germany?).

Prudential, realist statecraft does not make and implement policy according to a moral compass, but it is deeply respectful of the practical benefits of objectives and methods that politically important audiences in the circumstances deem to be just.

Bosnia: Scenario from Hell

There is no elementary formula for policymaking that can generate reliably sound advice for US policy towards Bosnia.

Theory can only help prepare individuals, groups, and institutions to make better decisions; it cannot itself provide those decisions. This essay has sought to outline how ethical considerations and moral argument in general intrude upon statecraft.

If there is any approximation to a moral imperative for realist statesmen, it is the necessity to act to preserve a balance, or a favorable imbalance, of power. Certainly the perpetration of atrocities by foreign thugs would not, as atrocities, attract more than sincere denunciation and perhaps modestly punitive actions on the part of the US Government (witness Sino-US relations, post Tiananmen Square).

Bosnia is the "Scenario from Hell" for the Clinton Administration. The case for US military intervention is moral, and political-ethical, yet massively unpersuasive. The moral case makes itself in the preponderance of atrocious behavior by Serbian thugs; behavior which, in moral terms, should both be stopped and punished. The political–ethical case for US intervention reposes centrally in the unwelcome consequences of inaction. Namely, there would be an accurate perception, that *the* super power, *the* principal guardian of a yet-to-emerge new international order, had failed to step up to a critical test of its leadership and tenacity.

While unfortunately, perhaps, the military case against US military intervention in the former Yugoslavia is overwhelming, that negative case readily lends itself to plausible ethical justification. Broadly speaking, it is not enough merely to intend to do good. In addition, there has to be a reasonable expectation that one actually, on balance, would do good.

While there are people who claim that the United States must do right – that is, protect Bosnian Moslems, punish Serbian thugs – in practice regardless of consequences, such people rarely command the heights of policymaking.

Strategy dicates no Bosnia intervention

Consequential, strategic reasoning over US policy towards Bosnia must advise powerfully against intervention. Bosnia, narrowly, and the former Yugoslavia, generally, comprise a several-sided civil conflict wherein, in real terms, everyone will lose. At present, the United States (and individual allies, NATO, and the Western European Union) is losing prestige because of her unmistakable impotence. That loss, however, is trivial compared with the loss of reputation for effectiveness that surely would follow failure of a serious American bid to shape beneficially the course of local events in the Balkans.

With the exception of a sense of moral outrage, literally every ingredient that tends to shape and propel policy successfully is lacking for the United Sates over Bosnia. Moral outrage is a feeling, it is not a policy. The United States does not know what its objectives ought to be in the former Yugoslavia; it does not know how to secure those as-yet-undefined objectives; it has no allies of note willing to stand up and be counted and make important contributions to the uncertain task; and it would be bound to disappoint the extravagant expectations of all (well-armed) local combatant parties.

Moral outrage or not, "Scenarios from Hell" should be avoided like the plague.

Part IV
War and the future

12 What is war?

A view from strategic studies
[2005]

I believe that the claims and arguments itemized in the following paragraphs are widely shared among those of us who are proud to wear the label "strategist," but since I have no authority to speak for anyone other than myself, this has to be a strictly personal statement. In summary form, I attempt to explain the most vital elements in the strategist's (at least, this strategist's) credo.

First, what is war? The question is easily answered. The heart of the matter was explained very adequately by Clausewitz and by Hedley Bull. The great Prussian tells us that "war is thus an act of force to compel our enemy to do our will," and that it "is nothing but a duel on a larger scale."[1] Bull follows Clausewitz and writes that "war is organised violence carried on by political units against each other."[2] War has many dimensions beyond the political, but its eternal essence is captured by Clausewitz and Bull. If the force is not applied for political purposes, then it is not war. It may be sport, or crime, or banditry of a kind integral to local culture, but it is not war. War, its threat and its actuality, is an instrument of policy.

Second, in what ways does war change? Clausewitz advises that war has two natures, objective and subjective.[3] The former is war's permanent, universal nature. The "climate of war," for example, is inalienable from war of any character in any period. That "climate" comprises "danger, exertion, uncertainty, and chance."[4] By way of contrast, war's subjective nature is ever liable to change; sometimes rapidly and sometimes much more slowly. War is distinctively war, no matter what are the weapons, who are the belligerents, or what are the issues. Many scholars have not been careful in their use of language. War cannot change its nature, any more than my cat can become a dog. If war changes its nature, it becomes something else. This is not a pedantic academic point. If the changing character of war is confused with change in the nature of war, wholly unrealistic expectations are encouraged.

Third, how do strategic studies relate to war? As the dean of American strategists, Bernard Brodie, once affirmed, "strategy is nothing if not pragmatic... Above all, strategic theory is a theory for action."[5] Strategic studies, and therefore "strategists" (i.e., not those who practice and execute strategy), exist because of the peril of war. Strategists are in the peace (with security) business, at least as much, if not more so, than were those "useful idiots" (Lenin) who demonstrated for peace via unilateral nuclear disarmament and the like, during the Cold War.

As pragmatic people, we strategists worked to prevent war, usually by deterrence, sometimes by inducement. I have been in strategic studies for thirty-seven years, but I can claim to have been in peace studies also. I do not concede the "peace" label to folk who are antistrategic or astrategic.

Fourth, how do strategic studies contribute to defense planning? Because war is a permanent feature of human history, an enduring reality or possibility, it has to be treated as a condition to be lived with, mitigated when feasible, and avoided at some costs. It is not a problem that can be solved. Much, probably most, of the scholarly literature on the causes of war is quite worthless, and offers no signal advance on Thucydides, with his deadly tryptich of "fear, honour, and interest."[6] Particular wars can be studied and perhaps prevented, but not war itself. War does not have a great general cause. If it did, some bright PhD student would have uncovered it and written the thesis of the ages en route to collecting a Nobel Peace Prize. Since war, like taxes, will always be with us, our societies have to prepare to wage it, in this substantially self-help international system of ours. We "strategists," proudly and honourably, serve our polities to help them prepare as well as may be for strategic challenges in the future. For more than thirty years I have advised the US Government, especially in the realm of nuclear planning. In the early 1980s, the American Catholic Bishops reluctantly endorsed nuclear deterrence as a regrettable necessity but declined to endorse the means (weapons and strategy):[7] as if one could in good conscience will the end but not the essential means to that end.

Fifth, is history cyclical or arrow-like? Many scholars, including some strategists, are of the opinion that we are now in an era of "new wars," as contrasted with the "old wars"[8] that appeared to fit a misreading of Clausewitz's "remarkable trinity."[9] He did not claim that war was the product of the ever varying interplay among "the people...The commander and his army," and "the government." That was his secondary trinity. The primary trinity was passion (violence, hatred, enmity), chance and probability, and subordination to reason, or policy.[10] One can locate appalling discussions of an allegedly "post-Clausewitzian" present and future. Such a future is not possible, should anyone be in any doubt. What I am leading up to is the arguable, but plausible, claim that today we are witnessing two "transformations." First, there is the narrowly military transformation, propelled predominantly by the exploitation of information technology. Second, there is, or may be, a transformation of war far more broadly. There are persuasive writings that describe revolutions in strategic affairs, in security affairs, and in attitudes to the military. There is much to be said in praise of this literature. Lawrence Freedman, Jeremy Black, and James Kurth, not to neglect Martin van Creveld and Edward Luttwak, have made valuable contributions to this view.[11] I have to register the point, however, that most of us who regard ourselves as professional strategists are not thoroughly persuaded that the "new wars," or the cultural transformation in ideas and attitudes that we can identify today, constitute the whole of the future of war. As a strategist, I believe that attitudes and behavior are driven very much by context and its perceived necessities. In a long era of peace, when our part of the world is not seriously menaced by death and destruction on the large-economy scale associated with interstate conflict (I am trying to avoid major diversion into the murky waters of terrorism and counterterrorism), we are at liberty to indulge our preferences. Wars, if waged at all, should be blessed by the UN Security Council, should be brief and successful, and should be all but free of casualties, both ours and theirs. Some people, who should know better, look out on the world of today, see a cultural and political transformation of warfare, and believe they are seeing a hopeful trend for the future. In fact, all that they are seeing is a relatively benign international political and strategic context. Contemporary history does not require us, we somewhat debellicised Europeans, to be ferocious and bloodthirsty in desperate self-defense.[12] Long may this continue, al Qaeda notwithstanding. Of course, this era, like all such, will come to an end.

A strategist's worldview[13]

The views expressed in this essay lend themselves to terse summation.

1   War, and warfare, will always be with us: it is a permanent feature of the human condition.
2   War, and warfare, has an enduring, unchanging nature but a highly variable character. It follows that history is our best, albeit incomplete, guide to the future.
3   Irregular warfare between states and non-state foes may well be the dominant form of belligerency for some years to come, but interstate war, including great power conflict, will return to trouble us. While we focus, laser-like, on al Qaeda and its franchised associates, the next cycle of balance of power antagonism, between the United States and China, is taking shape.
4   The political context is the principal, though far from sole, driver of the incidence and character of war. Above all else, warfare is political behavior, albeit conducted by military means.
5   Warfare is social and cultural, as well as political, behavior. As such it has to reflect the characteristics of the communities that wage it.
6   War and warfare do not always change in an evolutionary linear fashion. Surprise is not merely possible, or even probable, it is certain.
7   Efforts to control, limit, and regulate war, and therefore warfare by international political, legal, and normative-ethical measures and attitudes are well worth pursuing. However, the benefits from such endeavors will always be fragile, vulnerable to overturn by the commands of perceived belligerent necessity.

A strategist's prognosis for the twenty-first century

Since strategic studies lives on the oxygen provided by history, current and future anticipated, it seems most appropriate that this final essay in the collection should close with some direct commentary on the strategic future. These few paragraphs should be read not so much as specific prediction but rather as illustrative indicators of this strategist's expectations of the future.

US national security policy is driven by the US role in the world. For so long as America is inclined, or obliged, to behave as the global sheriff, as the state that takes in the really dirty washing for the world, it must be capable of dealing with all, and I mean all, kinds of threats.[14] As a culture, America is not particularly adept at thinking inclusively. Instead it likes to make choices, pick a winner, and be conceptually absorbed by the dominant menace of the decade. I will advance the claims, first, uncontentiously, that US national security policy in this new century needs to be able to assist allies to deal with insurgencies and terrorism. Second, eventually the United States will need to defeat political and strategic challenges of the highest order from a coalition of anti-hegemonic great powers. The age of great power conflict is far from over. While we hope for an orderly and peaceful twenty-first century, already we can discern some of the rivalries and issues that could render the future far from orderly and peaceful. Apart from among Islamic jihadists, ideological rivalry has ceased to poison world politics, but recall the lethal triad specified by Thucydides: "fear, honour, and interest." This deadly trio will continue to work hard to ensure that Americans live in "interesting times." Also, US foreign policy is anything but a value-free, non-ideological zone. Although I, in common with many other strategists, am a neoclassical realist, not many American politicians are in our nonideological camp. The United States is not a satisfied, status quo polity.[15] Its public culture, with its values of democracy, freedom, and open markets, is apt to be revolutionary in some parts of the world.

It is usually difficult to think beyond the contemporary context. Even when sincere efforts to do so are made, more often than not the specified future looks very much like today "only more so." Alas, history's nonlinearities, or major surprises, often ambush our expectations. What I am about to suggest are not quite predictions, but they are proposed as serious possibilities worth thinking about. First, I suggest that in decades to come we in what we still refer to as "the West" will look back on these early years of the twenty-first century as something of a Golden Era for world order. That may seem bizarre, not to say eccentric, given the current insurgency in Iraq and the global struggle against al Qaeda. However, this century is likely to witness additional geopolitical and other developments that have serious negative implications for our security. If one complains today about America's crusading zeal, its proclivity for going its own way when it believes its vital interests, defined broadly, are at stake, one could do worse than remind oneself of what may well be coming in the years ahead. Let me offer a few specifics.

- Geopolitically, today's unipolar imbalance of power will probably be replaced by the return of a bipolar balance. China, possibly in de facto or formal alliance with Russia, could well construct and lead an anti-American hegemonic coalition. I expect this to occur.
- If EU-Europe registers irregular progress towards true statehood, NATO will not survive. "Europe," perhaps minus Britain, will be a free-floating

geopolitical player, possibly neutral, possibly not, in the dominant power struggle of the period between the United States and China.

- For the first time since August 1945, world politics is very likely to have to learn to cope with the consequences of actual nuclear use, possibly by an irregular player (a terrorist or insurgent group), possibly by a regional power in desperation. The efforts to prevent and roll back the diffusion of Weapons of Mass Destruction (WMD) are important, worthwhile, but ultimately certain to be futile. The incentives to proliferate will be too serious to be overridden. Those incentives are well covered by, guess what, the Thucydidean trio of "fear, honour, and interest," yet again.

- Finally, we know that the world's climate is changing, in part, at least, because of human agency. We know, also, that it is too late to reverse the process of global warming. Should the climate change abruptly, the geo-political consequences could well be fatal for any condition that we would term, normatively, of world order. There could be mass starvation and, as a consequence, mass migration. Territory, arable land, and water would be at a premium.

***

But today, none of the dire developments just outlined have occurred. The United States, for good or ill, though mainly the former, is unchallengeably the principal guardian of world order. A hostile great power coalition has yet to coalesce, let alone mature. NATO is intact, if strained, and the ill consequences of European super-statehood remain in the future. Thus far, nuclear and biological war are only grim possibilities, whereas the emerging climatic crisis is still only emerging. It is for those reasons that I urge a look on the bright side, because the future almost certainly is going to be a great deal worse than today.[16] In the immortal words of Yogi Berra, "The future ain't what it used to be!"

Notes

Introduction: holding the strategy bridge

1 I grapple with this difficulty in my book, *Another Bloody Century: Future Warfare* (London: Weidenfeld and Nicolson, 2005).

2 C. von Clausewitz, *On War*, M. Howard and P. Paret (eds and trans), (Princeton, NJ: Princeton University Press, 1976), esp. book 2.

3 R. Aron, "The Evolution of Modern Strategic Thought," in A. Buchan (ed.), *Problems of Modern Strategy* (London: Chatto and Windus, 1970), esp. p. 25.

4 B. Brodie, *War and Politics* (New York: Macmillan, 1973), p. 452.

5 B. Heuser, *Reading Clausewitz* (London: Pimlico, 2002), p. 12.

6 See B. Brodie, "Strategy as a Science," *World Politics*, 1 (1949), pp. 476–88; and T.M. Kane, *Military Logistics and Strategic Performance* (London: Frank Cass, 2001).

7 P. Anderson, quoted in A. Koestler, *The Ghost in the Machine* (London: Pan, 1970), p. 77.

8 C. Ryan, *A Bridge Too Far* (New York: Simon and Schuster, 1995). The bridge in question was that over the Rhine at Arnhem. Ryan's book is about the poorly conceived and atrociously executed "Operation Market Garden" of September 1944, whereby Montgomery sought to secure an invasion road into Germany for the single powerful thrust that he urged relentlessly upon Eisenhower.

9 C. Gray, *Modern Strategy* (Oxford: Oxford University Press, 1999), ch. 1.

10 For example, see F.C. Iklé "After Detection – What?" *Foreign Affairs*, 39 (1961), pp. 208–20, for a perfect illustration of what I mean.

11 B. Brodie, "The Continuing Relevance On War," in Clausewitz, *On War*, p. 53.

12 Ibid. p. 89.

13 I answer the critics and discuss Clausewitz's continuing relevance in my essay, "Clausewitz, History, and the Future Strategic World," in W. Murray and R.H. Sinnreich (eds), *The Past as Prologue: History and the Military Profession* (Cambridge: Cambridge University Press, forthcoming).

14 Brodie, "Continuing Relevance On War," p. 54.

15 Heuser, *Reading Clausewitz*, p. 10.

16 Clausewitz, *On War*, pp. 606, 85. A.J. Echevarria II, *Globalization and the Nature of War* (Carlisle, PA: Strategic Studies Institute, US Army War College, 2003), offers an outstanding discussion of the two natures of war.

17 Clausewitz, *On War*, p. 605.

18 A. Wohlstetter, "The Delicate Balance of Terror," *Foreign Affairs*, 37 (1959), pp. 211–34. I offer a critique in my essay "The Holistic Strategist," *Global Strategy*, 7 (1992), pp. 171–82. This was a critical review of the *festschrift* to Wohlstetter's impressive and important professional contribution, A.W. Marshall, J.J. Martin, and Henry S. Rowen (eds), *On Not Confusing Ourselves: Essays on National Security Strategy in Honor of Albert and Roberta Wohlstetter* (Boulder, CO: Westview Press, 1991).

19 See Brodie's somewhat bitter lament in *War and Politics*, ch. 10.

20 C. Gray, "The Continued Primacy of Geography," *Orbis*, 40 (1996), pp. 247–59; "Inescapable Geography," in Gray and G. Sloan (eds), *Geopolitics, Geography, and Strategy* (London: Frank Cass, 1999), pp. 161–77; and "In Defence of the Heartland: Sir Halford Mackinder and His Critics on Hundred Years On," in B. Blouet (ed), *Global Strategy: Mackinder and the Defense of the West* (London: Frank Cass, 2005), pp. 17–35.

21 See M. Desch, "Culture Clash: Assessing the Importance of Ideas in Security Studies," *International Security*, 23 (1998), pp. 141–70; and J. Glenn, D. Howlett, and S. Poore (eds), *Neorealism Versus Strategic Culture* (Aldershot, UK: Ashgate, 2004). For a potent counterblast see Jeremy Black's brilliant analysis in *Rethinking Military History* (London: Routledge, 2004).

22 R.H. Scales, Jr, "Culture-Centric Warfare," *US Naval Institute Proceedings*, 130 (2004), pp. 32–6, is a sign of the times – and a tribute to Aron's insight!

23 C.S. Gray, *The MX ICBM and National Security* (New York: Praeger, 1981), "A Case for Strategic Defense," *Survival*, 27 (1985), pp. 26–40; and "The Influence of Space Power upon History," *Comparative Strategy*, 15 (1996), pp. 293–308.

24 I believe that this is a fair reading of L. Freedman, *The Evolution of Nuclear Strategy*, 3rd edn (Basingstoke, UK: Palgrave Macmillan, 2003), ch. 29.

25 Clausewitz, *On War*, pp. 184–5.

26 A.H. de Jomini, *The Art of War* (London: Greenhill Books, 1992), p. 70.

27 C. Gray, *The Leverage of Sea Power: The Strategic Advantage of Navies in War* (New York: Free Press, 1992).

28 See C. Gray, *Explorations in Strategy* (Westport, CT: Praeger, 1996), chs. 7–9; and especially J. Kiras, *Rendering the Mortal Blow Easier: Special Operations and the Nature of Strategy* (London: Routledge, 2006).

29 R.K. Betts, "Should Strategic Studies Survive?" *World Politics*, 50 (1997), pp. 7–33, was a slightly late, but still valuable, period piece that has much continuing merit.

30 I wince slightly at the title of my 2002 book, *Strategy for Chaos: Revolutions in Military Affairs and the Evidence of History* (London: Frank Cass). In composing the subtitle I was guilty of appearing to ignore the problematic and contestable nature of historical data selected as "evidence." I do not believe I was under any illusion as to the ambivalence of historical experience, but I concede that inadvertently I probably have given that impression.

31 See also D. Jablonsky, "Why Is Strategy Difficult?," in G.L. Guertner (ed.), *The Search for Strategy: Politics and Strategic Vision* (Westport, CT: Greenwood Press, 1993), pp. 3–45; C.S. Gray, "On Strategic Performance," *Joint Force Quarterly*, 10 (1995–96), pp. 30–6; R.K. Betts, "Is Strategy an Illusion?" *International Security*, 25 (2000), pp. 5–50; and R.K. Betts, "The Trouble with Strategy: Bridging Policy and Operations," *Joint Force Quarterly*, 29 (2001–02), pp. 23–30.

32 In my *Strategy for Chaos* I argued that the conduct of an RMA should be regarded as strategic behavior. Three works of special merit on this overwritten subject are W. Murray, "Thinking about Revolutions in Military Affairs," *Joint Force Quarterly*, 16 (1997), pp. 67–76; L. Freedman, *The Revolution in Strategic Affairs*, Adelphi Paper No. 318 (London: International Institute for Strategic Studies, 1998); and M. Knox and W. Murray (eds), *The Dynamics of Military Revolution, 1300–2050* (Cambridge: Cambridge University Press, 2001).

33 Black, *Rethinking Military History*, p. 225.

34 R. Strassler (ed.), *The Landmark Thucydides: A Comprehensive Guide to "The Peloponnesian War,"* R. Crawley (trans.), rev. edn (New York: Free Press, 1996), p. 43.

35 I vented my frustration at the futility of the arms control exercise in a book with an exceptionally uncompromising title, *House of Cards: Why Arms Must Fail* (Ithaca, NY: Cornell University Press, 1992).

36 See H.A. Winters, *Battling the Elements: Weather and Terrain in the Conduct of War* (Baltimore, MD: Johns Hopkins University Press, 1998).

37 M.C. Libicki, "The Emerging Primacy of Information," *Orbis*, 40 (1996), pp. 261–74, strives with mixed success to demote the significance of the spatial dimension to strategy. See my "Inescapable Geography."

38 K. Booth, *Strategy and Ethnocentrism* (London: Croom Helm, 1999); and C.S. Gray, *Nuclear Strategy and National Styles* (Lanham, MD: Hamilton Press, 1986).

39 M. Burleigh, *The Third Reich: A New History* (London: Macmillan, 2000), offers a distinctly cultural interpretation. In a different way so also does R. Bessel, *Nazism and War*, London: Weidenfeld and Nicolson, 2004, which argues fairly persuasively that war was very much what Nazism was all about. The most interesting argument for war being preeminently a cultural rather than a strategic phenomenon is advanced in J. Keegan, *A History of Warfare* (London: Hutchinson, 1993). I am unconvinced, but respectful.

40 I realize that here I am exceeding the bounds of careful scholarship in several ways. If truly pressed I could argue that Hitler's ideas were merely unreasonable, they were not irrational. In order to secure a great continental empire run by and for pure-bred Aryans, Nazi Germany needed to wage war against any and all threats to that vision. To state the matter thus is to stretch the reasonable meaning of a strategic approach, because although there is an awareness of the means–ends nexus, there is certainly no semblance of a prudent calculation of the realm of the practicable.

1 Across the nuclear divide – strategic studies, past and present [1977]

This article was prepared under a grant from the Ford Foundation as part of a much larger work, *Strategic Studies and Public Policy* I would like to thank my colleague at the Hudson Institute, Lewis Dunn, for his helpful comments.

1 Bernard Brodie, *War and Politics* (New York: Macmillan, 1973), p. 64.

2 See Colin S. Gray, *Strategic Studies and Public Policy: The American Experience* (Lexington, KY: University Press of Kentucky, 1982).

3 Prominent among the stronger statements affirming the reality of Soviet civil defense programs is Leon Gouré, *War Survival in Soviet Strategy: USSR Civil Defense* (Washington, DC: University of Miami Center for Advanced International Studies, 1976).

4 Annual Defense Department Report, FY 1976 and 1977 (Washington, DC: Government Printing Office, 1976), p. 1–10.

5 Donald C. Watt, *Too Serious a Business: European Armed Forces and the Approach to the Second World War* (London: Temple Smith, 1975), ch. 4; Michael Howard, *The Continental Commitment: The Dilemma of British Defence Policy in the Era of the Two World Wars* (London: Temple Smith, 1972), chs 5–6; and Richard D. Challener, *The French Theory of the Nation in Arms, 1866–1939* (New York: Russell and Russell, 1965), ch. 6. A usefully detailed study of German rearmament problems is Edward L. Homze, *Arming the Luftwaffe: The Reich Air Ministry and the German Aircraft Industry, 1919–1939* (Lincoln, NE: University of Nebraska Press, 1976).

6 See Watt, *Too Serious a Business*, pp. 31–3. But, it should not be forgotten that in the so-called Peace Ballot of Autumn 1934, 10 million people in Great Britain favored the imposition of economic sanctions against an aggressor so labeled by the League of Nations, while 6 million were willing to endorse military sanctions. This was hardly evidence of a country in the grip of pacifist sentiment.

7 Henry Kissinger, *Nuclear Weapons and Foreign Policy* (New York: Harper and Brothers, 1957), ch. 10.

8 See Colin S. Gray, *Geopolitics and East–West Relations*, HI-2577-P (Croton-on-Hudson, NY: Hudson Institute, January 1977).

9 The B-36 was, of course, developed prior to the success of the Manhattan Project (in part as a hedge against the possibility of failure or undue lead-time slippage with the B-29 and also with a view to transoceanic power projection should Great Britain be defeated).

10 William T.R. Fox *The Super Powers* (New York: Harcourt, Brace, 1944).

11 "Crisis slide" is a concept developed in Coral Bell, *The Conventions of Crisis: A Study in Diplomatic Management* (London: Oxford University Press, 1971), pp. 14–15.

12 On the possible scale of the change in warfare implied in PGM development, see John T. Burke, "Smart Weapons: A Coming Revolution in Tactics," *Army*, XXIII, 2 (February 1973), pp. 14–20; Edward B. Atkeson, "Is the Soviet Army Obsolete?" *Army*, XXIV, 5 (May 1974), pp. 10–16; and James F. Digby, *Precision-Guided Weapons*, Adelphi Paper, No. 118 (London: International Institute for Strategic Studies, Summer, 1975). The appropriateness of the analogy with the machine gun may be appreciated in a judgment by William McElwee: "It was the lavish provision of machine guns to their infantry regiments which was to give the Germans their nearly decisive tactical superiority in 1914." *The Art of War: Waterloo to Mons* (London: Weidenfeld and Nicolson, 1976), p. 304. Even McElwee is misleading: German infantry was not lavishly provided with machine guns compared with British infantry – the Germans simply employed the weapons more intelligently.

13 Good examples of the social scientific value of detailed historical study are Robert Art, *The Influence of Foreign Policy on Seapower: New Weapons and Weltpolitik in Wilhelminian Germany*, Sage Professional Paper in International Studies, Vol. 2, No. 02–019 (Beverly Hills: Sage, 1973); Vincent Davis, "The Politics of Innovation: Patterns in Navy Cases," in Richard G. Head and Ervin J. Rokke (eds), *American Defense Policy* (Baltimore, MD: Johns Hopkins, 1973), pp. 391–406; and Elting E. Morison, "A Case Study of Innovation," *Engineering and Science Monthly*, XIII, 7 (April 1950), pp. 5–11.

14 Thucydides, *The Peloponnesian War* (London: Cassell, 1962), pp. 30–1, 54–5, 93, 154.

15 The *Pax Britannica* was a good deal less robust than contemporary and subsequent romantic navalists believed. A superb discussion is G.S. Graham, *The Politics of Naval Supremacy: Studies in British Maritime Ascendancy* (Cambridge, England: Cambridge University Press, 1965). Also useful is Paul M. Kennedy, *The Rise and Fall of British Naval Mastery* (New York: Scribner's, 1976).

16 Bernard Brodie, *The Absolute Weapon: Atomic Power and World Order* (New York: Harcourt, Brace, 1946), pp. 95–9.

17 Probably the most powerful work in this genre was Emery Reves, *The Anatomy of Peace* (New York: Harper and Brothers, 1946). It is a mystery how an otherwise intelligent man could believe that Stalin might just acquiesce in the voluntary absorption of the Soviet Union into a democratically structured federal world state.

18 See Ernest R. May, *"Lessons" of the Past: The Use and Misuse of History in American Foreign Policy* (New York: Oxford University Press, 1973).

19 Satirical illustration of this point is made in W.C. Hall, "A Medal for Horatius," in Head and Rokke (eds), *American Defense Policy*, pp. 681–3.

20 See Arthur Lee Burns, *"Ethics and Deterrence: A Nuclear Balance Without Hostage Cities?"* Adelphi Paper No. 69 (London: Institute for Strategic Studies, July 1970).

21 Whether or not the professional ethics of the "Christian Knight" (as developed and propagandized by Pope Gregory VII and Bishop Bonizo of Sutri in the eleventh century) had any net moderating effect upon military behavior is very much a moot point. See Hans E. Mayer, *The Crusades* (London: Oxford University Press, 1972), pp. 20–1. The temper of medieval military practice is well conveyed in John Beeler, *Warfare in Feudal Europe, 730–1200* (Ithaca, NY: Cornell University Press, 1971); and Desmond Seward, *The Monks of War: The Military Religious Orders* (St Albans, Herts, England: Paladin, 1974, first published in 1972).

22 See Raphael Littauer and Norman Uphoff (eds), *The Air War in Indochina*, rev. edn (Boston, MA: Beacon, 1972).

23 It is quite possible that the connection between public lack of enthusiasm for the war and daily television coverage is no more substantial than the assertion that it "stands to reason." Brodie, *War and Politics*, p. 290. A powerful charge of systematic bias against a major television network in the United States is presented and argued in Ernest W. Lefever, *T.V. and National Defense: An Analysis of CBS News, 1972–1973* (Boston: Institute for American Strategy Press, 1974).

24 I have developed this argument in "Foreign Policy – There Is No Choice," *Foreign Policy*, 24 (Fall 1976), pp. 114–27.

25 For example, see F.W. Lanchester, *Aircraft in Warfare: The Dawn of the Fourth Arm* (London: Constable, 1916).

26 Bernard Brodie, "The Scientific Strategists" in Robert Gilpin and Christopher Wright (eds), *Scientists and National Policy-Making* (New York: Columbia University Press, 1964), p. 241. Brodie does not advocate a benign neglect of pre-nuclear theory and practice – quite the contrary. See Bernard Brodie *Strategy in the Missile Age* (Princeton, NJ: Princeton University Press, 1959), pp. 19–20.

27 Brodie, "The Scientific Strategists," p. 242.

28 Despite its overwritten features, there is a value in Charles Fair, *From the Jaws of Victory* (London: Weidenfeld and Nicolson, 1972, first published in 1971).

29 Israeli armor was committed piecemeal and naked of infantry or artillery support.

30 A useful, brief appraisal is Jay Luvaas, *The Education of an Army: British Military Thought, 1815–1940* (London: Cassell, 1964), ch. 8.

31 See John Erickson, *The Road to Stalingrad: Stalin's War with Germany*, Vol. 1 (London: Weidenfeld and Nicolson, 1975), p. viii.

32 James Rosenau (ed.), "Moral Fervor, Systematic Analysis and Scientific Consciousness in Foreign Policy Research," *The Scientific Study of Foreign Policy* (New York: The Free Press, 1971), p. 31.

33 Alexander George and Richard Smoke, *Deterrence in American Foreign Policy: Theory and Practice* (New York: Columbia University Press, 1974).

34 Fairly pure statements of the doctrine are George Rathjens: "The Dynamics of the Arms Race," *Scientific American*, 220, 4 (April 1969), pp. 15–25; and *The Future of the Strategic Arms Race: Options for the 1970s* (New York: Carnegie Endowment for International Peace, 1969). Critical texts include Albert Wohlstetter, *Legends of the Strategic Arms Race*, USSI Report 75–1 (Washington, DC: United States Strategic Institute, 1975); and Colin S. Gray, *The Soviet–American Arms Race* (Lexington, MA: Lexington Books, 1976).

35 One is reminded of Brodie's comment on Foch, an earlier propagandist: "The historical knowledge he possessed was always at the command of his convictions." *Strategy in the Missile Age*, p. 41.

36 Edward Mead Earle (ed.), *Makers of Modern Strategy: Military Thought from Machiavelli to Hitler* (Princeton, NJ: Princeton University Press, 1941). Overall, this book merits its enduring high reputation. However, the contributions on Liddell-Hart (chapter 15), on "Japanese Naval Strategy" (chapter 19), and on "Hitler: The Nazi Concept of War" (Epilogue), are notably weak.

37 Ibid., Earle, "Introduction," p. XI.

38 George H. Quester, *Deterrence before Hiroshima, The Airpower Background of Modern Strategy* (New York: John Wiley, 1966); Robert E. Osgood and Robert W. Tucker, *Force, Order, and Justice* (Baltimore, MD: Johns Hopkins Press, 1967); Barry Steiner, *Arms Races, Diplomacy, and Recurring Behavior: Lessons from Two Cases*, Sage Professional Paper in International Studies, Vol. 2, No. 02–013 (Beverly Hills: Sage, 1973). A recent work of considerable value whose authors tend to eschew deliberate and direct identification of pre- and post-1945 linkage, is Klaus Knorr (ed.), *Historical Dimensions of National Security Problems* (Lawrence, KA: The University Press of Kansas, 1976).

39 George and Smoke, *Deterrence in American Foreign Policy*, p. 14.
40 For example, see Edward N. Luttwak, *The Grand Strategy of the Roman Empire: From the First Century A.D. to the Third* (Baltimore, MD: Johns Hopkins, 1976).
41 Brodie, *Strategy in the Missile Age*, p. 28.
42 Ibid.
43 It is not implied here that Brodie has been uncritical towards the schema devised by his strategic colleagues since 1945. Indeed, as Michael Howard claims, he "has remained aloof from all the fashionable fads of civilian strategic analysis"; in "Two serious a matter: politicians and the Pentagon," *The Times Literary Supplement*, September 6, 1974, p. 946 (a review of Brodie's *War and Politics*).

2 New directions for strategic studies? How can theory help practice? [1992]

An earlier version of this essay appeared in Desmond Ball and David Horner (eds), *Strategic Studies in a Changing World: Global, Regional and Australian Perspectives* (Canberra: Strategic and Defence Studies Center, Research School of Pacific Studies, Australian National University, 1991).

1 Carl von Clausewitz, *On War*, Michael Howard and Peter Paret (eds and trans.) (1832; Princeton, NJ: Princeton University Press, 1976), p. 141.
2 Robert Jervis, *The Meaning of the Nuclear Revolution: Statecraft and the Prospects of Armageddon* (Ithaca, NY: Cornell University Press, 1989), pp. 177–8.
3 Barry Buzan, *People, States and Fear: An Agenda for International Security Studies in the Post-Cold War Era*, 2nd edn (Boulder, CO: Lynne Rienner, 1991), esp. pp. 3–12.
4 Philip Guedalla, *Collected Essays, III: Men of War* (London: Hodder and Stoughton, n.d. [but mid-1920s]), p. 47.
5 Buzan, *People, States and Fear*, 23–5. Although, in my opinion, Buzan is wrong in opposing a marriage between strategic and international security studies, he is wrong for the right reason. Specifically, Buzan does not want to dilute the distinctive "military focus [that gives strategic studies both] intellectual and social coherence but also a use-ful – indeed vital – role in the division of labour within the field as a whole," p. 24. That is a good argument for an unsound case.
6 John Chipman, "The Future of Strategic Studies: Beyond Even Grand Strategy," *Survival*, 34, 1 (Spring 1992), p. 100.
7 Ibid.
8 Stephen M. Walt is surely correct when he argues that "obviously, scholarship in social science need not have immediate 'policy relevance'. But tolerance for diverse approaches is not a license to pursue a technique regardless of its ultimate payoff; the value of any social science tool lies in what it can tell us about real human behaviour." "The Renaissance of Security Studies," *International Studies Quarterly*, 35, 2 (June 1991), p. 223. *Ab extensio*, Walt's sensible judgment about tools also must apply to the research product of the tools in question. Walt's survey article indeed affirms the reciprocal value of somewhat detached scholarship and a concern to be suitably, not unduly, policy relevant.
9 See Colin S. Gray, *Strategic Studies and Public Policy: The American Experience* (Lexington, KY: University Press of Kentucky, 1982); and *Strategic Studies: A Critical Assessment* (Westport, CI: Greenwood, 1982).
10 See Dean Wilkening and Kenneth Watman, *Strategic Defenses and First Strike Stability*, R-3412-FF/RC (Santa Monica, CA: RAND, November 1986); Glenn A. Kent, Randall J. DeValk, and David E.Thaler, *A Calculus of First-Strike Stability (A Criterion for Evaluating Strategic Forces)*, RAND Note (Santa Monica, CA: RAND, April 1989). Robert Jervis has identified what is wrong with the RAND (or perhaps more accurately the Glenn Kent) school of defense analysis: "The focus on vulnerability

and first-strike incentives is excessively mechanistic. States start wars for political objectives, not because they see an opportunity or fear that the other side does." "Arms Control, Stability, and Causes of War," *Daedalus*, 120, 1 (Winter 1991), p. 178. This single sentence by Jervis, if found plausible, threatens to unravel the taut, but fragile, theory of stable deterrence which drives much of arms control thinking.
Marc Trachtenberg has offered a similar judgment.

> [F]or the group [of RAND strategists led by Albert Wohlstetter] as a whole, the great problem of international politics, the problem of war and peace, was reduced to the problem of behaviour during times of crisis and after the outbreak of hostilities. The purely military side of war causation, as [Bernard] Brodie later complained, became the focus of analysis, as though war itself were not in essence a political artifact.

"Strategic Thought in America, 1952–1966," in Trachtenberg, *History and Strategy* (Princeton, NJ: Princeton University Press, 1991), p. 45.

11 For my full critique of arms control theory, see Colin S. Gray, *House of Cards: Why Arms Control Must Fail* (Ithaca, NY: Cornell University Press, 1992). Patrick Glynn, *Closing Pandora's Box: Arms Races, Arms Control, and the History of the Cold War* (New York: Basic Books, 1992), also assaults the intellectual center of gravity of false theory. Stripped bare, the argument about arms control reduces usefully to competition between rival paradoxes. The paradox which has propelled modern arms control is the clever complex – even ironical – proposition that cooperation is necessary and possible between antagonistic states precisely because they are antagonistic. See Thomas C. Schelling and Morton H. Halperin, "Introduction," in *Strategy and Arms Control* (New York: Twentieth Century Fund, 1961). This attractive paradox is denied both by an opposing logical paradox and by the evidence of four decades of strategic arms-limitation experience (from 1922 to 1938, and 1972 to the present). The opposing paradox posits that arms control is unattainable by the states which most obviously need it, for the same reasons, and approximately to the same degree, that they need it.

12 A point well made in Jervis, *Meaning of the Nuclear Revolution*, pp. 69–70.

13 From the status almost of a "fringe" idea in the late 1970s and early 1980s, strategic culture is in danger of becoming fashionable as an explanatory tool in the 1990s. See Carl G. Jacobsen (ed.), *Strategic Power: USA/USSR* (New York: St Martin's Press, 1990), pt. 1, "Strategic Culture in Theory and Practice"; Yitzhak Klein, "A Theory of Strategic Culture," *Comparative Strategy*, 10, 1 (January–March 1991), pp. 3–23; and, for a yet more imperial scope, Michael Vlahos, "Culture and Foreign Policy," *Foreign Policy*, 82 (Spring 1991), 59–78. As with theories of bureaucratic politics and geopolitics, the line between powerful tool and reductionist strait-jacket is likely to prove a fine one for strategic culture.

14 Robert M. Gates, "American Leadership in a New World," prepared address to the American Publishers' Association, May 7, 1991, p. 3.

15 Barry R. Posen and Stephen Van Evera, "Defense Policy and the Reagan Administration: Departure from Containment," *International Security*, 8, 1 (Summer 1983), p. 42. Jeffrey Record was no less critical and rather less restrained in his language:

> In sum, the Reagan Administration's declared military strategy is not only militarily defective. It is also foolishly ambitious, betraying an unbridgeable abyss between aspirations and resources. Indeed, if strategy is the calculated relationship of ends and means, the strategy of worldwide war is not a strategy at all.

"Jousting with Unreality: Reagan's Military Strategy," *International Security*, 8, 3 (Winter 1983–84), p. 19.

16 Both at the time in the mid 1980s and today in retrospect, I was and remain convinced that much of the criticism of the global war planning (for deterrence), which found its way very regularly into the pages of *International Security*, was narrowly continentalist

in viewpoint and thoroughly inappropriate for the mixed maritime-continental, and Atlantic-Pacific, alliance led by the United States. See Colin S. Gray, *Maritime Strategy, Geopolitics, and the Defense of West* (New York: Ramapo Press, 1986); and, for the long view, *The Leverage of Sea Power: The Strategic Advantage of Navies in War* (New York: Free Press, 1992). The views of which I was and remain critical are well represented in the following articles: John J. Mearsheimer, "Why the Soviets Can't Win Quickly in Central Europe," *International Security*, 7, 1 (Summer 1982), pp. 3–39; Barry R. Posen, "Inadvertent Nuclear War? Escalation and NATO's Northern Flank," *International Security*, 7, 2 (Fall 1982), pp. 28–54; Joshua M. Epstein, "Horizontal Escalation: Sour Notes of a Recurrent Theme," *International Security*, 8, 3 (Winter 1983–84), pp. 19–31; and John J. Mearsheimer, "A Strategic Misstep: The Maritime Strategy and Deterrence in Europe," *International Security*, 11, 2 (Fall 1986), pp. 3–57.

17 A useful, interpretation friendly to the strategy shifts cited here is Samuel P. Huntington, "U.S. Defense Strategy: The Strategic Innovations of the Reagan Years," in Joseph Kruzel (ed.), *American Defense Annual, 1987–1988* (Lexington, MA: Lexington Books, 1987), pp. 23–43.

18 See Albert Carnesale and Charles Glaser, "ICBM Vulnerability: The Cures Are Worse Than the Disease," *International Security*, 7, 1 (Summer 1982), pp. 70–86; and Charles L. Glaser, "Why Even Good Defenses May Be Bad," *International Security*, 9, 2 (Fall 1984), pp. 92–123. A useful book-length study critical of the Reagan years is Daniel Wirls, *Buildup: The Politics of Defense in the Reagan Era* (Ithaca, NY: Cornell University Press, 1992).

19 Walt, "Renaissance of Security Studies," p. 220. Emphasis added.

20 Stephen M. Walt, *The Origins of Alliances* (Ithaca, NY: Cornell University Press, 1987), p. 282.

21 For reasons that I present in detail in my *Leverage of Sea Power*, one always has to beware of grand theorists who are willing to leap from general (i.e., most cases) truth to specific historical judgment.

22 In company with global weather, the Israeli-Palestinian conflict, and the intercommunal strife in Northern Ireland, the causes of war/conditions for peace will long continue to frustrate the earnest seeker after "truth." The state-of-the-art may be sampled in Robert I. Rotberg and Theodore K. Rabb (eds), *The Origin and Prevention of Major Wars* (Cambridge: Cambridge University Press, 1989); Jack S. Levy, "The Causes of War: A Review of Theories and Evidence," in Philip E. Tetlock, Jo L. Husbands, Robert Jervis, Paul C. Stern, and Charles Tilly (eds), *Behaviour, Society, and Nuclear War* (New York: Oxford University Press, 1989), pp. 209–333; and Trachtenberg, *History and Strategy*, ch. 2, "The Coming of the First World War: A Reassessment."

23 Schelling and Halperin, for example, lamented that "sophistication [that is, *their* world view] comes slowly [to others!]." *Strategy and Arms Control*, p. 142.

24 Kurt Gottfried and Bruce G. Blair (eds), *Crisis Stability and Nuclear War* (New York: Oxford University Press, 1988), e.g., is a worthy collaborative effort which falls into wisdom occasionally (e.g., p. 160), but overall succeeds in adhering to the erroneous notion of a clockwork strategic universe.

25 The outstanding recent analysis is Robert Gordon Kaufman, *Arms Control During the Pre-Nuclear Era: The United States and Naval Limitation Between the Wars* (New York: Columbia University Press, 1990). The full cost of the inter-war naval arms limitation venture, however, can only be appreciated with reference to the consequences for the Royal Navy in the Second World War. See Correlli Barnett, *Engage the Enemy More Closely: The Royal Navy in the Second World War* (New York: Norton, 1991), pp. 22, 24, 43, 64–5, 78, and 218.

26 This Napoleonic concept is endorsed as a U.S. "strategic principle" in Gen. Colin L. Powell, chairman, Joint Chiefs of Staff, *National Military Strategy, 1992* (Washington, DC: Joint Chiefs of Staff, 1992), p. 10.

> Once a decision for military action has been made half-measures and confused objectives extract a severe price in the form of a protracted conflict which can cause needless waste of human lives and material resources, a divided nation at home, and defeat.

There speaks the authentic professional military voice of the junior officers of the Vietnam years.

27 See Clausewitz, *On War*, 88, for the original thought.

28 Even among German politicians there is widespread recognition that the CSCE process has none of the attributes critical for the successful functioning of a security system. If one lists the many reasons why NATO has worked as well as it has, one finds that the CSCE enjoys no overlap with that list.

29 Classic errors in the analysis of collective security are perpetrated in Charles A. Kupchan and Clifford A. Kupchan, "Concepts, Collective Security, and the Future of Europe," *International Security*, 16, 1 (Summer 1992), pp. 114–61.

30 On levels of analysis see the structure and argument of Edward N. Luttwak, *Strategy: The Logic of War and Peace* (Cambridge, MA: Harvard University Press, 1987). Luttwak overworks the "paradoxical logic" which he suggests, correctly, pervades "the entire realm of strategy" (p. 4). This book, nonetheless, is a dazzling achievement.

31 By analogy, a person who is incompetent but very energetic is likely to wreak far more harm than is someone who is incompetent but lazy.

32 Herman Kahn, *On Thermonuclear War*, 2nd edn (1960; New York: Free Press, 1969), p. 7, n. 2.

33 The terms of the INF treaty constituted a direct challenge to the equality-of-risk idea so central to NATO's political cohesion, they were an affront to German strategic preferences, and they endorsed a trend – of denuclearization – which undermined the political legitimacy of NATO strategy.

34 The various methodologies that aid force planning could suggest to the contrary, but do not be fooled. Henry C. Bartlett, "Approaches to Force Planning," *Naval War College Review*, 37, 3 (May–June 1985), pp. 37–48; Robert P. Haffa, Jr, *Rational Methods, Prudent Choices: Planning U.S. Forces* (Washington, DC: National Defense University Press, 1988); and Henry C. Bartlett and G. Paul Holman, Jr, "Strategy as a Guide to Force Planning," *Naval War College Review*, 41, 4 (Autumn 1988), pp. 15–25, all have value but share a lack of convincing grasp of the essentially indeterminate nature of the activity of force planning.

35 Winston S. Churchill, *The World Crisis, 1911–1918*, vol. 2 [of 2] (London: Odhams Press, 1938), p. 1442.

36 These themes pervade my book, *War, Peace, and Victory: Strategy and Statecraft for the Next Century* (New York: Simon and Schuster, 1990).

37 Geoffrey Till, *Maritime Strategy and the Nuclear Age* (London: Macmillan Press, 1982), p. 224.

38 Correlli Barnett, *The Swordbearers: Studies in Supreme Command in the First World War* (London: Eyre and Spottiswoode, 1953), p. 195.

39 See Ken Booth's "classic," *Strategy and Ethnocentrism* (London: Croom Helm, 1979).

40 Arthur J. Marder, *From the Dardanelles to Oran: Studies of the Royal Navy in War and Peace, 1915–1940* (London: Oxford University Press, 1974), 61.

41 See Scott D. Sagan, "The Origins of the Pacific War," *Journal of Interdisciplinary History* 18, 4 (Spring 1988): 905–6, 917.

42 R. Coupland, *The War Speeches of William Pitt the Younger* (Oxford: Clarendon Press, 1915), p. 16.

43 Neta C. Crawford could not be more wrong than in her claim that the current new (or fourth) "wave" of theorizing in strategic studies, *allegedly unlike* the second and third "waves" (1954–66 and 1971–early 1980s, respectively), has been stimulated by external events. "Once and Future Security Studies," *Security Studies*, 1, 2 (Winter 1991),

p. 291. Second-wave theorizing was kick-started by the Eisenhower administration's nuclear-heavy "new look" in defense policy and strategy, while third wave theorizing was energized by SALT 1, failure in Vietman, and the rise of the Soviet Union apparently to true superpower status.

44 For example, John J. Mearsheimer, "Back to the Future: Instability in Europe After the Cold War," *International Security*, 15, 1 (Summer 1990), p. 5–56.

45 The self-serving convenience of this belief has not escaped my notice.

46 Walt, "Renaissance of Strategic Studies"; Buzan, *People, States and Fear*; Chipman, "Future of Strategic Studies"; and Crawford, "Once and Future Security Studies."

47 The subjectivity of this judgment is as obvious as it is inescapable. There was a brief flurry of interest in strategy in the United States in the mid-to-late 1980s, but the fortuitous ending of the Cold War drew a political veil over that phenomenon. Strategic thinking comes naturally neither to the U.S. government nor to the American so-called strategic studies community. Some of the reasons why are discussed in Aaron L. Friedberg, "Can the United States Act Strategically?" *The Washington Quarterly*, 14, 1 (Winter 1991), pp. 5–23.

48 Gates, "American Leadership in a New World," p. 3. The idea of a "New World Order" lies buried in the sands of a Middle East which cannot be reordered even by a United States proven to be strong in battle, if not necessarily wise in war.

49 John Terraine, "Lessons of Coalition War: 1914 and 1939," *RUSI Journal*, 134, 2 (Summer 1989), p. 62.

50 See Anthony Clayton, *The British Empire as a Superpower, 1919–39* (Athens, GA: University of Georgia Press, 1986); and John Robert Ferris, *Men, Money, and Diplomacy: The Evolution of British Strategic Policy, 1919–26* (Ithaca, NY: Cornell University Press, 1989).

51 Francis Fukuyama, "The End of History?" *The National Interest*, 16 (Summer 1989), pp. 3–18; and *The End of History and the Last Man* (New York: Simon and Schuster, 1992).

52 Edward N. Luttwak, "An Emerging Postnuclear Era?" *The Washington Quarterly*, 11, 1 (Winter 1988), pp. 5–15.

53 John Mueller, *Retreat from Doomsday. The Obsolescence of Major War* (New York: Basic Books, 1989).

54 Martin van Creveld, *The Transformation of War* (New York: Free Press, 1991).

55 Crawford, "Once and Future Security Studies," p. 309.

56 Ibid., p. 307.

57 Clausewitz, *On War*, p. 141.

58 Keith B. Payne, *Missile Defense in the 21st Century: Protection Against Limited Threats, Including Lessons from the Gulf War* (Boulder, CO – Westview Press, 1991), pp. 113–26, is very much to the point, as – in much broader perspective – is Richard K. Betts, "The Concept of Deterrence in the Postwar Era," *Security Studies* 1, 1 (Autumn 1991), pp. 25–36.

59 Lawrence Freedman, *The Evolution of Nuclear Strategy* (London: Macmillan, 1981), pp. xvi. Jervis circles the same point in *Meaning of the Nuclear Revolution*, p. 78.

60 For example, as in Colin S. Gray, "From Defense Philosophy to Force Planning: The Strategic Forces," *Defence Analysis*, 7, 4 (December 1991), p. 363–72.

3 History for strategists: British sea power as a relevant past [1994]

1 See Andrew D. Lambert, *The Crimean War: British Grand Strategy against Russia, 1853–56* (Manchester, UK: Manchester UP, 1990), ch. 24. The Russian side is handled admirably in John Shelton Curtiss, *Russia's Crimean War* (Durham, NC: Duke UP, 1979).

2 Geoffrey Till, *Maritime Strategy and the Nuclear Age* (London: Macmillan, 1982), pp. 224–5.

3 John Francis Guilmartin, Jr, *Gunpowder and Galleys: Changing Technology and Mediterranean Warfare at Sea in the Sixteenth Century* (Cambridge. UK: Cambridge University Press, 1974), ch. 1, "The Mahanians' Fallacy."

4 Alfred Thayer Mahan, *The Influence of Sea Power upon History, 1660–1783* (London: Methuen, 1965; first published in 1890), pp. viii and v, resp.

5 See John H. Pryor, *Geography, Technology, and War: Studies in the Maritime History of the Mediterranean, 649–1571* (Cambridge, UK: Cambridge University Press, 1988), pp. 57–86.

6 Geoffrey Marcus, *Quiberon Bay: The Campaign in Home Waters, 1759* (London: Hollis and Carter, 1960), p. 66. In another work, Marcus called the close blockade of Brest "a revolution in naval strategy": *Heart of Oak: A Survey of British Sea Power in the Georgian Era* (London: Oxford University Press, 1975), p. 20.

7 J.F.C. Fuller argued, "[t]he main bases and the main theatre of war were fixed by geography and logistics, and no juggling with fronts could alter this..." *The Conduct of War, 1789–1961: A Study of the Impact of the French, Industrial, and Russian Revolutions on War and Its Conduct* (London: Eyre & Spottiswoode, 1961), p. 162. Also see John Terraine, *The Western Front, 1914–18* (London: Hutchinson, 1964), pp. 90–113.

8 See David F. Trask, *The United States in the Supreme War Council: American War Aims and Inter-Allied Strategy, 1917–1918* (Middletown, CT: Wesleyan University Press, 1961), pp. 13, 146.

9 Carl von Clausewitz, *On War* Michael Howard and Peter Paret (eds and trans) (Princeton, NJ: Princeton University Press, 1976; first published in 1832), p. 204. Emphasis in original.

10 See Josiah Ober, *Fortress Attica: Defense of the Athenian Land Frontier, 404–332 BC* (Leiden: E.J. Brill, 1985), pp. 36–7.

11 Eric Grove, *The Future of Sea Power* (Annapolis, MD: Naval Institute Press, 1990), p. 138.

12 Julian S. Corbett, *Some Principles of Maritime Strategy* (Annapolis, MD: Naval Institute Press, 1988; first published in 1911).

13 Halford J. Mackinder, *Democratic Ideals and Reality* (New York: Norton, 1962; first published in 1942), pp. 241ff. See W.H. Parker, *Mackinder: Geography as an Aid to Statecraft* (Oxford: Clarendon Press, 1982), ch. 6; and Geoffrey Parker, *Western Geopolitical Thought in the Twentieth Century* (New York: St Martin's Press, 1985), ch. 3.

14 The clearest exposition is Robert Jervis, *The Meaning of the Nuclear Revolution: Statecraft and the Prospect of Armageddon* (Ithaca, NY: Cornell University Press, 1989), ch. 1.

15 Mackinder, *Democratic Ideals and Reality*, p. 242, n. 13.

16 Writing of his British fellow-countrymen in the nineteenth century, Mackinder said: "They knew what it was to enjoy sea-power, the freedom of the ocean, but they forgot that sea-power is, in large measure, dependent on the production of the base on which it rests, and that East Europe and the Heartland would make a mighty sea base." Ibid., p. 138.

17 Chester G. Starr, Jr, *The Roman Imperial Navy, 31 BC–AD 324* (Westport, CT: Greenwood Press, 1975; first published in 1941), p. 167. For two centuries the Roman Navy kept the principal commercial routes in the Mediterrarean clear of what had been the perennial scourge of piracy, p. 173. Not until the nineteenth century was the Mediterranean again to be as free of pirates as it was in the first two centuries of the Christian era.

18 See Ronald Lewin, *Hitler's Mistakes* (London: Leo Cooper, 1984), pp. 113–19.

19 Quoted in John Terraine, *The Road to Passchendaele: The Flanders Offensive of 1917 – A Study in Inevitability* (London: Leo Cooper, 1984: first published in 1977), p. 10. Emphasis added.

20 Martin Wight. *Power Politics* (New York: Holmes and Meier. 1978), p. 78. Wight is simply interpreting Mackinder, he is not endorsing the proposition.
21 Quoted in Adm. Sir Peter Gretton, *Maritime Strategy: A Study of Defense Problems* (New York: Praeger, 1965), p. 43.
22 Wight, *Power Politics*, p. 77, n. 20.
23 Mahan, *Influence of Sea Power upon History, 1660–1783* p. 29, n. 4.
24 "What if the Great Continent, the Whole World-Island or a large part of it, were at some future time to become a single and united base of sea-power? Would not the other insular bases be outbuilt as regards ships and outmanned as regards seamen? ... must we not still reckon with the possibility that a large part of the Great Continent might some day be united under a single sway, and that an invincible sea-power might be based upon it?" Mackinder, *Democratic Ideals and Reality*, p. 70, n. 13.
25 The idea of a "natural" as contrasted with an artificial, sea power, was developed in Adm. Sir Herbert Richmond, *Sea Power in the Modern World* (London: G. Bell, 1934), ch.1.
26 The Persian Empire was a great naval power, not a natural sea power in Richmond's sense.
27 See Halford J. Mackinder, *Britain and the British Seas* (Oxford: Clarendon Press, 1915; first published in 1906), chs 1, 18.
28 Cited in Norman Gibbs, "British Strategic Doctrine, 1918–1939," in Michael Howard (ed.), *The Theory and Practice of War* (London: Cassell, 1965), p. 190.
29 An outstanding recent discussion is N.A.M. Rodger, "The Continental Commitment in the Eighteenth Century," in Lawrence Freedman, Paul Hayes, and Robert O'Neill (eds), *War, Strategy, and International Politics: Essays in Honour of Sir Michael Howard* (Oxford: Clarendon Press. 1992), pp. 39–53.
30 Winston S. Churchill, *The Second World War, Vol. 1: The Gathering Storm* (London: Guild Publishing, 1985; first published in 1948), pp. 186, 187.
31 Piers Mackesy, "Problems of an Amphibious Power: Britain against France, 1793–1815," in Merrill L. Bartlett (ed.), *Assault from the Sea: Essays on the History of Amphibious Warfare* (Annapolis, MD: Naval Institute Press, 1983), p. 61.
32 Daniel A. Baugh, "British Strategy during the First World War in the context of Four Centuries: Blue-Water versus Continental Commitment," in Daniel M. Masterton (ed.), *Naval History: The Sixth Symposium of the US Naval Academy* (Wilmington, DE: Scholarly Resources, 1987), pp. 85–110.
33 Corbett, *Some Principles of Maritime Strategy*, pt. 1, chs 3–6; and Basil Liddell Hart, *The British Way in Warfare* (London: Faber, 1932). For a powerful critique of "the British [limited, maritime] way in warfare" thesis, see Michael Howard (ed.), "The British Way in Warfare: A Reappraisal," *The Causes of Wars and Other Essays* (London: Unwin Paperbacks. 1984; first published in 1983), pp. 189–207. David French, *The British Way in Warfare, 1688–2000* (London: Unwin Hyman, 1990), is workmanlike.
34 For Haig's manpower problems on the eve of the German Spring Offensive of 1918, see John Terraine, *Douglas Haig: the Educated Soldier* (London: Hutchinson, 1963), ch. 11; but see Tim Travers, *How the War was Won: Command and Technology in the British Army on the Western Front, 1917–1918* (London: Routledge, 1992), p. 36, for a much less sympathetic opinion.
35 John Terraine, *A Time for Courage: The Royal Air Force in the European War, 1939–1945* (New York: Macmillan, 1985), p. 682.
36 See Herbert Rosinski's brilliant 1946 essay on "New York The Strategy of Japan," in Rosinski (ed.), *The Development of Naval Thought* (Newport, RI: Naval War College Press, 1977), ch. 6.
37 See Piers Mackesy, *The War in the Mediterranean, 1803–1810* (Westport, CT: Greenwood Press, 1981; first published in 1957); Donald D. Horward, "British Sea power and Its Influence Upon the Peninsular War (1808–1814)," *Naval War College*

Review, 31, 2 (Fall 1978), pp. 54–71; and David Syrett, "The Role of the Royal Navy in the Napoleonic Wars After Trafalgar, 1805–1814," *Naval War College Review*, 32, 5 (September–October 1979), pp. 71–84.

38 Paul M. Kennedy, *The Rise and Fall of British Naval Mastery* (New York: Scribner's, 1976), p. 147.

39 See Gerald S. Graham, *The Politics of Naval Supremacy: Studies in British Maritime Ascendancy* (Cambridge, UK: Cambridge University Press, 1963), pp. 96–125; and C.J. Bartlett, "Statecraft, Power and Influence," *Britain Pre-eminent: Studies of British World Influence in the Nineteenth Century* (New York: St Martin's Press, 1969), pp. 172–93.

40 Parker, *Mackinder* p. 175, n. 13.

41 John Terraine, "Lessons of Coalition Warfare: 1914 and 1939," *RUSI Journal*, 134, 2 (Summer 1989), p. 62.

4 Why strategy is difficult [1999]

1 J.F. Lazenby, *Hannibal's War: A History of the Second Punic War* (Warminster, UK: Aris and Phillips, 1978), p. 275.

2 Carl von Clausewitz, *On War*, Michael Howard and Peter Paret (eds and trans.) (Princeton, NJ: Princeton University Press, 1976), pp. 566–73. See also Antulio J. Echevarria II, "Clausewitz: Toward a Theory of Applied Strategy," *Defense Analysis*, 11, 3 (December 1995), pp. 229–40.

3 Clausewitz, *On War*, p. 204; Antoine Henri de Jomini, *The Art of War* (London: Greenhill Books, 1992), p. 70.

4 This argument is the central theme of Colin S. Gray in *Modern Strategy* (Oxford: Oxford University Press, 1999).

5 Clausewitz, *On War*, pp. 119–21.

6 Samuel B. Griffith, *On Guerrilla Warfare* (New York: Praeger, 1961), p. 31.

7 Rudolf von Caemmerer, *The Development of Strategical Science During the 19th Century*, Karl von Donat (trans.) (London: Hugh Rees, 1905), pp. 171–2.

8 Holger H. Herwig, *The First World War: Germany and Austria-Hungary, 1914–1918* (London: Arnold, 1997), pp. 96–106, is excellent.

9 Williamson Murray, "Does Military Culture Matter?" *Orbis*, 43, 1 (Winter 1999), p. 37.

10 See Martin van Creveld, *Fighting Power: German and U.S. Army Performance, 1939–1945* (Westport, CT: Greenwood, 1982).

11 Clausewitz, *On War*, p. 128.

12 For lengthy musings, see Edward N. Luttwak, *Strategy: The Logic of War and Peace* (Cambridge: Harvard University Press, 1987). Luttwak argues that what works well today may not tomorrow exactly because it worked well today. Because Clausewitz insists war is essentially a duel, one may face an enemy capable of reacting creatively to one's moves and perhaps even anticipate them.

13 Caemmerer, *Strategical Science*, p. 276.

14 Clausewitz, *On War*, p. 178.

15 This is a fair reading of the underlying premise of airpower theory. See Giulio Douhet, *The Command of the Air*, Dino Ferrari (trans.) (New York: Arno Press, 1972), p. 50; and John A. Warden III, "Success in Modern War: A Response to Robert Pape's *Bombing to Win*," *Security Studies*, 7, 2 (Winter 1997/98), pp. 174–85. To the air strategist targeting is strategy.

16 Caemmerer, *Strategical Science*, p. 275.

17 André Beaufre, *An Introduction to Strategy* (London: Faber and Faber, 1965), p. 22.

18 Clausewitz, *On War*, p. 75.

19 Lawrence Freedman, *The Evolution of Nuclear Strategy* (New York: St Martin's Press, 1981), p. 433.

20 Clausewitz, *On War*, p. 75.
21 Dominick Graham and Shelford Bidwell, *Coalitions, Politicians and Generals: Some Aspects of Command in Two World Wars* (London: Brassey's, 1993), chs 9–16, is pitilessly Anglo-Canadian in its critical view of Eisenhower as commander and serves as a partial corrective to the "patriotic" school of military history of the European campaign that finds undue favor among American writers such as Stephen E. Ambrose in *The Victors: Eisenhower and His Boys: The Men of World War II* (New York: Simon and Schuster, 1998).

5 From Principles of Warfare to Principles of War: a Clausewitzian solution [2005]

1 Carl von Clausewitz, *On War*, Michael Howard and Peter Paret (eds and trans.) (Princeton, NJ: Princeton University Press, 1976), p. 578.
2 Since there is no point to tactical and operational activity save that provided by strategy in support of policy, weakness in the latter is certain to result in American military effort failing to secure its just political rewards. In war after war, military victory, at least success, had disappointing consequences. Consider the course of the two World Wars, of Vietnam in 1968–70, and the two wars with Iraq. It is commonplace to observe that in the twentieth century Germany was very proficient, indeed was unmatched, at fighting, but was exceedingly incompetent at the strategic and political conduct of war. To a lesser degree, the same judgment can be made about the United States. The fact that the United States usually was on the winning side tends to obscure the merit in this uncomfortable comparison.
3 See Russell F. Weigley, *The American Way of War: A History of United States Military Strategy and Policy* (New York: Macmillan, 1973); Samuel P. Huntington, *American Military Strategy*, Policy Papers in International Affairs No. 28 (Berkeley, CA: Institute of International Studies, University of California, Berkeley, 1986); and Antulio J. Echevarria II, *Toward an American Way of War* (Carlisle, PA: Strategic Studies Institute, US Army War College, March 2004).
4 Historian Peter Browning is usefully clear on this distinction.

> Warfare is the act of making war. War is a relationship between two states or, if a civil war, two groups. Warfare is only a part of war, although the essential part. Military history is the history of war, though it more usually concentrates on the history of warfare.

Peter Browning, *The Changing Nature of Warfare: The Development of Land Warfare from 1792 to 1945* (Cambridge: Cambridge University Press, 2002), p. 2. It is sadly ironic that an author so alert to the distinction between war and warfare should fail to grasp the difference between the changing nature and character of warfare.
5 Echevarria, *Toward an American Way of War*.
6 Clausewitz, On War, p. 85. His subjective nature of war is what we mean by war's character.
7 Ibid., p. 606.
8 Ibid., p. 593.
9 Recall that this was the "third test" specified by then Secretary of Defense, Caspar Weinberger, on November 28, 1984, among his criteria for the use of force.

> "THIRD, if we do decide to commit forces to combat overseas, we should have clearly defined political and military objectives. And we should know precisely how our forces can accomplish those clearly defined objectives. And we should have and send the forces needed to do just that. As Clausewitz wrote, "no one starts a war – or rather, no one in his senses ought to do so – without first being clear in his mind what he intends to achieve by that war, and how he intends to conduct it".

The full text is provided in Michael I. Handel, *Masters of War: Classical Strategic Thought*, 3rd edn (London: Frank Cass, 2001), pp. 310–11. This Weinberger "test," though eminently sensible and explicitly Clausewitzian, has the weakness of directing attention to the war itself rather than to its intended consequences. The Secretary's Doctrine was admirable in several respects, but it did not reveal a wholly persuasive grasp of the connection between war and peace.

10 Clausewitz, On War, p. 605.

11 Strategy is very difficult to do well. As Clausewitz warns, "[e]verything in strategy is very simple, but that does not mean that everything is easy." Ibid., p. 178. First, however, one needs to have a strategy and to function strategically. Nonetheless, there are times when belligerents are unable to perform strategically. In 1940 after the fall of France, Britain had no strategy other than to stay in the war and keep fighting as best it could, hoping for something to turn up. That something needed to take the form of German mistakes and an American alliance. Britain was extraordinarily fortunate in the course of events in 1941. Its "strategy" of holding on was, of course, enabled by its insular geography. For a parallel case with a less happy outcome for the principal, after the defeat at Stalingrad Germany had no strategy. It had no practical choice other than to fight on, hoping, as did Britain in 1940–41, that something would turn up. Since negotiated war termination was precluded by the Allied adoption of the policy of unconditional surrender, the Third Reich might only have been saved had the Allies started fighting each other before Germany was totally defeated. See Richard Bessel, *Nazism and War* (London: Weidenfeld and Nicoloson, 2004), p. 116.

12 It might be argued that criticism should not be leveled at the transformation project, since the strategic issue is how and for what purposes the products of that project will be used. However, the transformation debate, as with the RMA debate which preceded it, resembles a strategy-free zone. Moreover, the much touted shift to capabilities, from threat, based on defense planning, is a clear sign that political purpose is not exactly in the ascendant. After all, strategy is the bridge between military power and that political purpose. Transformative defense planning to cope with capabilities is, in effect, an autistic military exercise.

13 Clausewitz, *On War*, p. 128 (emphasis in the original).

14 On strategy, apart from Clausewitz see Sun-tzu, *The Art of War*, Ralph D. Sawyer (trans.) (Boulder, CO: Westview Press, 1994); J. C. Wylie, *Military Strategy: A General Theory of Power Control* (Annapolis, MD: Naval Institute Press, 1989); Colin S. Gray, *Modern Strategy* (Oxford: Oxford University Press, 1999); Richard K. Betts, "Is Strategy an Illusion?" *International Security*, 25 (Fall 2000), pp. 5–50; and Edward N. Luttwak, *Strategy:* the Logic of War and Peace, rev. edn (Cambridge, MA: Harvard University Press, 2001).

15 See Jonathan M. House, *Combined Arms Warfare in the Twentieth Century* (Lawrence, KS: University Press of Kansas, 2001); and Stephen Biddle, *Military Power: Explaining Victory and Defeat in Modern Battle* (Princeton, NJ: Princeton University Press, 2004).

16 The cutting edge of scholarship on the relationship between culture and the diffusion of new military means and methods is to be found in Emily O. Goldman and Leslie C. Eliason (eds), *The Diffusion of Military Technology and Ideas* (Stanford, CA: Stanford University Press, 2003).

17 Michael C. Desch casts a skeptical eye over culturalist explanations of strategic behavior in "Culture Clash: Assessing the Importance of Ideas in Security Studies," *International Security*, 23 (Summer 1998), pp. 141–70.

18 Martin van Creveld, *The Transformation of War* (New York: Free Press, 1991).

19 Colonel Thomas X. Hammes, USMC, *The Sling and The Stone: On War in the 21st century* (St Paul, MN: Zenith Press, 2004), esp. p. 2. Hammes explains that "[f]ourth-generation warfare (4GW) uses all available networks – political, economic, social, and military – to convince the enemy's political decision makers that their strategic goals

are either unachievable or too costly for the perceived benefit." He then proceeds beyond his culminating point of victory and claims, unhistorically and consequently unsoundly, that "[u]nlike previous generations of warfare, it [4GW] does not attempt to win by defeating the enemy's military forces. Instead, via the networks, it directly attacks the minds of enemy decision makers to destroy the enemy's political will." Quite innocently, Hammes and the 4GW school have stumbled upon a permanent feature in the history and lore of war.

20 *Clausewitz, On War*, p. 75 (emphasis in the original). A leading historian of Roman military practices informs us that

> [i]n a very real sense any war in this period [100 BC–AD 200] was a conflict between the respective wills to fight on of the peoples involved. A war was decided when one of the participants admitted defeat and was no longer prepared to continue the fight.

Adrian Keith Goldsworthy, *The Roman Army at War, 100BC–AD200* (Oxford: Oxford University Press, 1996), p. 103.

21 9 Principles of War, download from http://www.wpi.edu/Acdemics/Depts/MilSci/BTSI/prinwar.html (accessed January 20, 2005).

22 John M. Collins, *Military Strategy: Principles, Practices, and Historical Perspectives* (Washington, DC: Brassey's, 2002), p. 81. By far the most comprehensive and scholarly study of the provenance, development, and (very limited) variety, in the Principles, is the excellent book by John I. Alger, *The Quest for Victory: The History of the Principles of War* (Westport, CT: Greenwood Press, 1982).

23 Clausewitz, *On War*, p. 605.

24 For example, in 1944–45 President Roosevelt, General Marshall, and General Eisenhower were all guilty of approaching the admittedly formidable task of defeating Nazi Germany as a strictly military undertaking. The postwar geopolitical consequences of that determination were dire indeed. NATO's lack of geographical depth for defense was attributable in part to the fact that the Red Army was needlessly conceded too forward a hold on Central Europe. Of course, American leaders had powerful reasons to discount political considerations in their conduct of the war against Germany. They included a concern to minimize American casualties; worry lest US and Soviet armies came to blows, as might have happened had US forces pushed on to Berlin; and an overriding desire to conclude the defeat of Germany as rapidly as possible, so that US forces could be transferred to the Pacific. However, none of these reasons suffice to excuse an unsound approach to the conduct of the war in Europe.

25 Clausewitz, *On War*, p. 75.

26 The most virulent culturalist critic of Clausewitz today is British popular historian, John Keegan. See his books: *A History of Warfare* (London: Hutchinson, 1993); and *War and Our World: The Reith Lectures, 1998* (London: Hutchinson, 1998). Van Creveld also mounts a culturalist assault on Clausewitz in *The Transformation of War*.

27 Bernard Brodie, *War and Politics* (New York: Macmillan, 1973), p. 332. Also see the brilliant short book by Ken Booth, *Strategy and Ethnocentrism* (London: Croom Helm, 1979). This is a neglected minor classic.

28 A recent black-comic novel about the Allied Bomber Offensive in the Second World War expressed this tenth Principle precisely.

> Whoever said truth is the first casualty [of war] arrived late on the scene. The first casualty of war is the plan... The first plan always fails. Usually the second plan does, often the third, too. Then, with a bit of luck, the next plan works, and we win.

Derek Robinson, *Damned Good Show* (London: Cassell, 2002), p. 302.

29 Carl von Clausewitz, *Principles of War*; Hans W. Gatzke (trans.), *Roots of Strategy, Book 2* (Harrisburg, PA: Stackpole Books, 1987), p. 367. The full title of this brief early work is "The Most Important Principles For the Conduct Of War To Complete

My Course Of Instruction Of His Royal Highness The Crown Prince [Frederick William of Prussia]."

6 Nuclear strategy: the case for a theory of victory [1979]

1 The actual execution of SIOP-level attacks upon Soviet population and economic targets, on the canonical scale advertised in the late 1960s, would be either an act of revenge (and without political purpose), or – as initiative – would likely trigger a Soviet response in kind. Assured destruction would leave an adversary's (presumably surviving) political leaders with nothing left to lose. Prominent among the political weaknesses of assured destruction reasoning is the consideration that just as not all credible threats need deter (if the threat is insufficiently awesome), so not all awesome threats need deter (if they are insufficiently credible).

2 President Carter, in his State of the Union Message for 1979, advertised the "overwhelming" deterrent influence that reposed in only one *Poseidon* SSBN (nominally bearing 160 reentry vehicles of 40 kt: 16×10). The president neglected to mention that although 40 kt warheads could destroy a lot of buildings, it was not obvious that one *Poseidon* SSBN could accomplish anything very useful by way of forwarding the accomplishment of US war aims. "Transcript of President's State of Union Address to a Joint Session of Congress," *The New York Times*, January 24, 1979, p. A. 13.

3 See US Congress, House Committee on Armed Services, *Full Committee Consideration of Overall National Security Programs and Related Budget Requirements, Hearings*, 94th Congress, 1st session (Washington, DC: US Government Printing Office, 1975), testimony of Edward Aldridge.

4 See Benjamin S. Lambeth, *How to Think About Soviet Military Doctrine*, P-5939 (Santa Monica, CA: Rand, February, 1978), pp. 15–16.

5 On the rationales for the "magic fractions" of damage that permeated assured destruction reasoning in the 1960s, see Alain C. Enthoven and K. Wayne Smith, *How Much is Enough? Shaping the Defense Program, 1961–1969* (New York: Harper and Row, 1971), chs 5–6.

6 NATO's 23/30 guideline is a case in point. For planning convenience, a baseline "threat" had to be identified in order to ensure that NATO did not underestimate its possible operational problems. It was assumed, as a guideline only – *not* as a strategic prediction – that the Warsaw Pact would take 30 days to mobilize for war in Europe and that NATO would identify the character of the threat only 7 days into the Pact mobilization, thereby granting 23 days for countermobilization. The thirty-day assumption was never intended to stand as a judgment that the Soviet Union would attack *only* after such a lengthy period of mobilization, rather it was intended to generate a large, as opposed to a more modest, theater threat. Almost needless to say, 23/30 came to assume doctrinal significance.

7 As James Schlesinger once said:

> [b]ut I might also emphasize, Mr. Chairman, that doctrines control the minds of men only in periods of non-emergency. They do not necessarily control the minds of men during periods of emergency. In the moment of truth, when the possibility of major devastation occurs, one is likely to discover sudden changes in doctrine.

Testimony in US Congress, Senate Committee on Foreign Relations, *Nuclear Weapons and Foreign Policy, Hearings*, 93rd Congress, 2nd session (Washington, DC: US Government Printing Office, 1974), p. 160.

8 In *The Alliance and Europe: Part II: Defence With Fewer Men, Adelphi Paper* No. 98 (London: IISS, Summer 1973), p. 20 and *passim*.

9 The "two camps" premise is not defended in detail in the text because (1) it is very close to being a self-evident truth, and (2) such an exercise in description would divert

the discussion away from ideas and towards a summary of debate – with details required that are really of secondary importance, at most, to the theme of the chapter. Opinion, of course, exists on a spectrum. However, this author predicts that if one designed a simple questionnaire containing, say, ten "litmus paper-type" test questions of an either/or character, and submitted this questionnaire to 100 members of the US national security community, inside and outside of government, there would be little cross-voting by individuals between "liberal" and "conservative" replies. Moreover, if one knew what an individual's final judgment was on SALT II, yea or nay, that fact would be extremely helpful in predicting his/her position on a wide range of other security issues.

10 In some important respects, it is more accurate and more satisfactory, at least for the limited purposes of this chapter, to talk of two schools, really loose coalitions of functional allies, of thought, than it would be to attempt to design a sophisticated multidimensional categorization of attitude and opinion. The latter implies a commitment to an accuracy in personal detail that verges upon the trivial and yet which could never really be complete. Probably the most satisfactory attempt at the categorization and analysis of strategic attitudes was Robert A. Levine, *The Arms Debate* (Cambridge, MA: Harvard University Press, 1963). However, even this excellent book suffered from the vices of its virtues. The very comprehensiveness of its coverage compelled the author to take at least semiserious note of opinions that are of no policy relevance.

11 See Edward Luttwak's contribution to "The Great SALT Debate," *The Washington Quarterly*, 2, 1 (Winter 1979), particularly pp. 84–5.

12 US strategic nuclear planning was essentially unrevised from the Kennedy years until the early 1970s. See Desmond J. Ball, *The Strategic Missile Program of the Kennedy Administration, 1961–1963*. Unpublished manuscript (no date), pt. 3, ch. 2. For a definitive judgment we will have to await the eventual publication of the war plans (SIOPs), of the 1960s under the auspices of the Freedom of Information Act.

13 The concept of strategic culture is a fascinating one and is as obvious as it has been neglected. For a brief and interesting introduction to the subject, see Jack L. Snyder, *The Soviet Strategic Culture: Implications for Limited Nuclear Operations*, R-2154-AF (Santa Monica, CA: Rand, September 1977). The protracted SALT history has served to diminish enthusiasm for the strategic intellectual convergence thesis, but the US government is only at the beginning of attaining a due appreciation of the policy implications of the distinctive strategic culture thesis. This is one of those cases of rediscovery of the wheel. Most American strategic thinkers have always *known* that there was a uniquely "Soviet way" in military affairs, but somehow that realization was never translated from insight into constituting a serious and enduring factor influencing analysis, policy recommendation, and war planning.

14 Naval arms limitation by treaty in the 1920s and 1930s (with its heavy focus upon battleships and, eventually, cruisers should stand as a classic lesson for all time). Also, it is worth recalling Bernard Brodie's judgment on the complex naval competition of the last decades of the nineteenth century.

> It is very likely that a more costly and politically more dangerous competition was avoided because the Powers permitted the building to go on steadily, subject only to self-imposed restraints, which in a period of such rapid obsolescence of new material were certain to be very real.

Benard Brodie, *Sea Power in the Machine Age* (Princeton, NJ: Princeton University Press, 1941), p. 254. A brilliant contemporary analysis of the unintended damage that can be wrought through the (mis)-control of technology is Edward N. Luttwak," SALT and the Meaning of Strategy," *The Washington Review of Strategic and International Studies*, 1, 2 (April 1978), pp. 16–28.

15 Carl von Clausewitz, "The Continuing Relevance of *On War*," *On War*, Michael Howard and Peter Paret (eds and trans.) (Princeton, NJ: Princeton University Press, 1978), p. 49.

16 "Mutual Deterrence and Strategic Arms Limitation in Soviet Policy," *International Security*, 3, 1 (Summer 1978), pp. 112–47. For a preliminary reply to Garthoff, see the commentary by Donald G. Brennan in *International Security*, 3, 3 (Winter 1978–79).

17 Assured destruction may have residual merit today in the strict context of deterring a Soviet counter-societal assault, but US strategic forces have the same formal extended-deterrent duties that they have always had. As the Soviet Union has canceled the more obvious US strategic nuclear advantages, and as the United States continues to decline to seek to secure some measure of strategic superiority, so the attempt has been made to design "strategy offsets" for the adverse trend in the basic weapons balance. Very selective nuclear strike options, countereconomic recovery targeting, selective counter military (and perhaps, in the 1980s, counterpolitical control) targeting, are all – to some degree – endeavors to effect an end run around the logical implications of an eroding military balance. This problem is well described with reference to the probable needs of NATO-Europe in Lawrence Martin's contribution to "The Great SALT Debate," *The Washington Quarterly*, 2, 1 (Winter 1979), pp. 29–37.

18 The title of chapter 9 of his *magnum opus, War and Politics* (New York: Macmillan, 1973). The historical boundaries of Bernard Brodie's career as a theorist of nuclear affairs were marked by *The Absolute Weapon* (New York: Harcourt, Brace, 1946), pp. 21–110; and "The Development of Nuclear Strategy," *International Security*, 2, 4 (Spring 1978), pp. 65–83.

19 Note the scorn which Brodie pours upon the idea of "war-winning strategies" in "The Development of Nuclear Strategy," p. 74. Nonetheless, a little earlier Brodie did observe that civilian scholars have "almost totally neglected" the question of "how do we fight a nuclear war and for what objectives?" – if deterrence fails (ibid., p. 66).

20 Probably the most powerful single exposition of "the Schlesinger doctrine" was Schlesinger's testimony in US Congress, Senate Committee on Foreign Relations, Subcommittee on Arms Control, International Law and Organization, *U.S.–U.S.S.R. Strategic Policies, Hearing*, 93rd Congress, 2nd session (Washington, DC: US Government Printing Office, March 4, 1974).

21 The strategic flexibility theme was much criticized by representatives of the first school of deterrence theory (see Herbert Scoville, "Flexible MADness," *Foreign Policy*, 14 (Spring 1974), pp. 164–77, and Barry Carter, "Nuclear Strategy and Nuclear Weapons," *Scientific American*, 230, 5 (May 1974), pp. 20–31), but those representatives – reasonably enough, from their perspective – did not offer the most telling line of criticism: namely, that strategic flexibility, however desirable in and of itself (a view which Scoville and Carter did not share), does not constitute, or even approximate, a strategy.

22 See Lynn E. Davis, *Limited Nuclear Options: Deterrence and the New American Doctrine, Adelphi Paper* No. 121 (London, CA: IISS, Winter 1975–76); and Desmond Ball, *Déjà Vu: The Return to Counterforce in the Nixon Administration* (Los Angeles, CA: California Seminar on Arms Control and Foreign Policy, December, 1974). The Davis characterization, with its focus upon limited nuclear options (LNOs), is very substantially misleading as to the basic thrust of NSDM 242.

23 See Martin's essay on "The Great SALT Debate," *The Washington Quarterly*, 29–37.

24 For examples, see George W. Rathjens, "Flexible Response Options," *Orbis*, XVIII, 3 (Fall 1974), pp. 677–88; and Herbert Scoville, " 'First Use' of Nuclear Weapons," *Arms Control Today*, 5, 7–8 (July–August 1975), pp. 1–3.

25 Scoville, " 'First War' of Nuclear Weapons," p. 2.

26 Assessment of trends in the strategic balance tend to be driven to a non-marginal degree by the doctrinal preferences of the assessor: somehow, people manage to find their beliefs supported by statistics. Nonetheless, it is difficult to analyze the contemporary strategic balance and find much comfort therein (almost regardless of one's doctrinal preferences). A group of analysts in ACDA has succeeded in achieving this quite remarkable goal. See *U.S. and Soviet Strategic Capability Through the Mid-1980s: A*

Comparative Analysis (Washington, DC: US Arms Control and Disarmament Agency, August, 1979). Needless to say, there are several important premises that one has to grant for the analysis to turn out as it does. Gloomier prognoses for the United States include: Santa Fe Corporation, *Measures and Trends: U.S. and U.S.S.R. Strategic Force Effectiveness*, DNA 4602Z (Washington, DC: Defense Nuclear Agency, March, 1978); John Collins, *American and Soviet Military Trends since the Cuban Missile Crisis* (Washington, DC: Center for Strategic and International Studies, Georgetown University, 1978); and John Collins and Anthony Cordesman, *Imbalance of Power: An Analysis of Shifting U.S.–Soviet Military Strengths* (San Rafael, CA: Presidio, 1978).

27 This thesis is argued forcefully in Paul H. Nitze, "Deterring Our Deterrent," *Foreign Policy*, 25 (Winter 1976–77), pp. 195–210. On the subject of possible Soviet responses to American selective strike options see Benjamin S. Lambeth, *Selective Nuclear Options in American and Soviet Strategic Policy*, R-2043-DDRE (Santa Monica, CA: Rand, December, 1976). Also note the very brief discussion in Harold Brown, *Department of Defense Annual Report, Fiscal Year 1979* (Washington, DC: US Government Printing Office, February 2, 1978), pp. 55–6, 62. Rather more interesting is Harold Brown, *Department of Defense Annual Report, Fiscal Year 1980* (Washington, DC: US Government Printing Office, January 25, 1979), pp. 77–8. These two paragraphs, weak though they are, constitute the strongest Posture Statement language in favor of (second-strike) hard-target counterforce that has been seen for well over a decade.

28 *Statement of Secretary of Defense Robert S. McNamara on the Fiscal Year 1968–72 Defense Program and 1968 Defense Budget* (Washington, DC: US Government Printing Office, January 23, 1967), chapter II; and *Statement of Secretary of Defense Robert S. McNamara on the Fiscal Year 1969–73 Defense Program and the 1969 Defense Budget* (Washington, DC: US Government Printing Office, January 22, 1968), chapter II. Also see Jerome H. Kahan, *Security in the Nuclear Age: Developing U.S. Strategic Arms Policy* (Washington, DC: Brookings, 1975), pp. 94–106.

29 Counter-recovery targeting was not, of course, invented in the 1970s. In 1967, Robert McNamara said that "it seems reasonable to assume that in the case of the Soviet Union, the destruction of, say one-fifth to one-fourth of its population and one-half to two-thirds of its industrial capacity *would mean its elimination as a major power for many years*." (Emphasis added). *Statement Secretary of Defense Robert S. McNamara on the Fiscal Year 1968–72 Defense Program and 1968 Defense Budget*, p. 39. Counter-recovery targeting has come, in the 1970s, to imply attacks on a more discrete character than those suggested in McNamara's words.

30 General George Brown, then Chairman of the Joint Chiefs of Staff was very explicit on this subject. "We do not target population *per se* any longer. What we are doing now is targeting a war recovery capability." Quoted in *The Defense Monitor*, VI, 6 (August 1977), p. 2.

31 On the contrary, the current Secretary of Defense has written as follows:

> I am not persuaded that the right way to deal with a major Soviet damage-limiting program would be by imitating it. Our efforts would almost certainly be self-defeating, as would theirs. We can make certain that we have enough warheads – including those held in reserve – targeted in such a way that the Soviets could have no expectation of escaping unacceptable damage.

Department of Defense Annual Report, Fiscal Year 1979, p. 65. Of course the United States *could* impose unacceptable damage upon the Soviet Union, but there is no good reason to believe that the current administration (1) knows what unacceptable damage means in Soviet terms; (2) would be willing to fund a US strategic posture capable of imposing truly unacceptable damage; or (3) would be capable of understanding that *our* offensive strategy will avail us very little if *our* domestic assets are totally at risk.

32 This author sees some merit in Bernard Brodie's comment (on the targeting of war recovery capability) that "[w]hatever else may be said about this idea, one would have

to go back almost to the fate of Carthage to find an historical precedent." "The Development of Nuclear Strategy," p. 79.

33 "Kissinger's Critique [of SALT II]," *The Economist*, February 3, 1979, p. 18. Kissinger watchers should note that their subject traditionally has been as poor a strategic theoretician as he has been a strong foreign policy analyst.

34 This idea has had some US official status for at least five years, but its detailed meaning has never been probed rigorously.

35 The Soviet imperial thesis has been advanced strongly by Richard Pipes. See *Russia Under the Old Regime* (New York: Scribner's, 1974); and "Détente: Moscow's View," in Pipes (ed.), *Soviet Strategy in Europe* (New York: Crane, Russak, 1976), pp. 3–44.

36 It is one thing if the Soviet state is able, as in The Great Patriotic War, to assume the mantle of defender of Mother Russia and if the general populace discerns no reasonable political alternative to Soviet power. It is quite another if the external enemy is being combatted militarily far from home, if "that enemy" seeks intelligently to exploit the latent fragilities of the Soviet system, and if the military damage suffered on Soviet soil is very substantially confined to Soviet-state type targets.

37 A very persuasive recent discussion of this area is C.N. Donnelly, "Tactical Problems Facing the Soviet Army: Recent Debates in the Soviet Military Press," *International Defense Review*, II, 9 (1978), pp. 1405–12. Also see Peter Vigor, *The Soviet View of War, Peace, and Neutrality* (London: Routledge and Kegan Paul, 1975), pp. 14–15 and *passim*.

38 For an expansion upon this argument see Colin S. Gray, "The Strategic Forces Triad: End of the Road?" *Foreign Affairs*, 56, 4 (July 1978), particularly pp. 771–8.

39 A brief clear statement of this thesis permeated Robert McNamara's statement introducing the supposedly China-oriented *Sentinel* ABM system. "McNamara Explanation of 'Thin' Missile Defense System," *The Washington Post*, September 19, 1967, p. A. 10. Also see Wolfgang K.H. Panofsky, "The Mutual-Hostage Relationship between America and Russia," *Foreign Affairs*, 52, 1 (October 1973), pp. 109–18. Interestingly enough, some of the more intense denials of McNamara-Panofsky reasoning seem to focus unduly upon the tactical merits of particular weapon systems.

40 John Erickson, "The Chimera of Mutual Deterrence," *Strategic Review*, IV, 2 (Spring 1978), p. 16. Also very useful is the discussion in Fritz Ermarth, "Contrasts in American and Soviet Strategic Thought," *International Security*, 3, 2 (Fall 1978), pp. 138–55.

41 Policymakers in Washington might profit from frequent reminders of Clausewitz' definition of strategy. Strategy teaches "*the use of engagements for the object of the war*" (emphasis in the original). *On War*, p. 128.

42 As Alexis de Tocqueville and many lesser commentators have observed, the conduct of foreign policy is not, and (given its political structure) cannot be, an American forte. For a sense of perspective, it is worth noting that very few countries can wage long, *losing* (or perpetually inconclusive) wars and emerge with little, if any, domestic damage. If Americans feel ashamed, in different ways, over their Vietnam record, they should consider what the war in Algeria did to France. Admittedly, Algeria was a true *colonial* war, but still it was a case of a democracy attempting to cope with the consequences of military success and political defeat. Any American president should know that the only kind of war his country can fight, and fight very well, is one where there is a clear concept of victory – analogically, the marines raising the flag on Mt Suribachi is the way in which a president should think of American wars being terminated. The more distant the Mt Suribachi analogue from the case at hand, the more doubtful a president should be over committing US forces to action. The US public could have understood, and almost certainly would have approved, the US Marine Corps seizing Hanoi (intact or rubble – no matter) in 1965 or 1966, and *compelling* Ho Chi Minh (or a successor – again, no matter) to sign a peace treaty. That would be victory. American academic theorists of "limited" (and "sublimited") war in the late 1950s and early 1960s simply failed to understand their own country. Most Americans believe that if wars are not worth winning (in fairly classical terms), they are not worth fighting.

43 See T.K. Jones and W. Scott Thompson, "Central War and Civil Defense," *Orbis*, 22, 3 (Fall 1978), pp. 681–712; and Director of Central Intelligence, *Soviet Civil Defense* (Washington, DC: CIA, July 1978). This latter study claims that Soviet casualties (only half of which would be fatalities) could be held to "the low tens of millions," though only under the most favorable conditions for the Soviet Union (p. 4). Some Boeing civil defense studies have suggested, by way of contrast, that under the most favorable conditions Soviet population fatalities would be less than ten million. Most commentators agree that a proper mix of offensive and defensive programs should make a dramatic difference to the prospects of early postwar recovery.

44 John Newhouse, *Cold Dawn: The History of SALT* (New York: Holt, Rinehart and Winston, 1973), p. 4. Also of interest is Raymond L. Garthoff, "Salt 1: An Evaluation," *World Politics*, XXXI, 1 (October, 1978), particularly pp. 3, 24.

45 It is beginning to be fashionable to concede that the West will have to endure several years of unusual peril in the early 1980s, in terms of military balances considered narrowly, but that condition will be transformed in the latter half of the decade as the US strategic force posture accommodates cruise missiles, a follow-on ICBM and, eventually, the Trident 2 SLBM. A similar phenomenon is claimed for the trend in the theater balance in Europe: NATO's long-term defense program should have a very noticeable cumulative impact by the mid- to late 1980s. This author grants the *possible* validity of this theory, but is disturbed by the fragility of almost all of its premises. Henry Kissinger has commented persuasively on the early to mid-1980s being "a period of maximum peril" in "Kissinger's Critique," p. 20.

46 The US Department of Defense, in its declaratory policy, and even more in its actual operational planning (though *not* in its force acquisition), stands squarely between the two schools. DoD planning *looks* as though it is about the serious prosecution of war, but (a) the proper means are lacking, and (b) (to repeat a now familiar refrain) there is no theory of Soviet defeat to be discerned.

47 Soviet offensive-force development will, on current trends, pose an unacceptably high threat to the prelaunch survivability of the US ICBM force by the early 1980s (for contrasting analyses of this problem see John D. Steinbruner and Thomas M. Garwin, "Strategic Vulnerability: The Balance Between Prudence and Paranoia," *International Security*, I, 1 (Summer 1976), pp. 138–81, and Colin S. Gray, *The Future of Land-Based Missile Forces*, *Adelphi Paper* No. 140 (Winter 1977)), while the Soviet Union continues to invest very heavily in active and passive defense of its homeland – thereby rejecting the thesis that it is desirable for Soviet assets to be at nuclear risk as hostages to the prudent behavior of Soviet (and American and Chinese) leaders.

48 On this subject see Paul C. Warnke "Apes On A Treadmill," *Foreign Policy*, 18 (Spring 1975), pp. 12–29.

49 Brown, *Department of Defense Annual Report, Fiscal Year 1980*, pp. 77–8.

50 It is difficult to tell a convincing story in support of SALT II, when the strategic doctrine that provides the political meaning in the strategic force posture is very uncertain. On what basis can one assess adequacy?

51 For examples, see Daniel O. Graham, "The Decline of U.S. Strategic Thought," *Air Force Magazine*, 60, 8 (August, 1977), pp. 24–9; and Luttwak, "SALT and the Meaning of Strategy." The scope for *strategic* thinking may, of course, be reduced if one discerns no, or hardly any, political value in military action at the level of *nuclear* operations. In the words of Fritz Ermarth: "For many years the prevailing U.S. concept of nuclear war's consequences has been such as to preclude belief in any military or politically meaningful form of victory." "Contrasts in American and Soviet Strategic Thought." *op. cit.*, p. 144. One might reformulate Clausewitz' definition of strategy so as to read "the use of [*the threat*] of engagements for the object of the war" (*On War*, p. 128, my addition in brackets) in order to accommodate the *strategy* of deterrence and compellence, but there is grave danger in the judgment offered by Bernard Brodie in 1946: "Thus far the chief purpose of our military establishment has been to win

wars. From now on its chief purpose must be to avert them. *It can have almost no other useful purpose," The Absolute Weapon*, p. 76. This is a prime example of a good idea becoming a poor idea when it is taken too far: at worst, it is a doctrinal formula for losing wars.

52　Two as yet unpublished manuscripts discuss the rise of (civilian) nuclear-age strategic theorizing in great detail. These are James King, *The New Strategy*; and my own *Strategic Studies and Public Policy: The American Experience*.

53　Bernard Brodie, *Strategy in the Missile Age* (Princeton, NJ: Princeton University Press, 1959).

54　Brodie, "The Development of Nuclear Strategy," p. 79.

55　See Richard Pipes, "Why the Soviet Union Thinks It Could Fight and Win a Nuclear War," *Commentary*, 64, 1 (July, 1977), pp. 21–34.

56　See US Congress, House of Representatives, Committee on Armed Services, *Civil Defense Review, Hearings*, 94th Congress, 2nd session (Washington, DC: US Government Printing Office, 1976), pp. 206–67.

57　For an unsympathetic but useful review of revisionist arguments on Soviet civil defense, see William H. Kincade, "Repeating History: The Civil Defense Debate Reviewed," *International Security*, 2, 3 (Winter 1978), pp. 99–120.

58　Richard Burt, "U.S. Moving Toward Vast Revision of Its Strategy on Nuclear War," *The New York Times*, November 30, 1978, pp. A1, A7; Bernard Weinraub, "Pentagon Seeking Shift in Nuclear Deterrent Policy," *The New York Times*, January 5, 1979, p. A5; and Richard Burt, "Carter Shifts U.S. Strategy for Deterring Nuclear War," *The New York Times*, February 10, 1979, p. 5. As Mark Twain said of the story of his alleged death: these reports are highly exaggerated.

59　The next sentence is intriguing. "However, this policy is contingent on similar Soviet restraint." *The Strategic Arms Limitation Talks, Special Report* No. 46 (Washington, DC: The Department of State, July, 1978), p. 3. This official logic fails, even on its own terms, if US strategic forces are not vulnerable to preemptive attack.

60　But it had its intellectual genesis in the late 1950s. For examples, see Thomas C. Schelling: "Surprise Attack and Disarmament," in Klaus Knorr (ed.), *NATO and American Security* Princeton, NJ: Princeton University Press, 1959), ch. 8; "Reciprocal Measures for Arms Stabilization," in Donald G. Brennan (ed.), *Arms Control, Disarmament, and National Security* (New York: Braziller, 1961), ch. 9.

61　"Carter Shifts U.S. Strategy for Deterring Nuclear War."

62　Clansewitz, *On War*, p. 605.

63　In his valuable study of the counterforce debate of the early 1970s, Desmond Ball quotes an Air Force general as claiming (in February 1973) that the SIOP was "never reworked under (President) Johnson. It is still basically the same as 1962." *Déjà Vu: The Return to Counterforce in the Nixon Adminstration*, p. 17.

64　Such a war might not be tripped by a military accident that related to political intention on neither side. It might pertain to matters of vital interest to both sides. In short, the US defense community might discover that it did have political goals that far transcended Brodie's prediction that the earliest possible war termination would likely be the superordinate objective (see Note 54).

65　Classic "period-piece" statements of the arms-race stability thesis were George W. Rathjens, *The Future of the Strategic Arms Race: Options for the 1970s* (New York: Carnegie Endowment for International Peace, 1969); and "The Dynamics of the Arms Race," *Scientific American*, 220, 4 (April 1969), pp. 15–25.

66　Strange to note, the theory of arms race dynamics that featured as its centerpiece the proposition that each side acts and reacts in a fairly mechanistic fashion in pursuit of a secure assured destruction capability has now been discredited pretty well definitively by the historical facts, but the strategic policy premises that flow from that flawed theory have not been over-hauled thoroughly. Since virtually all US commentators agree that the Soviet Union is not attracted to MAD reasoning, the long-familiar "instability" case against urban-area BMD and non-marginal civil defense provision is simply wrong. We are still in search of an adequate explanatory model for the strategic arms competition. See Colin S. Gray, *The Soviet–American Arms Race* (Lexington, MA: Lexington, 1976).

67 To have a serious civil defense program does not mean that a country is preparing for war, any more than equipping a ship with lifeboats means that the shipping line is preparing to operate the ship in a dangerous manner.

68 An argument central to the case against urban-area ABM defense was that its banning by treaty would break the action–reaction cycle of the arms race: the Soviet Union would not need to develop and deploy offensive forces to overcome such an American deployment (in order to preserve their assured destruction capability). It is a matter of history that the ABM treaty banned the ABM defense of US cities, but Soviet offensive force improvements have marched steadily onward. The action–reaction thesis was logical and reasonable; it just happened to be wrong (it neglected the local color, the domestic engines of the arms competition).

69 If US MX/MPS should induce the Soviet Union to proceed down a similar path, then stability (by anyone's definition) would be promoted. Rubles spent on MPSs are rubles not spent on missiles and warheads. It is true that an MPS system in place might attract the Soviet Union to producing large numbers of missiles, undetected, to be surge-deployed in a period of acute need. However, the Soviet government can produce ICBMs secretly now – in the absence of an MPS system they could be fired from pre-surveyed "soft" sites. The verification argument against MX/MPS is not a telling one, but – as a hedge – deployment of a fairly thin (preferentially assigned) ballistic missile defense system around the MPS could purchase an extraordinary degree of leverage *vis-à-vis* any secretly (or suddenly) deployed Soviet missiles. See Colin S. Gray, *The MX ICBM: Multiple Protective Structure (MPS) Basing and Arms Control*, H1-2977-P (Croton-on-Hudson, New York: Hudson Institute, February, 1979).

70 On the political meaning of strategic power, see Edward N. Luttwak, *Strategic Power: Military Capabilities and Political Utility, The Washington Papers*, Vol. IV (Beverly Hills, CA: SAGE, 1976).

71 Noteworthy endeavors since the mid-1970s include Robert Jervis, "Deterrence Theory Revisited," *World Politics*, XXXI, 2 (January 1979), pp. 289–324; Patrick Morgan, *Deterrence: A Conceptual Analysis* (Beverly Hills, CA: SAGE, 1977); and Richard Rosecrance, *Strategic Deterrence Reconsidered, Adelphi Paper* No. 116 (London: IISS, Spring 1975). Even well-considered judgments published as recently as 1975 can look a little fragile in 1979. Consider these words of Professor Rosecrance:

> Thus it is possible to say that although the deterrent requirements that were deemed necessary to protect Europe in the 1950s are probably not currently being met, they may not have to be met. An improvement in the Soviet–Western relationship makes them less necessary now than they were then.
>
> (Ibid., p. 36)

8 Arms control does not control arms [1993]

1 See E.A. Thompson, *A History of Attila and the Huns* (Oxford: Clarendon Press, 1948), p. 180. For evidence that the prohibition was still in effect one hundred years later, see Procopius, Vol VI, *The Anecdota*, H.B. Dewing (trans.) (Cambridge, MA: Harvard University Press, 1960), pp. xxv, 291, 293.

2 Winston S. Churchill, *The Gathering Storm* (London: Penguin, 1985; first published in 1948), p. 92.

3 Ambassador Ronald F. Lehman II, "The U.S. and the Future of Arms Control," *America's Role in a Changing World*, Adelphi Paper No. 256 (London: IISS, Winter 1990–91), p. 49.

4 See Turner Johnson, *Just War Tradition and the Restraint of War. A Moral and Historical Inquiry* (Princeton, NJ: Princeton University Press, 1981), pp. 128–9; See also Philippe Contamine, *War in the Middle Ages* (Oxford: Basil Blackwell, 1986), p. 274.

5 Lewis A. Dunn, *Containing Nuclear Proliferation*, Adelphi Paper No.263 (London: IISS, 1991).

6 For example, see Kurt M. Campbell, Ashton B. Carter, Steven E. Miller, and Charles A. Zraket, *Soviet Nuclear Fission: Control of the Nuclear Arsenal in a Disintegrating Soviet Union* (Cambridge, MA: John F. Kennedy School of Government, Harvard University, 1991).

7 An outstanding recent analysis is Robert Gordon Kaufman, *Arms Control During the Pre-Nuclear Era: The United States and Naval Limitations between the Wars* (New York: Columbia University Press, 1990).

8 Comprehensive assault upon the ideas behind, and the attempted practice of, arms control is launched in Patrick Glynn, *Closing Pandora's Box Arms Races, Arms Control, and the History of the Cold War* (New York: Basic Books, 1992); and Colin S. Gray, *House of Cards: Why Arms Control Must Fail* (Ithaca, NY: Cornell University Press, 1992).

9 For a valuable reassessment of the early years, see Jennifer E. Sims, *Icarus Restrained: An Intellectual History of Nuclear Arms Control, 1945–60* (Boulder, CO: Westview, 1990).

10 See Jerome H. Kahan, *Security in the Nuclear Age: Developing U.S. Strategic Arms Policy* (Washington, DC: Brookings, 1975).

11 See Bruce G. Blair, *Strategic Command and Control: Redefining the Nuclear Threat* (Washington, DC: Brookings, 1985).

12 See, for example, Joseph S. Nye, Jr, "Arms Control and International Politics," *Daedalus*, 120, 1 (Winter 1991).

13 Thomas C. Schelling, *The Strategy of Conflict* (Cambridge, MA: Harvard University Press, 1960), title of ch. 9.

14 This issue and related topics are handled persuasively in Marc Trachtenberg, *History and Strategy* (Princeton, NJ: Princeton University Press, 1991), ch. 1, "Strategic Thought in America, 1952–1966."

15 Bernard Brodie, *Sea Power in the Machine Age* (Princeton, NJ: Princeton University Press, 1941), p. 336.

16 A judgment advanced vehemently but convincingly in Correlli Barnett, *Engage the Enemy More Closely: The Royal Navy in the Second World War* (New York: W.W. Norton, 1991).

17 Alexei G. Arbatov, "We Could Have Done Better," *The Bulletin of the Atomic Scientists*, 47, 11 (November 1991), p. 37.

18 Louis J. Halle, *The Elements of International Strategy: A Primer for the Nuclear Age* (Lanham, MD: University Press of America, 1984), p. 73.

19 For example, Kurt Gottfried and Bruce G. Blair, *Crisis Stability and Nuclear War* (New York: Oxford University Press, 1988), pp. 3–4, 160.

9 Geography and grand strategy [1991]

An earlier version of this article was published in John B. Hattendorf and Malcolm H. Murfett (eds), *The Limitations of Military Power* (London and New York: Macmillan and St Martin's Press, 1990).

1 As, for example, when Jonathan Dull considered Mahan's "general conditions affecting sea power" with reference to Britain's enemies and judged that:

> In seeing these enduring strengths and weaknesses, one is struck by the near impossibility of overcoming the impersonal forces of economic growth and

decline, of geography and demography that underlie sea power. *These are factors that virtually foreordained the defeats of the German, Japanese, and Italian navies during the Second World War.*

(Emphasis added)

"Mahan, Sea Power, and the War for American Independence," *The International History Review*, 10, 1 (February, 1988), p. 67.

2 See Douglas Edward Leach, *Arms for Empire: A Military History of the British Colonies in North America, 1607–1763* (New York: Macmillan Company, 1973); Allan R. Millet and Peter Maslowski, *For the Common Defense: A Military History of the United States* (New York: Free Press, 1984), chs 1–2; and John Shy, "Armed Force in Colonial North America: New Spain, New France, and Anglo-America," in Kenneth J. Hagan and William R. Roberts (eds), *Against All Enemies: Interpretations of American Military History from Colonial Times to the Present* (New York: Greenwood Press, 1986), pp. 3–20.

3 Jeremy Black argues in his "Introduction" to Black and Philip Woodfine (eds), *The British Navy and the Use of Naval Power in the Eighteenth Century* (Leicester: Leicester University Press, 1988), that "[t]here was nothing inevitable about British victory in the colonial and transoceanic struggles" (p. 26). Similarly, belief in the inevitability of British defeat should have been shaken by Piers Mackesy, *The War for America, 1775–1783* (Cambridge, MA: Harvard University Press, 1964).

4 It may be recalled that during the Revolutionary War the British government could not decide, or remain decided for very long, whether to concentrate the fleet in home waters, as per the traditional strategy, or in American waters. London did neither, with unfortunate consequences. On Britain's geostrategic problems and opportunities in the nineteenth century, see Kenneth Bourne, *Britain and the Balance of Power in North America, 1815–1908* (Berkeley, CA: University of California Press, 1967), particularly p. 409. Also useful are Alfred Thayer Mahan (ed.), "Considerations Governing the Disposition of Navies," *Retrospect and Prospect: Studies in International Relations, Naval and Political* (London: Sampson Low, Marston and Company, 1902), pp. 139–205; and C.J. Bartlett "Statecraft, Power and Influence," (ed.), *Britain Preeminent: Studies of British World Influence in the Nineteenth Century* (New York: St Martin's Press, 1969), pp. 172–93.

5 This is not to forget the strength of the continentalist urge in the Nine Years' War, in the War of Spanish Succession, and again in the War of Austrian Succession. Still less is it to forget the historic, if transient, policy reversal effected during the First World War, when Britain elected, for a variety of reasons, to provide and wield a mighty continental sword of her own. However, the British continental sword initially intended to win the peace had to be employed to win the war as well. In prewar planning it had been thought that the provision of 100,000 professional British soldiers at the right time and place in a continental war could have a quite disproportionate impact upon the course of events. It so happened that, more by luck than judgment, the BEF's imprudently far-forward assembly area close to the Franco-Belgian border placed it unexpectedly in the path of von Kluck's First Army. London could scarcely have pre-planned such an opportunity for glory, or disproportionate impact. As Britain and the other combatant countries painfully learnt the nature of modern war, a mass British army was envisaged (in London) as the eventual instrument of allied victory. Unfortunately for that army, the fighting effectiveness of the leading continental allies collapsed, or all-but-collapsed, prematurely, leaving the BEF with the unenviable task of playing the lead role against a still undefeated German army. Amidst a vast litera- ture, see John Terraine, *To Win a War: 1918, the Year of Victory* (New York: Doubleday and Company, 1981); Trevor Wilson, *The Myriad Faces of War: Britain and the Great War, 1914–1918* (Cambridge: Polity Press, 1986); David French, *British Strategy and War Aims, 1914–1916* (London: Allen and Unwin, 1986); and Tim Travers, *The Killing*

Ground: The British Army, the Western Front and the Emergence of Modern Warfare,
1900–1918 (London: Allen and Unwin, 1987).

6　For example, see John M. Sherwig, *Guineas and Gunpowder: British Foreign Aid in
the Wars with France, 1793–1815* (Cambridge, MA: Harvard University Press, 1969).

7　See John Creswell, *British Admirals of the Eighteenth Century: Tactics in Battle*
(London: George Allen and Unwin, 1972).

8　The Western Allies could not conclude the Second World War in Europe with victory
in the Battle of the Atlantic, but the achievement of that victory in the late spring and
summer of 1943 was a precondition for victory in the war as a whole. For a recent
study, see Dan van der Vat, *The Atlantic Campaign: The Great Struggle at Sea,
1939–1945* (London: Hodder and Stoughton, 1988).

9　See Julian S. Corbett, *The Campaign of Trafalgar* (London: Longmans, Green and
Company, 1910), ch. 26. On the persisting debate over the strategic utility of the Royal
Navy, see Charles John Fedorak, "The Royal Navy and British Amphibious Operations dur-
ing the Revolutionary and Napoleonic Wars," *Military Affairs*, 52, 3 (July 1988), pp. 141–6.

10　See the editors' "Introduction" and Colin S. Gray, "Sea power and Landpower," in
Roger W. Barnett and Gray (eds), *Sea power and Strategy* (Annapolis, MD: Naval
Institute Press, 1989).

11　For example, see Jack L. Snyder, *The Soviet Strategic Culture: Implications for Limited
Nuclear Operations*, R-2154-AF (Santa Monica, CA: RAND Corporation, September
1977); Ken Booth, *Strategy and Ethnocentrism* (New York: Croom, Helm, 1979);
Colin S. Gray, *Nuclear Strategy and National Style* (Lanham, MD: Hamilton Press,
1986); Joseph Rothschild, "Culture and War," in Stephanie G. Neuman and Robert E.
Harkavy (eds), *The Lessons of Recent Wars in the Third World: Vol. II, Comparative
Dimensions* (Lexington, MA: Lexington Books, 1987), pp. 53–72; and the essays in
Williamson Murray and Alvin Bernstein (eds), *The Making of Strategy: Rulers, States,
and War* (Cambridge: Cambridge University Press, 1994).

12　See Brian D. Dailey and Patrick J. Parker (eds), *Soviet Strategic Deception* (Lexington,
MA: Lexington Books, 1987).

13　See Colin S. Gray, "Strategy in the Nuclear Age: The United States, 1945–1990," in
Murray and Bernstein (eds), *The Making of Strategy*.

14　Very much to this point is John Shy (ed.), "The American Military Experience: History
and Learning," *A People Numerous and Armed: Reflections on The Military Struggle
for American Independence* (Oxford: Oxford University Press, 1976), pp. 225–54.

15　Christopher Donnelly, *Red Banner: The Soviet Military System in Peace and War*
(Coulsdon, Surrey: Jane's Information Group, 1988), p. 13.

16　The Byzantine Empire's strategic discretion and subtlety had a way of vanishing when
strategic opportunity for military conquest beckoned. The theory, or myth, of universal
empire all-but-drove Byzantium beyond the culminating point of victory. For example,
in the late tenth and early eleventh centuries, at the apogeé of imperial fortunes, the
invaluable buffer states of Bulgaria, Armenia, and Georgia were critically weakened.
See Romilly Jenkins, *Byzantium: The Imperial Centuries, AD 610–1071* (Toronto:
University of Toronto Press, 1987; first published in 1966), p. 312.

17　See Ira D. Gruber, "The Anglo-American Military Tradition and the War for American
Independence," in Hagan and Roberts (eds), *Against All Enemies*, pp. 21–46.

18　An outstanding treatment is Ray Allen Billington, *America's Frontier Heritage*
(Albuquerque, NM: University of New Mexico Press, 1986; first published in 1963).

19　Denis W. Brogan, *The American Character* (New York: Alfred A. Knopf, 1944), p. 150.
Emphasis in original.

20　A recent history of the American Civil War argues that "all three branches of the art of
war – logistics, strategy, and tactics – played crucial and interrelated roles ... but more
or less their relative importance was in that order." Herman Hattaway and Archer Jones,
How the North Won: A Military History of the Civil War (Urbana, IL: University of
Illinois Press, 1983), p. 720.

21 See Duncan S. Ballantine, *U.S. Naval Logistics in the Second World War* (Princeton, NJ: Princeton University Press, 1947).

22 For example, Admiral Edward Hawke's close blockade of Brest in 1759 depended critically upon resupply at sea. See Geoffrey Marcus, *Quiberon Bay: The Campaign in Home Waters, 1759* (London: Hollis and Carter, 1960), ch. 8; and Ruddock F. Mackay, *Admiral Hawke* (Oxford: Clarendon Press, 1965), ch. 13.

23 James D. Watkins, P.X. Kelley and Hugh K. O'Donnell, Jr, John F. Lehman, Jr, and Peter M. Swartz, *The Maritime Strategy* (Annapolis, MD: US Naval Institute, January 1986); and Norman Friedman, *The U.S. Maritime Strategy* (London: Jane's Publishing Company, 1988).

24 See Daniel Baugh: "Great Britain's 'Blue Water' Policy, 1689–1815," *The International History Review*, 10, 1 (February 1988), pp. 33–58; and "Why did Britain Lose Command of the Sea During the War for America?" in Black and Woodfine (eds), *The British Navy and the Use of Naval Power in the Eighteenth Century* (Leicester: Leicester University Press, 1988), pp. 149–69. For the theory, see Julian S. Corbett, *Some Principles of Maritime Strategy* (Annapolis, MD: Naval Institute Press, 1972; first published in 1911), chs 3–6; and Basil Liddell Hart, "The Historical Strategy of Britain," *The British Way in Warfare* (London: Faber and Faber, 1932), ch. 1.

25 In his powerful essay, "The British Way in Warfare: A Reappraisal," Michael Howard claims that "a commitment of support to a Continental ally in the nearest available theatre, on the largest scale that contemporary resources could afford, so far from being alien to traditional British strategy, was absolutely central to it." Howard, *The Causes of Wars and Other Essays* (London: Unwin Paperbacks, 1984; first published in 1983), p. 200. Also see Michael Howard, *The Continental Commitment: The Dilemma of British Defence Policy in the Era of the Two World Wars* (London: Temple Smith, 1972); and Paul M. Kennedy, *The Rise and Fall of British Naval Mastery* (New York: Charles Scribner's Sons, 1976), particularly p. 88. Kennedy comments critically on Baugh's "blue-water" thesis in "The Influence and the Limitations of Sea Power," *The International History Review*, 10, 1 (February 1988), pp. 8–10.

26 See Jeremy Black, *Natural and Necessary Enemies: Anglo-French Relations in the Eighteenth Century* (London: Gerald Duckworth and Company, 1986); and John Brewer, *The Sinews of Power: War, Money and the English State, 1688–1783* (New York: Alfred A. Knopf, 1989). Brewer quotes Baugh (supra n. 24) with approval on "blue-water strategy" (p. 257, fn. 94), but adheres to the now-traditional continentalist-leaning interpretation of British grand strategy.

27 As much, of course, could not have been claimed for the US' allies in Europe and Asia. See Fred Kaplan, *The Wizards of Armageddon* (New York: Touchstone, 1984; first published in 1983), p. 295. As Kaplan records, a Department of Defense study in August–September 1961 "concluded that a [U.S.] counterforce first-strike was indeed very feasible, that we would pull it off with high confidence" (p. 299, also see p. 301). But, see Richard K. Betts, *Nuclear Blackmail and Nuclear Balance* (Washington, DC: Brookings Institution, 1987), pp. 96–102, 159–72.

28 Edward N. Luttwak, "An Emerging Postnuclear Era?" *The Washington Quarterly*, 11, 1 (Winter 1988), pp. 5–15.

29 See William E. Odom, "The Kremlin's Strategy to De-Nuclearize NATO," *Air Force Magazine*, 72, 3 (March 1989), pp. 40–45.

30 John Mueller: "The Essential Irrelevance of Nuclear Weapons: Stability in the Postwar World," *International Security*, 13, 2 (Fall 1988), pp. 55–79; and *Retreat from Doomsday: The Obsolescence of Major War* (New York: Basic Books, 1989).

31 Halford J. Mackinder, *Democratic Ideals and Reality* (New York: W.W. Norton 1962). This book contains (*inter alia*) Mackinder's three key geopolitical essays, dating from 1904, 1918–1919 (the long title essay), and 1943. See W.H. Parker, *Mackinder: Geography as an Aid to Statecraft* (Oxford: Clarendon Press, 1982); and Colin S. Gray, *The Geopolitics of Super Power* (Lexington, KY: University Press of Kentucky, 1988), ch. 2.

32 It is worth noting that although the English erred in transferring the lessons of the Dutch Wars to the conflict with France, the Dutch had erred in attempting to transfer their long experience of maritime conflict with Imperial Spain to the new conflict with England. The Dutch learned very painfully that the kind of underarmed, shoddily constructed and unprofessionally officered fighting fleets (comprised largely of hastily converted merchantmen) that had been good enough to cope with a geostrategically very disadvantaged Spain, amounted to a prescription for defeat in war with England. See J.R. Jones, "The Dutch Navy and National Survival in the Seventeenth Century," *The International History Review*, 10, 1 (February 1988), pp. 18–32. Also useful are G.J. Marcus, *A Naval History of England: I, The Formative Centuries* (Boston, MA: Little, Brown and Company, 1961), ch. 5; and Peter Padfield, *Tide of Empires: Decisive Naval Campaigns in the Rise of the West: Vol I, 1481–1654* (London: Routledge and Kegan Paul, 1979), ch. 6.

33 Prior to the great reforms in national financial administration in England in the 1690s (see Brewer, *The Sinews of Power*), London's center of gravity in war lay in the shortness of its purse.

34 See Etienne Taillemite, *L'Histoire ignorée de la marine française* (Paris: Librarie Académique Perrin, 1988).

35 See Jonathan R. Dull, *The French Navy and American Independence: A Study of Arms and Diplomacy, 1774–1787* (Princeton, NJ: Princeton University Press, 1975), pp. 343–4. England's public finances could cope with the extraordinarily expensive simultaneous wars with the American colonists and with France, Spain, and Holland, but the finances of France were strained beyond management by any facsimile to standard operating procedures.

36 Carl von Clausewitz, *On War*, Michael Howard and Peter Paret (eds and trans) (Princeton, NJ: Princeton University Press, 1976; first published in 1832), p. 88.

37 Ibid., p. 579.

38 It is unhistorical to speculate about "might have beens." Suffice it to say that: *had* Hitler adhered to a theory of victory in war, rather than a campaign; *had* he been willing to gamble very boldly when faced with salt water; and *had* he not succumbed to wishful thinking concerning Britain's demoralization when bereft of its allied (French) continental sword – he might, but only might, have set the true basis for winning the war by invading Britain in the summer of 1940. Needless to say, the historian, blessed with hindsight, discerns fewer attractive choices for Germany in the summer of 1940 than did Hitler at that time. A cross-channel invasion conducted on a "come as you are" basis, with a navy rendered all but *hors de combat* in Norway, an army in need of rest and refit, and an air force likewise ragged around the edges, looked to be a tremendous gamble. We know that virtually any risk would have been worth accepting in return for the solid prospect of eliminating Britain from the war. Hitler could not know the future, but great statesmanship was not required in order to perceive the peril of unfinished business in the West (and South, given Britain's imperial interests).

39 See Gerhard Ritter, *The Schlieffen Plan: Critique of a Myth* (London: Oswald Wolff, 1958; first published in 1956); Martin van Creveld, *Supplying War: Logistics from Wallenstein to Patton* (Cambridge: Cambridge University Press, 1977), ch. 4; L.C.F. Turner, "The Significance of the Schlieffen Plan," in Paul Kennedy (ed.), *The War Plans of the Great Powers, 1880–1914* (London: George Allen and Unwin, 1979), pp. 199–221; and Jehuda L. Wallach, *The Dogma of the Battle of Annihilation: The Theories of Clausewitz and Schlieffen and Their Impact on the German Conduct of Two World Wars* (Westport, CT: Greenwood Press, 1986), pp. 87–125.

40 Each of Germany's three great offensives in the West – 1914, 1916, and 1918 – did enormous, and ultimately cumulatively, fatal damage to her prospects for achieving a tolerable war outcome. Partial success can indeed be devastating. (1) The partial success of the modified Schlieffen Plan encouraged German aspirations for the complete

victory that had eluded them in 1914. But, that success guaranteed French commitment to *guerre totale* and had the effect of ensuring that British (and later American) policy and strategy, if such is not to exaggerate, would be hostage to French preferences. (2) Falkenhayn's great, truly absurd offensive against the French Army at Verdun, had the (entirely predictable) consequence of imposing damage upon the German Army, which could be absorbed less readily than could the damage to the French, in the total context of the anti-German coalition. The German Army was ruined in 1916 at Verdun and on the Somme. (3) The spring offensive of March 1918 was a gambler's throw wherein the retrained and somewhat rearmed tactical cutting edge of the German Army was sacrificed in a series of operationally, let alone strategically, inept lunges loosely designed to unhinge the British from the French armies. The salient created by the incomplete success of spring 1918 lengthened the German front and set the stage for the great allied counteroffensives of the late summer and the autumn.

41 This point is well argued in the early study, F.H. Hinsley, *Hitler's Strategy* (Cambridge: Cambridge University Press, 1951), ch. 1. Also see Anthony Martienssen, *Hitler and His Admirals* (London: Secker and Warburg, 1948), chs 2–3. But, see Wilhelm Deist, *The Wehrmacht and German Rearmament* (Toronto: University of Toronto Press, 1981), ch. 5; Jost Dülffer, "Determinants of German Naval Policy, 1920–1939," in Wilhelm Deist (ed.), *The German Military in the Age of Total War* (Leamington Spa: Berg Publishers, 1985), pp. 152–70; and Holger H. Herwig, "The Failure of German Sea Power, 1914–1945: Mahan, Tirpitz, and Raeder Reconsidered," *The International History Review*, 10, 1 (February 1988), particularly pp. 87–95.

42 Jürgen E. Förster writes that "[d]runk with victory over France, the senior army leadership planned the invasion of the Soviet Union as a Blitzkrieg in every respect." "The Dynamics of *Volksgemeinschaft:* The Effectiveness of the German Military Establishment in the Second World War," in Allan R. Millett and Williamson Murray (eds), *Military Effectiveness: Vol. III, The Second World War* (Boston, MA: Allen and Unwin, 1988), p. 195. Hitler informed his senior military courtiers on July 31, 1940 that, beginning in May 1941, he intended to smash the USSR in a five-month campaign. However, as early as "mid-June 1940, quite independently of Hitler, Halder [Army Chief of Staff] began to plan first for an offensive–defensive, and then for a preventive military blow at Russia to force her to recognize the dominant role of Germany in Europe" (p. 194).

43 See Holger H. Herwig, "From Tirpitz Plan to Schlieffen Plan: Some Observations on German Military Planning," *The Journal of Strategic Studies*, 9, 1 (March 1986), pp. 53–63; and Stig Förster, "Facing People's War: Moltke the Elder and Germany's Military Options After 1871," *The Journal of Strategic Studies*, 10, 2 (June 1987), pp. 209–30.

44 Donald Kagan, *The Fall of the Athenian Empire* (Ithaca, NY: Cornell University Press, 1987), p. 423.

45 Sparta lacked the manpower, the expertise, and the wealth to add a first-class fleet to her first-class army. Allied, and truly mercenary, manpower and skills, glued together with Persian gold, were necessary for the fashioning of a naval instrument capable of defeating the Athenians at sea. Even then, Spartan victory required first that Athens go a long way towards ruining herself with the great expedition to Sicily in 415–413 BC, second that several signal defeats be absorbed en route to final success, and third that the Athenians behave with extreme tactical imprudence. Overall, the Spartan victory at Aegospotami in 404 BC was not exactly foreordained.

46 On strategic behavior in, and connections among, levels of analysis, see Edward N. Luttwak, *Strategy: The Logic of War and Peace* (Cambridge, MA: Harvard University Press, 1987). Also see Colin S. Gray, *War, Peace, and Victory: Strategy and Statecraft for the Next Century* (New York: Simon and Schuster, 1990).

47 The two most useful studies in English are Paul S. Dull, *A Battle History of the Imperial Japanese Navy (1941–1945)* (Annapolis, MD: Naval Institute Press, 1978);

and H.P. Willmott, *The Barrier and the Javelin: Japanese and Allied Pacific Strategies, February–June 1942* (Annapolis, MD: Naval Institute Press, 1983).

48 See S.J. Lewis, *Forgotten Legions: German Army Infantry Policy, 1918–1941* (New York: Praeger Publishers, 1985), pp. 162–7. Also valuable are Albert Seaton, *The Russo-German War, 1941–45* (New York: Praeger Publishers, 1970), ch. 15; and James Lucas, *War on the Eastern Front, 1941–1945: The German Soldier in Russia* (London: Jane's Publishing Company, 1979).

49 Seaton claims that

> [a]t the end of the war the equipment holding of the Soviet Armed forces amounted to 665,000 motor vehicles. Of these, 427,000 had been provided mainly from US sources during the war years; contemporary evidence indicates that over 50 percent of all vehicles in Red Army service were of American origin. These trucks, together with the thousands of locomotives and railway flats [respectively 1,900 and 11,000], gave to the Red Army the strategic and tactical mobility required to destroy the German forces.

The Russo-German War, 1941–45, p. 589. Also see Albert Seaton, *International Aid Statistics, World War II: A Summary of War Department Lend Lease* (Washington, DC: International Branch, H.Q., Army Service Forces, War Department, no date [probably 1946]); T.H. Vail Motter, *United States Army in World War II, The Middle East Theater: The Persian Corridor and Aid to Russia* (Washington, DC: US Government Printing Office, 1952), appendix A, table 2, pp. 484–5; and Robert Huhn Jones, *The Roads to Russia: United States Lend-Lease to the Soviet Union* (Norman, OK: University of Oklahoma Press, 1969).

50 Clausewitz, *On War*, p. 359.

51 Mahan, *Retrospect and Prospect*, p. 168.

52 The differences and similarities between combat on land and at sea are summarized persuasively in Wayne P. Hughes, Jr, *Fleet Tactics: Theory and Practice* (Annapolis, MD: Naval Institute Press, 1986), pp. 143–4.

53 See Colin S. Gray, *Space as an Environment for War* (Fairfax, VA: National Security Research, 1989).

54 See Simon P. Worden and Bruce P. Jackson, "Space, Power, and Strategy," *The National Interest*, 13, (Fall 1988), pp. 43–52, and John L. Piotrowski, "Space Warfare Principles," unpublished paper, August 1988.

55 See Bruce Palmer, Jr, *The 25-Year War: America's Military Role in Vietnam* (Lexington, KY: University Press of Kentucky, 1984), pp. 43, 57–8, 122, 176–8. Palmer notes, unarguably, that

> [a]lthough at times North Vietnamese execution of its strategy was faulty, their concept was brilliant. Basically, the strategy took advantage of the long, narrow geographic configuration of South Vietnam that made the country very vulnerable to penetration from its land border flank, and that in the northern and central regions provided very little depth between the generally wild and sparsely inhabited border areas and the heavily populated coastal region. The strategy also took advantage of the geopolitical weaknesses of South Vietnam and exploited the high foot and sampan mobility of main force units of Vietcong and NVA infantry (pp. 180–1).

56 The outstanding study remains Jeter A. Isely and Philip A. Crowl, *The U.S. Marines and Amphibious Warfare: Its Theory and Its Practice in the Pacific* (Princeton, NJ: Princeton University Press, 1951).

57 The measure of JCS dissaffection from the principles guiding the higher direction of the war, may be gauged with reference to the fact that, reportedly, on August 25, 1967, they planned to resign en masse the following day. The further fact that they did not resign on August 26, 1967, apparently is attributable to a distinctly arguable view of military discipline and of respect for civilian policymaking (however erroneous). See Mark Perry, *Four Stars* (Boston, MA: Houghton Mifflin Company, 1989), pp. 160–6.

58 In the ancient and medieval eras the Southern European-Middle Eastern, generally Mediterrean, focus of strategic history yielded a systemic advantage for land power as a basis for, or means to evade, sea power. Galley warfare in the narrow land-girt Middle Sea was a very different phenomenon indeed from the exercise of maritime strategy in an open-ocean setting. See Chester G. Starr, *The Influence of Sea Power on Ancient History* (New York: Oxford University Press, 1989); and, for the medieval period, Archibald R. Lewis, *Naval Power and Trade in the Mediterranean, A.D. 500–1100* (Princeton, NJ: Princeton University Press, 1951); Archibald R. Lewis and Timothy J. Runyan, *European Naval and Maritime History, 300–1500* (Bloomington, IN: Indiana University Press, 1985); and John H. Pryor, *Geography, Technology, and War: Studies in the Maritime History of the Mediterranean, 649–1571* (Cambridge: Cambridge University Press, 1988). In ancient, medieval, and even early modern times, land powers succeeded in acquiring more than offsetting sea power. This was true for the Spartans, the Macedonians, the Romans, the Arabs, and the Ottoman Turks. However, since the sixteenth century, when the Turks greatly overmatched imperial Venice at sea, no great land power has achieved and sustained first-class sea power.

59 See Gray, *The Geopolitics of Super Power*.

60 Jenkins wrote that "those walls, during centuries, suffered as little damage from sieges as a dog suffers from fleas" (p. 231), *Byzantium*. For a useful description of the walls of Constantinople, see J.B. Bury, *History of the Later Roman Empire from the Death of Theodosius I to the Death of Justinian, Vol. I* (New York: Dover Publications, 1958), pp. 67–73.

61 Strictly speaking, the Anatolian plateau was the key to the strength of the empire.

62 Even when the empire was far advanced in military decline, geography and military engineering combined to pose the severest of challenges to the besiegers of Constantinople. The stories of the only two successful assaults in 1000 years are best told in Edwin Pears, *The Fall of Constantinople: Being the Story of the Fourth Crusade* (New York: Harper and Brothers, 1886); and Steven Runciman, *The Fall of Constantinople, 1453* (Cambridge: Cambridge University Press, 1965).

63 See G.J. Marcus, *Heart of Oak: A Survey of British Sea Power in the Georgian Era* (London: Oxford University Press, 1975), ch. 2.

64 See the important collection of essays in Ciro E. Zoppo and Charles Zorgbibe (eds), *On Geopolitics: Classical and Nuclear* (Dordrecht: Martinus Nijhoff, 1985).

10 Strategic culture as context: the first generation of theory strikes back [1999]

This chapter is adapted from a chapter in my book *Modern Strategy* (Oxford, 1999). I am most grateful to Jim Wirtz of the Naval Postgraduate School, Monterey, California, and to James Kiras of the Centre for Security Studies, University of Hull, for their invaluable comments. Also I must thank two anonymous reviewers for this Journal who both made most useful comments.

1 The postulate of three generations is offered by Alastair Iain Johnston, "Thinking about Strategic Culture," *International Security*, 19, 4 (1995), pp. 36–43; *Cultural Realism: Strategic Culture and Grand Strategy in Chinese History* (Princeton, NJ: Princeton University Press, 19, 4 (1995)), pp. 4–22; "Cultural Realism and Strategy in Maoist China," in Peter J. Katzenstein (ed.), *The Culture of National Security: Norms and Identity in World Politics* (New York: Columbia University Press, 1996), pp. 221–2. n. 8. Although the generations overlap, the peak of their intellectual activity respectively can be associated primarily with the late 1970s, the 1980s, and the 1990s. It is worth mentioning that gathering together even all of these "generations" would make only a small party. Whereas first generation scholars by and large were looking for a more Russian, and Soviet, USSR, than contemporary policy and strategic theory recognized, second generation scholars sought the cunning coded messages behind the language of

strategic studies, and the third generation appears primarily to be interested in research ability. The current, or third, wave of cultural theorizing has many elements. In a recent article, Michael C. Desch identifies four strands as dominant: "organizational, political, strategic, and global." "Culture Clash: Assessing the Importance of Ideas in Security Studies," *International Security*, 23, 1 (1998), p. 142.

2 Martin Hollis and Steve Smith, *Explaining and Understanding International Relations* (Oxford: Oxford University Press, 1990).

3 This discussion draws heavily upon the excellent analysis in Michael Cole, *Cultural Psychology: A Once and Future Discipline* (Cambridge, MA: Harvard University Press, 1996), pp. 131–7.

4 Bernard Brodie, *War and Politics* (New York, 1973), p. 332.

5 Works from the first generation include Jack L. Snyder, *The Soviet Strategic Culture Implications for Limited Nuclear Operations*, R-2154–AF (Santa Monica, CA: RAND, September 1977); Colin S. Gray, "National Style in Strategy: The American Example," *International Security*, 6, 2 (1981), pp. 21–47; *Nuclear Strategy and National Style* (Lanham, MD: Hamilton Press, 1986); *War, Peace and Victory: Strategy and Statecraft for the Next Century* (New York: Simon and Schuster, 1990), esp. ch. 2; Carnes Lord, "American Strategic Culture," *Comparative Strategy*, 5, 3 (1985), pp. 269–93; and Carl G. Jacobsen (ed.), *Strategic Power: USA/USSR* (New York: St. Martin's Press, 1990), pt. 1.

6 I am pleased to acknowledge the inspiration provided by Michael Howard, "The Forgotten Dimensions of Strategy," *Foreign Affairs*, 57, 5 (1979), pp. 975–86. I have developed my thoughts on the dimensions of strategy in "RMAs and the Dimensions of Strategy," *Joint Force Quarterly*, 17 (Autumn–Winter 1997–98), pp. 50–4.

7 Carl H. Builder, *The Masks of War: American Military Styles in Strategy and Analysis* (Baltimore, MD: Johns Hopkins University Press, 1989); Deborah D. Avant, *Political Institutions and Military Change: Lessons from Peripheral Wars* (Ithaca, NY: Cornell University Press, 1994); Elizabeth Kier, *Imagining War: French and British Military Doctrine between the Wars* (Princeton, NJ: Princeton Universiry Press, 1997). The review article by Theo Farrell, "Figuring Out Fighting Organizations: The New Organizational Analysis in Strategic Studies," *The Journal of Strategic Studies*, 19, 1 (1996), pp. 122–356, is strongly recommended reading, as also is another review article by Farrell, "Culture and Military Power," *The Review of International Studies*, 24 (1998), pp. 407–16.

8 I apologize for the neologism of "encultured," but it would seem to be licensed at least implicitly by the long recognized words, accultured and acculturation. If one can be accultured, as the Oxford and Webster's dictionaries allow, logically initially one must have been encultured. In order to transfer one's culture, first one must have a culture to be transferred.

9 Raymond Williams, "The Analysis of Culture," in John Storey (ed.), *Cultural Theory and Popular Culture: A Reader* (Hemel Hempstead, UK: Harvester-Wheatsheaf, 1994), p. 56.

10 The distinction that I draw between "preparation for war" and "war proper," is, of course, borrowed from Carl von Clausewitz, *On War*, Michael Howard and Peter Paret (eds and trans) (Princeton, NJ: Princeton University Press, 1976), p. 131.

11 Johnston, *Cultural Realism*, p. 8.

12 Johnston, "Thinking about Strategic Culture," pp. 36–9; *Cultural Realism*, pp. 7–10.

13 Johnston, "Thinking about Strategic Culture," p. 45.

14 Leslie A. White, *The Concept of Cultural Systems: A Key to Understanding Tribes and Nations* (New York: Columbia University Press, 1975), p. 4, n.

15 Robert B. Bathurst, *Intelligence and the Mirror: On Creating an Enemy* (London: SAGE Publications, 1993), p. 24.

16 Clyde Kluckholn and William H. Kelly, "The Concept of Culture," in Charles C. Hughes (ed.), *Custom-Made: Introductory Readings for Cultural Anthropology*, 2nd edn (Chicago: Rand McNally, 1976), p. 188.

17 Marvin Harris, *Cultural Materialism: The Struggle for a Science of Culture* (New York: Random House, 1979), p. 47.

18 Johnston, *Cultural Realism*, pp. 12–13.
19 Gray, *Nuclear Strategy and National Style*, ch. 2.
20 Dean Peabody, *National Characteristics* (Cambridge: Cambridge University Press, 1985); Edward L. Keenan, "Muscovite Political Folkways," *The Russian Review*, 45 (1986), pp. 115–81; and Emilio Willems, *A Way of Life and Death: Three Centuries of Prussian–German Militarism, An Anthropological Approach* (Nashville, TN: Vanderbilt University Press, 1986), are all useful.
21 This idea helps drive Johnston's methodology in *Cultural Realism*.
22 Ibid., p. 8.
23 Desch, "Culture Clash," has as its central theme comparison of the utility of culturalist and realist theories of international relations. To my mind, to draw a distinction between realism and culturalism is to miss the point that strategy and security always is "done" by people and organizations who must function within the domain of cultural influences.
24 Edward T. Hall, *Beyond Culture* (Garden City, NY: Anchor, 1977), chs 6–8.
25 Bathurst, *Intelligence and the Mirror*, ch. 3.
26 John Mueller, "The Impact of Ideas on Grand Strategy," in Richard Rosecrance and Arthur A. Stein (eds), *The Domestic Bases of Grand Strategy* (Ithaca, NY: Cornell University Press, 1993), p. 48.
27 Ibid., p. 62.
28 Johnston, "Thinking about Strategic Culture," p. 63. He is no less severe in "Cultural Realism and Strategy in Maoist China," pp. 221–2. Interestingly enough, while Desch (in "Culture Clash," p. 170) judges the Cold War wave of theory "largely discredited," that "wave of cultural theorizing had the virtue of making clear empirical predictions that made it possible to test its theories against both real-world evidence and alternative theories," (p. 158). Johnston, by contrast, finds us Cold War theorists guilty of purveying untestable theories.
29 Edward N. Luttwak, *Strategy: The Logic of War and Peace* (Cambridge, MA: Harvard University Press, 1987).
30 Barry S. Strauss and Josiah Ober, *The Anatomy of Error: Ancient Military Disasters and Their Lessons for Modern Strategists* (New York: St. Martin's Press, 1990), pp. 6–7.
31 Barry D. Watts, *Clausewitzian Friction and Future War*, McNair Paper 52 (Washington, DC: National Defense University Press, October 1996), esp. ch. 8.
32 Bathurst, *Intelligence and the Mirror*, p. 121.
33 Adda B. Bozeman, *Politics and Culture in International History* (Princeton, NJ: Princeton University Press, 1960), p. 324. This book is the genuine article as an under-recognized classic.
34 Bathurst, *Intelligence and the Mirror*, p. 125.
35 Colin S. Gray, "Strategy in the Nuclear Age: The United States, 1945–1991," in Williamson Murray, MacGregor Knox, and Alvin Bernstein (eds), *The Making of Strategy: Rulers, States, and War* (Cambridge: Cambridge University Press, 1994), pp. 589–98. Bruno Colson, *La culture stratégique Américaine: L'influence de Jomini* (Paris, 1993). is not without merit.
36 Johnston, "Cultural Realism and Strategy in Maoist China," pp. 221–2. Emphasis in original.
37 Dennis Kavanagh, *Political Culture* (London, 1972), p. 10.
38 Basil H. Liddell Hart, *The British Way in Warfare* (London: Faber and Faber, 1932), ch. 1. Michael Howard, *The Continental Commitment: The Dilemma of British Defence Policy in the Era of the Two World Wars* (London: Temple Smith, 1972); Hew Strachan, "The British Way in Warfare Revisited," *The Historical Journal*, 26, 2 (1983), pp. 447–61; "The British Way in Warfare," in David Chandler (ed.), *The Oxford Illustrated History of the British Army* (Oxford: Oxford University Press, 1994), pp. 417–34, visit the relevant issues.
39 Arthur Schlesinger, Jr, "Back to the Womb? Isolationism's Renewed Threat," *Foreign Affairs*, 74, 4 (1995), pp. 2–8.

40 Richard Holbrooke, "America, a European Power," *Foreign Affairs*, 74, 4 (1995), p. 38.

41 Hew Strachan, "The Battle of the Somme and British Strategy," *The Journal of Strategic Studies*, 21, 1 (March 1998), pp. 79–95.

42 Ken Booth, *Strategy and Ethnocentrism* (London: Croom Helm, 1979), is essential.

43 David Fraser, *And We Shall Shock Them: The British Army in the Second World War* (London: Hodder and Stoughton, 1983): Martin van Creveld, *Fighting Power: German and US Army Performance, 1939–1945* (Westport, CT: Greenwood Press, 1982); Michael D. Doubler, *Closing with the Enemy: How GIs Fought the War in Europe, 1944–1945* (Lawrence, KS: University Press of Kansas, 1994).

44 Alfred Thayer Mahan, *The Life of Nelson: The Embodiment of the Sea Power of Great Britain*, (Boston: Little Brown, 1897), chs 22–3; Julian S. Corbett, *The Campaign of Trafalgar* (London, 1910).

45 Peter Burke, *Popular Culture in Early Modern Europe*, rev. edn (Aldershot, UK: Ashgate, 1994), p. xxii.

46 Strauss and Ober, *Anatomy of Error*, pp. 9–10. Emphasis added.

47 A forthcoming book addresses the pertinent issues superbly: A.J. Bacevich and Brian Sullivan (eds), *The Limits of Technology in Modern War*.

48 Gray, *Nuclear Strategy and National Style*, p. 35.

49 Bathurst, *Intelligence and the Mirror*.

50 Gerald Segal, "Strategy and 'Ethnic Chic,'" International Affairs, 60, 1 (1983–84), pp. 15–30. Michael I. Handel, *Masters of War: Classical Strategic Thought* (London: Frank Cass, 1996) p. 3. For the opinion that there are contrasting broadly Western and Eastern, or Oriental, strategic cultures, see Victor Davis Hanson, *The Western Way of War: Infantry Battle in Classical Greece* (London: Hodder and Stoughton, 1989), and John Keegan, *A History of Warfare* (London: Hutchinson, 1993).

51 Bathurst, *Intelligence and the Mirror*, pp. 25–6.

52 Clausewitz, *On War*, p. 141. Emphasis in original.

53 Johnston, *Cultural Realism*.

54 Colin S. Gray. *Explorations in Strategy* (Westport, CT: Greenwood Press, 1996), pt. 3.

55 Gray, *Modern Strategy*, ch. 12.

56 See Susan L. Marquis, *Unconventional Warfare: Rebuilding US Special Operations Forces* (Washington, DC: Brookings Institution Press, 1997).

57 Wolfgang Wegener, *The Naval Strategy of the World War*, Holger H. Herwig (trans.) (Annapolis, MD: Naval Institute Press, 1989), is a powerful German statement of the importance of geography to naval power.

58 Brian Bond, *British Military Policy between the World Wars* (Oxford: Oxford University Press, 1980).

59 Harry G. Summers, Jr, *On Strategy: A Critical Analysis of the Vietnam War* (Novato, CA: Presidio Press, 1982); Andrew F. Krepinevich, Jr, *The Army and Vietnam* (Baltimore: Johns Hopkins University Press, 1986); Robert Buzzanco, *Masters of War: Military Dissent and Politics in the Vietnam Era* (Cambridge: Cambridge University Press, 1996); H.R. McMaster, *Dereliction of Duty: Lyndon Johnson, Robert McNamara, the Joint Chiefs of Staff and the Lies That Led to Vietnam* (New York: Harper Collins, 1997); Michael A. Hennessy, *Strategy in Vietnam: The Marines and Revolutionary Warfare in I Corps, 1965–1972* (Westport, CT: Greenwood Press, 1997); and Jeffrey Record, "Vietnam in Retrospect: Could We Have Won?" *Parameters*, 26 (1996–97), pp. 51–65. US defeat in Vietnam appears to have been so overdetermined that some powerful arguments suggesting, and evidence for, US success in Vietnam has yet to receive a decent hearing. Dale Walton, *The Myth of Inevitable U.S. Defeat in Vietnam* (London: Frank Cass, 2002) a step in the right direction of more balanced scholarship.

60 Clausewitz, *On War*, p. 579.

61 J.C. Wylie. *Military Strategy: A General Theory of Power Control*, John B. Hattendorf (ed.) (Annapolis, MD, 1989), ch. 5, "The Existing Theories," p. 42.

62 Gray, *Explorations In Strategy*, p. 156.

63 Bathurst, *Intelligence and the Mirror*, ch. 3; Hall, *Beyond Culture*, chs 6–8.

12 What is war? A view from strategic studies [2005]

1 C. von Clausewitz, *On War*, M. Howard and P. Paret (eds and trans.) (Princeton, NJ: Princeton University Press, 1976), p. 75.

2 H. Bull, *The Anarchical Society: A Study of Order in World Politics* (New York: Columbia University press, 1977), p. 184.

3 Clausewitz, *On War*, p. 85.

4 Ibid., p. 104.

5 B. Brodie, *War and Politics* (New York: Macmillan, 1973), p. 452.

6 R. Strassler (ed.), *The Landmark Thucydides: a comprehensive guide to The Peloponnesian War* R. Crawley (trans.), rev. edn (New York: Free Press, 1996), p. 43.

7 See The National Conference of Catholic Bishops, *The Challenge to Peace: God's Promise and Our Response*, pastoral letter printed as a special supplement to the *Chicago Catholic*, June 24 and July 1, 1983.

8 Mary Kaldor, *New and Old Wars: Organized Violence in a Global Era* (Cambridge: Polity Press, 1999); Mary Kaldor, "Elaborating the 'new war' thesis," in I. Duyvesteyn and J. Angstrom (eds), *Rethinking the Nature of War* (London: Frank Cass, 2005), pp. 210–24; and H. Münkler, *The New Wars* (Cambridge: Polity Press, 2005).

9 Clausewitz, *On War*, p. 89.

10 See Jan Willem Honig, "Strategy in a Post-Clausewitzian Setting," in G. de Nooy (ed.), *The Clausewitzian Dictum and the Future of Western Military Strategy* (The Hague: Kluwer Law International, 1997), pp. 109–21.

11 L. Freedman, *The Revolution in Strategic Affairs*, Adelphi Paper No. 318 (London: International Institute for Strategic Studies, 1998); J. Black, *War and Disorder in the 21st Century* (New York: Continuum, 2004); J. Kurth, "Clausewitz and the Two Contemporary Military Revolutions: RMA and RAM," in B.A. Lee and K.F. Walling (eds), *Strategic Logic and Political Rationality: Essays in Honor of M.I. Handel* (London: Frank Cass, 2003), pp. 274–97; M. van Creveld, *The Transformation of War* (New York: Free Press, 1991); and E. Luttwak, "Towards Post-Heroic Warfare," *Foreign Affairs*, 75 (1996), 33–44.

12 I am grateful to Major General Jonathan Bailey of the British Army, who made this telling point in a most powerful and persuasive manner in a seminar he gave at the University of Reading in 2004.

13 This shortlist, which summarizes my worldview, comprises the basic architecture of argument in my recent book, *Another Bloody Century: Future Warfare* (London: Weidenfeld and Nicolson, 2005). Each item is explained and defended at length in that book.

14 For a full explanation of the claims in the text see my book, *The Sheriff: America's Defense of the New World Order* (Lexington, KY: University Press of Kentucky, 2004).

15 See A.J. Bacevich, *American Empire: The Realities and Consequences of U.S. Diplomacy* (Cambridge, MA: Harvard University Press, 2002). In a perceptive review of my book, *The Sheriff*, Dr Bacevich accused me of understating the role of values in US foreign policy. *The International History Review*, XXVII (2005), pp. 216–18. On balance, I find that there is some justice in his complaint. While I certainly did not deny the importance of values, or ideology, and indeed I have campaigned for a quarter century on behalf of the salience of culture, I must admit that sometimes I can fail to pay ideology the homage that it deserves.

16 For those who enjoy a serious disaster plot, in fact a whole barrel load of them, the best place to begin is with the grim musings of a distinguished scientist, the British Astronomer Royal, M. Rees, in his book, *Our Final Century: Will Civilization Survive the Twenty-First Century?* (London: Arrow Books, 2003). And I thought that strategic studies had become the new dismal science.

Suggested reading

The 37 items in this short list have important things to say about strategic theory, strategists, and the value of ideas for policy, which is what the subject is all about. The selection is, of course, personal. If you read and ponder on these works you could not fail either to improve your understanding and hence mature as a theorist, or to raise your game as an official consumer of strategic ideas.

Aron, R., *Peace And War: A Theory of International Relations* (New York: Doubleday, 1966).

Beaufre, A., *An Introduction to Strategy* (London: Faber and Faber, 1965).

Betts, R.K., "Should Strategic Studies Survive?" *World Politics*, 50 (1997), pp. 7–33.

—— "Is Strategy an Illusion?" *International Security*, 25 (2000), pp. 5–50.

Beyerchen, A., "Clausewitz, Nonlinearity, and the Unpredictability of War," *International Security*, 17 (1992–93), pp. 59–90.

Black, J., *Rethinking Military History* (London: Routledge, 2004).

Bond, B., *The Pursuit of Victory: From Napoleon to Saddam Hussein* (Oxford: Oxford University Press, 1996).

Brodie, B., *Strategy in the Missile Age* (Princeton, NJ: Princeton University Press, 1959).

—— *War and Politics* (New York: Macmillan, 1973).

Buchan, A. (ed.), *Problems of Modern Strategy* (London: Chatto and Windus, 1970).

Builder, C., "Keeping the Strategic Flame," *Joint Force Quarterly*, 14 (1996–97), pp. 76–84.

Clausewitz, C. von, *On War*, M. Howard and P. Paret (eds and trans) (Princeton, NJ: Princeton University Press, 1976).

Foster, G.D., "On Strategic Theory and Logic," review of Edward N. Luttwak, "Strategy: The Logic of War and Peace," *Strategic Review*, 15 (1987), pp. 75–80.

—— "A Conceptual Foundation for a Theory of Strategy," *The Washington Quarterly*, 13 (1990), pp. 43–59.

—— "Research, Writing and the Mind of the Strategist," *Joint Force Quarterly*, 11 (1996), pp. 111–15.

Gray, C.S., *Modern Strategy* (Oxford: Oxford University Press, 1999).

—— *Strategy for Chaos: Revolutions in Military Affairs and the Evidence of History* (London: Frank Cass, 2002).

—— *Another Bloody Century: Future Warfare* (London: Weidenfeld and Nicolson, 2005).

Handel, M.I., *Masters of War: Classical Strategic Thought*, 3rd edn (London: Frank Cass, 2001).

Howard, M., *Studies in War and Peace* (London: Temple Smith, 1970).

—— *The Causes of Wars and Other Essays* (London: Counterpoint, 1983).

—— *The Lessons of History* (New Haven, CT: Yale University Press, 1991).

—— *The Invention of Peace and the Reinvention of War* (London: Profile Books, 2001).

Iklé, F.C., "The Role of Character and Intellect in Strategy," in A.W. Marshall, J.J. Martin, and H.S. Rowen (eds), *On Not Confusing Ourselves: Essays on National Security Strategy in Honor of Albert and Roberta Wohlstetter* (Boulder, CO: Westview Press, 1991), pp. 312–16.

Jomini, A.H. de, *The Art of War*, reprint of 1862 edn (London: Greenhill Books, 1992).

Katzenstein, P.J. (ed.), *The Culture of National Security: Norms and Identity in World Politics* (New York: Columbia University Press, 1996).

Liddell Hart, B.H., *Strategy: The Indirect Approach* (London: Faber and Faber, 1967).

Luttwak, E.N., *Strategy: The Logic of War and Peace*, rev. edn (Cambridge, MA: Harvard University Press, 2001).

Murray, W. and Sinnreich (eds), *The Past Is Prologue: History and the Military Profession* (Cambridge: Cambridge University Press, 2006).

Murray, W., Knox, M., and Bernstein, A. (eds), *The Making of Strategy: Rulers, States, and War* (Cambridge: Cambridge University Press, 1994).

Paret, P. (ed.), *Makers of Modern Strategy: From Machiavelli to the Nuclear Age* (Princeton, NJ: Princeton University Press, 1986).

Strassler, R. (ed.), *The Landmark Thucydides: A Comprehensive Guide to "The Peloponnesian War,"* R. Crawley (trans.), rev. edn (New York: Free Press, 1996).

Sun-tzu, *The Art of War*, R.D. Sawyer (trans.) (Boulder, CO: Westview Press, 1994).

Van Creveld, M., *The Transformation of War* (New York: Free Press, 1991).

Waltzer, M., *Just and Unjust Wars: A Moral Argument with Historical Illustrations*, 3rd edn (New York: Basic Books, 2000).

Watts, B.D., *Clausewitzian Friction and Future War*, McNair Paper 68, rev. edn (Washington, DC: Institute for National Strategic Studies, National Defense University, 2004).

Wylie, J.C., *Military Strategy: A General Theory of Power Control*, J.B. Hattendorf (intro.) (Annapolis, MD: Naval Institute Press, 1989).

Index

ABM Treaty *see* Anti-Ballistic
  Missile Treaty
Aegean Sea 59
Afghanistan 162
airpower 54–5, 59, 117, 139; impact on
  outcome of war 61; United States 140
Alexander the Great 62, 64
Algeria 162
amphibious warfare 149
anathematization 122
Anderson, Poul 3
Anglo-German naval agreement
  (1935) 123
Anti–Ballistic Missile (ABM) Treaty
  (1972) 124
Antwerp 70
Arab–Israeli War (1973) 26–7
Arbatov, Alexei 128
arms acquisition: political motivation 11
arms control 4, 6–7, 8, 11–12, 36, 41, 49,
  109, 120, 125–6; current scene 124–5;
  evidence for theory 29; failure 130–3;
  historical experience 122–4; lessons
  128–30; paradoxes 121–2; practical
  concerns 126–7; and stability 127–8
arms race 19
arms supply 120
Aron, Raymond 2
assured destruction 105, 109, 110, 111;
  see also mutual assured destruction
Athens 59, 60, 70, 64, 69, 70, 147
atomic bombs 18, 25, 142
atomic energy 17–18
Austria 67
Austrian War of Succession (1740–48)
  67, 70

B-1 bombers 106
balance-of-power policy 55, 66, 72, 178

ballistic missile defense (BMD)
  system 94, 109
ballistic missiles 139
Barca, Hannibal 74
Barnett, Correlli 46
Bathurst, Robert B. 155, 158, 163, 167
Baugh, Daniel A. 68
Beaufre, Andre 78
Black, Jeremy 11, 186
Black Sea 59
BMD system *see* ballistic missile
  defense system
Bosnia 12–13, 77, 170, 173, 174–5,
  179, 180–1
Bosphorus 54, 59
Bozeman, Adda B. 158
Britain 65, 128, 145, 147, 164; alliances
  137–8; alliance with France 67;
  continental allies 69, 141–2; cultural
  preconception 160–1; fleet deployment
  150; insular geographical setting
  138–9; manpower 68–9; naval arms
  regime 127; sea power 55, 56,
  65–71; strategic culture 141, 159–60,
  168; strategy in 1920s 50; and
  United States 55
Brodie, Bernard 2–3, 5, 6, 22, 31, 96,
  104, 127, 152, 185
Brogan, Denis 141
Bull, Hedley 185
Burma 68
Burt, Richard 106
Buzan, Barry 34, 48
Byzantium 64, 141, 149–50

Caemmerer, Rudolf von 76
Cambodia 149
Carter, Jimmy 38, 105, 106
Carthage 64, 74

Ceylon 70
CFE Treaty *see* Conventional Forces in
   Europe Treaty
chemical weapons 20
China 67, 128, 187
Chipman, John 34, 48
Churchill, Winston 44, 62, 67, 120
Cicero 74
Clausewitz, Carl von 1, 2, 3, 5, 6, 8, 13,
   26, 30, 36, 74, 75, 77, 79, 81, 83, 84,
   87, 106, 145, 164, 165, 175, 185, 186
coalition politics 49, 73, 149, 160
Cold War 6, 9, 36–7, 41, 47; arms
   control agreements in 124; end
   50–1, 61
collateral damage 24
collective morality 175–6
collective security 49
communications 76
Conference on Security and Cooperation
   in Europe (CSCE) 41–2
conscription 68
Conventional Forces in Europe (CFE)
   Treaty 42, 49, 128
Corbett, Sir Julian 60, 68, 141, 142
counter-economic recovery theory 97–8,
   99, 105
counter-military targeting 105–8
Crawford, Neta C. 48, 50, 51
cruise missiles 19, 33, 91, 107, 129, 139
CSCE *see* Conference on Security and
   Cooperation in Europe
cultural preconception 160–1
culture 7, 12, 113, 153, 154, 157–61; and
   geography 139–42; modern strategy
   161–8; and strategic behavior 151–2,
   154–7; of United States 188
cyberwar 114, 115

damage limitation 94, 110
Dardanelles Straits 54, 59
defense budget: United States 44
defense policy: fault-tolerant 52
defense policy, American 38, 83; 1970s
   and 1980s 141; Bush administration
   48; Carter administration 106; Reagan
   administration 38–9; and superpower
   nuclear peace 39–40
defense policy, British: 1920s 50
Desch, Michael 156
disarmament 11, 12, 122; *see also* arms
   control
Donnelly, Christopher 140
Dunn, Lewis A. 122

Earle, Edward Mead 30, 31
Eastern Europe 99
Eastwood, Clint 52
Egypt 70
Eisenhower, Dwight 79
Elizabeth I, Queen 63
environmental specialization 27
Erickson, John 100
ethics 12–13, 23–5, 170; alternative
   approaches 171–2; public vs. private
   170–1; of realism 175–80
ethnic cleansing 173
Europe: balance of power politics 66,
   146; political context for security 50
Evera, Stephen Van 38
The Evolution of Nuclear Strategy
   (Freedman) 79

Five Power Treaty (1922) 128
fleet train 141
flexibility 103
Foch, Ferdinand 30
force 171, 179
Ford, Gerald 98
Ford, Henry 56
foreign policy 172–3
Fourth-Generation Warfare (4GW) 84
Fox, William T.R. 20
France 68, 69, 71, 128, 137–8, 145;
   alliance with Britain 67; Egyptian
   expedition 70; imperial France 65, 78;
   sea power 66
Franco, Francisco 62
Freedman, Lawrence 52, 79, 186

4GW *see* Fourth-Generation Warfare
galley warfare 54, 56, 57
Gates, Robert 49
geography 7, 12, 64, 137, 167; and
   character of conflict 144–8; influence
   on grand strategy 137–9, 148–50;
   Russian 140, 147; and strategic culture
   139–42
geophysical environments 142, 149
geopolitics 7, 54, 65–6, 72
George, Alexander 29
Germany 130, 142, 165, 174; imperial
   Germany 146; strategic behavior 153;
   threat 75; *see also* Nazi Germany
glasnost 38
Gorbachev, Mikhail 43
grand strategy 65, 69, 157, 168; British
   72; influence of geography 137–9,
   148–50

Greece, ancient 59
Grey, Sir Edward 66
Griffith, Samuel 76
Grove, Eric 59
Guilmartin, John 56
Gulf War (1991) 46, 140

Haig, Sir Douglas 68
Hall, Edward T. 167
Halle, Louis J. 130
Hammes, Thomas X. 84
Harris, Marvin 155
Hart, Sir Basil Liddell 68, 141, 142
Hawaii 70
Hawke, Sir Edward 57
historical experience 60–1, 166–7;
    relevance 65
history 1, 2, 5–6, 56–7, 186–7; arms
    control 122–4; future 13; and
    strategy 9, 10, 54, 55–65; utility 9,
    21–3, 56
Hitler, Adolf 12, 30, 31, 62, 145,
    146, 171
Holbrooke, Richard 160
Hollis, Martin 151
Howard, Michael 141, 142
Hundred Years War 142
Huns 140
Hunt, Kenneth 93

ICBM *see* intercontinental
    ballistic missiles
Imperial Navy (Japan) 58
industrial mobilization 109
information-led warfare 114, 115–16,
    118–19
INF Treaty *see* Intermediate-Range
    Nuclear Forces Treaty
Instructions for Superior Commanders
    (Moltke) 77
intercontinental ballistic missiles (ICBM)
    3, 7, 91, 103, 129; MX ICBM 7, 106,
    107, 110
Intermediate-Range Nuclear Forces (INF)
    Treaty (1987) 43, 124
international politics 19–20
Iraq 51
isolationism 160
Israel 51, 146, 164
Italy 68, 128, 130

Japan 47, 72, 128, 130, 147; imperial
    Japan 70, 162, 147
Jervis, Robert 36

Johnston, Alastair Iain 151, 152–3,
    154–5, 156, 159, 164
Johnson, Lyndon 149
Jomini, A.H. de 75
Jones, T.K. 104
justice 171, 172, 178

Kagan, Donald 147
Kahn, Herman 43
Kavanagh, Dennis 159
Kellogg-Briand Pact (1928) 123
Kelly, William H. 155
Kennan, George 37
Kennedy, Paul 71, 141, 142
Kissinger, Henry 98
Kitchener, Lord 75
Kluckholn, Clyde 113, 155
Kroeber, A.L. 113
Kurth, James 186
Kuwait 51

land power 144; *see also* sea
    power–land power relations
League of Nations 123
Lehman, Ronald 120
LeMay, Curtis 140
limited war 41, 70
lock-in political gains 128
London treaties (1930 and 1936) 123
Luttwak, Edward 186

Macedonia 64
Machiavelli, Nicolo 30
Mackesy, Piers 67
Mackinder, Halford J. 7, 61, 63, 64, 72
McNamara, Robert 29, 94, 98, 102
MAD *see* mutual assured destruction
Mahan, Alfred Thayer 57, 63, 64
Makers of Modern Strategy (Earle)
    29–30
Manhattan Project 20
man power: Britain 68–9
Marcian, Emperor 120, 122
maritime defiles 59
maritime power: Britain 10
maritime strategy 8, 149, 163; United
    States 65–6, 141
media 24
Mediterranean region 54, 56, 59, 62
military power 2, 43, 77, 83, 104;
    effectiveness 79; principal
    forms 142
military space operations 60, 117
military strategy 65, 86

Missile Technology Control Regime (MTCR) (1987) 120
Moltke, Helmuth Graf von 77
Montgomery, Sir Bernard 63, 68
Moore, Sir John 68
moral authority 173–5
Morgan, John 1–2
Morocco Crisis I (1905) 67
MPS *see* multiple protective structure
MTCR *see* Missile Technology Control Regime
Mueller, John 157
multiple protective structure (MPS) 110
mutual assured destruction (MAD) 92, 94–5, 98, 105; decline of 100–3
MX ICBM 7, 106, 107, 110

Napoleon Bonaparte 31, 78, 141
national interests 179–80
National Security Decision Memorandum *see* NSDM
national strategic performance 81
NATO *see* North Atlantic Treaty Organization
naval arms limitation regime 123–4, 127
naval power: Soviet Union 65–6
Nazi Germany 59, 78, 144, 145–6; culture 12; U-boat bases 62
Nelson, Horatio 161
Netherlands 69, 71
New World Order 49
Nivelle, Robert 46
Nixon, Richard 98
Non-Proliferation of Nuclear Weapons Treaty (NPT) (1968) 120
North Atlantic Treaty Organization (NATO) 37, 62, 63, 71, 77, 93, 141, 142, 143, 188, 189
NPT *see* Non-Proliferation of Nuclear Weapons Treaty
NSDM (National Security Decision Memorandum) 242 97, 105; nuclear deterrence 6, 25, 40–1, 51–2, 69, 93–4, 96–7, 142–3, 173, 186; punishment-oriented 100, 101, 102–3; revisionist claims 103–5
nuclear divide 28, 29
nuclear policy: United States 93
nuclear strategies 4, 8, 10–11, 40–1
nuclear targeting 11, 96, 107
nuclear war 91–2, 93
Nuclear Weapon Employment Policy (NUWEP) 92

nuclear weapons 19, 22, 149; and grand strategy 142–5
nuclear-weapon states 20–1
NUWEP *see* Nuclear Weapon Employment Policy

Ober, Josiah 158, 162
oil embargo 47
Operation Desert Storm 41
Operation Felix 62
order 171, 179
Osgood, Robert 30
Ottoman Turkey 64
Owens, William 76

parity principle 128
Parker, W.H. 72
peace: and arms control 120; and war 82–3
Peace of Amiens (1802–03) 147
Peloponnesian War 147
People, States and Fear (Buzan) 34
perestroika 38
Persia 59, 60, 64
personal morality 175–6
Peters, Ralph 118–19
PGM *see* precision-guided munitions
physical geography 12; strategic significance 59–60
Pitt, William, the younger 47, 139
political motivation 6–7; arms acquisition 11
Portugal 71
Posen, Barry R. 38
power: arrogance 72
precision-guided munitions (PGM) 21–2
prisoners of war 24
prudence 23, 176
Prussia 67
public safety 35, 36
Punic (Hannibal's) War II (218–201 BC) 64, 74

al Qaeda 187, 188
Quester, George 30

RAF *see* Royal Air Force (Britain)
Reagan, Ronald 38
Realpolitik 176
recovery economy: targeting 97–8, 102
Revolution in Military Affairs (RMA) 11, 113; definition and concept 113–14; schools of thought 114–18
RMA *see* Revolution in Military Affairs

Rome 62, 64, 140–1
Roosevelt, Franklin Delano 47
Rosenau, James 28
Royal Air Force (RAF) (Britain) 68;
  fatalities 69
Royal Navy (Britain) 57, 62, 67, 68, 70,
  72, 138
Russia 47; geography 140, 147; strategic
  culture 165; *see also* Soviet Union
Ryan, Cornelius 4

SAC *see* Strategic Air Command
SALT (Strategic Arms Limitation Talks)
  93, 103, 128
SALT II (Strategic Arms Limitation Talks)
  91, 94, 103
Saxe 30
Schlesinger, James 96, 97
Schlieffen, Alfred Graf von 76
Schlieffen Plan 145–6
scholarship 3, 48; critical function 43–4
Scipio Africanus 74
Scoville, Herbert 97
SDI (Strategic Defense Initiative) 7, 38
sea power 54–5, 59, 138–9, 144; British
  experience 55, 56, 65–71; France 66;
  relevance 59–60; Soviet Union 63; and
  technology 60
sea power–land power relations 54, 56,
  57, 60, 61–5, 71
sea warfare: medieval 54
security 10, 11, 34; political context 50;
  revolution 117
security, American 188; relevance of the
  British experience 66
security community 164–5
security studies 34–5
selective nuclear options 97, 101
Seven Years War (1756–63) 65, 67
Sherman, William Tecumseh 140
Sicily 59, 70
Single Integrated Operational
  Plan *see* SIOP
SIOP (Single Integrated Operational
  Plan) 45, 91, 105, 106, 107, 108;
  SIOP-62 142
SLBM *see* submarine-launched ballistic
  missiles
Smith, Steve 151
Smoke, Richard 29
social assets 105, 108, 109
Some Principles of Maritime Strategy
  (Corbett) 60
Southeast Asia 75, 148–9

Soviet Union 20, 50, 78, 104, 130, 142,
  145, 163, 164, 172; and Cold War
  36–7; demise 23–4, 37–8, 61; focus on
  World War II and its lessons 27–8;
  impairment of state functioning
  99–100; recovery economy 97–8, 102;
  threat 75
space warfare 148
Spain 69
Sparta 59, 60, 64
special operations forces 9, 164, 167
Spykman, Nicholas J. 7
stability 105, 108–10; arms control
  concept of 127–8, 130, 131–2
stable deterrence 41
Stalin, Josef 37
START (Strategic Arms Reduction Talks)
  41–2, 43, 45, 128
statecraft 1, 3, 17; Britain 63, 66;
  Japan 47
Steiner, Barry 30
Strategic Air Command (US) 96–7
strategic arms limitation 41
Strategic Arms Limitation Talks *see* SALT
Strategic Arms Reduction Talks *see*
  START
strategic behavior 151, 162–3; and culture
  12, 151–2, 154–7; Germany 153
strategic culture: classification 166–8;
  dysfunctional elements 165–6
Strategic Defense Initiative *see* SDI
strategic education 52
strategic stability 94
strategic studies 9, 13, 17, 139, 187;
  continuing necessity 9–10; contribution
  to defense planning 186; impact upon
  official choices for policy and strategy
  40, 41, 45–6; intellectual legacy of Cold
  War-era 40, 41–2; new direction
  46–51; old vs. new thinking 52;
  political framework 48; pre-nuclear
  heritage literature 29–32; pre-nuclear
  origins 25–8; profession 35–6;
  vs. security studies 34–5; and
  war 185–6
strategic theory 2–3, 13; and practice
  4–5, 35, 42–4, 51–3
strategy 1–2, 4, 9; complex 77–8;
  definition 78; difficulties 10, 74–6,
  77–8; dimensions 153–4, 168–9; and
  history 55–65; need 91–4; operational
  realities 79–80; pre-nuclear 17–18, 21;
  pre-nuclear history 32–3; vs. moral
  imperative 172–3; and war 118

strategy, American: relevance of British maritime experience 55, 71–3
Strategy in the Missile Age (Brodie) 31–2
strategy, Soviet 101
Strauss, Barry S. 158, 162
submarine-launched ballistic missiles (SLBM) 129
subsidization of allies 63, 67, 68
success 80
Sun-tzu 5, 26, 113, 158
superiority 110–12
superpowers 38; changing relationship 50; strategic prowess 102–3
Syria 67

taboo promotion 122
technology 7–8; consequences 8; importance in war 117–18; and nature of war 83–4; navigational 60; and strategic difficulties 76–7
telegraphy 76
Terraine, John 49, 68, 73
Theodosius II 150
Thucydides 11–12, 26, 186, 188
Till, Geoffrey 56
training 78
Tucker, Robert 30
Tukhachevsky, Marshal 27

ULTRA intelligence 47, 118
unilateralism 160
United States 20, 83, 128, 160, 165, 170, 187, 189; air power 140; arms control policy 129; and Britain 55; civilian strategic experts 35; coalition politics 160; culture 188; defense debate 114; geography and strategic culture 137, 141, 148–9; golden age of strategic thought 103–4; intervention in Eurasia 67; military problem in Southeast Asia 75; naval power 64; performance in war 81; policy towards Bosnia 180–1; relative decline 47; special operations 164; strategic nuclear posture 93; victory in cold war 36–7; WWI, dispatch of expeditionary force 58
United States Marine Corps 70
Urban II, Pope 122
USSR *see* Soviet Union

Van Creveld, Martin 84, 186
Vietnam 26, 101, 107, 148–9, 162, 165

Walt, Stephen M. 39, 48
war 106–7, 187; Clausewitzian understanding of nature of war 2, 3, 5, 6, 82, 185; concept and definition 84, 114, 185; contextual analysis 86–7; distinction between warfare and 82; importance of technology 117–18; militarily effective prosecution 102, 103–5; nature and character 82; nature and technology 83–4; and peace 82–3, 86; Soviet posture 109–10; and strategic studies 185–6; and superpowers 20–1
warfare 10, 86, 187; American way 140, 165, 166; British way 68, 141; information-led 115–16, 118–19; means and methods 83–4; principles of 81; regular and irregular 84–5
war plans 45, 170; United States 92
war, principles of 1, 10, 81; Army Field Manual FM-3 Military Operations 85–6; new style 86–7; reinvention 82
Washington Treaty (1922) 123
Watts, Barry 116
weapon effectiveness 21–2
Weapons of Mass Destruction (WMD) 189
Westmoreland, William 75
White, Leslie A. 155
Wight, Martin 63
Wilkinson, Spenser 27
Williams, Raymond 153
WMD *see* Weapons of Mass Destruction
World Disarmament Conference (1932–34) 123
World War I 57–8, 123; British manpower 68, 69; United States intervention 67
World War II 18; military strategies 27–8; naval staff studies 47; strategic geography 145–6
Wylie, J.C. 167

Yamamoto, Isoroku 58
Yugoslavia 170, 181